I0559187

You CAN
Overcome

Truth, Values, and Wisdom for Living

You CAN Overcome

Truth, Values, and Wisdom for Living

Hermann Eben

EQUIP PRESS

Colorado Springs

Copyright © 2024 Hermann Eben and GR8 Solutions Group
All rights reserved.

Printed in the United States of America

No part of this publication may be reproduced, stored in, or introduced into a retrieval system, or transmitted in any form or by any means (electronic, mechanical, photocopying, recording, or otherwise) without the prior permission of the publisher except for the use of brief quotations in a book review or scholarly journal.

First Printing: 2024
Paperback ISBN: 978-1-966923-05-3
ePUB ISBN: 978-1-966923-06-0

GR8 Solutions Group
242 Spring Park Drive, Suite A
Midland, Texas 79705
www.gr8relate.com; *www.gr8leaders.com*; *www.gr8grp.com*

Ordering Information:
Special discounts are available on quantity purchases by corporations, associations, educators, and others. For details, contact the publisher at the above-listed address.
U.S. trade bookstores and wholesalers: Please contact GR8 Solutions Group at +1 (432) 682-6823 or email *heben@gr8grp.com*.

CONTENTS

HERMANN EBEN

How to Use This Book

You have the right book if you want to know the fundamental values, principles, and tools that help you orient your life to be an *Overcomer*. With this material, you can grow your life skills to experience the abundant life you have been given (2 Peter 1:3). It will benefit your entire life. These Godly principles prepare you for overcoming here and receiving your inheritance in heaven.

This information has no foundation in fads—it is proven, practical, and powerful—built on God's Word. Applying this material shifts your focus to Jesus Christ's example to help you become an *Overcomer*.

1. **Read Individually or in a Group**
    You can work through this book on your own or with a small group. We recommend a group setting, as constructive feedback is invaluable for growth.
2. **Review and Discuss**
    After finishing a chapter, answer the questions at the end of each chapter and discuss it with your group. You can cover one chapter per week or follow a schedule that works best for your group.

HERMANN EBEN

ACKNOWLEDGMENTS

Everything in this book is a compilation of material from "GR8 Relationships" (*https://gr8relate.com*) and "GR8 Leaders" (*https://gr8leaders.com*). The GR8 Relationships material helps you create superior biblical relationships, "Pursuing Their Best—Freedom in Relationships." The GR8 Leaders information helps leaders "Build superior cultures with great leaders."

Each website has nearly five hundred online, instructive, short videos to help you apply what you learn. Both have hundreds of informative blogs, and the GR8 Relationships information is entirely FREE—all courses, TV shows, podcasts, and blogs.

Both of our websites have benefitted from the hours of labor from Paul Moore, Karl Munt, and Matt Montgomery for years. And I am very grateful to them.

But none of this would exist without the grace, strength, and work of Jesus Christ, the support of my dear wife, Louie, and the generosity of Tim Dunn, who provided the resources of the Next Step Discipleship Ministries studio.

Finally, the Moment of Truth information in chapter 7, "*Overcomers Create a Culture of Truth*," provides an overview of the Moment of Truth process. If you want the details from the creators of the process, read the book *Managerial Moment of Truth* by Robert Fritz and Bruce Bodaken.

HERMANN EBEN

Introduction

Are you trying to survive in today's fallen world? Do you trust God's truth, values, and wisdom in His Word? Do you stand for His truth, values, and wisdom? Are you persevering with His truth, wisdom, and values in difficult times?

Overcomers answer *no* to the first question because they are not trying to survive; they live abundant lives. They answer *yes* to the last three questions because they are in the game, on the battleground, not sitting around and hoping someone else does the work. Most importantly, they do not depend on their courage and perseverance but rely on Jesus. *Overcomers* overcome because they choose the life of Jesus in them to live through them. And living has nothing to do with a better or easier life because *Overcomers* focus on the best life, the abundant life we have been given (2 Peter 1:3).

Overcomers are not reactionary to society and events around them. They create change like a catalyst. Their thinking, actions, feelings, and life contrast to the world. Their lives depend on the power of Jesus, who is unchanging and not reactionary. Yet, unlike Jesus, *Overcomers* will fail at times. *Overcomers* always come back to depending on Jesus to live their everyday lives.

It will take Jesus' transcendent values to face the challenges that public schools have created by mandating inappropriate materials for children to read. Some of them are a far cry from God's truth.

It will take Jesus' wisdom to relate to those who feel they have a personal right to end the life of an unborn child because the child isn't convenient. It will take Jesus speaking the truth through you to people who feel they have a right to choose whether they are a man, woman, or neither, and those pushed into changing their gender. It will take Jesus' values to speak through you with gentleness and forgiveness to those who later regret what they did.

It will take Jesus through you to speak truth to church leaders who are improperly tolerating rather than loving people who are in sin. Love shares the truth (Ephesians 4:15), but tolerance puts up with evil to get along. Jesus' values and wisdom always showed up by steering people to the way of truth. Did Jesus forget His values when He was angry and overturned the tables in the temple? No, He was demonstrating them because He was adamant about showing people the truth. His overwhelming love for people (pursuing their best) meant He was showing them the perfect way to live.

If you believe the gospel of Christ and believe the Bible to be absolute truth, the "Who said so," then you are likely challenged and maybe discouraged by many things in society today. That is normal for most Christians.

However, there is a difference between a believer and an *Overcomer*. A believer may know a little or a lot about the truth, values, and wisdom in this book, but an *Overcomer* exemplifies them.

We will explore critical principles for Christians that *Overcomers* hear, obey, and proclaim to others. These are not the only principles of the Christian life but have and will continue to change relationships, marriages, and lives. They will help a believer become an *Overcomer*.

The purpose of this book is to provide you with practical principles, tools, and truth, which will help you radiate the image of Christ to those around you and become or continue on the path of an *Overcomer*.

I hope you will let Jesus enhance your relationship with Him by becoming dependent upon Him to live through you daily. He will gladly help you learn and experience the benefit of the information herein as you walk with Him in a fallen world.

Fortunately, my editor (Ann Lovett) and manager (Tina Jacobson) are more relational and better with books than I am. So we have started each chapter with a story of someone living in a modern, fallen world and the choices and decisions they face. You likely face some of the same situations. We hope the story will make the concepts and tools presented herein more applicable to your life.

CHAPTER 1

HANNAH, THE *OVERCOMER*?

Hannah has always tried to walk as a Christian, even though she often finds that in Corporate America, it's not an easy road. She put herself through college by working part-time jobs. She graduated in three years due to her rigorous class schedule, something she is proud of. Educated in marketing and finance, she has worked hard to climb the corporate ladder. Her exceptional relational skills have helped propel her to the top of the insurance firm where she works.

Hannah's husband, Mark, is an attorney in a large downtown law firm. They have two children—Megan, age five, and Jade, age nine. She intended to stay home with her kids, but she and her husband need to work to support the lifestyle they want for their family. Both girls attend the neighborhood elementary school.

Today in her position at work, and now as a mom with kids in school, she finds herself torn between standing up for her faith and belief in how God created men and women, yet walking in grace with people.

At her daughter's school, the parent organization has raised concerns about some of the mandated materials in the curriculum and books available in the library. Hannah has been very vocal about the fact that the materials present ideas that are not age-appropriate for her young family. At a recent PTO meeting, one of the teachers accused her of being racist in front of everyone. When she challenged the teacher, the principal stopped the interchange and said they needed to maintain harmony. Hannah was livid because she felt the accusation was unfounded and just a rote theme in many places in the world. She felt like the principal was scolding her for trying to stand up for herself and her children.

Several times in the last two years, she and Mark had discussed possibly home-schooling the girls. They wanted more control over their daughters' environment and education. Hannah wanted her girls to be able to pray to start the day and maybe even study the Bible. Hannah had learned about prayer from her grandmother, who prayed for Hannah and her family to accept Jesus as their personal Savior every day. Even when Hannah was getting in trouble in high school, her grandmother always showed love and grace toward her. Hannah felt like her grandmother was a model of putting others' needs first, which was always an inspiration to Hannah.

Four months ago, Hannah stepped into her role as Vice President of Marketing at the insurance firm. Several members of her team were very vocal about their gay lifestyles. Two of the women on her team lived together. They loved to tell stories about how they met on the marketing team as friends. Then they realized the deep love they had for each other and moved in together. Hannah felt like they were always pushing an agenda that she did not agree with and was out of place at work, but she wasn't sure how to handle it.

One evening, after a particularly rough day, Mark noticed that Hannah seemed to be distressed about something.

"What's bothering you, Hannah?" he asked gently.

Hannah sighed deeply and said, "You know I've always been good with people, and building relationships has been my strong suit. That is one of the reasons I have excelled at my job. But now I feel pressured to embrace ideas that conflict with my beliefs."

"What's going on?" he asked.

"These two women on my team dominate staff meetings with their personal stories, emphasizing that they are glad to live in a state where they can be married. They bash conservatives in the legislature. I try to steer the conversation away from the political talk because I know others on the team don't agree with these two, but the other team members are afraid to speak their opinions."

"How do you know the other people on the team don't agree?" Mark asked.

"One of them, Mary, has confided in me that these women are always testing her. One time Mary mentioned going to church and how her faith was important. One of the women challenged her by saying, 'Well, I used to go to a church like yours until all those Bible thumper people just ruined the place. I moved to a Methodist church that accepts us just as we are. The pastors are gay men who encourage us to live the way God created us.'"

Mark looked at her empathetically and said, "Unfortunately, that is the world we live in these days. I know that goes against what you believe; it goes against what I believe, but legally, our hands are tied."

Hannah continued, "I try to show love and grace without agreeing with their lifestyle. I don't dare share my conservative views. It's almost like I'm a criminal."

Mark didn't say anything and nodded his head in agreement.

About a week later, Mark and Hannah discussed the situation at the girls' school and concluded it was time to enroll them in a private Christian school. Hannah, the budget master of the family, poured over their income and expenses and knew they would have to bring in more income and cut their expenses to afford to put the girls in private school.

The next day at work, her boss called her into his office for an impromptu meeting. She sat down in the chair in front of his desk and a sick feeling overwhelmed her.

"Hannah, you are a valuable asset to our company, and I appreciate what you have done for our department. We've had some major restructuring, and we are anticipating a merger deal. We are eliminating your position," he explained.

"How long do I have?" Hannah asked, trying to remain calm.

"Today is your final day. We will give you a month's severance and provide outplacement services."

Hannah felt her face turn bright red and flush with heat.

She told her boss, "You know that is not enough time or severance for someone at my level."

Her boss said, "I don't really have a choice. I've negotiated for you as much as I could."

Hannah looked at him and silently shook her head. She stood up and left his office.

He never really went to bat for me. He's always been scared and just towed the company line. Why do I have to have such a dud of a boss? she thought.

Hannah felt anger and disbelief wash over her. She called Mark right away, but he didn't answer. She left a message to call her back, but he didn't.

When she got home that evening after the kids were asleep, she let Mark know what was going on.

"I got let go today. I only have a month's severance," she said with little emotion.

"Oh man, I'm sorry to hear that. What happened?" Mark asked.

"You know it's the typical corporate line to keep them out of legal trouble: 'We are restructuring and eliminating the position.'"

"I'm sorry, Hannah. I know how hard you worked for them," Mark said in a quiet tone.

"I'm going to go read and go to bed," Hannah said as she left the room.

Hannah couldn't sleep. She was so angry she couldn't see straight or stop thinking about what had happened.

She cried out to God and said, "What are we supposed to do?! We are trying to live a Christian life and raise our kids the right way, but the world is against us!"

Questions
1. Hannah is a Christian, but is she an *Overcomer*?
2. Was she trying to fix things or trying to depend on God through prayer and being responsible?
3. How can we know when we are depending on God instead of ourselves?

OVERCOMERS HEAR, OBEY, AND ENDURE WITHOUT FEAR

Key Lesson: *Overcomers are Believers, but all Believers are not Overcomers.*

OVERCOMERS ARE DIFFERENT

Did you know the sportswear giant Nike gets its name from the Greek word for *"Overcomer"*?

The expression "He who overcomes" (Revelation 2:26; 3:21) actually translates the Greek verb, nikaō, the noun form of the word nikē. The verb and noun refer to winning, being victorious, and overcoming an opponent.

A Nike Christian is an overcomer, one who perseveres in faith and good works. That is what we are called to be. The Holy Spirit enables all believers to be victorious (2 Peter 1:3), but victory is not automatic. We must be doers of the Word, and not hearers only, if we are to be Nike Christians (James 1:22)—Wilkin, R. (2003). The Road to Reward: Living Today in the Light of Tomorrow (p. 57)

Can buying a pair of Nike shoes instantly make you an *Overcomer*? Obviously not. God's Word is the path to victory and how you can become an *Overcomer*! However, it should not be surprising that people have different views about *Overcomers*. Three common beliefs are:

- *Overcomers* are believers who are finally justified at death because they continued in the faith.
- *Overcomers* are every Christian.
- *Overcomers* are faithful Christians.

Excellent scholars have commented and battled over their interpretation of God's Word as they support their view. Each view indicates how you see other critical biblical issues. Hopefully, if you disagree with my chosen view, you will find some merit in this chapter and, most importantly, future chapters.

You will soon see my definition of an *Overcomer*, which applies to all three beliefs. But first, it is essential that you know I believe *Overcomers* are faithful Christians.

Overcomers Overcome What?

In one sense, all believers are *Overcomers*.

> *1 John 5:4-5 (NKJV)—For whatever is born of God overcomes the world. And this is the victory that has overcome the world—our faith. Who is he who overcomes the world, but he who believes that Jesus is the Son of God?*

Isn't that great news?

When you believe in or trust that Jesus's death, burial, and resurrection paid for your sins, you overcome the second death (eternity in hell) through the power of Christ.

> *It is certainly true that all Christians are Overcomers in the sense that all Overcomers have believed in Christ and are therefore justified. . . . However, . . . not all who are Overcomers in the sense of personal salvation live like Overcomers in their practical lives. In the book of Revelation, John addresses all true Christians, and challenges them to become Christians who overcome, and challenges them to live like who they are, promising them rewards if they do, and in five instances, loss if they do not.—Dillow, J. C. (2018). Final Destiny: The Future Reign of the Servant Kings, 4th edition. Grace Theology Press*

The same power of God demonstrated in Jesus' payment for and victory over your sins, removal of them, and establishment of you as a child of God is now in you. According to Romans 8:11, the same power that raised Christ from the dead is in you! It is dynamic. The power in you, Jesus' life, and the Holy Spirit make it possible to choose righteousness and overcome (have victory over) the temptation and sin you face daily.

That victory over the temptation to sin is the essence of being an *Overcomer*.

All believers have His power to hear His Word and let Him live through them by doing as He says in His Word.

That means you have Christ's power to overcome your flesh, your sin nature, or any time you decide to make everything about yourself—what we label "Flashing your ME." Only Christ's life in you can remove your selfishness, confusion, and sin at any moment of your life.

Overcomers are faithful in their walk with Jesus to overcome their sin nature. They more often do what God says and rely on Christ's life in them to choose against the flesh. Notice the two words "more often," implying the continuing sanctification process of Jesus' power to make an *Overcomer* look more like Him.

An *Overcomer* will have setbacks, but they will progress again when they faithfully return and follow God's Word. That is why this is a good statement to remember.

In every circumstance, the quicker I thank God for His PERFECTION, the quicker He restores the wisdom, peace, and power of Jesus' life and the Holy Spirit in and through me.

That contains the essence of an *Overcomer*, which is different than the definition of an *Overcomer*, which you will learn later.

Overcomers Are Running for the Prize

But wait! Are all believers *Overcomers*? No, *Overcomers* are believers, but all believers are not *Overcomers*. The difference between justification and sanctification explains why.

Justification means that your sins no longer count against you, and God makes you righteous. Sanctification is God's ongoing and daily work in your life. If all believers were *Overcomers*, numerous warnings to choose righteousness, like Romans 6:13-23, would be unnecessary.

To further explain the difference, consider the *gift* and the *prize*. The *gift* of becoming a child of God is free for those who believe in the death, burial, and resurrection of Jesus Christ (John 3:16, 1 Corinthians 15: 3-5). The *prize* is the reward or inheritance available based on how much a Christian applies God's Word and lets Christ live through them during their life. The apostle Paul was referring to the *prize* when he said,

> *2 Timothy 4:7-8 (NKJV)—I have fought the good fight, I have finished the race, I have kept the faith. Finally, there is laid up for me the crown of righteousness, which the Lord, the righteous Judge, will give to me on that Day, and not to me only but also to all who have loved His appearing.*

If these distinctions are unclear, many passages in God's Word will confuse you and encourage you to think you must earn or validate your eternal life in Heaven instead of only receiving a gift from God. It is easy to confuse passages that urge you to strive, work, or do something as how you earn or validate the *gift*.

Overwhelmingly, those passages are about pursuing the *prize* instead of validating or earning the *gift*. Remember that the *gift* is free, as stated in Ephesians 2:8-9 (NKJV).

*For by grace you have been saved through faith,
and that not of yourselves; it is the gift of God,
not of works, lest anyone should boast.*

However, the *prize* is a reward for choosing righteousness and the life of Christ, as seen in 2 Timothy 4:7-8.

Satan wants to confuse believers to make them ineffective in their walk and prevent them from experiencing the abundant life they have been given (2 Peter 1:3). He creates fear about their future in eternity by getting them to think the *gift* was not free. He also encourages judging other believer's actions to determine whether someone *really* is a believer.

So take a moment. What voice are you hearing?

Overcomers and the Seven Churches

The apostle John often used the words *overcome* and *overcomes*. The most well-known occurrences are in Revelation chapters 2 and 3, describing promises made to *Overcomers*.

*Revelation 2:7 (NKJV)—He who has an ear, let him
hear what the Spirit says to the churches. To him
who overcomes I will give to eat from the tree of life,
which is in the midst of the Paradise of God.*

*Revelation 2:11 (NKJV)—He who has an ear, let him
hear what the Spirit says to the churches. He who
overcomes shall not be hurt by the second death.*

*Revelation 2:17 (NKJV)—He who has an ear, let him hear
what the Spirit says to the churches. To him who overcomes
I will give some of the hidden manna to eat. And I will give
him a white stone, and on the stone a new name written
which no one knows except him who receives it.*

*Revelation 2:26 (NKJV)—And he who overcomes,
and he who keeps My deeds until the end, to him
I will give authority over the nations.*

*Revelation 3:5 (NKJV)—He who overcomes shall be
clothed in white garments, and I will not blot out his
name from the Book of Life, but I will confess his
name before My Father and before His angels.*

*Revelation 3:12 (NKJV)—He who overcomes, I will make him
a pillar in the temple of My God, and he shall go out no more.
I will write on him the name of My God and the name of the*

city of My God, the New Jerusalem, which comes down out of heaven from My God. And I will write on him My new name.

Revelation 3:21 (NKJV)—To him who overcomes I will grant to sit with Me on My throne, as I also overcame and sat down with My Father on His throne.

Revelation 21:7 (NKJV)—He who overcomes shall inherit all things, and I will be his God and he shall be My son.

(A Note to the Reader: Please study the above promises to understand their meanings fully. This chapter and this book will not discuss and explain the promises. Instead, this book aims to equip you with practical principles, tools, and truths that will help you radiate the image of Christ to those around you. In other words, these are things **Overcomers** do.

I highly recommend the two books listed below for a comprehensive and precise understanding of the promises and the difference between believers and **Overcomers**. These resources offer valuable insights from God's Word that will encourage you to be an Overcomer. For example, understanding the significance of the Book of Life (Revelation 3:5) can profoundly inspire your daily walk with the Lord.

- DILLOW, J. C. (2018). *FINAL DESTINY: THE FUTURE REIGN OF THE SERVANT KINGS*, 4TH EDITION. GRACE THEOLOGY PRESS. (SEE CHAPTER 43)
- WILKIN, R. N. (1999). *CONFIDENT IN CHRIST: LIVING BY FAITH REALLY WORKS*. GRACE EVANGELICAL SOCIETY.)

The first seven of the eight verses listed above are part of God's message to each of the seven churches in Revelation chapters 2 and 3. The short messages to each church contain powerful and practical insights for all churches. They also contain many references to individuals or *Overcomers* ("he who overcomes").

Dr. John Walvoord, a leading scholar on the book of Revelation, has summarized the messages to the seven churches in the following table. The headings highlighted in gray are my additions.

	Hear			Obey	Endure without Fear
	Christ	Commendation	Rebuke	Exhortation	Promise
Ephesus (Revelation 2:1–7)	Holds the seven stars in His right hand and walks among the seven golden lampstands.	Deeds, hard work, perseverance. Does not tolerate wicked men. Hates the practices of the Nicolaitans.	Has forsaken her first love.	Remember; repent; do the things you did at first.	Will eat from the tree of life.
Smyrna (Revelation 2:8–11)	The first and the Last, who died and came to life again.	Suffers persecution and poverty.	—	Do not be afraid. Be faithful, even to the point of death.	Will receive a crown of life; will not be hurt by the second death.
Pergamum (Revelation 2:12–17)	Has the sharp, double-edged sword.	Remains true to Christ; does not renounce her faith.	People there hold the teachings of Balaam and of the Nicolaitans.	Repent.	Will receive hidden manna and a white stone with a new name on it.
Thyatira (Revelation 2:18–29)	The Son of God, eyes are like blazing fire, and feet are like burnished brass.	Deeds, love, faith, service, perseverance, doing more than at first.	Tolerates Jezebel with her immorality and idolatry.	Repent; hold on to what you have.	Will have authority over the nations; the morning star.
Sardis (Revelation 3:1–6)	Holds the seven spirits of God and the seven stars.	Deeds; the reputation of being alive.	Dead.	Wake up! Strengthen what remains. Remember what you received, obey it, repent.	Will be dressed in white; will be acknowledged before My Father and His angels.
Philadelphia (Revelation 3:7–13)	Holy and true, holds the key of David.	Deeds, keeps Christ's word, and does not deny His name, endures patiently.	—	Hold on to what you have.	Overcomers will be pillars in the temple; the name of God, of the New Jerusalem, and of Christ's new name, will be written on them.
Laodicea (Revelation 3:14–22)	The Amen, the faithful and true witness, the Ruler of God's creation.	—	Lukewarm. Wretched. pitiful, poor, blind, and naked.	Buy from Christ refined gold, white clothes, and eye salve. Be earnest, repent.	Overcomers will eat with Christ; will rule with Christ.

Please use this information for self-examination. You can identify with each church because the message highlights critical battles between your flesh and the Holy Spirit. Choices in those battles define the difference between an *Overcomer* and a believer. Viewing the passage as a message to believers makes it beneficial for self-examination. That is why I placed Church in parentheses and added believer in the following.

1. Careless, Loveless Believer (Church)
   a. **Overcome** by repenting and returning to a close relationship with Christ.
   b. **Promise**: Having a rewarding, personal, and close relationship with God.

2. Persecuted Believer (Church)
   a. **Overcome** by enduring without fear and being faithful even to death.
   b. **Promise**: Receiving a victor's crown for finishing well.

3. Compromising Believer (Church)
   a. **Overcome** by repenting from belief in lies and false teachings.
   b. **Promise**: Receiving hidden nourishment (truth), a special reward, and a new name.

4. Corrupt Believer (Church)
   a. **Overcome** by holding fast to the truth till Christ returns.
   b. **Promise**: Reigning with Christ and having the Morning Star for light and discernment.

5. Dead Believer (Church)
   a. **Overcome** by waking up, repenting, obeying what you know, and watching for Christ's return.
   b. **Promise**: Being clothed in righteousness, associated with and recognized by God and the angels.

6. Faithful Believer (Church)
   a. **Overcome** by holding on to the truth, looking for Christ's coming, and continuing to endure.
   b. **Promise**: Being raptured from the hour of trial and becoming a vital fixture in New Jerusalem with whom God identifies.

7. Lukewarm, Foolish Believer (Church)
   a. **Overcome** by earnestly repenting, clothing in righteousness, and seeing through God's eyes.
   b. **Promise**: Dining with Christ now and sitting with Christ later on His throne.

How many of those do you identify with? What needs repentance and letting Christ live through you?

Hopefully, learning more about *Overcomers* will help you make different choices from now on.

Overcomer Definition

Finally, it is time to create a working definition of the word *Overcomer*. Definitions of words are critical for clarity and understanding. Earlier, you saw that I believe an *Overcomer* is a faithful believer. That is useful but not as concrete or specific as I desire for my life. If you would please indulge me, let me walk you through my journey of building my definition of an *Overcomer*.

Several years ago, I listened to a message about the seven churches. Toward the end of the message, a phrase stuck in my mind. I do not remember the speaker saying it, but it became my early definition of an

Overcomer. It eventually became the first item of eight daily reminders I speak to myself because it is a prayer for everyone on the prayer list. The definition was:

Hear, then do, and do not fear—especially loss or death.

I have benefited, and hopefully, those I have counseled and coached have benefited from that definition. However, after my initial study about *Overcomers*, I changed *do* to *obey* and added *endure*. That added clarity and strengthened the phrase to fit what I was learning. The new definition became:

Hear, obey, and endure without fear of loss or death.

Dr. Walvoord's table helped me better define an *Overcomer* since it references some of their most essential scriptures.

The column title *Exhortation* is defined as a strong urge or appeal to action—a short reflection on that definition encouraged me to connect exhortation to *obey* in my definition. Then I connected *hear* to the *Christ, Commendation,* and *Rebuke* column titles because *Overcomers* must hear the vital information in each column.

The final connection of *endure without fear* to the *Promise* column title requires seeing the promise as a reward. The potential for a reward often enhances endurance and reduces or removes the impact of fear. When someone knows a reward is available, they can more easily endure without fear.

Those changes were strengthened after additional reflection and research. So let's examine each part of the definition to arrive at a better one.

Hear and Obey

An *Overcomer* considers *hear*ing and *obeying* functionally connected when looking at God's Word.

An example of that is a story about a man seeking to be the pastor of a church. He preached an impressive sermon on his first visit. The people loved it and voted for him to become their new pastor. However, they were surprised when, on his first Sunday there, he preached the same sermon and even more surprised when he preached it again the following week. After he preached the same sermon the third week in a row, the leaders met with him to find out what was happening. The pastor assured them, "When you start living out this sermon, I'll continue to my next one."

It is best to connect *hear* and *obey* when speaking about God's Word and *Overcomers*. Just because you hear God's Word does not mean you obey it.

Notice the parable of the two builders.

> *Matthew 7:24,26 (NKJV)—Therefore whoever hears these*
> *sayings of Mine, and does them, I will liken him to a wise*
> *man who built his house on the rock . . . But everyone who*
> *hears these sayings of Mine, and does not do them, will*
> *be like a foolish man who built his house on the sand.*

Jesus, the ultimate *Overcomer*, came to announce a new world order utterly different from how people were living. He repeatedly spoke of forgiveness, servanthood, humility, and unconditional mercy and grace. Two thousand years later, Jesus repeats the same message. When we embrace the authority, reign, and rule of Jesus our King, we will experience a profound transformation in our lives, bring glory to His name, and bless others.

God's new world order requires hearing His Word and obeying it for both the *gift* and the *prize*. If your hearing does not include a subsequent obeying, the hearing bears no fruit in your life. That is the essence of Satan's knowledge of God's Word; he hears it and does not do it.

Unfortunately, many Christians are like the people God spoke about to Ezekiel.

> *Ezekiel 33:31 (NKJV)—So they come to you as people*
> *do, they sit before you as My people, and they hear your*
> *words, but they do not do them; for with their mouth they*
> *show much love, but their hearts pursue their own gain.*

That is the opposite of an *Overcomer* who hears and obeys.

Jesus never insists on your obedience. He never says, "You will obey me." He leaves you completely free to choose, so free that people spat in His face and killed Him, and yet He did not prevent it. But once He creates His life in you through His redemption, you will have new insights to see His right to absolute authority over you. Your eyes open to see and acknowledge that "You are worthy, O Lord . . ." (Revelation 4:11).

However, your flesh, or sin nature refuses to bow down or obey the worthy One. Meeting someone more holy than you and not recognizing their worthiness is a revelation or display of your sin nature. God teaches you by using these people who are even a little holier than you are. And He continues to do so until you agree that your worthiness comes only from Christ, not you. Then the whole attitude of your life can become one of obedience to Him.

The word obedience does not indicate the world's view of duty or dominance. Like submission, obedience is a voluntary choice to do what another desires or requires. Obedience does not imply compliance against someone's will. That would be subjection or domination.

Furthermore, obedience is not natural. Somehow, Christ learned obedience. Since Christ is equal with the Father, "I and My Father are one" (John 10:30), the Father did not force Him to become our Savior. ". . . though He was a Son, yet He learned obedience by the things which He suffered" (Hebrews 5:8). The Son was obedient and became our Redeemer even though He was equal with the Father.

> *Philippians 2:3-9 (NKJV)—Let nothing be done through selfish ambition or conceit, but in lowliness of mind let each esteem others better than himself. Let each of you look out not only for his own interests, but also for the interests of others.*
>
> *Let this mind be in you which was also in Christ Jesus, who, being in the form of God, did not consider it robbery to be equal with God, but made Himself of no reputation, taking the form of a bondservant, and coming in the likeness of men. And being found in appearance as a man, He humbled Himself and became obedient to the point of death, even the death of the cross. Therefore God also has highly exalted Him and given Him the name which is above every name . . .*

Your obedience reveals the level of your growth in grace and overcoming. If the Lord insisted on your obedience, He would become a taskmaster. He never insists on obedience, but obedience is simple when you see Him as He reveals Himself and change your view of Him as you learn to obey Him. Each act of obedience teaches you about the worthiness of what God says is right and who He is.

That is the life of an *Overcomer.*

Isn't Something Missing?

What seems to be missing between *hearing* and *obeying*? You may enjoy asking that question when you use the proposed *Overcomer* definition to discuss overcoming with others.

It is profound that the parable of the Two Builders comes immediately after the Sermon on the Mount. Jesus presented an amazingly different way of life, vastly different from anything taught before, and He concluded with ". . .whoever hears these sayings of Mine, and does them. . ."

The word *hears* in that phrase means "to receive communication from someone." So what is missing? What would you expect to follow *hears* before Jesus states *and does*? *Understand* seems to be missing. But it is not part of the definition of these two words, *hears* or *does*.

You can argue that *understand* is implied, yet taking it literally strengthens your walk with the Lord so you can overcome.

Does that seem to contradict the idea that you learn obedience? That may be true, but learning obedience does not mean that you understand before you obey. Learning will occur most often after the experience or teaching. As an *Overcomer*, you reinforce current obedience with past obedience, which encourages future obedience as you continue to learn of the greatness of God.

Hear and obey also gives you insight and enlightenment in obedience because you see how it ties to and helps you understand previous obedience. God's Word is interwoven, and obeying one part gives insight into others. Obeying is counterintuitive since it has the foundation of faith. We see the physical and material world, but faith is about the "conviction of things not seen" (Hebrews 11:1).

Therefore, it is essential to connect *hear* and *obey*.

Endure Without Fear

Enduring or persevering are excellent words for *Overcomers*. Endurance is not their own; otherwise, they would not persist in times of trouble.

> *Proverbs 24:10 (NKJV)—If you faint in the day*
> *of adversity, your strength is small.*

In the long term, *Overcomers* endure, even though it may not be every moment. Those moments become learning times to show them they were not overcoming, and that is most often linked directly to the powerful impact of fear.

Fear is not always bad. It helps when you live in the first phrase in the following verse, and it hurts if you are in the second part.

> *Proverbs 1:7 (NKJV)—The fear of the LORD is the beginning*
> *of knowledge, but fools despise wisdom and instruction.*

Satan uses fear to implement his only strategy, which is "Did God really say. . .?" The moment of doubt about God's perfection becomes an opportunity for Satan to interrupt your progress by deceiving you to no longer endure through the current circumstance.

> *Galatians 6:7-8 (NKJV)—Do not be deceived, God is not*
> *mocked; for whatever a man sows, that he will also reap. For*
> *he who sows to his flesh will of the flesh reap corruption, but he*
> *who sows to the Spirit will of the Spirit reap everlasting life.*

That is a reminder of the truth of Romans 6:13-23. Whatever you sow in your thoughts will reap a harvest, good or bad.

When you are deceived, you do not think God will do what He says. In the context of fear, if you fear something other than God, you will sow corruption. If you sow obedience to God, it will be life-giving.

The Power Source

Hearing, Obeying, and Enduring without fear depend on a power source far exceeding your willpower. Without it, you are easily deceived when Satan pushes the door open and whispers, "If God cared about you, you would have a much better life." That is especially true when enduring.

What is this crucial power source?

In Dr. Walvoord's table, notice that Christ is the heading of the first column under *Hear*. That is not only profound but also the foundation for all remaining columns. While the earlier definition works, I find hearing, obeying, and enduring easier when I remember that I have Christ's power to do those things. Because of what Jesus has done for us, He is the new power source.

The power source is the tipping point for *Overcomers* because you either trust Christ's power or something else, often yourself. However, dealing with "self" becomes tricky and easily misconstrued without relying on God's Word.

For example, "dying to self" is a good concept, but it may be distorted into trying to eliminate who I am or my humanity. That misapplication leads to the need for a monastery, strict discipline, seclusion, and even beating, depriving, and driving ourselves—more often our bodies—into submission. It requires rules to keep self in line. Even personalities enter the picture and are determined as better or worse as it relates to the self.

Notice that it leaves the power in something other than Christ through us. It is a version of trying to make myself better instead of being transformed into the image of Christ.

But God tells us through the apostle Paul that the idea of dying to self is about the power source. Jesus' life in us is the new power source. He tells us that the old power source is no longer your only option.

> *Romans 6:2 (NKJV)—How shall we who*
> *died to sin live any longer in it?"*

A child of God has not "died to sin" in the way we think about death. A helpful definition of dead is "separated from" or "apathetic." Christ's death, burial, and resurrection unplugged the old power source for our "earth suit." As God's child and creation, we now have two power options: the sin nature or Christ's life (new man, new nature).

The apostle Paul refers to the old power source as self, old man, flesh, sin nature, etc. As God's child, we can now plug into what our PERFECT Father God created us to be. It is about transformation into either "what is that good and acceptable and perfect will of God" (Romans 12:2) or "a depraved mind" (Romans 1:28). *Overcomers* choose the Romans 12:2 path.

Another view is about the identity we have of ourselves. Is our identity in Christ or something else? That is an accurate view, but I prefer concrete pictures. For example, which energy outlet am I plugged into? Which faucet am I connecting myself to? It is like having two outlets available: one labeled "world," which varies in voltage and reliability, and the other labeled "Christ," which has perfect, clean, reliable power. Or two faucets, one with sewage and the other with pure water.

Overcomers listen to the voice of the Holy Spirit, who lets us know which power source we are connected to.

Finally, Christ living through us does not eliminate who you are. Being renewed into the image of Christ makes us into the best of who we were created to be.

The Authority

Return to the parable of the Two Builders and look at how the people responded.

> *Matthew 7:28-29 (NKJV)—And so it was, when Jesus had ended these sayings, that the people were astonished at His teaching, for He taught them as one having authority, and not as the scribes.*

For those who accepted that He had authority, would you agree that it would be easier for them to obey? Is it easier to obey the speed limit when the police or the authorities are around? Yes, because they represent the consequences of disobeying authority.

If those people accepted Jesus as their authority, they do not need to understand. The same is true for you. It is time to obey because God is the one who knows and understands everything. That does not mean I am against understanding. Understanding comes later, mainly if you accept that He is the authority who is perfect.

God Is PERFECT

Earlier in my walk with the Lord, I studied God's attributes. The study was daunting because the human mind is finite. It was complex because of the many extraordinary ways to speak about who God says He is and what He does.

Years later, God helped me when I thought about how scholars refer to God's attributes as His "perfections." That became my profound and simplifying moment because it combined all God's attributes into one word that applies to all He is and does.

Consider some of the ways a dictionary defines perfect.

- Complete, unblemished, faultless
- Lacking nothing essential to the whole, complete of its nature or kind
- Being without defect or blemish
- Thoroughly skilled or talented in a certain field or area; proficient
- Completely suited for a particular purpose or situation
- Complete, thorough, utter
- Pure, undiluted, unmixed
- Excellent and delightful in all respects

It became a straightforward way to think and speak about God, especially His role in my circumstances. "He is *PERFECT*, so this situation is for my *best!*"

Seeing God as having authority is critical, but seeing Him as *PERFECT* can elevate *hear*ing, *obeying*, and *enduring* to *want to* instead of *have to*. If I knew the authority setting the speed limit was perfect, I might speed less often. If they had perfect knowledge, it would be easier to obey even without understanding.

It is even more applicable to our obedience to God's Word. He is *PERFECT*, and it is best for me to *hear* and *obey* all He says.

When you include God's perfection in the definition, it becomes

God is PERFECT. So hear, obey, and endure
without fear of loss or death.

Pursues My Best Through Me

If you have read any other books in the GR8 Relationship or Leaders series or read or listened to our blog/podcasts, you know that we often talk about the *Problem*.

Everyone has the *Problem* embedded in them. What is it?

We make everything about ME!

The power of marketing and advertising has the problem as its foundation because of an acronym marketers know people are thinking — WIIFM — "What's In It For Me?" God created us and knows our thoughts will quickly turn toward ourselves. That is why it is crucial to be in His Word. It is full of promises for those who accept the *Overcomer* path rather than something less.

The simplicity of removing WIIFM thinking is in this powerful verse for *Overcomers.*

> *Galatians 6:9 (NKJV)—And let us not grow weary while doing good, for in due season we shall reap if we do not lose heart.*

But how can I endure doing what is good when I do not see any positive results? In other words, "What's in it for me?" God answers, ". . . you shall reap if you do not lose heart." A harvest is waiting for you if you do not lose heart.

The incredible reality is God is *PERFECT*, and Jesus' perfect life is available to me—not like a Harry Potter wand. However, I can be a conduit through which His perfection can flow to the people around me and into the circumstances where He has placed me. The simplicity of endurance has nothing to do with your ability or strength. It is all about trusting in Jesus' power to live through you.

> *Ephesians 2:10 (NKJV)—For we are His workmanship, created in Christ Jesus for good works, which God prepared beforehand that we should walk in them.*

Your *PERFECT* Father God created you for good works. Better yet, He pursues your best in every part of your life. Nothing can separate you from His love (pursuing your best), as Paul states in Romans 8:37-39. You can choose God's power to endure and walk in the good works and what is best for you.

> *Philippians 2:12-13 (NKJV)—Therefore, my beloved, as you have always obeyed, not as in my presence only, but now much more in my absence, work out your own salvation with fear and trembling; for it is God who works in you both to will and to do for His good pleasure.*

Work out, not work for, your salvation. You choose to be a conduit for the life of Christ to flow through you to those around you. Your *PERFECT* Father God works in you for your best and His good pleasure. You could say He is pleased when you let Christ live through you.

> *Philippians 4:13 (NKJV)—I can do all things through Christ who strengthens me.*

The context for that verse is about contentment, so it is about trusting in Christ's ability, not ours. We experience rest when trusting in God's ability and anxiety when trusting in "ME."

It is essential that *Overcomers* recognize that the crucial power source for overcoming is Christ's life in them. It is their new life, Christ's Life, in them that overcomes, not their strength. It is the "Not I, but Christ" principle at work. It is Christ's life through them.

> *2 Corinthians 4:7, 11 (NKJV)—But we have this treasure*
> *in earthen vessels, that the excellence of the power*
> *may be of God and not of us . . . that the life of Jesus*
> *also may be manifested in our mortal flesh.*

Finally, it is appropriate to remove the last part of the original definition — "of loss or death." While fearing loss, especially death, is natural, the apostle Paul reminds us that fear is irrelevant when walking with Christ. King David agrees, as he tells us in Psalm 23:4 (NKJV):

> *Yea, though I walk through the valley of the shadow*
> *of death, I will fear no evil; for You are with me;*
> *Your rod and Your staff, they comfort me.*

With those thoughts, the definition becomes

God is PERFECT and pursues my best through me.
So hear, obey, and endure without fear.

The first part of the definition helps people see the *Overcomer's* power source. The second part identifies the *Overcomer's* fundamental actions.

When discussing an *Overcomer*, you can state the last part (hear, obey, and endure without fear) and then ask how an *Overcomer* can do that. It creates a discussion leading to the first part of the definition.

With the definition of an *Overcomer*, the remainder of the book presents Godly truth, wisdom, and values to *hear*. When you choose to *obey*, you will display the actions of an *Overcomer*. When you *endure*, you will display the heart of an *Overcomer* to a lost and dying world. God has promised us extraordinary rewards in eternity and the blessings of the fruit of the Holy Spirit now as we overcome.

Overcomers remember the simplicity of faith in both our becoming God's child and the process of being transformed into the image of Christ. It takes faith to become God's child and faith to let Jesus live through us. Faith is in both justification and sanctification. **Overcoming is not about how much discipline you have but about faith that Jesus will work through you!** You will not hear, obey, and endure without fear unless Jesus does it through you. When we try to do it, we focus on "ME." **Overcoming is God's work in us, not our work!**

Please endure without fear and trust that He will strengthen and renew you as He lives His life through you.

Overcomers Benefit from Structure

Overcomers need the benefit of structure to hear, obey, and endure without fear. The *Overcomer* structure demands different behavior unless you are already an *Overcomer*. Structure is a profound principle impacting your life. Once you learn about it, you will see how often it affects you.

When Winston Churchill said, "We shape our buildings, thereafter they shape us," he was talking about the power of structure.

Physical and mental structures constantly demand action from you, but you seldom notice them. Everything in life follows a structure, most importantly, what and how you think. What you think creates the most powerful structures in your life. What you think about drives your actions and feelings.

The principle of structure needs only three words to explain its importance.

Structure demands behavior

Structure creates the *path of least resistance*. Most often, the phrase means

> ". . . the easy way out. But what we mean is that energy
> moves where it is easiest for it to go. —Robert Fritz*

You can better understand structure when you apply it to real situations. For instance, consider one drop of rain that hits the top of a mountain. It has no choice about what will happen next because it will follow "the path of least resistance." Assuming the mountaintop is exceedingly small, how many ways can that drop go down the mountain?

Some say, "Any number of ways." But it can go down only *one* way. It will follow *the path of least resistance*. That drop of rain will flow in the direction where it is easiest to go. Think of a time when you spilled water on a table. What happened? The water either puddled or flowed off the table. The tabletop's angle demanded that the water's behavior stay or flow.

The structure of a room creates a path of least resistance for how you enter that room. Coming in through a door rather than climbing through a window is easiest. The structure of a car determines how you will interact with it. The steering wheel and pedals demand you sit close to the driver's seat to drive. Your shoe demands that you put the right one on the right foot and the left one on the left foot; otherwise, it will be uncomfortable. Even how you sit in a chair is determined by its design.

So structure demands behavior and creates the path of least resistance. But you could fight the structure. For example, you could get into a room by tunneling through the floor, breaking through a wall, or making a hole in the ceiling instead of using the door. It would be rare for you to do that because it *takes more physical and mental energy.*

While picturing physical structures is easy, the more powerful ones are in your mind. If you break a hole in the wall of a room to enter, you most likely will need to ignore your values first. You probably do not value tearing up property to enter a room in a way other than through the door. That is a good illustration of the structure or power of thinking. So the word structure in this book most often talks about what and how you think.

Structure and THP

THP is an easy way to use the power of structure! THP stands for THERE, HERE, PATH. A detailed explanation of this is in Chapter 13.

- THERE—Where you want to be or go.
- HERE—Where you are now.
- PATH—Steps or actions to get from HERE to THERE (this is seldom a straight line).

You create the path of least resistance *only when THERE and HERE are clear.*

A simple example of THP would be sitting in a chair.

- THERE—You want to rest your legs.
- HERE—You are standing up, and your legs are tired.
- PATH—You look for a chair or place to sit, walk to the chair, turn around, and sit down.

The THP Chart to the right illustrates that.

The PATH will be different if either THERE or HERE are different. If you do not want to "rest your legs" (THERE), you do not need a path of action to lead to that end result. If you do not want to rest your legs because you are already sitting, your HERE has changed, which requires a different THERE and PATH.

Finally, the following principle is critical to the path of least resistance:

Where you look, you tend to go

That applies to all your goals and wants, even sitting in a chair. In the example above, looking at the chair and walking to it is easier than looking elsewhere. The same is true when driving, riding a bicycle, or riding a horse. My wife tells me that horse riding instructors tell you that where you look changes your body position, influencing the horse and what you do as you ride. Looking at where you want to go helps you integrate where you are with where you want to be. That helps create the path to get where you want to be.

You influence your current and future actions by having a clear end result.

Glorify God Structure

Overcomers want to glorify God in all that they do. The graphic illustrates that with THP. It shows how focusing on what God states is most important will influence actions or the PATH.

If you focus your attention on **Reflect** Christ NOW . . .

> *1 Corinthians 10:31 (NKJV)—Therefore, whether you eat or drink, or whatever you do, do all to the glory of God.*

. . . and **Reign** with Christ LATER

> *Revelation 20:6 (NKJV)—Blessed and holy is he who has part in the first resurrection. Over such the second death has no power, but they shall be priests of God and of Christ, and shall reign with Him a thousand years.*

. . . then actions like those in the PATH in the graphic will be part of your life.

If your THERE is to Glorify God, it demands actions that God desires to do through you (Philippians 2:12). Actions such as 1) depend upon Him, 2) grow in Him through the eight steps of personal transformation (2 Peter 1:5-8), 3) have an eternal not temporary view of life, 4) operate in your God-given design, and, above all, 5) love others—pursue their best.

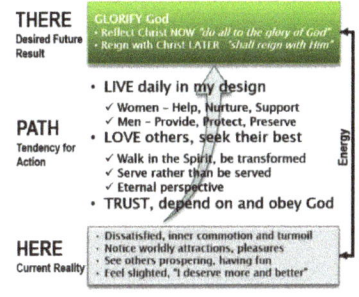

Battling Structures—Glorify God or Glorify ME

Because of your sin nature, many things can distract you from Glorifying God. The reality is all those distractions fall into the category of trusting something other than God. Before I go further, everyone has a *fundamental choice* or decision every day.

Will I trust God or something other than God?

Keeping it simple helps you escape Satan's trap when he asks, "Did God really say?" Satan wants you confused, thinking life is complex when it is not. Everything comes down to whether *you trust God or not.*

Romans 6 and 7 show both sides of the fundamental choice. The struggle between trusting God and trusting something other than God is evident.

> *Romans 7:15 (NKJV)—For what I am doing, I do*
> *not understand. For what I will to do, that I do*
> *not practice; but what I hate, that I do.*

In Romans 7:25, the Apostle Paul further states the following:

> *So then, with the mind I myself serve the law of*
> *God, but with the flesh the law of sin.*

Those verses show you another structure working to capture your attention. Remember the statement, "Where you look, you tend to go?" Romans 6 and most of the Bible provide that clear message to you as a child of God—blessings or cursings, righteousness or unrighteousness. Where are you looking?

> *Deuteronomy 30:19 (NKJV)—I call heaven and earth as*
> *witnesses today against you, that I have set before you*
> *life and death, blessing and cursing; therefore choose life,*
> *that both you and your descendants may live . . .*

That message is the same in the New Testament.

> *Romans 6:13 (NKJV)—And do not present your members*
> *as instruments of unrighteousness to sin, but present*
> *yourselves to God as being alive from the dead, and your*
> *members as instruments of righteousness to God.*

The graphic presents two structures available to you right now.

Whatever is happening in your life now is your current reality (HERE)—the bottom rectangle. That is the common element for both structures. You have two options (two THEREs).

Everything that happens next depends on which THERE you look at.

Remember, structure demands behavior. If you look at "Glorify, Satisfy ME, Now!" the behaviors and actions in your life will be similar to the PATH on the left. You present yourself to unrighteousness, trust something other than God, and ignore the explicit instructions of God's Word.

If you choose to look at "Glorify GOD," vastly different actions and behaviors show up in your life. Those actions and behaviors focus on a future benefit driven by a desire to *reflect* Christ now, allowing you to prepare to *reign* with Him later.

Choosing the Glorify GOD structure is not simply better—**it is the difference between life and death**.

> *Romans 6:23 (NJKV)—For the wages of sin is death, but the gift of God is eternal life in Christ Jesus our Lord.*

Remember, that verse is not for unbelievers but for believers. Choosing the Glorify ME structure does not mean you have lost your salvation. It means you experience the consequences of the sin nature just like the unbeliever who is a slave to sin. You decided to be a slave to sin even though you are no longer sin's slave.

> *Romans 6:16 (NKJV)—Do you not know that to whom you present yourselves slaves to obey, you are that one's slaves whom you obey, whether of sin leading to death, or of obedience leading to righteousness?*

These two structures are REAL. *Where are you looking?*

ME or WE Structures

The ME and WE structures are like the battling structures of Glorify ME or Glorify God. These structures highlight your most significant problem as a person or an *Overcomer*—ME!

You are either elevating ME above others or overcoming. The ME structure has values and actions that fit your sin nature and Satan.

Serve ME—Committed to INFLUENCE others to get THERE	Serve WE—Committed to INFLUENCE others to get THERE
Satisfy personal purpose and goals – value power and position, results tell a story about ME	Satisfy organization purpose and goals – value people and self-governance, results tell a story about US

Problems, challenges, changes, limited resources, overwhelmed

> *Isaiah 14:13-14 (NKJV)—For you have said in your heart: "I will ascend into heaven, I will exalt my throne above the stars of God; I will also sit on the mount of the congregation on the farthest sides of the north; I will ascend above the heights of the clouds, I will be like the Most High."*

You can never be an *Overcomer* when your focus is selfish and self-absorbed because that is what *Overcomers* overcome. That means your values do not align with God's. On the other hand, when you pursue the best for others, you have a WE mindset and an *Overcomer* structure. Godly values, principles, and actions are still needed, but the foundation is solid.

Be honest with yourself. If you look at "Serve ME" as the world does, your actions and words will show it. Your actions and words will also show if you are in the "Serve WE" structure.

> *Jeremiah 17:9-10 (NKJV)—The heart is deceitful above all things, and desperately wicked. Who can know it? I, the Lord, search the heart, I test the mind, even to give every man according to his ways, according to the fruit of his doings.*

Who you are will appear as the "fruit of [your] doings," which the Lord sees and judges. Words also tell what is in your heart.

> *Matthew 12:34 (NKJV)—Brood of vipers! How can you, being evil, speak good things? For out of the abundance of the heart the mouth speaks.*

> *Matthew 15:18 (NKJV)—But those things which proceed out of the mouth come from the heart, and they defile a man.*

You know it is true. People see whether you are in the ME or WE structure, and God already knows.

So thinking about overcoming as a Christian, are you turning to Him, depending on Him and His Word to figure out where to go, or are you self-focused as you look at the problem or challenge? *Overcomers* use the structure of God's Word and the power of Christ's life in them to keep looking in the right direction (where you look, you tend to go) and focus on overcoming rather than being defeated. And importantly, they are not striving to do it by their power; instead, they choose the power source of Jesus living through them.

SUMMARY

Overcomers are believers, but not all believers are *Overcomers*. *Overcomers* are *faithful* believers. Believers who hear, obey, and endure without fear will become *Overcomers* because they obey God's Word instead of their sin nature. Any believer can be an *Overcomer*.

Justification versus sanctification makes the difference in whether a believer in Christ is an *Overcomer*. *Justification* means that your sins no longer count against you, and God makes you righteous. *Sanctification* is God's ongoing and daily work to change you into Christ's image, which is the *Overcomer's* path. The power source for overcoming is trusting a perfect God to live Christ's life through you. That power energizes you to hear, obey, and endure without fear. You become a child of God through faith in Christ's death, burial, and resurrection. You become an *Overcomer* through faith in Christ's life working in and through you.

An *Overcomer's* primary thinking follows the Glorify God structure. However, they will face situations where they choose the Glorify ME structure. If they continue in that ME structure, it will impact their rewards in eternity. If they look back to their perfect God and choose by faith the power of the life of Christ in them, they will confess and restore fellowship with God, and they will be back on the *Overcomer* path.

Even believers, though they are given the Bible, the living Word to guide them, are not always *Overcomers* because they don't walk in the fullness of their faith, in deep relationship with God.

Are you only a justified Christian, or are you also allowing God to make you an *Overcomer* as He lives through you? Is your path in life focused on glorifying God or glorifying you?

The remainder of this book is about principles, truth, wisdom, and tools that help us overcome. While some chapters may appear to lean more on the idea of discipline or self-control, none of the following information works best without the complete trust in the life of Christ and the Holy Spirit working in and through us.

Overcomers QUICKStart

Overcomers Definition

God is PERFECT and pursues my best through me.
So HEAR, OBEY, and ENDURE without fear

Overcomers Recipe

God created man with the critical ability for faith. All of man's existence demonstrates faith in something. Unfortunately, too few have faith in the correct object—God, the PERFECT Creator, Master, and Father! The *Overcomer's* recipe uses that foundation and the elements of the definition of an *Overcomer*.

Each ingredient stands alone, but all are required to be an *Overcomer*. Notice the recurring theme of faith.

HEAR about Jesus's death, burial, and resurrection—HEARING turns to Faith.

Both the Believer and the *Overcomer* have faith in the death, burial, and resurrection of Jesus Christ (Romans 10:17). The *Overcomer* has further faith that Jesus will live through them to allow them to look more like Him.

Faith in God and His Word as the Authority—HEAR to grow.

The *Overcomer* begins the journey by trusting that God's Word is true and God is the authority. Faith in Christ's life in the *Overcomer* is the power and the foundation to allow Christ to live through you and enjoy the fruit of the Holy Spirit.

Faith that God is Perfect and wants what is BEST for ME—HEAR and OBEY to overcome.

Overcomers hear more of God's Word, see the benefits of obedience, and start accepting God's perfection, preeminence, and priority in life and eternity. As they accept that God is perfect and wants their BEST, they trust more often that He allows circumstances and people in their lives to transform them into the image of Jesus Christ. Instead of trusting their understanding (Proverbs 3:5-6), they learn to hear and obey God. *Overcomers* continue to learn how to rest by faith in Christ's power through them.

Faith in God's Promises of Inheritance and Rewards—ENDURE.

Overcomers start to believe God's promises, rewards, and inheritance are waiting for them in heaven. They accept that life is like running a race to receive the prize (1 Corinthians 9:24), so they eliminate weights that hinder them from enduring as they run the race (Hebrews 12:1). The most significant weight is the lack of faith that a believer is a "new creature, and only God can overcome our self-life, "ME." No one can be an *Overcomer* without accepting by faith that Christ will gladly live through them. Dismantle the pretense that you can do it.

Faith in Christ's Power in and Through Me—ENDURE without fear.

Overcomers who abandon their lives to the power of Christ's life and the Holy Spirit in and through them make a critical and eternal life decision. They realize that Christ's life in them is the only reliable resource to become an *Overcomer*. They renew their mind to be an *Overcomer* when they accept God's Perfection and Christ's Power. He renews their strength, mind, and courage to see He is the Victor through them. His power in them allows participation in His victory as a co-victor. Enduring without fear only occurs when an *Overcomer* rests in the power of Christ living through them. There is nothing to fear since Christ has already overcome all obstacles and sits at the right hand of God.

Discussion Questions

1. How are *Overcomers* different from Believers?
2. What is the primary element that *Overcomers* overcome?
3. Explain the "Gift and the Prize."
4. Which of the seven churches in Revelation could be you? Why?
5. What are your thoughts about an *Overcomer* hearing and obeying even if they do not understand?
6. What difference do you see between enduring and enduring without fear?
7. What would change if you consistently reminded yourself that God is PERFECT?
8. What examples can you think of that might verify the problem is "Making everything about ME?"
9. What difference do you see between Christ "in" you and Christ "through" you?
10. Explain "Structure demands behavior."
11. What do you think about THP?
12. Explain the need for clarity about HERE.
13. Explain the phrase, "Where you look, you tend to go."
14. Look at the battling structures (ME or WE). What are some life lessons you could learn from that chart?

CHAPTER 2

WHO'S IN CHARGE?

Michael always loved being in charge from the time he was a young child. He was always the captain of any team he was on and excelled in school and sports. God called Michael to ministry in his early college years. He attended seminary, where he met his wife, and they married after graduating. His wife, Georgia, was always supportive of his call to lead a church. She knew he had all the tools to be a great leader.

When Michael was about 40 years old, after serving in several churches in smaller communities, he was called to pastor a large church in a metropolitan area. He and Georgia were excited to make the move and adjust to a larger church in a city.

Six months in, Michael discovered a faction of people in church leadership who had been in the church for over 30 years. All of them were close friends who did not want change. Michael knew his ability to lead a church through change would keep this one alive and thriving.

The team who hired him said they wanted him to come in and draw younger people who desperately needed to understand living in a personal relationship with Christ. They had noticed a young generation wandering and confused about God and His love and grace.

Michael hired an executive coach to help him navigate the situation. He was careful to choose a Christian coach who professed Christ as Savior. He and the coach focused on how he could get the dissenting leaders in the church to respect him and treat him like their leader. The coach took him through some behavioral assessments that would help him influence others in the church, and in their coaching sessions, they discussed scriptures that supported Michael commanding respect as the senior pastor.

After several months of coaching, the atmosphere started to shift, and the group that had resisted what he was trying to do in the beginning started to support him. He found that rather than disagreeing with him in leadership meetings and challenging everything he said, they softened and volunteered to lead certain committees and serve as advocates for the programs that Michael wanted to implement.

One evening after this shift, as Michael drifted off to sleep, he prayed, "Thank you, Lord, for delivering me from the trial and helping me move forward with programs that I know will help the church grow and prosper."

Questions

1. Is Michael an *Overcomer*?
2. What does he do that indicates that he's an *Overcomer*?
3. What scriptures could the coach use to help Michael command respect as a senior pastor?

Overcomers Trust God as the Only Authority

Key Lesson: *God is the ONLY authority! Overcomers are a channel of God's authority and steward it to benefit others.*

Your thinking and actions change when you see God as the **only** authority. First, you open your ears to *hear* and *obey* because He is THE authority. Second, you see satisfaction and comfort entirely different than before. Finally, you see how Godly authority used correctly benefits people and does not abuse them.

God Is THE Authority

Overcomers do not operate based on their authority. Instead, they completely trust God's authority. They believe He is the priority and the ONLY authority, first in all things, which is the purpose of the first commandment.

The following verses are a small sample of what God tells us about Himself.

> *Exodus 20:3 (NKJV)—You shall have no other gods before Me.*

> *Job 42:1-2 (NKJV)—Then Job answered the LORD and said: "I know that You can do everything, and that no purpose of Yours can be withheld from You.*

> *Proverbs 21:1 (NKJV)—The king's heart is in the hand of the Lord, Like the rivers of water; He turns it wherever He wishes.*

> *Isaiah 40:13-14, 25 (NKJV)—Who has directed the Spirit of the Lord, or as His counselor has taught Him? With whom did He take counsel, and who instructed Him, and taught Him in the path of justice? Who taught Him knowledge, and showed Him the way of understanding? To whom will you liken Me, or to who shall I be equal? says the Holy One.*

> *Daniel 4:34-35, 39 (NKJV)—For His dominion is an everlasting dominion, and His kingdom is from generation to generation. All the inhabitants of the earth are reputed as nothing; He does according to His will in the army of heaven and among the inhabitants of the earth. No one can restrain His hand or*

say to Him, "What have You done?" Therefore know this day,
and consider it in your heart, that the Lord Himself is God in
heaven above and on the earth beneath; there is no other.

1 Timothy 6:15-16 (NKJV)— . . . which He will manifest in
His own time, He who is the blessed and only Potentate, the
King of kings and Lord of lords, who alone has immortality,
dwelling in unapproachable light, whom no man has seen or
can see, to whom be honor and everlasting power. Amen.

Revelation 19:16 (NKJV)—And He has on His robe and on His
thigh a name written: KING OF KINGS AND LORD OF LORDS.

Even though God is THE authority and has the supreme right and ability to do whatever He desires, He does not force His will on anyone. We remain free to choose for or against Him. No one knows how God can be in control, from the germs to the galaxies, yet we still have freedom of choice.

Overcomers accept that truth, hear Him, and obey Him because He is THE authority and sovereign over all creation. Without that clarity, it is impossible to be an *Overcomer*. Why? What is the *Overcomer* overcoming? Self, the sin nature, or the desire to make everything about ME.

When an *Overcomer* overcomes, they depend on God, not themselves. They hear and obey because God is THE authority and our caring Father who wants what is best for His children.

GOD'S AUTHORITY IS COMFORTING

If you are unwilling to hear and obey God, comfort and contentment will be fleeting. The flesh craves satisfaction and comfort but seeks it from what is temporal, leading to unexpected consequences like regrets, grief, and addictions.

But trusting God's Word and truth produces unexpected comforts and benefits like the fruit of the Spirit. It is entirely counterintuitive because God's ways are much better than ours.

Isaiah 55:8-9 (NKJV)—"For My thoughts are not your thoughts,
nor are your ways My ways," says the LORD. "For as the
heavens are higher than the earth, So are My ways higher
than your ways, And My thoughts than your thoughts."

The willingness of your flesh to doubt and not trust a PERFECT God makes it easy to be skeptical of truth and, most likely, all of God's Word.

However, in those times of surrender to the Holy Spirit, the *Overcomer* in you hears and obeys, then notices that while the situation has not changed, there is a positive change, even peace and comfort. Accepting that God's ways are higher is obedience, which can eventually lead to an increased understanding of who God is and how trustworthy He is.

> *There is no attribute more comforting to His children than that of God's sovereignty. Under the most adverse circumstances, in the most severe trials, they believe that sovereignty has ordained their afflictions, that sovereignty overrules them, and that sovereignty will sanctify them all. There is nothing for which the children ought to more earnestly contend to than the doctrine of their Master over all creation—the Kingship of God over all the works of His own hands—the Throne of God and His right to sit upon that throne . . . for it is God upon the Throne whom we trust.—C. H. Spurgeon*

In a fallen world, it is too easy to see everything falling apart and become a doomsday prophet. That is the essence of discomfort, encouraging worry, which is disrespectful and disobedient to God.

> *Philippians 4:6-7 (NKJV)—Be anxious for nothing, but in everything by prayer and supplication, with thanksgiving, let your requests be made known to God; 7 and the peace of God, which surpasses all understanding, will guard your hearts and minds through Christ Jesus.*

Accepting that God is on His throne, in control of everything, even though it does not look like it, is immensely comforting because someone needs to be in control! Those are the times God challenges you to hear, obey, and endure without fear, and you overcome the flesh's desire to believe lies about God.

God's Authority Requires Stewardship

You may assume you are an authority because you have a title in a business or church. Be cautious; that was the mistake of the Pharisees, Scribes, and the religious leaders of the day during Jesus Christ's time.

> *Luke 20: 46-47 (NIV)—Beware of the scribes, who desire to go around in long robes, love greetings in marketplaces, the best seats in the synagogues, and the best places at feasts, who devour widows' houses, and for a pretense make long prayers. These will receive their condemnation.*

That is not God's view of authority. Since He is THE authority, stewarding His authority is required. Authority is like money or possessions. They are not yours. They are God's. *Overcomers* are good stewards of God's authority. That means anyone in a position of authority is only **a channel of authority**, not the authority.

If you want to be an *Overcomer*, Jesus Christ has a message for you.

> Matthew 20:26 (NIV)—*Not so with you. Instead, whoever wants to become great among you must be your servant.*

You are a good steward of God's authority when you maximize others' freedom, use authority with gentleness, and use authority to serve.

Maximize Others' Freedom

Authority Is NOT About Control

The Greek word for authority is *exousia*. It indicates "freedom of choice." So a person with significant authority has the maximum freedom of choice. On the other hand, the one under authority most often has their freedom limited.

That is how it works in the world, but that is not how God wants you to use His authority—His channel of authority. Since God is the only authority, look at how He used His authority with us.

> Galatians 5:1 (NKJV)—*Stand fast therefore in the liberty by which Christ has made us free, and do not be entangled again with a yoke of bondage.*

See it? God used His authority through the death of Jesus Christ the Son to set us FREE! That means the example God set for us as channels of His authority is to use His authority to provide freedom, not control.

That means authority is NOT about "ME." It is not about your position or your power. It encourages, even creates, freedom of choice for those under your channel of authority. It does not mean there are no boundaries or consequences for people who do not follow the rules. When used correctly, authority allows people to cross boundaries and experience the consequences, just as God deals with you.

Control does work. However, control works mainly in the short term, relying on fear. If you can maintain fear in people, you can control them until they are brave enough to fight back or rebel. What control fails to create is self-governance. It may create compliance, but not much more. Control gets people to comply with the minimum requirements, **but they do not pursue excellence.**

Control completely misapplies God's authority. God gave you freedom and wants to transform you (2 Peter 1:5). Following Him produces the fruit of the Spirit (Galatians 5:22), which includes self-control, not external control.

Authority IS About Developing

When you accept your role as a channel of authority, you can focus on valuing and developing people instead of using your authority to control people.

Are you focused on developing people like the Apostle Paul? Will you help them become *Overcomers*?

> *2 Corinthians 10:8 (NKJV)—. . .our authority, which the Lord gave us for edification and not for your destruction.*

> *2 Corinthians 13:10 (NKJV)—. . .the authority which the Lord has given me for edification and not for destruction.*

Paul's example is so good to follow because he used power, but it was God's, not his power. He followed the "power from the outside, not the inside" principle (more on this later). That frees you to relate to others appropriately. You do not just try to "get along" because the POWER of God shares the truth (power) in love (relate)—Ephesians 4:15.

POWERFUL	RELATIONAL
• Power comes from God, not us; given, not deserved; use it wisely • Power comes from God's Word to build up and free others, not control • The power of God frees Leaders to RELATE	• Paul related God's, not his own, power as he led • Paul related meekness and gentleness to the people • Paul would not "lord it over your faith" (2 Cor. 1:24) • Paul would "lower myself to elevate you" (2 Cor. 11:7)

When you think authority is about control, you will try to use God's Word to support your power or desire to control. That means you will probably misuse the following verses and graphs. (The graphic is for marriage, but the principles apply to any level of authority.)

Ephesians 5:23 (NKJV)—For the husband is head of the wife, as also Christ is head of the church . . .

Chain of Command

H = Husband
W = Wife

*1 Corinthians 11:3 (NKJV)—But I want you to know
that the head of every man is Christ, the head of
woman is man, and the head of Christ is God.*

The reality is God's image involves both Power and Relating. Yes, Ephesians 5:23 is entirely true, but what is His purpose as the head?

It is for the PROTECTION of the followers!

That means using power FOR the benefit of the wife and followers. That is true of Jesus. He is THE authority AND He is our Savior! Powerful and Relational. He uses His power FOR us, not Himself.

So a summary of the graphics is as follows:

- The POWER of Authority is from God, not us
- Trusting His Power frees leaders to RELATE (Phil. 2:12)
- Spiritual authority is OVER for Protection and Guidance (Powerful)
- Spiritual authority is BESIDE for Development and Support (Relational)

Use Authority Gently

Fueled by Meekness and Gentleness

*2 Corinthians 10:1-2 (ESV)— . . . by the meekness and
gentleness of Christ—I who am humble when face to face
with you, but bold toward you I am when away! I beg of
you that when I am present I may not have to show boldness
with such confidence as I count on showing against some
who suspect us of walking according to the flesh.*

How clear can Paul be about the proper use of authority? Paul was the channel of the authority of God. Jesus is THE Authority and is "meek and gentle" in His dealings with us. His unlimited power is used for our benefit because He is meek and gentle.

That does not mean that He is timid! A good definition of meekness is "power under control." Jesus' vast power is not destructive like the power of a bomb. Instead, His power is like electricity that powers our lights and other beneficial tools and appliances. When you use the power of God's authority, you do not try to change people—that is Christ's role. You hope, pray, encourage, exhort, and rebuke, but leave the change to God and them.

Paul did not try to control the Corinthians. Instead, he invited them to consider the truth but did not demand it, even though he could have done so with his position. Why not? Because the authority is not Paul's, he used Christ's authority the same way Christ would.

Each of the following is about treating people as Jesus would—with meekness and gentleness.

> *2 Corinthians 1:24 (ESV)—Not that we lord it over your faith, but we work with you for your joy*

> *2 Corinthians 2:8 (NKJV)—I urge you to reaffirm your love for Him*

> *2 Corinthians 8:8 (ESV)—I say this not as a command, but to prove by the earnestness of others that your love also is genuine*

> *2 Corinthians 11:7 (NKJV)—Did I commit sin in humbling myself so that you might be exalted?*

Our Power Is Unnecessary

Since authority is about freedom and you are only a channel of God's authority, you can start using God's authority more effectively. Follow Paul's example with the Corinthian church.

> *2 Corinthians 13:2-4 (NKJV)—2 I have told you before, and foretell as if I were present the second time, and now being absent I write to those who have sinned before, and to all the rest, that if I come again I will not spare—3 since you seek a proof of Christ speaking in me, who is not weak toward you, but mighty in you. 4 For though He was crucified in weakness, yet He lives by the power of God. For we also are weak in Him, but we shall live with Him by the power of God toward you.*

What Paul says may not be clear, so the table below will help.

PERCEPTION	REALITY
Christ does not speak through Paul	(He does, let me prove it to you)
Christ won't deal with our sin	Christ is mighty in you, deals with sin and disobedience
Christ died on the cross, was weak, not strong	Christ was strong, He won and is alive by the Power of God
Paul is weak, so we do not need to listen to him	Yes, we are weak just like Christ!
Paul has no power	We will use God's power when dealing with you

Therefore, "I will not spare you" – "God will not spare you."

The Corinthians were questioning Paul's authority. Paul asked them to deal with people who were sinning, but they did not because they did not believe Christ was speaking to them through Paul. They did not think Christ was concerned about their sin, so they ignored Paul and Christ. They also may have questioned the power of Christ to deal with their sin.

So Paul states that Christ ". . . is not weak toward you, but mighty in you." In other words, Paul tells them they do not understand who Christ is and His power.

He goes on to say, and I paraphrase, "Yes, He died on the cross, which may appear that He was weak, not strong, but you are missing the power of God that raised Christ from the dead, and now He lives by the power of God."

So far, this is a good lesson for leaders to correct errors when noticed, share the truth, and leave it with God to change a person's life.

Now it gets even better! The Corinthians were mistaken about the power of Christ. They were also mistaken about the power of Christ directed at them through Paul. So my paraphrase is:

> "Since you are mistaken about Christ—He is not weak but extremely powerful. So you might say, I am weak, just like Christ is weak! But I do not need to be strong because Christ's power will deal with you. Therefore, when I say, 'I will not spare you,' it means God will not spare you. I am not the power; I am just a messenger or channel of the power."

What a fantastic message for *Overcomers* who follow Christ! If you rely on your power, you do it completely wrong. **Be like Paul. He depended on Christ's authority and power, not his own.**

The Power Source Makes the Difference

The world's view of authority has its roots attached to ME: pride, my position, and my power. Being the power or the authority is the primary focus of your sin nature—linked to the world system—which Satan rules.

But God's view is drastically different—the only authority is God. Authority channels value humility because authority is not theirs. It is God's. It is not about you but being a good steward of His authority.

World's View	God's View
• "I said"	• "God says"
• OVER	• UNDER
• Envy	• Content
• Getting	• Giving
• Restricting	• Developing
• Rules and laws	• Grace and freedom
• Being served	• Serving
• Being protected	• Protecting

Along with that different view of authority comes the big difference between the world's emphasis and God's. Look at some of the differences in the table.

If you have the world's view, your power source is you and your ability to control others. But God's way is quite different! Your power source is God, who works through you.

Consider this great principle: "Always find the power from the outside, not the inside."

First, it means you clearly understand what God wants! Then you apply what God wants to those under and around you. As a channel of authority in an organization, your power source is the purpose, core values, rules, and expectations. You do not need to act powerfully. Instead, you let those elements be the power. Control or anger is unnecessary. You point them to the organization's values, which is the power you use.

Try that approach; your attitude will improve when approaching someone needing correction. Why? Because it is not about you against them or winning. It is about helping them overcome by remembering what the organization needs from them. People who see themselves as authority channels for God are taking excellent steps to become *Overcomers*, servants, and people helpers.

Use Authority to Serve

Servants Not Dictators

As a reminder, authority is misunderstood and misused. Attention focuses on being the authority, so the world's view of authority is self-absorbed, which misuses it. If people do not do what the authority wants, the structure demands defensiveness and lets people know who is the boss, the one in charge.

You are not an *Overcomer* or servant leader when you try to prove you are the authority. You are a dictator, reacting and responding, not leading. Leading is not about you! It is about serving, so *Overcomers*—

- Follow THE Leader, do what HE says is correct and best, and are not dependent on or trying to please followers or others.
- Think about their relationship with God first and consider followers and others second.
- Value followers enough to develop them and invite and encourage them to self-governance.
- Apply the power of God's Truth and relate or share the Truth with others who may follow.
- Focus on THERE, HERE, and PATH . . . and invite others to go THERE, see HERE, and walk (act, learn, adjust on) the PATH.

Overcomers Do Not "Have to" Serve

Please do not miss this point. If you "should, must, have to" serve, you will create a problem for yourself and those around and under you. At a minimum, you will decrease your energy to serve because you do it from obligation, not want. More about this is in chapter 9—Values Freedom.

If you serve because you "have to," you can easily have a bad attitude and expect others to show their appreciation for what you do. Satan wants you to think that way because he knows you will focus on yourself, not others. You choose to serve or not, but do not serve because you believe you "have to."

> *"The Army, with its emphasis on rank and medals and efficiency reports, is the easiest institution in the world in which to get consumed with ambition. Some officers spend all their time currying favor and worrying about the next promotion — a miserable way to live. But West Point saved me from that by instilling the ideal of service above self — to do my duty for my country even if it brought no gain at all. It gave me far more than a military career — it gave me a calling."—It Doesn't Take a Hero, General H. Norman Schwarzkopf*

Paul's Use of God's Authority—(2 Corinthians 11)

Finally, here is a summary of Paul's style, as shown in 2 Corinthians 11. I challenge you to study it further to see how his style fits Jesus.

- Cares deeply for and identifies with those he served (1–2)
- Offers protection to & exhorts those he served (3-4, 12-15)
- Unwavering and sober about abilities & position (5-6)

- Defends the position and ministry, but not himself (defensive=about ME)
- Refuses to burden or depend on those he served (7–11)
- Speaks the truth and communicates clearly with them (16-21)
- Suffers for those he served (22-27)
- Boasts in and trusts God, not himself (28-31)

DISCUSSION QUESTIONS

1. What is the difference between God's view of authority and man's?
2. What is the difference between a channel of authority versus being the authority?
3. What example can you use to explain the difference?
4. What three words help you remember how to be a Godly authority channel?
5. Explain the benefits of freedom for you as the leader and the followers.
6. Explain how God uses His authority for freedom, not control.
7. Explain what is happening in 2 Corinthians 13:2-4.
8. Explain the principle: "Always find the power from the outside, not the inside."
9. What can be wrong with "having to lead"?

Chapter 3

Get the Work Done, No Matter What it Takes

Sam is the manager of a retail store of a small electronics firm in a large city. He reports to a vice president at the firm, who works in the corporate office in another city. Sam joined the company about two years ago. He is accountable to the vice president for meeting sales goals and cost containment. Sam manages 10 employees who are paid by the hour and work in shifts, as well as two salaried assistant managers. The assistant managers are supposed to schedule the hourly employees and manage them while they are working their shifts serving customers. In addition, they are responsible for ordering inventory, balancing the store's books regarding inventory, and sales tax and revenue. One of these assistant managers, Ashley, has been with the company in this retail location for a year, and Bill has been with the company for 10 years.

In the last few weeks, Sam has noticed that two employees consistently arrive late for their shifts and do not complete their duties at work. This creates long lines at checkout counters and frustrated customers who can't get their questions answered. He schedules a meeting with his assistant managers, Ashley and Bill.

"Ashley, Bill, thanks for meeting with me. Over the last few weeks, I have noticed that Justin and Tiffany are typically late for work and don't seem to complete tasks they are supposed to, including sweeping the supply room and being available to help customers."

Ashley says, "I know what you mean. Often, I have to work late because I'm interrupted all day to help customers. I literally walk the floor about every hour to make sure no customers are standing around with no one to help them."

Sam asks, "Have you spoken to them about this?"

Ashley says, "Not really. When I try, they just get mad and start gossiping about me with the other workers. It's just easier to do the work myself. Everything gets done faster that way."

Bill says, "Oh, you know those two employees are just kids. They don't have a work ethic. They just show up to get paid and do the minimal amount of work possible."

Sam asks Bill, "How do you deal with employees who are not pulling their weight?"

Bill says, "Well, you can't really make somebody work harder if they don't want to. Most of our customers come in and know what they want, so I don't think people are getting upset about not having someone to answer a question."

Sam encourages Bill to consider the burden that thinking puts on other workers and new customers who want advice on what to buy and want to understand the differences in product brands.

Six months later, Ashley calls a meeting with Sam. Here's how the conversation goes.

"Sam, I'm ready to quit! Bill doesn't do anything. When I come to work, he is supposed to have updated the inventory reports and cash register receipts. He is supposed to do it at the end of the day, but most of the time, he doesn't get around to it. I have worked so hard to make this store a great place for customers, but it feels like I'm doing everything! The employees don't even do their jobs."

Sam looks at her with concern and asks, "Have you said anything to Bill or the employees about this?"

Ashley answers, "Of course not. I don't want to rock the boat, and he doesn't listen to me anyway. Sam, you need to do something right away. I know you have the power to fix this through corrective action or hiring different people."

Sam says, "Ashley, you are a smart person and a hard worker. I appreciate what you do. Part of your job is to manage the employees during their shifts. So you need to talk to them about your expectations."

Ashley, "Well, okay."

After that meeting, Ashley does not talk to the employees or Bill. She continues to stay late to get all of the work done, even taking on some of Bill's tasks because she can do it faster. She would rather know that the job is done right and on time. She feels she is putting the company above herself. In the evening, she complains to her husband about how she is doing all the work, and her resentment grows.

Questions

1. Is Ashley showing self-control, also called self-governance? What did she say or do that influenced you to answer yes or no?
2. What did she do to pass up immediate gratification for future benefits?
3. How do you think her actions will impact the store and Ashley in the long-term?
4. What could Sam do differently to demonstrate self-governance and leadership?

Overcomers Choose the Holy Spirit Over Self

Key Lesson: *Pass up immediate gratification for future benefits. You do the right thing when no one is watching.*

What Is Self-Governance?

Before reading this chapter, please note that I firmly believe the Christian life involves personal responsibility. Still, it requires Christ living through us, "Not I, but Christ" (Galatians 2:20). So we have Christ's power to strengthen us as He lives through us (Philippians 2:12) and the responsibility to run the race to win (1 Corinthians 9:24, Hebrews 12:1). Both are true and part of an Overcomer's life. This chapter focuses more on personal responsibility and reminds us that we are to "walk in the Spirit, and you will not fulfill the lust of the flesh (Galatians 5:16).

Are You Asking...
- Why is this happening to me?
- Why do we have to make these changes?
- Why aren't more people working as hard as me?
- Why don't we have a clear strategy and clear goals?
- Why is my boss not taking the time to develop me?

It is reasonable to ask, "What's wrong with any of those questions?"

Those questions show your attitude, which is the same as how you think! What is the emphasis of those questions? You are complaining about problems.

Or Are You Asking . . .
- What can I do to help things get better?
- How can I help create a solution?
- What can I do to help us become more productive?
- How can I communicate better with the team?
- How can I help the team?

Notice the vast difference in the implied attitude. The earlier questions were primarily, "Why is this happening to ME?" However, the latter set of questions takes a different approach, asking, "Since we are in this reality, what role can I play to help it change?"

Which person do you want to be? Which person would you like to be around? There is freedom in the latter set of questions. It implies you have a Choose and Create mindset rather than React and Respond.

Not only does it imply an attitude of freedom, but it also implies self-governance. That is a critical value that will increase your freedom and benefit others.

Self-Governance Defined

The dictionary says this is self-governance:
- Exercising control or rule over oneself
- Characterized by self-discipline or self-control
- Control of emotions, desires, and actions by one's own will

Those definitions show the way we use the word. Self-control is an essential synonym for self-governance. With that in mind, our definition of self-governance is

Passing up immediate gratification for future benefits.

Think about how that will impact your life. If you develop the strength to think about future benefits more than current satisfaction, you experience more freedom. Why? Because you make a choice rather than being controlled by an immediate desire. You also display the spirit and actions of an *Overcomer.*

Proverbs 25:28 (NKJV)—Whoever has no rule over his own spirit is like a city broken down, without walls.

An excellent addition to the definition is

Doing the right thing when no one is watching.

You focus on a life of good values. You do the right thing even when there is no one to reward or punish you.

Why Is Self-Governance Needed?

Roy Baumeister wrote an excellent book titled *Willpower.* That term is similar to self-governance. In his book, he gave some outstanding research on the benefits of self-control or self-governance.

Increases What Is Good

People who demonstrate more self-governance increase positive elements in their lives. His research shows that all parts of your life are impacted positively by increased self-control. It directly correlates to higher future income, better grades, lower teen pregnancy rates, less anxiety, less depression, better health, and almost everything else most people want for themselves.

1. It is a better predictor of GPA than IQ or SAT scores.
2. It rates a manager more favorably by subordinates and peers.
3. It makes you good at forming and maintaining secure, satisfying attachments with other people.
4. It makes you better at empathizing with others and seeing their perspective.
5. It helps you be more stable emotionally—less prone to anxiety, depression, paranoia, eating disorders, drinking problems, and more.
6. It helps you remove anger or get angry less often and be less aggressive when angry.
7. It aids better physical health and even healthier teeth.
8. It aids better financial health.
9. It aids stability in marriage and relationships.
10. It helps keep you out of prison.

Overall, lower self-control leads to being sicker, poorer, and more likely to spend time in prison.

Think about that! Most things that people want are directly associated with self-control. And most of the things that people do not want are associated with a LACK of self-control.

The benefits for an *Overcomer* follow the same pattern but are substantially better. Each of the seven churches in Revelation chapters 2 and 3 has significant promises attached to overcoming.

• Eat from the tree of life
• Receive a crown of life
• Will not be hurt by the second death
• Receive hidden manna
• Receive a white stone and a new name on it
• Authority over nations
• Receive the morning star
• Be dressed in white
• Acknowledged before God the Father and His angels
• Be pillars in the temple
• Name of God, the city of God, and Jesus new name written on them
• Eat with Christ
• Rule with Christ

That list is simultaneously incomprehensible and incredible to me. I will benefit as I study it. For now, I know that Jesus said it, which makes it beyond my imagination (Ephesians 3:20) and available to me! If you want those things, you will pass up immediate gratification for the future rewards created by your PERFECT God. That lists God's rewards to you for hearing, obeying, and enduring without fear.

Helps Avoid Problems

One of the most interesting statements made in *Willpower* is **people with higher degrees of self-control do not tend to use their self-control**. That seems contradictory, but here is why it is true.

Generally, self-control is critical when temptation is looming. You are on the edge of the slippery slope to sin because of temptation. You need substantial self-control to back away from the edge when in temptation's grip. And backing away is difficult and unlikely. Therefore, you end up sliding down the slippery slope to the pit of sin.

However, people with elevated self-control do not use it because **they do not go near the edge**! Self-governance is best for keeping you away from the edge! You develop structures of behavior that eliminate the need to use massive amounts of self-control in an emergency.

When you stay away from the edge, you participate with God in what He has created you to do.

> *Ephesians 2:10 (NKJV)—For we are His workmanship,*
> *created in Christ Jesus for good works, which God*
> *prepared beforehand that we should walk in them.*

Helps You Get More Done

Finally, self-governance is critical for organizations. It increases the capacity of individuals without adding more people. Less oversight is needed when people follow through on their tasks. When everyone oversees their responsibility, the organization's capacity expands. That is why organizations with self-governing people get more done.

Overcomers are self-governing, and they constantly teach and encourage self-governance. It is critical for you and the church.

> *Colossians 3:23-25 (NKJV)—23 And whatever you do, do it*
> *heartily, as to the Lord and not to men, 24 knowing that from*
> *the Lord you will receive the reward of the inheritance; for*
> *you serve the Lord Christ. 25 But he who does wrong will be*
> *repaid for what he has done, and there is no partiality.*

Obeying that statement increases the reality of the following for you:

*Matthew 25:21 (NKJV)—His lord said to him, 'Well done, good
and faithful servant; you were faithful over a few things, I will
make you ruler over many things. Enter into the joy of your lord.'*

Unlimited Supply

Based on those benefits, I want that!

Here is a big problem, though. Everyone has self-control, but it is a limited supply. People can develop and demonstrate incredible willpower like David Blaine, who

- Fasted for 44 days and lost 54 pounds
- Stood for 35 hours 80 feet in the air without a safety harness, atop a round pillar 22 inches wide
- Spent 63 sleepless hours encased in a block of ice
- Was entombed in a coffin with 6 inches of headroom for 7 days, consuming nothing but water
- Spent 44 days above the Thames River sealed in a transparent box, with temperatures ranging from subfreezing to 114 degrees.

Researchers also found that self-control was high for the things people focused on, but other areas of their lives showed minimal self-control. Willpower might be in part of our lives but completely devoid elsewhere.

They also call willpower or self-control energy. The "Oh WOW light" flashed when I first read that. That is exciting because you have unlimited self-control as a child of God.

Think about it. A child of God has the Holy Spirit. The Holy Spirit is a being, not an "it," and He is the power or energy to live the life of Christ in you. How does that translate into an inexhaustible supply of self-control?

*Galatians 5:22-23 (NKJV)—But the fruit of the Spirit is love,
joy, peace, longsuffering, kindness, goodness, faithfulness,
gentleness, self-control. Against such there is no law.*

The Fruit of the Spirit is love, joy, peace, patience, kindness, goodness, gentleness, faithfulness, and WHAT? **SELF-CONTROL.**

You have an inexhaustible supply of self-control as you walk in and with the Spirit of God. Here is how I look at my life; it may also work for you. Any area of my life that shows a lack of self-control means I am trying to manage that area alone or not walking with the Lord in that part of my life.

If you want more self-control, it is time to pay attention to how much you are walking with the Lord. The Holy Spirit is an inexhaustible supply of self-governance. He is the only one who can control your SELF. You cannot do it, and neither can I.

How to Increase Self-Governance

As stated, walking in the Spirit is the key. Below are five critical actions to help increase your self-governance.

Pursue the Best for Others

Self-absorption is the most significant danger to self-governance, which is the opposite of Overcoming. There is no doubt that we are selfish, self-absorbed creatures. Any doubt about that is not paying attention to the reality of evil in the world. Your environment plays a part, but not as much as our built-in nature that "makes everything about ME." You do not have to teach children to lie or be deceptive.

When you pursue the best for others, it encourages a service orientation as opposed to self-gratification. Self-governance encourages Overcoming and WE, not ME.

Focus on Your Next Step to THERE

Sometimes the change you want will take a long time. And when your desired transformation is long-term, you may not have enough energy to keep going. That is where milestones and clear short-term targets will help you focus your energy.

Also, review the fantastic Primary and Secondary Choices tool in the "Overcoming Irresponsible Freedom" chapter. When you bring your focus back to shorter-term milestones, limit yourself to 1 to 3 tasks each day or week. That helps you achieve and enhance self-governance one day or step at a time.

Measure Your Progress

Even focusing more on the short-term, you still need to measure progress. Ensure that your long-term and short-term goals are measurable based on objective evidence, not subjective feelings.

When measuring, having an accountability partner or partners is always good. Self-governance wants feedback, which is valuable for self-examination if accepted as valid until proven otherwise.

Practice, Improve, Reward

There is a vast difference between self-esteem and self-governance. Self-esteem hurts you, and self-governance helps you. If you want secular research on the difference, read Chapter 9 in *Willpower*. If you want more information and the biblical perspective, go to gr8relate.com and search for this podcast—"Satan Loves This—Do You? You can listen to the podcast and download a document with the same title.

Self-esteem thinks well of self without verifiable evidence. Self-governance has proof for you and probably others. You can reward yourself when you achieve milestones or reach your goal. That can be a big help as you improve your self-governance. Ultimately, self-governance is mostly its own reward.

KEY ACTION—Pre-decide

As you read earlier, one of the best ways to enhance self-governance is to learn how NOT to use it. Use your self-governance wisely.

You are probably in less control of your life than you think. You may also think you can dabble in questionable things and it will not hurt you. Most people believe that lie, which is why so many people end up addicted, divorced, or in prison.

How many men and women nowadays believe that a bit of porn will not hurt them. It is an epidemic for men in the world. How about drugs and alcohol? Addicts did not say to themselves, "I want to be addicted to drugs; I am going to find some!" No, they believed a lie like, "It will not happen to me. I want to feel different than I do right now."

You can eliminate many wrong choices when you pre-decide. That will help you stand back from the edge so you do not slide down the slippery slope.

> *James 1:14-15 (NKJV)—But each one is tempted when*
> *he is drawn away by his own desires and enticed.*
> *Then when desire has conceived, it gives birth to sin;*
> *and sin, when it is full-grown, brings forth death.*

Pre-deciding is a simple tool. You self-examine your weaknesses, temptations, and unGodly values. Before the event, you decide what you will do when you are wandering in the wrong direction. You create a simple action or plan to help you choose correctly. The best start for any plan is to memorize the following verses or at least the bolded portion.

> *1 Corinthians 10:4-5 (NKJV)—For the weapons of our*
> *warfare are not carnal but mighty in God for pulling down*
> *strongholds, casting down arguments and every high thing*
> *that exalts itself against the knowledge of God, **bringing***
> ***every thought into captivity to the obedience of Christ.***

When the temptation begins to blossom, you ask Jesus to take those thoughts away and depend on His strength to follow your pre-decided plan. It can be decisions about minor things, like when you get up in the morning or something as significant as monogamy.

Of course, you may say, "I will commit to doing the right thing, no matter what." That may be true, but it will not be as powerful as committing to a specific "right thing." For example, if you decide to be monogamous, what is your pre-decision about being with a person you are attracted to? You need clear guidelines to follow in that situation. Those guidelines become your first, and sometimes last, line of defense when tempted to violate your values.

Finally, Baumeister's research showed when people committed to what God or their "higher power" said, the probability of self-governance increased. Be sure about what God wants you to do and not do. *Overcomers* pre-decide to hear and obey God. That saves your self-governance for temptations that surprise you.

God's Word provides what He wants us to do right now! The entire Bible helps you pre-decide. For example:

> *James 5:9 (NKJV)—Do not grumble against one another, brethren, lest you be condemned. Behold, the Judge is standing at the door!*

God is the only authority and asks you to obey that now. He does not tell you to think about this later in your life. He invites you to that behavior now. How about pre-deciding to pursue their best instead of complaining and grumbling about them? The life of an *Overcomer* is about hearing and obeying. That means **now**.

God wants you to pre-decide to escape harmful consequences now and later. Whatever you do now will impact your eternity. Please choose life and righteousness.

> *Deuteronomy 30:19 (NKJV)—I call heaven and earth as witnesses today against you, that I have set before you life and death, blessing and cursing; therefore choose life, that both you and your descendants may live.*

A similar passage in the New Testament is Romans 6:12-14 (NKJV):

> *Therefore do not let sin reign in your mortal body, that you should obey it in its lusts. And do not present your members as instruments of unrighteousness to sin, but present yourselves to God as being alive from the dead, and your members as instruments of righteousness to God. For sin shall not have dominion over you, for you are not under law but under grace.*

It is time to choose the abundant life rather than the "death life" (Romans 6:23).

Are You Getting Too Close?

One of my favorite parts of *Willpower* is the example of hyperbolic discounting. What is that? You will see what it is shortly. If you are not pre-deciding, hyperbolic discounting hurts you. The book has the story of Eric Clapton's relapse as an alcoholic, which resulted from his not resisting the temptation to stop for a drink. It is an excellent illustration of how anyone can easily be undone by hyperbolic discounting.

> *"Think of Eric Clapton on that Saturday evening as a repentant sinner who is literally on the road to salvation, like the hero of Pilgrim's Progress, the seventeenth century allegory. Suppose that he, too, was journeying toward Celestial City. While traveling through the open countryside, he can see the city's far-off golden spires and keeps heading in their direction. This evening, he looks ahead and notices a pub strategically situated at a bend in the road so that it's directly in front of travelers. From this distance it looks like a small building, and he still keeps his eyes fixed on the grander spires of the Celestial City in the background. But as Eric the Pilgrim approaches the pub, it looms larger, and when he arrives, the building completely blocks his view. He can no longer see the golden spires in the distance. Suddenly, Celestial City seems much less important than this one little building. And thus, verily, our pilgrim's progress endeth with him passed out on the pub's floor."—Roy Baumeister, Willpower*

Using your hand is a simple way to illustrate what happens without pre-deciding. Look at an object or person near you. Now, hold up your hand, fingers closed together, with your arm fully extended and your palm toward your face. Look at the person and notice your hand blocks some of your view of them.

You should still be able to see them because your hand is not close enough to your eyes to entirely block your view of them. Now, pull your hand slowly closer to your eyes. Your view of them is blocked further as your hand approaches your eyes. Eventually, you will no longer see them and only see your hand.

That is what happens when you are in the presence of temptation. At first, it is just a part of your thinking, but as you continue, it becomes all you see. That is when temptation turns into actions that result in regrets.

If you do not want to get too close—**pre-decide**. If you have enough self-governance, you may not fall for the temptation. Do not take the chance! Pre-decide! Be as drastic as necessary to avoid getting too close. Think about your current temptations. Some may have already blossomed into full-blown addictions. It is not too late to pre-decide. It may be your first step out of your addiction.

Self-governance accepts the invitation to experience the abundant life that God has given to you.

> *2 Peter 1:2-4 (NKJV)—Grace and peace be multiplied to you in the knowledge of God and of Jesus our Lord, as His divine power has given to us all things that pertain to life and godliness, through the knowledge of Him who called us by glory and virtue, by which have been given to us exceedingly great and precious promises, that through these you may be partakers of the divine nature, having escaped the corruption that is in the world through lust.*

Learning more about Jesus and every statement in God's Word is an opportunity to use the self-control available from the Holy Spirit. When you see self-governance as just doing what God asks, here is a short list of ways that self-governance will help you.

1. Helps commitment to eternal rather than temporal things (Romans 2:7-9a)
2. Helps you transform into Christlikeness (2 Peter 1:5-8)
3. Encourages faith and dependence on God (Hebrews 11:6)
4. Helps maintain a proper view of self (Romans 12:3)
5. Helps the body of Christ, serving others with your gifts (Romans 12:4-9)
6. Helps you esteem others more than yourself (Philippians 2:3-4)
7. Helps you stay away from the slippery slope to sin (2 Timothy 2:22)
8. Aids contentment (1 Timothy 6:6)
9. MOST IMPORTANTLY—Helps you obey God (Proverbs 3:1-8)

There is maximum joy when you deny self and allow the Holy Spirit to control self!

THE TWO CIRCLES TOOL

Since self-governance is critical, it helps to know or remember when you are moving away from it. It also helps to have a tool to help you and others discover when self-governance is lacking. Making everything about ME is **the** problem for everyone, but it is hard to see sometimes. That is why the Two Circles tool is so valuable.

Think about a time someone complained to you. Maybe it was about being overworked and underpaid. Or it was about a friend who was mistreating them. Whatever their complaint, they are upset and want it fixed.

As you listened, you may have sympathized with them. You may have offered insights or tried to help them see things differently. But most often, no matter what wisdom you provide, they do not change their mind to see life differently. So they leave the conversation still struggling and complaining because they do not see reality. And worse, that person might be you.

Sometimes people need a listening ear. That allows them to adjust their thinking and move on. Other times, people get stuck wanting life to be different than it is—they are unwilling to accept reality. That fits our definition of pain—"not wanting it to be the way it is." That creates confusion, powerlessness, and no change—wanting it to be different but not living in reality about your choices.

That is where the Two Circlestool helps. Taking someone through the Two Circles helps them discover how to change for the better, accept reality, and get out of their flawed thinking.

Drawing and telling people about the Two Circles is a big mistake. That does not work well because the other person does not discover the truth for themselves. If you do not take the 10 to 15 minutes needed, you will often tell them about it instead of engaging them with questions. The following is a complete description of how you can use the tool. If you prefer to watch a video, go here: *https://vimeo.com/manage/videos/195051948*.

Do the exercise as if I am speaking to you to get the most out of the following. As we go through it, I will include comments to explain some points more thoroughly. The bold section titles provide the steps or a summary of the flow of the conversation.

At an opening in the conversation, I would say:

Draw the Two Circles

"Would you do a little exercise with me? It won't take long and may help clarify some things for you.

"Get a piece of paper and draw two circles side by side— left and right.

"Now, write 'ME' in the middle of both circles.

"Next, in the left circle, draw arrows from the circle inward to ME—the arrow's point is on ME.

"In the right circle, draw the arrows the opposite way; the arrow's point is at the circle."

If you are reading this, please do the exercise also. You will get more out of it. When doing this first step, do not offer more information than the above. Also, watch to make sure the person draws the arrows correctly.

Have them guess what the left circle means

*"You don't have much information, but what do you guess the **left** circle means?*

Most people will guess things like "I am the center," "Things are focused on me," "Things are pressing on me," or something similar. Sometimes people answer oppositely. "Things depend on me." I do not get that often, but it has happened.

Whatever the answer, acknowledge it and move to the next step.

Add Life, Circumstances, and People

"Let me give you some more information. Each circle represents Life, Circumstances, and People. Write the words Life, Circumstance, and People around each circle. (Give them enough time to write because writing around a circle can be difficult.)

"Now, what do you think the left circle means?"

At this point, they tend to guess more clearly. "I am the center of everything." "Everything is happening to me." If they say something other than that, have them explain. Also, some people want to go on and explain what they think the Right Circle means, but guide them back to the Left Circle and tell them you will talk about that in a few minutes.

"This Left Circle shows that we often think everything happens to ME. Or worse, life is all about ME."

"You just react and respond to what happens.

"Please write React/Respond above that left circle somewhere. Living in this Left Circle means you believe your role in life is determining what to do when things happen to you. You don't see choices clearly, especially when others mistreat you."

Since they have some basic information about reacting and responding, it is essential to tie their emotions into what is happening.

Engage their emotions

"If Life, Circumstances, and People are treating you great, how would you feel?"

Let them answer—and obviously, most people say something like "happy" or "good."

"What if everything is not great?"

Let them answer again.

"The Left Circle is like thinking, if I just had that new thing, that person in my life, etc., everything would be so good. And when those things aren't there, life is awful. You feel great if life, circumstances, and people treat you right.

"Now, if I am happy when things go well and sad when they do not, who or what controls me?"

You are now helping them see how a React/Respond lifestyle can progressively worsen.

Some people will answer the questions with, "I am in control," which is correct, but it shows they do not see what drives their emotions. Generally, all you need to say here is, "Yes, you are ultimately in control. We will talk about that, but when you are happy or sad, depending on the circumstances, what or who is in control at that point?" Give them time to answer the question because they need to discover they are handing their emotions over to other people and things.

"When we live this way, we become a 'Slave' to Life, Circumstances, and People. It is like handing the key to your emotions and life to another person. You are a slave at that point. That is another word that describes the Left Circle. So write 'Slave' underneath React/Respond."

Identify with Them

Identify with them at this point. Letting them know you occasionally live in this Left Circle is best. Say something like,

> *"But it gets worse. Before I tell you how it gets worse, I want you to know that I live in this Left Circle more than I prefer. Let me give you a couple of examples from my life.*

> *"Consider a time when I am driving along in my car, and someone pulls into my lane too quickly and too close to me. I have to press the brake pedal to keep from hitting them. What might be one of my reactions?"*

After some laughter and talking about those situations, I immediately add another example about when I went to our local supermarket to buy some items.

> *"Another time I was living in the Left Circle was when I needed a couple of items from my local supermarket. I was in a hurry, so I almost ran in, picked up the two items, and headed for the '15 Items or Less Lane'. When I arrived, the person in front of me had more than two items. How many things do you think they had?"*

That example always works; it is best to ask that last question. It sets up the punch line. I wait to get them to say several items, and then I say,

> *"They had 16 because I counted!"*

That provides some relief from being so serious and gives a precise point on how real this is in everyday life. You can use those examples or find your own to help people see that you are not providing this information from the "You need to be more like me" perspective. Everyone lives in the Left Circle; we need to learn how to live there less often.

Discuss being a Victim

> *"It gets worse because I am not only a Slave at that point, I am also a Victim. So please write 'Victim' underneath Slave. I see myself as a Victim."*

> *"There are real and perceived victims. Real victims suffer from some accident or abuse from another person. But even real victims can become perceived victims if they aren't careful.*

> *"This idea of being a Victim is essential. In fact, somewhere below the Left Circle, write this statement—'Victims can't be helped; they have to be rescued.' Again, 'Victims can't be helped; they have to be rescued.'"*

I will repeat it several times to ensure they have enough time to write the statement. Then I ask this important question.

"Why can't Victims be helped?"

Since I have done the Two Circles hundreds of times, I will also say

"This is a very tough question. Only two people have been able to answer correctly in the many times that I have asked this question. So what do you think—why can't a Victim be helped?"

The answers you get here will vary: "They don't want help." "They won't take personal responsibility for themselves." "They aren't living in reality." Most of the statements provided will be close, but it is rare for anyone to give the correct answer.

Many of the answers will be reasonable, so I will say something like,

"That is probably true, but that isn't why they can't be helped. The answer lies in seeing this from the victim's point of view."

Instead of providing the answer, return to your examples and show what a Victim is thinking.

What I have found works best is to take them back to my standing in the 15 Items or Less lane.

"Picture me standing at the supermarket in the 15 Items or Less lane. Do you have that picture? Describe it. What am I thinking? What am I focused on?"

That typically helps them get something tangible to help them understand the answer. Listen to their answers, and some of them may be getting close.

"So I am standing there and looking at the person's 16 items—I am unhappy because of their bad behavior. I am looking at the cashier who is accepting this lousy behavior. AND ALL OF THEIR BAD BEHAVIOR IS HURTING ME!"

At this point, I will typically point at the imaginary people around me and use a sweeping gesture from left to right and say

"I am saying, 'If you would just change your bad behavior, my life would be much better! I am doing life correctly, and you aren't, and you need to change now!'

"I am a Victim at that point, and I can't be helped because I am not the one who needs the help—EVERYONE ELSE needs the help. When everyone else changes—I am 'rescued.' When those people in the 15 Items or Less

lane or the people on the road get their behavior right—they throw me a life preserver and rescue me!

"When we are victims like that, and I do this more than I prefer, I am saying, 'I don't need to change because I am not doing anything wrong. Everyone else needs to make changes.'"

That is a critical point in the discussion of the Left Circle, and people tend to understand it. Most often, there is more talk about this. You want to ensure they understand by making additional statements like these.

"When we are in the Left Circle, we look at life, circumstances, and people and say, 'If you would just change, I'd be happy!' We won't see any need for our change because WE DO NOT BELIEVE WE ARE DOING ANYTHING WRONG. It is everyone else that is messed up, not me. Therefore, we can only be rescued when everything and everyone else changes for the better.

"That Victim thinking is like you being a pool ball on the pool table of life, and how does a pool ball move? It can't unless another ball or a cue stick hits it. When we live as victims, we complain about others 'hitting us' instead of seeing our role. 'I'm mad because they didn't treat me right.' It actually could have been for our benefit, but we do not see it because we are playing the role of a victim."

The One Critical Item

Please make this final point because it lays the groundwork for the actions they will need to take.

"There is one critical item that supports being a victim. What do you think that is?"

Sometimes people know the answer, but if they do not, say,

"Victims aren't living in REALITY! They can CHOOSE, no matter the circumstance. Victims start acting as if the only choice is for others to change their life for 'ME' to be happy."

Then I take them back to me standing in the 15 Items or Less Lane.

"What choices do I have as I stand there getting mad about others not paying attention to the rules?"

That often turns into a fun and funny discussion.

"I could go to another lane. I could start a fight. I could catch up on the gossip about the celebrities in the magazines. I could leave."

The more choices you discuss, the better. It helps drive home that you do not see options when you are a victim. All we can think about is how others need to change.

Emotions Are Your Signal

This is optional but helpful because it provides a way to identify when you are entering or may already be in the Left Circle.

I will say . . .

"There is one key I look for that tells me I am about to go into the Left Circle—negative emotions. From my experience, it is the best signal for me— probably 99 percent accurate."

If there is time and the discussion has been good, I will provide them with my experience of asking myself, "Am I making this about ME right now?"

"I have found that during those negative emotion times—I am making life about 'ME' and becoming a Victim of Life, Circumstances, and People.

"A friend (Tim Dunn) says, 'Your emotions are like the warning lights on your car's dashboard. They tell you something is wrong, so don't ignore them.' That is highly true in these situations. When you notice those negative emotions, you need to stop and open the hood of your mind to recognize that you need to get into reality and that you have a choice—YOU ARE NOT A VICTIM HERE!

"As Victor Frankl in his book Man's Search for Meaning tells us—no matter how bad your circumstances, you are the sole controller of your mind. How you think about this situation will make you a Victim who lives in the Left Circle or help you choose a better way of living."

Have them guess about the Right Circle

With that last statement, you have a good segue into talking about the Right Circle.

"We have talked about the Left Circle, so what do you think the Right Circle is about?"

At first, some people will answer that you control what happens. Obviously, that is wrong, but it is a place to further add humor, like

"So am I to strive to be the Master of the Universe?"

Bridge off their answer and say,

"Since the Left Circle says I am a victim of what happens to me, the Right Circle says life, circumstances, and people may not treat me well, but I will live my values anyway. If people aren't treating me well, I can still treat them well because I value that.

"Therefore, the Right Circle is about choosing. Write above the Right Circle—Choose/Create. Even though life, circumstances, and people are not what you desire, you still have choices. Living in the Right Circle means you are clear about what you can control, which is what?"

Most people answer they can only control what they do or themselves.

"Since you can only control yourself, you are free from trying to control or manipulate others.

"Please write Freedom underneath Choose/Create. Your life can be free from being controlled by what others think about you and what you think about them. You can be free of trying to make others do what you want and, more importantly, correct the past wrongs they did to you.

"Finally, write Values underneath Freedom. Instead of a Victim lifestyle, you live a Values lifestyle. Living what you value, even when others aren't."

Get feedback

It is time to see what they discovered. You ask a simple question and then talk about it.

"Which circle do you think you are in right now?

Only a couple of people said they were living in the Right Circle. Most people discover their Left Circle attitude.

It takes a deliberate choice and energy to live in the Right Circle. I'm betting that you would like to do that, too. What would change if you chose the Right Circle more?"

Use their answer to help them discover the reality of their choices. Hopefully, they see how much people and circumstances control their life when it could be different. Now, you can return to what they discussed before starting this exercise.

The Two Circles has been a great tool to help communicate the difference between being controlled and free, being a victim, or living your values.

Further, when people understand the two options, everyone wants to live in the Right Circle. Many even think they are, but using the contrast, they realize they are not.

How about you? What did you discover? Do you have any examples in the last couple of days that would show which circle you have been in? You may find that the Left Circle is where you have moved too often—not just visited. It is time to pack your belongings and move to the Right Circle. It is much less confusing there, even when things are not going as you desire.

THE FREEDOM V TOOL

The second self-governance tool is the Freedom V. It will help you live more often in the Right Circle. It is an excellent tool and principle because it lets you grasp how freedom and self-governance are linked. It is a simple, primarily visual tool, so it is relatively easy to explain and draw.

The table to the right of the Freedom V graph is unnecessary unless you want to provide more information. I seldom use the table unless I teach people about the Freedom V or have a more extended freedom discussion.

The two most essential elements are the V shape and the arrow in the middle.

Understanding the Graphic

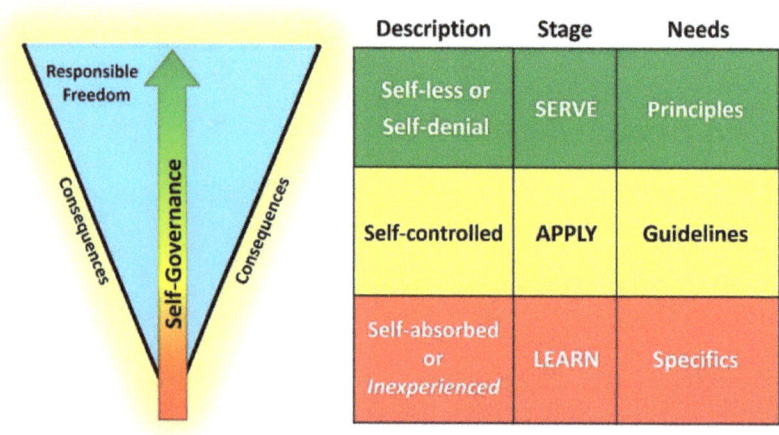

Description	Stage	Needs
Self-less or Self-denial	SERVE	Principles
Self-controlled	APPLY	Guidelines
Self-absorbed or Inexperienced	LEARN	Specifics

First, notice the V shape. The lines on the right and left are boundaries that define the limits of acceptable behavior. The boundaries are best when they are clear and bright. Nothing is left to speculation or conjecture. Boundaries need to be easily known and advertised.

Second, the space inside the V represents the area of Responsible Freedom. That is where you use your freedom correctly or within the accepted norms of the structure that demands behavior. The amount of freedom increases as you move up the V shape. The structure can be malevolent or benign, but there will still be a V shape. Even in the most disgusting dictatorships or gangs, some gain more freedom by not crossing the boundaries set by the structure. In those situations, freedom inside the V is often irresponsible by moral and ethical standards but demanded by the standards of the gang or dictator. Their idea of self-governance then fits their perverted standards.

Third, outside the V, there are consequences for crossing the boundaries. Once you cross the boundary, you move into the area of Irresponsible Freedom. Again, this applies to both good and bad value organizations or structures. Even evil organizations have their boundaries. Hopefully, the consequences are clearly stated when the boundaries are set and discussed.

Finally, the arrow in the middle represents self-governance. The color on the arrow represents the degree of self-governance demonstrated. At the bottom, it is lacking. The yellow and green represent the increase in self-governance as you move from bottom to top. And the colors directly correlate with the narrow or expansive freedom allowed.

When you abide by the rules of the structure and stay inside the boundaries, greater responsible freedom is available. In other words, the more self-governance, the more freedom is available.

In the graph above, the table to the right provides additional ways to look at the Freedom V. For example, you can divide self-governance into three overlapping levels.

- **Self-absorbed or Inexperienced**—From the bottom in the red into the yellow area. That would be someone who is either inexperienced, without knowledge about a topic, or ignores what is right. That is the Learning Stage. In that stage, people need specific rules and tighter controls. That does not mean you ignore the "why" of the rules.
- **Self-controlled**—From the middle yellow area into the green. That would be someone who exhibits an adequate level of self-governance. That can be measured in general or specific for

69

individual work or life situations. They are in the Apply Stage, where they mostly need guidelines since they understand the rules.

- **Selfless or Self-denial**—The top area of self-governance tends to work for the benefit of others. That is the Serve Stage, where people operate based on principles and know how to apply those principles to various life situations.

The Freedom V will work with any structure, especially for families and organizations with great values.

Application

A person with self-governance considers other people and their impact on them. They will stay within the V if the freedom inside the V is about excellent and Godly values.

Suppose you are responsible for a baby, and you are a wise parent desiring to act as God does with you. You would create tight boundaries for them because they do not have knowledge or experience with the way things work in the world. You would put them in controlled environments like a crib or playpen and help reduce the opportunity for them to harm themselves. At the same time, you would provide them enough freedom to see if they can learn how to stay within the boundaries.

You will still have relatively tight boundaries when the baby has grown into a toddler. They will be learning to stay within the boundaries for the freedom you give them and experiencing the consequences when they do not. The rules and expectations provided to them are an invitation to live wisely, not a way to ensure they know you are in charge. You would invite them to live by rules to help them escape the consequences. If you saw them moving toward a boundary, you would warn them but allow them to choose if the consequences were not too severe.

When a child grows older, you expand the boundaries as they show the ability to make the right choices. Since you have taught them how to recognize boundaries for themselves, they are hopefully making good choices while they are away from us at school, with friends, or by themselves. The more self-governance they show, the more freedom you allow. When they cross boundaries, you reduce their freedom by moving them down the V.

You might tell an older child, "Go where you want, be safe, and be home by nightfall." If that did not happen, and it was determined to be willful disobedience, you would move them down the freedom V until they demonstrated they would be home at the designated time.

The goal is to have the child set boundaries that are always inside God's clear boundaries.

If you remember, the definition of self-governance is "delaying immediate gratification for future benefit." Another practical way to see self-governance is setting boundaries for yourself rather than the authorities. Of course, those boundaries are within the overall boundaries set by God and His designated authority channels (Romans 13).

You love and value people when you commit to influencing them to be self-governing. You cannot do it for them. As much as you might want to control, it is often best to allow people to cross the boundary and suffer the consequences if not too severe for them or the organization. You can control the people you lead, but it is seldom the best action. Exercising personal freedom is essential to being human and learning to be self-governing after experiencing consequences.

If you learn to pre-decide, you become more self-governing and suffer fewer consequences.

It is time to revisit how freedom works best. First, Christ set us free to live a life of freedom, not bondage and obligation.

> *Galatians 5:1 (ESV)—It is for freedom that Christ has set us free. Stand firm, then, and do not let yourselves be burdened again by a yoke of slavery.*

Our definition of freedom is "acting without controlling or being controlled." Can you misuse freedom and be irresponsible with your freedom? Absolutely! Of course, if you decide to use your freedom irresponsibly and do anything you want, most likely, your freedom will become limited. Why? Because authorities can move you down the Freedom V with monetary consequences like fines or physical consequences like jail. God initiates His wrath through authority channels (Romans 13).

Please be self-governing and put your freedom underneath the higher value of LOVE. When you do that, **you limit your freedom by pursuing the best for others.**

> *Galatians 5:13 (ESV)—For you were called to freedom, brothers. Only do not use your freedom as an opportunity for the flesh, but through love serve one another.*

> *1 Corinthians 6:12 (NIV)—"I have the right to do anything," you say—but not everything is beneficial. "I have the right to do anything"—but I will not be mastered by anything.*

> *1 Corinthians 10:23 (RSV)—"All things are lawful," but not all things are helpful. "All things are lawful," but not all things build up.*

Romans 8:21 (ESV)— . . . that the creation itself will be set free from its bondage to corruption and obtain the freedom of the glory of the children of God.

Genesis 2:16-17 (ESV)—And the Lord God commanded the man, saying, "You may surely eat of every tree of the garden, but of the tree of the knowledge of good and evil you shall not eat, for in the day that you eat of it you shall surely die."

2 Peter 2:19 (ESV)—They promise them freedom, but they themselves are slaves of corruption. For whatever overcomes a person, to that he is enslaved.

Proverbs 25:28 (ESV)—A man without self-control is like a city broken into and left without walls.

DISCUSSION QUESTIONS

1. Write and memorize the definition of self-governance (it is similar to self-control).
2. What is an excellent addition to the definition?
3. Explain why people with higher self-governance do not tend to use it.
4. How can we get an unlimited supply of self-governance?
5. Explain what it means to "pre-decide." What is the key benefit when you pre-decide?
6. Explain what happens when you do not pre-decide by using your hand.
7. Do the Two Circles at least ten times. What is the benefit of engaging their emotions before discussing being a "slave?"
8. What are your examples to explain how you sometimes act like a victim? Ensure you clearly show how "you cannot be helped" and "have to be rescued."
9. What is the fiction that a person in the Left Circle has? What drives them to believe that fiction?
10. How do emotions fit into the two circles?
11. Clearly explain the elements of the Freedom V.
12. Explain how a person with a high degree of self-governance may need to be at the bottom of the Freedom V.
13. Explain the "Needs" column of the Freedom V.
14. What happens to your freedom when you put it underneath love?

Hermann Eben

HERMANN EBEN

HERMANN EBEN

74

CHAPTER 4

WHOSE NEEDS ARE YOU FOCUSED ON?

Larry and Dawn met in college and married soon after they graduated. They both worked in corporate jobs until they decided to start a family. Dawn was an account manager for a major sporting goods manufacturer, and Larry worked for a consumer-packaged goods company. When Dawn got pregnant with their first child, Larry insisted she stay home and take care of the family. He believed it was his responsibility to provide for the family and wanted her to spend her energy on the kids and their home.

Fast forward about thirty years later. Their kids are grown, out of the house, and have children of their own. All of them live in the same city. Larry decides to retire from his corporate job and work part-time as an ad-hoc business professor at a local college. They are set for retirement, so Larry tells Dawn she can continue to stay at home when he retires. Larry works from home in a space on the second floor of their home. When he has colleagues over to discuss projects at the college, Dawn always greets the guests at the door and asks what refreshments she can provide for them. She always has the refrigerator stocked with bottled water, tea, a variety of soda, and sparkling water.

Dawn has mentioned to Larry that she would like to get out of the house and find a job. He insists she doesn't need to.

In one conversation about this, he says, "We have plenty of money, so you don't need to work. You have worked so hard all these years raising the family. I think you should get a break and not have to work for pay. Besides, it's my responsibility to provide for the family."

Out of respect for Larry, she stops bringing up the subject.

They love to host their children and grandchildren on Sunday afternoons. Dawn always plans and cooks a great family-style meal, then plans activities for the grandchildren. Sometimes the activities are art projects, and other times, they are just swimming in the backyard pool. When they are swimming, she always goes out and takes responsibility for watching each child closely to make sure all of them are safe. Sometimes the parents go out and watch the grandchildren too, but they always depend on Dawn to be the responsible one.

Larry loves to invite colleagues and friends over for dinner. Sometimes he will do this at the last minute because he is sure Dawn can handle it, as she always has the refrigerator and pantry stocked. She never complains about these last-minute plans because she has never had to work and feels she owes it to Larry to do what works best for him.

One Sunday morning, Dawn is in the kitchen prepping for the noon meal. She and Larry typically go to church and Sunday School every Sunday. A heavy fatigue falls over her, and she tells Larry she just needs to go rest and skip church today.

Larry agrees and says, "Hey, why don't you skip cooking and we will just take the family out to eat after church?"

Dawn, the manager of the household budget, says, "Larry, I don't think that's a good idea since we are now on a fixed retirement income and we need to make it last."

"Okay, well, I just was trying to make it easier on you. Everyone was planning on swimming this afternoon. I don't want to disappoint them."

Dawn thinks to herself that if they all come over to the house, she will have to make the meal, make sure snacks and drinks are available, and watch the grandchildren as they swim in the pool. All of it makes her tired just thinking about it.

Larry says, "You can skip church, so by the time we all get here, you will be rested up."

Dawn agrees even though she knows she won't get much rest if she must cook the big meal and take care of the grandkids.

Larry says, "You are the best wife and grandma on the planet. I'm so glad you are willing to serve the family all the time."

Larry gets dressed for church and heads out of the house.

Dawn goes back to sleep and forgets to set an alarm. She wakes to the sound of Larry coming from the garage into the kitchen. Feeling really groggy from the deep sleep, she finds it hard to make herself jump out of bed.

"Dawn, Dawn?" Larry calls. "Are you okay?"

Dawn drags herself to the closet and puts on some clothes. She doesn't bother washing her face or putting on any makeup. She shows up in the kitchen and decides to put out food so that everyone can make their own sandwiches.

Larry, looking a little disappointed, says with a smile, "Oh rats, I was hoping you would make your delicious enchiladas for lunch. I know that's what you had planned."

"Sorry Larry, I forgot to set my alarm. This will be fine."

Larry looks down, trying to hide his disappointment, and doesn't say anything further. He goes back to their room and changes into something more comfortable for the afternoon.

When the kids and grandkids arrive, he greets them at the door and says, "So we have a little change of plans today! No enchiladas. Grandma was feeling tired. But we will still get to swim a little later this afternoon."

At the same time, all the grandkids shout, "Yea!"

Questions

1. Who is Larry focused on in this story?
2. What does he do and say that made you answer the first question the way you did?
3. Who is Dawn focused on in the story? What support do you have for your answer?
4. Do you see any potential problems in the relationship between Larry and Dawn?
5. If you do see problems, what do you suggest they do differently?
6. What role do truth and love play in their relationship?

OVERCOMERS PURSUE THE BEST FOR OTHERS

Key Lesson: *Your biggest problem—you make everything about "ME." The solution—pursue their best patiently, kindly, sacrificially, and unconditionally.*

AN OVERCOMER'S BIGGEST PROBLEM

Here is truly a sad thought. You seldom notice when you make everything about yourself. You see it when others are selfish and self-absorbed, but not when you do it. That may not be true for you, but it is true for me.

When others are selfish, it is like "ME" flashing on their forehead. But when you do it, you cannot see it—because it is on your forehead above your eyes! You can be selfish, not care about others, and have your "ME" flashing bright enough to light a house—but you do not see it.

Are You Acting Like a Baby?

A baby is a good picture of how THE PROBLEM works. Not the image of cuddly and innocent, but an out-of-control, screaming infant who wants something just because they do! That is another good name for the PROBLEM—**The Baby.**

The Baby plugs into the sin nature, which plugs into the world that Satan himself rules. **As the Baby, you take everything personally, making your ME flash.**

"Make Everything About ME"	
Be defensive	don't be teachable
Be self-absorbed	don't be considerate
Be self-indulgent	don't be self-controlled
Work on your self-esteem	don't accept who you are
Be a victim	don't make choices
Always be right	don't seek the truth
Seek revenge	don't forgive
Be manipulative	don't tell the truth
React and respond	don't choose and create
Be unilateral, self-serving	don't pursue their best

Defensiveness is the primary reaction of The Baby, especially when criticized. You live primarily by appetites, impulses, and pleasures. It is selfishness, self-absorption, and self-sufficiency—"It's all about ME."

It Is Built In

The PROBLEM is "ME" or self, the ***fundamental element Overcomers are overcoming!*** It is part of everyone and destroys an *Overcomer* if left unchecked. Those without the life of Christ are slaves to ME behavior. If you trusted Jesus's death, burial, and resurrection as the answer to your sins, you now have a choice—the fundamental choice—**trust God or trust something or someone other than God**. Present yourself to righteousness or unrighteousness (Romans 6:13).

When you act like a Baby, you do not have good thinking and truth as the foundation for your feelings and actions. You are driven by selfishness and immature thinking, just like a baby. So you react and respond to everything emotionally and are happy, satisfied, and content only if people and circumstances treat you like you require. In other words, you have a Left Circle lifestyle, only considering others when something is in it for ME and believing it is everybody's job to make ME happy.

Everyone sometimes acts like The Baby because of built-in desires to be accepted, included, significant, valued, close, secure, safe, cared for, and satisfied. Your ME flashes when you fear you will not get one of those desires. And if you do notice your selfishness, you excuse your behavior with statements like, "If I don't look out for myself, who will?" **Self-absorption is the default of your sin nature and the opposite of an Overcomer!**

There is no example of a time Jesus "flashed His ME." In fact, Jesus implied that self-absorption or self-pity was of Satan. Remember when Jesus told the disciples that He would suffer and die?

> *Matthew 16:21-23 (NKJV)—From that time Jesus began to show to His disciples that He must go to Jerusalem, and suffer many things from the elders and chief priests and scribes, and be killed, and be raised the third day.*

> *Then Peter took Him aside and began to rebuke Him, saying, "Far be it from You, Lord; this shall not happen to You!"*

> *But He turned and said to Peter, "Get behind Me, Satan! You are an offense to Me, for you are not mindful of the things of God, but the things of men.*

Jesus rebuked Peter for acting in a way that opposed God's plan, but it also implies that those things that God has placed in our life are not times to indulge in self-pity; instead, persevere with God's energy and grace to go through that dark valley (Psalm 23). That is the thinking and actions of an *Overcomer*.

If you are uncertain whether you tend to flash your ME or act like a Baby, then determine if you have ever asked yourself questions like these. "What's in it for me? What do they think about me? What is going to happen to me?" Or simply, "Well . . . what about me?" Bet you have!

A Better Question

Since flashing your ME comes from your sin nature, *Overcomers* choose to act differently. That only happens with the energy of the Holy Spirit. ***The sin nature cannot choose against itself.***

Try this to see if you are flashing your ME. When you are irritable, discontent, discouraged, depressed, or angry, ask yourself this simple question, "Am I making this about me right now?"

That is no longer an experiment for me. I know how self-absorbed I am. I did what I just asked you to do for about eight years. After asking that question for years, I stopped one day and tried to think of a time when I honestly answered, "No, I am not making this about ME." Guess what? I could not remember ONE time where I could honestly answer no. Even though I am probably more selfish than you, please try the exercise. More than likely, it will reveal results you will not like.

Because of that personal research and the tendency not to be objective, here is a better question when you have those negative emotions:

HOW am I making this about ME right now?

That is a much better question because you most likely are making everything about ME, so start looking for "how" you are doing it this time. Awareness of my negative emotions is a reliable alert to my selfish behavior. Being a "Baby" is THE PROBLEM for all relationships. Based on God's Word, **it is a severe problem that** *Overcomers* **want no part of**. Please memorize the following verse because it is essential to remind yourself how damaging the PROBLEM is.

> *James 3:16 (NKJV)—For where envy and self-seeking exist, confusion and every evil thing are there.*

And another excellent verse.

> *Ezekiel 33:31 (NKJV)—So they come to you as people do, they sit before you as My people, and they hear your words, but they do not do them; for with their mouth they show much love, but their hearts pursue their own gain.*

So what is the solution for *Overcomers* and all relationships?

Love Is the SOLUTION

What Is Love?

When you say you "love" someone, what are you saying? Reading God's Words about love is crucial since God's Word provides ". . . all things that pertain to life and godliness . . ." (2 Peter 1:3). Before you read the verses below, consider one of your relationships. If it is experiencing problems now, the following can be more beneficial.

Read the following verses slowly and reflect on that relationship.

> *I Corinthians 13: 4-7 (NKJV)—Love suffers long and is kind; love does not envy; love does not parade itself, is not puffed up; does not behave rudely, does not seek its own, is not provoked, thinks no evil; does not rejoice in iniquity, but rejoices in the truth; bears all things, believes all things, hopes all things, endures all things.*

Would doing those things help your relationships? Are those things happening in your relationships? You may have heard and read this passage many times, but biblical knowledge does not mean you are an *Overcomer*. Remember, *hear* and *obey*? Knowledge helps, but not until you apply it. And when your definition of love is more about ME than others, you will not obey those verses to be an *Overcomer*. It is typical to talk about love but not act according to God's description of love.

> *We have just enough religion to make us hate, but not enough to make us love one another.—Jonathan Swift*

> *A clear head and a deep understanding are of no value without a benevolent and charitable heart.—Matthew Henry*

Overcomers do things God's way.

World's View of Love

The world completely misses the beauty of love as God has described it. So many lousy definitions of the word love exist.

> *Love is friendship plus sex.—Havelock Ellis*

> *Love, as it exists in society, is nothing more than the exchange of two fantasies and the contact of two skins.—Nicolas Chamfort*

> *Many a man has fallen in love with a girl in a light so dim he would not have chosen a suit by it.—Maurice Chevalier*

The world's "love" is selfish. It encourages flashing your ME, seeking your good above theirs. It focuses on getting more than giving, which often results in controlling others to meet your desires.

Second, it is conditional. Selfishness requires attention to your needs; as long as that happens, you "love" them. Worse, the conditions keep changing because your expectations keep changing. When you first were attracted to them, the conditions were few. The expectations are much more intense and numerous now that you know them. It is no longer okay to have them say they love you; it requires scientific proof!

Finally, selfish and conditional love leads to temporary love. When you are unhappy, when things get uncomfortable or difficult in the relationship, or when you no longer feel loved or loving, "love" dies. It is as fleeting as magic fairy dust that gets blown away in high wind. It knows nothing of patience, kindness, sacrifice, and no conditions.

That thinking drives the idea of "falling in love." When you fall, it is not something you decide to do; it happens to you. A wave of feelings lifts you, sprinkles you with love dust, and poof, you are in love!

Yes, I do believe in "chemistry" between people. It is real, but that is attraction, not love. And if you "fall in love," watch out for the tumble when they "fall out of love" with you! They no longer love you when the love dust floats away on the wind of disagreement. In other words, "love" is a feeling that may not last.

When you look at the world's selfish, conditional, and temporary "love," you may not want it and desire love to be different. But is it? What is love?

God's View of Love

Here are most English definitions of "love" from Webster's Dictionary.
- A strong affection for one another
- Attraction based on sexual desire
- Affection based on admiration
- Warm attachment or devotion
- Unselfish, loyal, and benevolent concern for the good of another
- An amorous episode between two people
- A sexual embrace

One does get close to the 1 Corinthians description. Using 1 Corinthians 13 and Ephesians 5, you can create a good definition of love.

Pursuing their best (highest good) patiently, kindly, sacrificially, and unconditionally

What would be different in your life and relationships if you defined love that way? Practicing that definition solves the PROBLEM and all relationship mistakes you make. It also means you desire to be an *Overcomer*. Overcoming requires consistent practice of love, and it is the most crucial element for an *Overcomer* to hear and obey because that is the foundation of overcoming—becoming like Jesus.

Notice the definition says nothing about the one loved. It does not "pursue their best" as long as they pursue your best. It does not limit the suffering, kindness, and sacrifice in proportion to how well the other person behaves.

The supreme example is Christ, who perfectly practiced this definition. He loved you patiently, kindly, sacrificially, and unconditionally while you were still a sinner (Romans 5:6). You were spiritually dead (Ephesians 2:4, 5), His enemy (Romans 5:10)! There is no way you will ever be able to pay Him back or be worthy of His love. And still, He loves you and works through you to become an *Overcomer*!

He calls you to have this love for others. His example of love satisfies because it does not depend on how others treat you. This love transforms horrible relationships into beauty, hope, and freedom.

The next time you say, "I love you," ask yourself, "Am I willing to pursue their best patiently, kindly, sacrificially, and unconditionally?"

The critical difference between real love and the world's love is the word "**decision**." *Love is a decision to which your feelings respond.* Beyond attraction is where love exists, *a decision to pursue their best*.

Love Solves the PROBLEM

Overcomers pursue the best for the people. They—
- DO NOT demand that people change—they hope, pray, encourage, and sometimes exhort and rebuke.
- DO NOT depend on others for joy or happiness—their joy is from doing what God says is right.
- DO practice freedom and choice—both parties are free.
- DO serve the other person and tell them the truth, even when they may not want to hear it.

And most of all
- Practice a Godly definition of love.

A great relationship is best when both parties use a good definition of love, with no dependence on the other person to make you happy. It is a simple decision or choice to pursue their best. Your decision to love will be tested when they are not pursuing your best. And your decision will be tested when they are pursuing your best and telling you the truth, but you cannot see it or do not like it.

That is why you will see feelings, freedom, forgiveness, and confession in this book. Understanding the other items helps you maintain that decision. But nothing is more critical for *Overcomers* and relationships than your decision to apply that definition of love.

You cannot practice that definition for the long term using your strength. Your sin nature fights against practicing this definition of love. ONLY THE HOLY SPIRIT and the life of Christ in you provides the energy to maintain love for the long term. The Holy Spirit in you is the only way to become an *Overcomer*.

THE 15 COMPONENTS OF LOVE

Nothing or Something?

The classic passage in the Bible describing love is 1 Corinthians 13:4-7. As with all verses in the Bible, the context helps you understand the verses you are reading. Look at the first three verses in chapter 13.

> *1 Corinthians 13:1-3 (NKJV)—Though I speak with the tongues of men and of angels, but have not love, I have become sounding brass or a clanging cymbal. And though I have the gift of prophecy, and understand all mysteries and all knowledge, and though I have all faith, so that I could remove mountains, but have not love, I am nothing. And though I bestow all my goods to feed the poor, and though I give my body to be burned, but have not love, it profits me nothing.*

The Corinthian church had many problems, and these three verses reveal some of them. Paul talks about speaking in tongues, knowing mysteries, having knowledge, having faith, bestowing goods to the poor, and even burning their body. That last one sounds awful, but notice what Paul says about them.

- Speak with tongues of men and angels, but no love = "**I have become . . . clanging cymbal**"
- Gift of prophecy, understand all mysteries, all knowledge, all faith, but no love = "**I am nothing**"
- Bestow all goods, burn my body, but no love = "**it profits me nothing**"

What are they doing? The Corinthians were making everything about ME, and their ME was flashing. They wanted 1) to speak well and sound good (not be a clanging cymbal), 2) to be *somebody* because of their gifts (not be insignificant or nothing), and 3) to profit or get rewards because of their actions (not be without profit).

They claimed to be something special because their gift was better than another person's. But they were becoming **nothing**. Instead of helping the body with their gifts, they created problems because they were selfish and unloving. The more you invest in "ME," your return will be "nothing."

The beautiful description of love is in the context of people "making life about ME." They are clear examples of the PROBLEM, so God provides the SOLUTION. These first three verses contrast a self-absorbed life to the *Overcomers'* supernatural, Holy Spirit-energized, and others-focused life. God contrasts a life of **nothing** and a life with **meaning, purpose, and rewards**.

A meaningful life comes from "pursuing their best patiently, kindly, sacrificially, and unconditionally." It is a life driven by love, "the most excellent way." Not based on what you have but on pursuing their best.

Two Primary Components

God's love is nothing like the world's love. You could spend your entire life unpacking the biblical definition of love provided in 1 Corinthians 13:4-7. While you may be familiar with the verses, they are far more critical than something to read at weddings.

> *1 Corinthians 13: 4-8 (NKJV)—Love suffers long and is kind; love does not envy; love does not parade itself, is not puffed up; does not behave rudely, does not seek its own, is not provoked, thinks no evil; does not rejoice in iniquity, but rejoices in the truth; bears all things, believes all things, hopes all things, endures all things. Love never fails.*

The SOLUTION has 15 components. Some theologians think the first two elements, *suffering long* and *kind*, are the primary elements, and the following thirteen belong under one or the other. I like that idea, which is why ". . . patiently, kindly . . ." is part of the definition of love stated earlier.

#1—Love Suffers Long

> *Colossians 3:12-13 (NKJV)—Therefore, as the elect of God, holy and beloved, put on tender mercies, kindness, humility, meekness, longsuffering; bearing with one another, and forgiving one another, if anyone has a complaint against another; even as Christ forgave you, so you also must do.*

Patience is a great word, but the older term "longsuffering" or "suffering long" provides a clearer picture. "Patience" might suggest waiting calmly in a line or not responding when someone has been rude to you. Those are good things to do; Winston Churchill says, "By swallowing evil words unsaid, no one has ever harmed his stomach."

Suffering long, however, speaks of months and years, not minutes and hours. Suffering long is like the marathon runner who trains with dedication and endurance. Or how about the picture of a 70-year-old man who still prays for the salvation of his 45-year-old son? Maybe you have suffered long in years of difficulties with someone. Or maybe your spouse and friends have suffered long with you!

Love has an enormous capacity to be wronged time after time and not retaliate. When you love, you endure evil and injury without resentment, anger, or revenge. You put up with slights and neglect from the person you love. You wait and hope for the change in the other person rather than resent their behavior. You hope for their best and are not fearful of the worst. You wait, for years if needed, without demands, agendas, or expectations. That is the life of an *Overcomer*!

Suffering long is *not* a martyr-like face with a bad attitude, grudgingly gritting your teeth. It is not even patiently taking the pain you rightfully deserve. Peter makes this clear:

> *1 Peter 2:20-24 (NKJV)—For what credit is it if, when you are beaten for your faults, you take it patiently? But when you do good and suffer, if you take it patiently, this is commendable before God. For to this you were called, because Christ also suffered for us, leaving us an example, that you should follow His steps:*

> *"Who committed no sin, nor was deceit found in His mouth"; who, when He was reviled, did not revile in return; when He suffered, He did not threaten, but committed Himself to Him who judges righteously; who Himself bore our sins in His own body on the tree, that we, having died to sins, might live for righteousness—by whose stripes you were healed.*

The life of Christ and the energy of the Holy Spirit give you the power to suffer long and not give in to angry passions that focus on protecting yourself or getting your way rather than serving others. When you suffer long, you realize that God rewards you for waiting patiently for His timing. That is being an *Overcomer*.

Peter tells us about the reward of longsuffering. The capstone of Peter's instructions is to suffer long, whether the relationship is with unbelievers, governing authorities, masters/employers, or spouses.

> *1 Peter 3:8-10 (NKJV)—Finally, all of you be of one mind, having compassion for one another; love as brothers, be tenderhearted, be courteous; not returning evil for evil or reviling for reviling, but on the contrary blessing, knowing that you were called to this, that you may inherit a blessing. For "He who would love life and see good days, let him refrain his tongue from evil, and his lips from speaking deceit."*

The blessing you receive is loving life and having good days! That means the sacrifice of suffering long becomes, in one sense, no sacrifice at all!

#2—Love Is Kind

Most people value kindness, but its application is lacking. How often you practice it determines whether kindness is a word or a value. For example, you talk about kindness but seldom treat people well. That means it is a fake value, not real, just words.

Kindness is a critical component of love, life, and overcoming.

> *Ephesians 4:32 (NKJV)—And be kind to one another, tenderhearted, forgiving one another, even as God in Christ forgave you.*

Kindness demonstrates graciousness toward others. You show favor, respect, and consideration for others. You see and seek ways to do good for them. You give liberally, not expecting anything in return.

> *New Testament usage focuses on four facets of kindness: friendliness, compassion, helpfulness, and forbearance.—Dr. Ralph F. Wilson*

No wonder kindness is one of the crucial elements in describing love. Where suffering long is marked by the absence of anger when provoked, kindness is a special grace to go further and actively pursue their best.

> *James 3:17 (NKJV)—But the wisdom that is from above is first pure, then peaceable, gentle, willing to yield, full of mercy and good fruits, without partiality and without hypocrisy.*

The Old Testament uses a word for kindness translated as mercy or lovingkindness. Those two words often describe God's actions toward the nation of Israel, ever generous and forbearing. In the same way, He invites you to have a heart of kindness that desires and works for the benefit of others.

Life is mostly froth and bubble,
Two things stand like stone,
Kindness in another's trouble,
Courage in your own.—Adam Lindsay Gordon

Relationship of These Two Components

These two components are like mercy and grace. Suffering long is like mercy. Kindness is like grace. Suffering long withholds punishment. Kindness gives unmerited favor. Suffering long walks the mile without complaint or measuring stick. Kindness volunteers cheerfully to walk the second mile.

God shows longsuffering and mercy in not treating you as your sins deserve. He shows kindness and grace in giving you abundant life and blessings you could never earn.

If you adopt suffering long and kindness as values, you will offer your relationships the potential to blossom and reinforce your desire to overcome! Be honest, and do not rationalize your behavior with your answers to these questions. Am I putting up with slights and neglect? Am I inclined to show favor, no matter what? If you practice these two qualities, all the other attributes of love will likely become part of your life.

Thirteen Supporting Components to Be Something

#3—Love Does Not Envy

An excellent verse describing a self-absorbed life is James 3:16 (NKJV):

For where envy and self-seeking exist, confusion
and every evil thing are there.

The combination of envy and self-seeking is deadly to an *Overcomer*. Self-seeking, self-absorbed living is a common sickness for everyone; when you add envy, it becomes a nightmare.

Another word often combined with envy is jealousy. Both are elements of a self-absorbed life, but the focus of the two words is quite different. Envy focuses on what others have, while jealousy wants to keep others away from what you see as yours. It would be like saying, "I want what you have, and you stay away from what I have."

Love does not compare yourself to others that way. Why? Love is not about serving ME but about pursuing their best. It does not resent others for their gifts, honors, or material blessings but instead rejoices for and with them. It does not feel inferior because such feelings only come from comparison. If you feel inferior, you are comparing what you have to others, so envy may be lurking or already present.

In 1 Corinthians 12, Paul addressed envy, self-seeking, and jealousy related to spiritual gifts. When you read 1 Corinthians 12:4-7, the answer focuses on serving, not comparing. Overcoming means you fit into a body of believers to contribute rather than get.

The focus of love is external, serving, and pursuing their best. That requires a clear mind to remember that God has given you everything for life and godliness (2 Peter 1:3), so envy is lousy thinking and wasted energy.

#4—Love Does Not Parade Itself

A proud man is always looking down on things and people; and, of course, as long as you are looking down, you cannot see something that is above you.—C.S. Lewis

You probably know a time when someone is talking about how great they are but have accomplished much less than you. Your natural tendency is to look for an opening to describe your greatness. It is only fitting to let them know how they compare to you, right? Hopefully, that is not one of your common behaviors, but it will be when you follow your sin nature instead of the path of an *Overcomer*. Self-love, parading yourself, flashing your ME makes sure everyone else knows about ME!

Oh, how silly, I do not do that—or do I?" Be careful not to rationalize bad behavior. You want the truth, be an *Overcomer*, or you do not!

The Flashing ME happens in subtle ways, also. Even a good deed with the wrong motive can be your little parade. That is the difference between entertaining and hospitality. Entertaining is a show, while hospitality seeks to serve others with formal dishes or paper plates.

Philippians 2:3 (NKJV)—Let nothing be done through selfish ambition or conceit, but in lowliness of mind let each esteem others better than himself.

When you love, you are not interested in esteeming yourself; you are not boastful, arrogant, or a braggart because you want their best. More importantly, you want to glorify God. You do not consider yourself above others, honor yourself, or parade yourself because you know about your "I" problem.

#5—Love Is Not Puffed Up

What do you see when you picture a peacock? How about people calling attention to themselves? There is a difference between calling attention to yourself and just demonstrating the beauty of God's creation.

A peacock does not call attention to itself because it thinks it is better than other birds. It is doing it because it is fulfilling God's design. But calling attention to ourselves, as many athletes do, is not beautiful. It is ugly.

Love does not call attention to itself. It does not need to because it is pursuing their best. It is full of God's wisdom and focuses attention on Him. When you love, it can remind you how small you are, how great He is, and that He has gifted all you have by grace.

> *1 Corinthians 4:6-7 (NLT)—Now these things, brethren, I have figuratively transferred to myself and Apollos for your sakes, that you may learn in us not to think beyond what is written, that none of you may be puffed up on behalf of one against the other. For who makes you differ from another? And what do you have that you did not receive? Now if you did indeed receive it, why do you boast as if you had not received it?*

Love is full of joy for others. It is filled with concern for their highest good. Even if you are talented, accomplished, or powerful, it detracts from your accomplishments when you are filled with pride or obsessed with yourself.

> *Romans 12:10 (NKJV)—Be kindly affectionate to one another with brotherly love, in honor giving preference to one another*

#6—Love Does Not Behave Rudely

Rudeness is demeaning, thoughtless, or beyond the boundary of decency. That most likely describes one or more of your actions in the last few days. Satan loves to remind you of that behavior, dragging you down and accusing you of being no different than an unbeliever.

Satan has less to bring to your mind when you are not rude and thoughtless. But you cannot reduce those actions without the power of the Holy Spirit in your life. Yes, you may be able to reduce them temporarily but not in the long term because those are actions of the sin nature, and the Spirit wars against that behavior as you follow Him. He provides the energy to love, pursuing their best instead of being rude.

The mouth is an easy way to be rude.

> *Ephesians 4:29 (NKJV)—Let no corrupt word proceed out of your mouth, but what is good for necessary edification, that it may impart grace to the hearers.*

The Apostle James describes the power of the tongue in James 3:2-12, and you know the power from your own experience. Be careful of sarcasm. That is often rudeness, beyond the boundary of decency, with the sweet icing of humor.

On the other hand, love is courteous, respectful, considerate, and gallant. Love honors authorities, older adults, and those weaker than you. Love gives men the power to be gentle and protective of women and the capacity for women to be respectful, gracious, and pure to men.

Love does not value one person over another and respects every person's position, despite their behavior. God instituted governments (Romans 13); whether you like the government is irrelevant. You can work toward correcting and removing poor governing authorities, but do not become like them.

> *Reverence and respect to superiors.*
> *Kindness and consideration to inferiors.*
> *Courtesy and goodwill to all.—Matthew Henry*

Imagine the benefit you give to others in this rude, indecent world when you pursue the best for others.

#7—Love Does Not Seek Its Own

"Seeking its own" is the "lover of self" problem—the PROBLEM for everyone. The billions of dollars spent on the educational system and corporate training programs to promote self-esteem will work more against society than for it. If you accept God's Word, it is evident that all people are born with a sin nature that focuses on flashing ME rather than helping others. Research shows a clear correlation between hostility and high self-esteem, thus the reason you find criminals with high self-esteem. Pursuing your best often contradicts what others see as their best, increasing the probability of hostility.

Love and selfishness are opposites, even enemies, because they are representative of God and Satan. God is love, and Satan is prideful, self-absorbed, and flashing ME. Satan continually seeks his own way rather than depending on God. On the other hand, love never seeks to hurt or neglect others. It strives for others' welfare and satisfaction and pursues their highest good. The outstanding benefit is satisfaction and fulfillment for the one who loves.

Think about that. When you seek your own, you want satisfaction and fulfillment, but it is, at best, temporary because the self plugs into this world system, ruled by Satan, which is all temporary.

But when you pursue their best, you operate with an eternal perspective. That is where long-term, endless satisfaction and fulfillment live. When you pursue their highest good, your reward is eternal satisfaction.

Consider this scenario. You are selfish and self-absorbed, seeking satisfaction, so you indulge in your appetites, impulses, and pleasures. Since that fulfillment uses something temporary by nature, it can only provide what its nature allows. For example, eating a piece of fruit provides temporary satisfaction because it is temporary. Indulging in materialism, sex, drugs, and alcohol can only provide temporary satisfaction due to their physical and temporal properties.

Worse yet, the dependence on the temporary escalates because you want the satisfaction again. But the object of the satisfaction is temporary by nature and invariably produces less rather than more satisfaction as you rely on it. You can continue indulging your appetites, impulses, and pleasures and become addicted to that temporal satisfaction. You continue desiring satisfaction, but it is ultimately unrealized.

Suppose you pursue the best for another person, and it helps them. It may be satisfying to you and them. Or you do the same thing, and they do not benefit. How does that fit the temporal satisfaction issue?

Appreciation, or the lack of it, is a temporal element. Instead of needing acceptance or appreciation from people, trust God's eternal nature, perfection, and trustworthiness. How? In every situation, ". . . do all to the glory of God" (1 Corinthians 10:31). When you do what He wants, you plug into eternal satisfaction. He is the living water, contrasted against the earthly water that satisfies for a while, then satisfies less the more you drink, and then you get thirsty again.

You find lasting satisfaction when you place all your emotions and pleasure in doing what God asks. It is a satisfaction no longer dependent on life, circumstances, or people.

God rewards your desire to please Him when you serve others. Some people will thank you for your service, even though you did not seek their thanks. God's way blesses you for doing what He wants you to do. He also gives you peace and joy when others are displeased with you.

That is the Christian paradox. Losing your life will save it. Passing up selfish pleasures gives you everlasting rewards.

1 Timothy 6:18, 19 (NKJV)—Let them do good, that they
be rich in good works, ready to give, willing to share,
storing up for themselves a good foundation for the time
to come, that they may lay hold on eternal life.

#8—Love Is Not Provoked

The silliest things provoke people. Perhaps it is a group of little girls who insisted a boy is "bothering them" when he only grinned mischievously at them. Or maybe the same boy gets mad when his favorite cap is snatched and chases furiously after the cap-snatcher like a cat after a string.

But that does not have to be the way you act. You do not have to be a victim controlled by another person's behavior! The path to overcoming and freedom is love, which chooses not to react and respond to people or circumstances. You refuse to have buttons for people to push because buttons are ways you see yourself and want others to see you. Buttons are flashing your ME, which requires you to protect your ME. Love is an outward focus, so there is no ME to protect. Love trusts God to protect ME, so defensiveness is unnecessary.

There is a difference between defensive and defending. Defensive takes things personally, flashing your ME. Defending is like 1 Peter 3:15,

> *". . . be ready to give a defense to everyone who asks you a*
> *reason for the hope that is in you, with meekness and fear."*

Note the manner of the defense, "with meekness and fear." Defensive is when you have to be right, flashing your ME, but defending provides persuasive, truth-focused dialogue without inappropriate emotions.

There is a place for anger. For example, if a gang is beating a child or person, that is wrong, which may encourage your anger. But with anger, take great care (Ephesians 4:26).

Most of the time, anger grows from the root of the flashing ME. Slow down the next time you are angry and ask, "How am I making this about ME right now?" It will be a rare situation where you are not making it about ME.

It is critical to slow your thinking down. That helps you change your thinking to God's. He wants you to pursue their best, even if they misunderstand and mistreat you. Love is not provoked because it trusts completely in your PERFECT Father. It does not depend on superficial tactics like venting, hitting a punching bag, or screaming into a pillow. Those tactics may help temporarily but rarely provide a solution.

The only solution is confessing your self-seeking ways to God and asking Him to renew your mind to a loving perspective! Pursuing their best is always the best.

> *It corrects a sharpness of temper, sweetens and softens*
> *the mind, so that it does not suddenly conceive, nor long*
> *continue, a vehement passion. Where the fire of love is kept*
> *in, the flames of wrath will not easily kindle, nor long keep*
> *burning. Charity will never be angry without a cause, and will*
> *endeavor to confine the passions within proper limits, that they*
> *may not exceed the measure that is just, either in degree or*
> *duration. Anger cannot rest in the bosom where love reigns.*

*It is hard to be angry with those we love, but very easy to
drop our resentments and be reconciled.—Matthew Henry*

*To be a Christian means to forgive the inexcusable because
God has forgiven the inexcusable in you.—C.S. Lewis*

#9—Love Thinks No Evil

Love involves thinking no evil and not keeping a list of wrongs done. Godly actions flow from a mind focused intently on the goodness of God. Sooner or later, your thoughts will show themselves in your actions, whether evil or good.

*Philippians 4:8 (NKJV)—Finally, brethren, whatever things
are true, whatever things are noble, whatever things are
just, whatever things are pure, whatever things are lovely,
whatever things are of good report, if there is any virtue and
if there is anything praiseworthy—meditate on these things.*

While the sin nature drives evil thoughts, the mind seems especially attracted to evil when others have wronged you. You seldom dismiss those wrongs easily. Like Velcro, they stick in your mind and fuel bitterness, resentment, and grudges.

How much more love, joy, and peace would you have if you kept no record of wrongs? If you let go of resentment, grudges, hurts, and thoughts of vengeance? What freedom might come if you dropped your suspicions and plans for revenge instead, focusing on goodness and deeds of kindness? That is the power of forgiveness and overcoming, driven by the energy of the Holy Spirit and love.

Additionally, love is not inclined to suspect others of evil. That does not mean closing your eyes to evil, but simply not suspecting or assuming evil from others. Because of your flashing ME, comparison is built in; therefore, it is easier to believe something terrible about them, right? That is not loving because love does not compare. Love pursues their best and does not think evil of them. It pursues ways to help them.

#10—Love Does Not Rejoice in Evil

This is closely related to the above. Love takes no pleasure in anything wrong. Love is displeased when evil or pain comes to others, not happy when others sin, and not tolerant of evil. Clearly, it does not tolerate the lie that calls evil good and is unafraid of ridicule from standing for truth.

This quote is so relevant to Satan's strategy.

*Evil preaches tolerance until it is dominant, then
it tries to silence good.—Archbishop Chaput*

Do not confuse tolerating evil with tolerating mistakes. Love makes allowances for the errors and sins of others, loving even in their failings. At the same time, it grieves about evil, knowing it results in pain, grief, and destruction. Love hopes, prays, encourages, and sometimes exhorts and rebukes, pursuing the highest good for the other person.

Romans 12:9 (NKJV)—Let love be without hypocrisy.
Abhor what is evil. Cling to what is good.

11—Love Rejoices in Truth

Love rejoices when truth prevails. It is not about being right and winning arguments because that is flashing your ME. Instead, love rejoices in the truth for its own sake! Truth brings freedom and light and is always better for those you love. Love shares the truth and does not fear saying things that, though they may hurt for a time, are nonetheless the truth that can benefit the other person.

More importantly, when you hear the truth, you rejoice in hearing it, even though it may hurt. Love rejoices in truth because the truth is about freedom, the reason Christ died for us on the cross.

John 8:32 (NKJV)—And you shall know the
truth, and the truth shall make you free.

#12—Love Bears All Things

1 Peter 4:8 (NKJV)— . . . love covers a multitude of sins

Not only does God cover sin, but He also demonstrates patience. Both are part of "bearing all things." Thank goodness God loves like that! He hates sin but is patient as He sanctifies and helps you become an *Overcomer*. He is the example of how to relate to others. Love seeks to protect, focuses on the good, forgives wrongs, and works with people to help them overcome their faults. Love bears any difficulty willingly for the good of others and God's glory.

Not publishing the faults of others is challenging but more manageable than bearing the burden of their faults toward you. They may hurt you like Christ was hurt, but love "bears all things." It is a decision to trust your PERFECT Father God, which frees you to overcome by loving and caring for them when they do not care for you. That is supernatural, not natural. It is only possible when you trust God.

That truth is powerful and freeing because you focus on God's thinking, not their awful thinking. You fall into a trap when you think they need to change for your life to improve. Please do not enslave yourself and become a victim, depending on them to change. Instead, rely on your Lord God, Creator of the Universe, to care for them and you.

A picture of bearing all things is in Tolkien's *The Return of the King*. Frodo Baggins and Samwise Gamgee reach the most demanding stage of their quest—climbing Mt. Doom to destroy the evil Ring. Frodo, carrying the Ring, has no more strength to continue.

> *"Now for it! Now for the last gasp!" said Sam as he struggled to his feet. He bent over Frodo, rousing him gently. Frodo groaned, but with a great effort of will he staggered up; and then he fell upon his knees again. He raised his eyes with difficulty to the dark slopes of Mount Doom towering above him, and then pitifully he began to crawl forward on his hands.*

> *Sam looked at him and wept in his heart, but no tears came to his dry and stinging eyes. "I said I'd carry him if it broke my back," he muttered, "and I will!"*

> *"Come, Mr. Frodo!" he cried. "I can't carry it for you, but I can carry you and it as well. So up you get! Come on, Mr. Frodo dear! Sam will give you a ride. Just tell him where to go, and he'll go."*

> *As Frodo clung upon his back, arms loosely about his neck, legs clasped firmly under his arms, Sam staggered to his feet; and then to his amazement he felt the burden light. He had feared that he would have barely strength to lift his master alone, and beyond that he had expected to share in the dreadful dragging weight of the accursed Ring. But it was not so. Whether because Frodo was so worn by his long pains, wound of knife, and venomous sting, and sorrow, fear, and homeless wandering, or because some gift of final strength was given to him, Sam lifted Frodo with no more difficulty than if he were carrying a hobbit-child pig-a-back in some romp on the lawns or hayfields of the Shire.—J. R. R. Tolkien*

Are you willing to carry their burdens? *Overcomers* see it as a privilege because it is acting like Christ. It is lighter than you realize when you depend on God's strength to do it.

#13—Love Believes All Things

The disease of doubt will spring from fear. Faith in God is the antidote. That applies directly to your relationship with Christ and how you treat others. If you trust Him, you can know that God will use it for good in His PERFECTION, despite people doing good or bad. You need not be overwhelmed with pessimism and mistrust. And you do not need to be gullible, either.

Indeed charity does by no means destroy prudence, and, out
of mere simplicity and silliness, believe every word, Proverbs
14:15. Wisdom may dwell with love, and charity be cautious.
But it is apt to believe well of all, to entertain a good opinion
of them when there is no appearance to the contrary; nay,
to believe well when there may be some dark appearances,
if the evidence of ill be not clear.—Matthew Henry

When thinking about trust, people believe it must be earned. While that is true, gifting trust is significantly more common! Think about the last time you sat in a chair. Did you cautiously test its strength and inquire about the credentials and training of the craftsman or manufacturer? No, you just sat because you trusted it to be a good chair! There are so many examples in life like that. If trust is gifted and then unfulfilled, earning trust applies.

In the same way, you have the glorious opportunity to believe the best about people first and, even if proven wrong, to believe in God's PERFECT power, love, and redemption. That is the most crucial thought behind "believes all things." You depend on God to deal with people, so it frees you to believe in the best.

How about a thinking change? With extreme unwillingness, believe badly about others.

#14—Love Hopes All Things

While like the previous, "hopes all things" seems to express a significant challenge. Suppose there is evidence to doubt, to no longer believe. That is where hope enters: hope for returning to what is good and right. The facts reduced or removed trust, but hope still lingers.

When you pursue their highest good, you hope God will do marvelous works in them as He does in you. He turns a heart of cold stone into a vibrant soul passionate about Him, a Saul into a Paul, a slave-trading John Newton into a pastor and writer of Amazing Grace.

And when, in spite of inclination, it cannot believe well of
others, it will yet hope well, and continue to hope as long as
there is any ground for it. It will not presently conclude a case
desperate, but wishes the amendment of the worst of men,
and is very apt to hope for what it wishes.—Matthew Henry

[The Christian] does not think God will love us
because we are good, but that God will make us
good because He loves us.—C.S. Lewis

Are you willing to hope for their good, even if they choose a life of sin? If yes, that is love.

#15—Love Endures All Things

Nothing can stop love. Pain, suffering, loneliness, heartache, loss, and hatred are not strong enough to destroy love. Love has no price tag. Nothing compares to love because it will endure all and outlast all. It perseveres, holds fast, and stands firm in injury and terrible circumstances through God's strength for the sake of others. It overcomes all things.

> *Note, what a fortitude and firmness fervent love will give the mind! What cannot a lover endure for the beloved and for his sake! How many slights and injuries will he put up with! How many hazards will he run and how many difficulties encounter!—Matthew Henry*

> *Hebrews 12:2 (NKJV)—Looking to Jesus the author and finisher of our faith; who for the joy that was set before him endured the cross, despising the shame, and is set down at the right hand of the throne of God.*

The joy set before Christ was our redemption! In the same way, you can joyfully endure all things.

Be Something Eternally

Love Never Fails—Permanent & Perpetual

What a statement—love never fails! It is permanent and perpetual. No example, evidence, or fact shows love does not work. It not only works, but it is also eternal.

> *1 Corinthians 13:13 (NKJV)—And now abide faith, hope, love, these three; but the greatest of these is love.*

All things will be fulfilled, even faith and hope. Love, however, is everlasting! There is nothing temporary or faddish because it describes God Himself. God is love, and His love for us never fails.

But what about your love? Do you fall in and out of love? Is love temporary? Using our definition of love would mean you "fell into" pursuing their best patiently, kindly, sacrificially, and unconditionally.

Love is not mindless. Falling in and out of love is not love. When you see love as a decision, you might say, "I was attracted to them, and now I am no longer." Or "I was attracted to them, got to know them, and decided I did not want to pursue their best."

When you love, you participate in an ongoing story that will continue throughout eternity.

> *At the end of things, The Blessed will say, "We have never lived anywhere except in Heaven." And the lost will say, "We were always in Hell." And both will speak truly.—C.S. Lewis*

CURRENT REALITY ABOUT YOUR LOVE

Reality is your friend, so be objective when rating yourself in the following assessment. You do not need to share this with anyone, but sharing could be helpful if you are objective and want to change.

The statements use "always" and "never" to help you accurately assess yourself.

Score YOURSELF on how you relate to your SPOUSE or a SPECIAL relationship. Use a 1 to 10 scale, where 1 is worst, and 10 is best (10 = Never or Always in the statements below)	
1. I suffer long; I am patient—I always endure evil, injury, and provocation without being filled with resentment, anger, or revenge.	
2. I am kind—I am always gracious and do good for others.	
3. I do not envy; I am not jealous—I never compare myself to others, never suspect unfaithfulness, and never feel inferior because of comparison.	
4. I do not brag or boast—I never have an "I" problem and never judge or act like I am better than others.	
5. I am not puffed up or proud—I never call attention to myself, never puffed up about ME or my possessions.	
6. I do not behave rudely—I am always courteous, respectful, considerate, and polite.	
7. I do not seek my own—I am never self-seeking or self-absorbed and never have to have it my way.	
8. I am not provoked—I am never easily angered or react to what others are doing to me, and I always operate on Godly values.	
9. I think no evil—I never keep a list or think of wrongs done to me.	
10. I do not rejoice in evil—I never condone or tolerate evil or wrongdoing and never rejoice when it happens.	
11. I rejoice in truth—I am always delighted to see truth win, delighted when the truth is shared with me, and glad to get constructive criticism.	
12. I bear all things—I always protect others and never share their faults when speaking to others.	
13. I believe all things—I always trust, never suspicious or assuming, and I am reluctant to believe badly about others.	
14. I hope all things—I always hope for the best without controlling or manipulating.	
15. I endure all things—I always persevere in good and tough times and never feel compelled to talk about my problems.	

Look at the assessment and identify 1 or 2 items you want to improve. Write an action you could regularly take this month to help you score higher next time.

A COMMON PROBLEM

Finger Pointing

Do this simple exercise when leading a group or working with a couple. Ask the people to get together with another person, preferably their spouse or special relationship. Then ask the pairs to look at each other and point their index finger at each other.

As they point their finger at each other, ask one person to say, "If you would just change, I'd be happy." Then ask the other person to say, "If you would just change, I would be happy." Finally, ask them to repeat the exercise with both saying that phrase at the same time.

Generally, everyone laughs after the exercise. Most people agree they do it in their relationships, maybe not right now, but they have done it. The simplicity of this exercise emphasizes that the PROBLEM—making everything about ME, flashing our ME—is real.

Dr. Marlin Howe would say, *"To the degree to which we deny our own issues, we will find a scapegoat on which to dump them."* In my life, that has been true! It is easy to direct thoughts to the problems that others have when substantial changes are needed inside me. Everyone else is messed up, but not ME! Everyone else needs to change, but not ME!

A Critical Question

Think about your closest relationships. Do you think that if they changed, you would be happy or happier? Why is that thinking terrible for you? Because you ignore the change needed in your own life! That means you think, "They are the problem, not me."

You spend energy on changes needed for someone else but little energy on changes you need. You may think you need change, but not as much as they need it. Reality may tell a different story, but it is much easier to see problems in others and blame them for issues in your life.

The same principle is true of the typical relationship definition. It burdens the other person to do what is right instead of ensuring that you do what is right, regardless of whether they do.

Consider asking a critical question. "Am I seeking to change others or me?" Your answer shows if you value freedom or control. Freedom helps you accept, value, and love others as they are.

Judgmental

When speaking about judgment, it is about a self-righteous condemnation of the other person rather than an accurate appraisal of their character. So the definition of judgmental could be—***justice without mercy***.

God is the only one who can provide justice and mercy in the right proportion for each situation. We tend to condemn someone and be satisfied in our declaration of their guilt—without considering any mercy, much less getting the rest of the story.

The definition of love helps change our attitude and actions, but the following verse helps us repent because being judgmental has a big downside too.

> *Matthew 7:2 (NKJV)—With what judgment you judge, you will be judged; and with the measure you use, it will be measured back to you.*

That is not some strange theory; it is part of God's plan. Whatever judgment you give will be the way God judges you. Jesus said that the basis of life is justice—"with the measure you use, it will be measured back to you." God will measure or judge you similarly if you have been exacting, unforgiving, and harsh in your relationship with others. The way you judge others is how God will judge you. This eternal law works from God's throne down to us.

> *Psalm 18:25-27 (NKJV)—With the merciful You will show Yourself merciful; with a blameless man You will show Yourself blameless; with the pure You will show Yourself pure; and with the devious You will show Yourself shrewd. For You will save the humble people but will bring down haughty looks.*

Even more specifically:

> *Romans 2:1 (NKJV)—Therefore you are inexcusable, O man, whoever you are who judge, for in whatever you judge another you condemn yourself; for you who judge practice the same things.*

God looks at the act and the possibility of committing it, which He sees by looking at your heart. You see hypocrisy, deceit, and a lack of genuineness in others because those are in your heart. An excellent characteristic of a saint is humility, as evidenced by being able to say honestly and humbly, "Yes, those, as well as other evils, will be exhibited in me if it not for the grace of God. Therefore, I have no right to judge."

Who would dare to stand before God and say, "My God, judge me as I have judged others"? We have judged others as sinners—if God judged us similarly, He would condemn us to hell. Yet God judges us based on the miraculous atonement of the Cross of Christ.

It is time to look at your heart rather than "finding scapegoats." Let God deal with others and open your heart to God working on you. That is the best place to be!

Give It to God

Try another exercise since you tend to direct your energy into trying to change others, particularly your closest friends and relatives. This one will help you move away from being judgmental.

First, select any personal relationship you have. Write the changes you want to see in their life on some paper. Second, find a private place away from other people when finished writing. Third, fold the sheet of paper you used and put it into the palms of your hands, both palms facing up, not holding the paper. Then pray something like the following:

"Lord, You alone are the one responsible for changing people. If You desire to change (person's name), that is Your decision, Your will. I want Your will, not mine. I now give this list to You. I desire by Your grace that You change my focus and energy from trying to change (person's name) and focus that energy on doing what You want me to do for (person's name) and focus that energy on serving them. LORD, CHANGE ME. Lord, make me a faithful servant and Overcomer. I no longer want to waste energy trying to change (person's name). I want to love, accept, and value them where they are, even if they never change. Amen."

When you finish, throw the list away and spend some time writing what you think and feel now.

Hopefully, you will sense some relief because you released it to God, who is much more interested in them than you will ever be. The relief you experience depends on your view of God. You will have less relief if you do not believe He is PERFECT and wants to help.

On the other hand, if you know Him as He describes Himself in the Bible: perfect, powerful, and personal ". . . able to do exceeding, abundantly, above all that we ask or think . . ." (Ephesians 3:20), then your relief will be significant. Your view of God is critical to understanding who you are and how life works. The relief will be apparent as long as you continue to give the changes back to God.

When you trust God to work His best in others and treat them perfectly, it provides more energy for you to do the same. You can stop trying to change them and accept them as they are.

The heart of a relationship is to know others for who they are and still value, accept, and love them.—R. C. Sproul

Now you can start having a real relationship. Accept them for who they are. Relate to others as God relates to you. He values, accepts, and loves you as you are, not how you were or will be. That is not easy to understand, especially the love part.

Discussion Questions

1. What is the biggest hindrance to becoming an *Overcomer*?
2. What is the difference between being defensive and defending yourself?
3. What is a simple way to know you are probably "making everything about ME?"
4. Memorize James 3:16.
5. What question will help you when you have elevated negative emotions?
6. Quote the definition of Love proposed.
7. How does that definition solve the ME problem?
8. 1 Corinthians 13:4-8 lists 15 elements of love. Which two can be a summary of the other 13?
9. Memorize the quote from Archbishop Chaput. Explain the quote.
10. Explain how the "Finger Pointing" exercise works.

Chapter 5

Move Up or Move Out

Daniel and Perry have worked at a large retail chain for 15 years. They started at the same local store right after graduating from high school. During high school, Daniel excelled in sports, playing football and basketball and sometimes running track. Perry, on the other hand, wasn't very motivated in school. After being ridiculed in junior high, he avoided sports and didn't apply himself much academically.

After joining the company, Daniel attended night school for several years to earn his college degree. During that time, he met and married his wife, and now they have three children. Daniel worked his way up from being a checkout clerk to becoming the manager of the local store. He was always diligent and eager to learn. He volunteered to work on extra projects to learn the business and committed himself to understanding how other departments worked. His hard work ethic earned the respect of regional managers and those around him.

Perry joined the store about three months after Daniel. Unlike Daniel, who started work two weeks after graduating from high school, Perry took the summer off to spend time at the lake and with his girlfriend. At the end of the summer, his girlfriend broke up with him and announced that she was leaving town to go to college. Perry was devastated by this and didn't really do anything for several weeks. Still living at home with his parents, he spent weeks doing nothing, staying up late and sleeping in. His mom finally had enough and told him to get out and get a job. He reluctantly started working at the store in the stockroom, a job he disliked but preferred over his mother's nagging.

Five years later, Daniel was promoted to assistant store manager. By then, he knew Perry pretty well. Perry reported to one of the department managers at the store, who reported to Daniel. Daniel thought Perry was kind of lazy. While Daniel saw potential in Perry, he also noticed his lack of motivation. He knew that Perry didn't have a wife and children to support, so maybe he just needed some encouragement. Daniel tried to encourage him by offering opportunities to learn new things around the store, hoping Perry would seize the chance to grow.

One day during a break in a mandatory training session, Daniel struck up a conversation with Perry. "So how do you like the training so far?"

Perry gave a half-smile and said, "Well, for training, it's pretty good, but most of the time, training is just boring to me."

"How so?" Daniel asked.

"They just put somebody up there to give you a lot of information about how to 'be a good servant,'" Perry replied. "That guy doesn't know anything about this company, what it is like to work here, and the way we are treated. My boss is always micro-managing me to the point that I can't focus on the customers the way I want to."

Daniel nodded silently, telling himself not to judge his colleague, who never really showed any initiative to excel. *How can I help him?* he wondered to himself. *He's got tons of potential and is really smart. If I could get him to see that and motivate him, he could be a valuable asset to the team.*

About that time, the training was going to start again. Daniel said to Perry, "You could be a real asset to this company. I see how much you know about the products, and you go out of your way to help customers who are looking for a certain item, especially in the hardware department."

Perry shrugged and said, "Thanks, man. Nice try at the motivational talk." Then he grinned.

They walked back to the training. Perry continued to be bored and did not participate. Daniel, on the other hand, asked questions of the trainer and was generally very engaged with the trainer and the content.

Another five years passed, and Daniel became the store manager. Perry had quit twice to start his own construction business but always returned when business was slow. By this time, Perry was married, though he and his wife didn't have children.

The third time Perry came back, Daniel decided to have a heart-to-heart talk with him.

"Perry, I really admire that you are trying to start your own business; that takes a lot of guts," Daniel said. I've rehired you a couple of times because the regular customers like you. The thing is, if you just continue to think of this work as something to keep food on the table, I don't see how you will ever get promoted, and I am committed to that for everyone on my team. I don't want to see you helping people pick out the right screw to hold two boards together for the rest of your life. You can achieve so much more than that."

Perry was stunned at Daniel's blunt tone and didn't know what to say.

"Look," Daniel said, "I really want to help you be all the best you can be. You know when I was back in high school and started playing football, everyone said I was too small to succeed, but I proved them all wrong. My career was so much more than any of my coaches thought I could achieve. Don't you want more than just a clerk job?"

Perry stared at the floor for a moment, then looked Daniel in the eye and said, "So I guess this means you are not going to hire me this time."

"Perry, I'm doing this for your own good. You need to take care of your wife, and someday you may have kids. I don't think I'm helping you by continuing to hire you in a dead-end job."

Standing up, Perry said with a sarcastic tone, "Well, I guess with you, it's move up or move out."

With that, he walked out of the store.

Questions

1. Was Daniel's attitude confident or arrogant, especially in the last conversation?
2. Was Daniel focused on helping himself or helping Perry? What evidence could you provide?
3. Was Daniel trying to help Perry be an *Overcomer*?
4. What could Daniel have done better as a friend and leader?

Overcomers Are Humble, Sacrificial Servants

Key Lesson: *Value, develop, serve, and sacrifice, especially when leading.*

Value and Develop People

Greater Capacity

Overcomers value and develop people because they want them to experience the abundant life Jesus has given to believers. Look at the definitions of these words.

- Value: regard highly, think much of, respect and honor, esteem
- Develop: make something new, create by training and teaching

While love pursues their best, valuing and developing focuses on increasing a person's capacity, especially to overcome. When you do this, you fulfill some "one anothers" that God asks us to do for each other.

> *1 Thessalonians 5:11 (NLT)—So encourage each other and build each other up, just as you are already doing.*

> *Ephesians 4:12 (NKJV)— . . . for the equipping of the saints for the work of ministry, for the edifying of the body of Christ . . .*

It is easy to say, "I agree and am doing that." Maybe that is true, but now think about how much time you spend getting to know the people you work with or lead. Do you know their strengths, weaknesses, gifts, and personal goals?

Discovering those answers with just one person takes time, and you may think you are too busy to do that. Of course, that's flawed thinking because people who feel respected and accepted tend to be more satisfied with their work and perform at higher levels. That happens when you value and develop people.

Benefits of Valuing People

This graph is interesting research. Note the title "When Leaders Treat You with Respect, You're More Engaged." Valuing and developing people means you respect them. While this research is about leaders, it easily applies to relationships. *Overcomers* respect, value, and develop people because that is what God does.

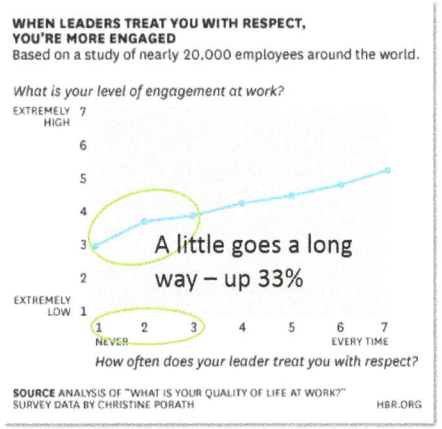

WHEN LEADERS TREAT YOU WITH RESPECT, YOU'RE MORE ENGAGED
Based on a study of nearly 20,000 employees around the world.

What is your level of engagement at work?

A little goes a long way – up 33%

How often does your leader treat you with respect?

SOURCE ANALYSIS OF "WHAT IS YOUR QUALITY OF LIFE AT WORK?" SURVEY DATA BY CHRISTINE PORATH   HBR.ORG

Look at the results of the research. People who felt their leader respected them had

- 56 percent better health and well-being
- 89 percent greater job enjoyment and satisfaction
- 92 percent greater focus and prioritization

Unfortunately, in the same study of 20,000 employees, 54 percent said they did not regularly get respect from their leaders.

Respect, value, and love are all closely related. It is time to do what God asks of you—love one another. There are big dividends for the church or any organization. Why? Because that is what God wants, and He is perfect. Yet selfish, self-absorbed minds do not take the time to encourage, respect, and love people. Valuing people helps them grow and develop.

The best benefit for others is when you value them enough to share the wisdom of God's Word. That gives them the opportunity for insight and self-governance to learn more.

> *Proverbs 9:9 (NKJV)—Give instruction to a wise man, and he will be still wiser; teach a just man, and he will increase in learning.*

> *Proverbs 15:14 (NKJV)—The heart of him who has understanding seeks knowledge, but the mouth of fools feeds on foolishness.*

Do you value people enough to help them grow and develop? *Overcomers* do that because they help others overcome.

Humility Pushes ME to the Back

Definition and Need

Humility is a difficult word and value for me because it is not true of me and is challenging to measure. If you use the English dictionary, humility is:

- Marked by meekness or modesty in behavior, attitude, or spirit
- Not proud or arrogant; modest, unpretentious, courteously respectful

Since the definition uses "meekness," here is an excellent working definition of humility.

Strength under control

That is the definition I learned for meekness, and it fits humility.

Assume you have walked from Cairo to Johannesburg, 5,479 miles or 8,818 kilometers. That would be amazing! Today, you are in a group of people who do not know you. They are all bragging about the longest walk they have taken. One person says the longest walk they ever took was 20 miles. Another person says, "I walked for 50 miles once," and another says 100 miles.

You congratulate them for doing it and ask them questions about it. But you feel no need to tell them you had walked for 5,479 miles. If asked, you would tell them, but you demonstrate humility, "strength under control." You do not try to make yourself appear better than other people.

Humility (strength under control) does not hide or flaunt strengths.

That fits with Jesus' advice.

> Luke 14:8-11 (NKJV)—When you are invited by anyone to a wedding feast, do not sit down in the best place, lest one more honorable than you be invited by him; and he who invited you and him come and say to you, "Give place to this man," and then you begin with shame to take the lowest place. But when you are invited, go and sit down in the lowest place, so that when he who invited you comes he may say to you, "Friend, go up higher." Then you will have glory in the presence of those who sit at the table with you. For whoever exalts himself will be humbled, and he who humbles himself will be exalted.

Even if you had high stature to sit in an honorable place, "strength under control" would not do that. Humility does not elevate yourself but allows others to do so. Notice that Jesus does not tell us to argue with the person about going "up higher." That implies that when you accept the offer, you are doing the right thing and still humble.

> *Romans 12:3 (NKJV)—For I say to you, through the grace given to me, to everyone who is among you, not to think of himself more highly than he ought to think, but to think soberly, as God has dealt to each one a measure of faith.*

What a great message to help stop making everything about ME!

Highly Underrated Value

Jim Collins wrote *Good to Great*. At the beginning of his research to find ten companies that were much better than their competition, he told his team not to pay any attention to the leaders of the companies. However, after reviewing the research, it was clear that each company had humble leaders. In his book, he defines the term Level 5 Leaders as "a paradoxical blend of personal humility and professional will."

He made this statement about Level 5 leaders.

> *Level 5 leaders channel their ego needs away from themselves and into the larger goal of building a great company. It's not that Level 5 leaders have no ego or self-interest. Indeed, they are incredibly ambitious—but their ambition is first and foremost for the institution, not themselves. — Jim Collins*

That last part is critical: humble servant leaders and *Overcomers* glorify God and strengthen the church, not "ME."

Key Action That Helps

The definition of humility, "strength under control," can still be challenging to understand and apply. How do you know that you are moving toward humility? How do you increase humility?

While not answering those questions directly, the critical action of humility is **serving** or **being service-oriented**. Serving is extremely practical. When you serve, you may be increasing your humility. Serving changes your view of humility as a great value and makes it real and active. That, of course, is part of being an *Overcomer*.

Confidence or Arrogance

Hearing someone tell someone to have "self-confidence" or be confident in their actions is well-intentioned. A typical coaching tactic in sports is asking someone to have some confidence. But think about this. How do you get confidence?

Most times, trying to generate some confidence is about having a "can-do attitude." In other words, you say, "Go try it," or, like in basketball, "You will miss every shot you do not take."

It is more helpful to refer to it that way. Because confidence primarily comes from the experience of doing something—if you did it well, you are more confident—if not well, you are less confident—that is why you need practice and repetition. You generate confidence the more that you do something well.

The problem then becomes, are you confident or arrogant? Look at the definitions of the two words. The definitions point to the intent of your heart.

- **Confidence**—the quality or state of being certain
- **Arrogance**—an attitude of superiority manifested in an overbearing manner or in presumptuous claims or assumptions

Which is it for you? Unfortunately for me, it is often arrogance. It is time to meditate on God's Word.

James 4:10 (NKJV)—Humble yourself in the
sight of the Lord and He will lift you up.

1 Peter 5:5 (NKJV)—Likewise you younger people, submit
yourselves to your elders. Yes, all of you be submissive
to one another, and be clothed in humility, for "God
resists the proud, but gives grace to the humble."

Overcomers want the blessing and "lifting" of the Lord. It will not happen when you are arrogant. It only happens with the humble.

SACRIFICE PROVES VALUING PEOPLE IS REAL

Definition and Need

Overcomers sacrifice and give up things they value for the good of the church and others.

Sacrifice is:

- Forfeiture of something highly valued for the sake of one considered to have a greater value
- To forfeit one thing for another thing considered to be of higher value

Consider that and look at most people who want to benefit from everyone else's sacrifice. If you want to be an *Overcomer,* sacrifice is essential. We define sacrifice as

Committed to giving up things you value to benefit the organization and others

The sacrifice fly or bunt is an excellent example for those who know about baseball. The batter is doing something for the team's betterment but may hurt their statistics.

Key Action That Helps

When you sacrifice, you move **commitment** to action, similar to obedience. Commitment is essential, but action like obedience is more important. No longer are you talking about doing what is best for the church; sacrifice shows you are living that value.

Jesus is the ultimate example of willingness to "incur personal costs" for the benefit of others. He is God and chose to give up everything for everyone.

> *Philippians 2: 4-8 (NKJV)—Let each of you look not only to your own interests, but also to the interests of others. Let this mind be in you which was also in Christ Jesus, who, being in the form of God, did not consider it robbery to be equal with God, but made Himself of no reputation, taking the form of a bondservant, and coming in the likeness of men. And being found in appearance as a man, he humbled Himself and became obedient to death, even the death of the cross.*

> *Romans 5:8 (NKJV)—But God demonstrates His own love toward us, in that while we were still sinners, Christ died for us.*

Jesus committed to helping us and served us with the ultimate sacrifice. He showed no ME attitude, which makes Him the ultimate *Overcomer.* All His actions and life proved that He loves and values people!

Big Benefits

It should not be surprising that people displaying self-sacrificial behavior are more highly regarded than others. When researchers studied leaders, they found that sacrificing leaders

> *". . . are considered by their followers to be more effective, charismatic, and legitimate than are self-benefitting leaders."—Hoogervorst, De Cremer, van Dijke, & Mayer, 2012*

What is even more critical is that those leaders

> ". . . *enhance followers' willingness to reciprocate the behavior of a self-sacrificial leader."—Choi and Mai-Dalton, 1999*

What huge benefits! Additionally,

> ". . . *participants elicited higher positive emotions and a stronger willingness to work together with the leader when the leader exhibited self-sacrifice rather than self-benefiting behavior . . . these effects were considerably stronger when the leader did not act in an autocratic (i.e., pushy) manner.—David De Cremer - The Leadership Quarterly 17 (2006) 79-93*

Overcomers will influence others, which is the essence of leadership because they hear, obey, and endure without fear. They are willing to sacrifice everything as Jesus did. It takes significant courage, which only comes from faith in Jesus' power and perfection, to live through you in your situation. *Overcomers* commit to their relationship with Jesus instead of any personal gain.

PRACTICE RESULTS AND RELATING

The Image of God

Finally, Results and Relating is a simple relationship approach that is easy to understand and implement. It will be more effective when you value people, are humble, and are willing to sacrifice for others.

It uses the image of God, which is a critical topic but not included in this book. To learn more about it, see course 02B in GR8 Relationships (gr8relate.com/video-courses/.

Using two words is an easy way to understand and apply our view of the image of God.

Powerful AND Relational

Overcomers understand how broadly those two words apply to relationships and life. When used correctly, *Overcomers* display God's image instead of distorting it. You distort God's image when you use primarily one word—just Results (powerful) or just Relational—excluding the other. The graphic can help.

The powerful and relational words are correct; you may want to use them instead of Results and Relating. For most people, it is easier to remember **Results** and **Relate**.

Here is how this works. The red bar on the black line can move to the right or left on the graphic or anywhere on the line. The graphic illustrates an *Overcomer*'s range of behavior with anyone in a situation.

- If the red bar is more on the left, you demonstrate more Results or powerful behavior.
- If the red bar is more on the right, you display more Relating or relational behavior.

Distorting God's Image

You impact all relationships through Results and Relating. If you overuse either, you hurt your ability to have a Godly relationship. It is critical to model God's behavior; He uses the perfect amount of Results AND Relating as He works with you.

Look at your behavior right now. Think about how you act in most situations when dealing with people. Do you more easily move toward the Results side of the switch, more powerful? If so, at the extreme, you might think or even say, "It's my way or the highway!" "Just get the job done!" or "If people get hurt, that's life."

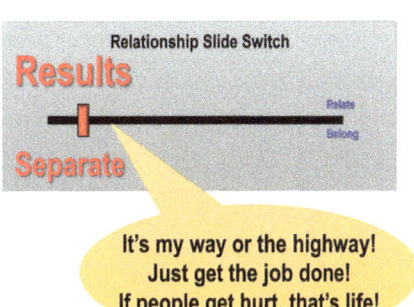

Your actions would be more dominant, aggressive, vocal, and maybe even angry toward others. But you can also be quiet and still be on the Results side. It is not about whether you are loud and vocal; it is about your development to focus more on work and activities and less on people. That means for you, results are the priority more than a relationship.

Your energy for Results values just that—results—not to the exclusion of relating, but as a priority to relating. You relate to people but focus more on results than the people. Relationships are secondary. The further to the left on the switch, the more you focus on results and less on people.

Or you may focus more energy on Relating (relational)—the right side of the switch. At the extreme, that would mean, "Let's just get along!" "Unity is all we need!" or "I just want everyone to feel good about each other!" Your development focuses on what happens to the people and less on the work and activities. You do not like to make things uncomfortable for anyone, especially yourself, and might even say you agree with someone when you do not just to maintain the relationship with them.

Relating energy values people not to the exclusion of results but as a priority to results. The further the bar moves to the right on the graphic, the less energy you have for results. Therefore, you spend more energy on getting along with people.

On the Relating side, manipulation can be the primary way to control people. For example, if you want to persuade someone, you will not try to force your idea on them. You would find a way to get what you want without them realizing it. By contrast, if you are on the Results side—you probably would dominate to get your way. On the extreme, you will use force and fear to control someone.

Reflecting God's Image

People tend to develop more on one side than the other—more Results or more Relating. But no matter how you develop, God wants you to reflect His image accurately.

> *2 Timothy 1:7 (NKJV)—For God has not given us a spirit of fear, but of power and of love and of a sound mind.*

You probably know which side you tend to use the most. If you are not sure, ask others. If you are more on the Results side, you may ignore important relational or people principles. When you want to move the switch more toward Relating, ask these questions:

- What principle about Relating am I ignoring?
- Am I caring for and about others?
- Am I considering the power of gentleness?
- Am I using the truth with mercy?
- Am I pursuing their best?

If you are on the Results side, please remember, "People get results." Results do not just happen; it takes people to generate the results needed. Finding better ways to relate to people helps you achieve your desired results.

Relationship Slide Switch

Results → Relate

Gentleness reduces barriers, force builds them. Use truth with mercy.

It is not wrong to require work from people to get results. However, if that is the only way you deal with people, you create a structure of rebellion. You can force people to do something, but it is a bad long-term strategy. That may get their compliance, but that is not what you want as an *Overcomer*. Instead, you want the full strengths of people to show up to help get the best results. You can move the switch toward Relating as you use gentleness, grace, and freedom because those things reduce barriers. When you add more Relating, it helps you understand the people.

On the other hand, maybe your tendency is more about Relating. You certainly can desire results, but relationships with people are more critical. You may not stand up and do what is right even when others are not. You might tend to "go along to get along."

If you want to move the switch more to Results, ask yourself questions like these:

- What principle about Results am I ignoring?
- Am I doing what is right, using good values?
- Am I relating without violating my values?
- Am I using truth for boundaries?
- Am I pursuing their best?

On the Relating side, you focus on people—you want to get along, belong, and be accepted. Sometimes the other person in the relationship may be on the Results side, taking advantage of you. Or they could be on the Relating side with you, which may mean you both ignore values, boundaries, and truth. Either situation requires work to increase the health of the relationship.

PROPORTION Not Balance

Identifying your tendency may create an undesirable reaction. It may make you think you need to move to the other side or even the extreme other side. However, once you try to operate on the other side, you find a lack of experience or less ability to act that way. That drives you back to your original tendency. When you go back, you feel that is wrong, so you swing back to the other side again. You start swinging back and forth from Results to Relating.

The swing occurs because you see one side as excluding the other. That is how relationships get distorted. The answer is not moving the switch to the other side or swinging back and forth—it is about using the right PROPORTION. Balance is NOT the objective!

God uses both His Power and His Relating in perfect PROPORTION. You can read about the times of His anger as much as His mercy. He knows how to use the perfect amount for each situation. Of course, we will never be perfect, but looking for proportion helps.

Finding the right proportion for each situation helps you develop your less preferred side.

Sometimes an extreme approach is best. Consider examples that require results or assertiveness. What if someone stepped in the path of an oncoming bus? You would yell or push them out of the way, right? You scream, "Watch out!" because Results are needed.

Or on the Relating side, if someone is in a tragic situation that seldom requires focusing on Results. It is a time to act like a mother caring for a newborn child, which needs a tender touch and great care.

When you use the right **proportion**, you change your thinking. You see the bigger picture about being an effective *Overcomer* rather than using the way you have developed. So you think:

- Others may need to change, but change is their responsibility
- Share the truth with and invite others to escape the consequences of not changing
- My job is not to change others but to pursue their best even if they do not change
- Getting things done is essential, but not if it hurts people
- Sharing the truth is important, but share the "truth in love"
- Harmony is good, but not at the expense of what is right
- Relate and belong with others, but not without boundaries
- Make choices based on values; do not react/respond

In closing, God designed men to be more on the Results side and women more on the Relating side. You can see that in Genesis 2. But no matter your design or development, *Overcomers* use the right proportion as God does.

Results need Relating, and Relating needs Results. The proportional use of both is best.

A mentor of mine, Dr. Marlin Howe, used a statement that may help you remember the need for proportion.

Men, be loving leaders! Women, be leading lovers!

Discussion Questions

1. What is a great reason to value and develop people?
2. What two skills are needed to get to know someone so you can help them grow or develop?
3. What is the shift in thinking any leader needs to make?
4. What is the definition used for humility?
5. Explain the definition and how it works in real life.
6. Explain how you can be highly ambitious, accomplished, talented, and HUMBLE.
7. Why is service a critical action for humility?
8. Explain the difference between confidence and arrogance.
9. What is a simple definition of sacrifice?
10. Explain whether a leader should sacrifice for a follower's THERE.
11. Explain the Results and Relating principle.
12. Do you see yourself as more Results or Relating?
13. Explain why proportion is a better word than balance for this principle.

CHAPTER 6

FORGIVE AND FORGET

Mary Anne and Andy met at their church's annual meeting. Both were in their 30s and had never been married; they hit it off right away and decided to attend a Discipleship Class together at the church. Their relationship blossomed, and in 18 months, they were married by their pastor in a small ceremony with family and a few close friends.

Because Mary Anne was 36, they wanted to start a family right away. After three years, and many medical procedures, they did not have children. Despite their struggles, Andy was firmly against adoption. He felt it was very important for them to carry their lineage to the next generation. Mary Anne didn't agree with his point-of-view, but she wanted to be supportive of her husband as head of their household.

As time passed, Mary Anne grew increasingly frustrated with Andy about his refusal to consider adoption. She had several friends who had adopted children and watched as they happily talked about their process. Daily, she thought about how many children needed a good home and felt that they could provide a loving home tor a child in need. Yet, every time she tried to bring up the subject, Andy just got mad and said he did not want to discuss it. Mary Anne's frustration grew into resentment.

Seeking advice, Mary Anne reached out to her girlfriend Joanie from work to complain. Joanie advised Mary Anne to stand up to her husband and not let him rule over her.

Their conversations became tense.

One evening, Andy asked, "Mary Anne, what do you want to do this weekend?"

Mary Anne, brimming with anger, snapped, "Andy, I don't care. You call all the shots in this family. You decide."

Andy, feeling his face flush, asked, "What is this about?"

Mary Anne's frustration boiled over, and she spoke in a harsh, angry tone, "C'mon, Andy, you know how much I want to have a family, but you won't allow us to."

Incredulously, he said, "I won't allow us to? You know that I am not the reason we cannot have children. I have supported you through every procedure we have tried. You know I would love to have a family too."

Crushed by guilt, Mary Anne ran from the room sobbing. She ran to the guest bedroom and locked the door. She threw herself on the bed and thought to herself. *I have ruined this marriage because I cannot get pregnant. I can't believe how mean Andy is acting to me, but I guess I am at fault. I guess I got what I deserved.*

Andy decided he should let his wife work this out herself. He knew if he knocked on the door, she would send him away. Andy thought, *All I did was ask her what she wanted to do this weekend, and this is what I get. I just don't understand her. Maybe this is just a woman thing.*

Andy felt he needed to get out of the house to regroup.

He went to the door of the guest room and said, "Mary Anne, I'm going to go out for a walk. I'll be back in 30 minutes."

Mary Anne continued to sob in a pile of guilt and shame.

The following weekend, their pastor gave a sermon on confession, based on 1 John 1:9 (NKJV)—"If we confess our sins, He is faithful and just to forgive us our sins and cleanse us from all unrighteousness." Mary Anne realized how angry and resentful she was at her situation of not being able to get pregnant. This was the root cause of many of the arguments between Andy and her. She reasoned, though, that it was her fault that she and her husband couldn't have kids, so what did she need to confess? She already labored with the guilt of causing their problems.

The pastor also talked about the meaning of repentance, to change thinking or turn from a behavior or mindset. Mary Anne thought to herself, *Well, Andy is the one who needs to do that. He keeps reminding me that I'm the one who keeps us from having kids.*

Meanwhile, Andy, also moved by the sermon, began reflecting on his behavior. He realized that he blamed his wife for them not having a family. Over the week that followed, he examined his behavior and attitude toward Mary Anne about nagging him to adopt when he didn't want to take that path. He was tired of her emotional outbursts and their constant fighting. One morning when he was reading his daily scripture, he stopped and confessed to God, "Forgive me, Lord. I have acted badly toward my wife."

In response, he felt the Lord whisper to him, "Yes, I forgive you. Now, confess your wrong thinking to Mary Anne and change how you act."

Andy felt some rebellion rise up inside of him. *Confess to her*? He thought that would be harder than confessing to God. He figured he could just change his behavior by not bringing the subject of family up. And if she did, he would just apologize for her disappointment.

Questions

1. Does it sound like Andy was repentant? What did he do to influence your answer?
2. Does it sound like Mary Anne is repentant? What did she do to influence your answer?
3. Does Mary Anne have real or false guilt?
4. What do you think would help this situation?

Overcomers Confess When They Are Wrong

Key Lesson: *Confession requires an internal change of heart.*

Confession and Guilt

You cannot survive without food, water, and sleep. No one disputes this. But I would like to add two activities to that list that *Overcomers* know are essential—confession and forgiveness! Those might not come to mind as naturally as the necessities listed, but let me assure you both are just as necessary for *Overcomers* as air and water.

Confession and forgiveness are critical because every *Overcomer* will sin against others and be sinned against by others. An *Overcomer* who does not confess and forgive lacks obedience and trust in the PERFECTION of God. It also proves that Jesus' life is not flowing through as much as He desires. An *Overcomer's* unconfessed sin or unforgiveness blocks the flow of Jesus' life and the Holy Spirit's work in them.

When you do not walk through those two gates, you stop or limit your progress as an *Overcomer* and damage your relationships with God and others. That is not hyperbole because those two actions demonstrate a dependence on God or something other than God. This and the following chapter are critical elements for *Overcomers*.

Definition of Confession

Confession is admitting you have done something wrong; often, that means you hurt others. It does not matter who you are; wrongs need confession and forgiveness in every relationship. When you sin, God asks you to confess your sins to Him and the people you harmed.

Webster's Dictionary defines confession as follows: "To tell, to make known, to admit." The second part of the definition is: "To acknowledge a sin to God or to a priest." That is a surprisingly good definition, but it is not complete.

Consider the definition offered by Strong's Exhaustive Concordance: "To concede, not refuse, to promise, to not deny, or to admit and declare oneself guilty."

That is a more Christian and complete definition. Why? Because the definition describes an action you will not want to take. No person naturally wants to admit or even believe they are guilty until they finally understand that, in Christ, they no longer need to defend themselves. Once you get this embedded in your heart and soul, you more easily own the fact that you sinned, hurt God and others, and need to confess.

The definition of confession we will use ties confession and repentance together.

Confession is the external act of an internal change of heart.

What I confess comes out in words to God and reflects my values and belief in God's Word. It says I do not want to continue this type of behavior. I do not want to do that anymore. This definition of confession reflects the reality of physical laws. Two objects cannot occupy the same space at the same time.

Consequently, if you accept God's values, you expel the rebellious part that does not want to repent. It is both a spiritual and natural law of the universe. It is simply reality.

Order of Confession

The order is critical to understanding and applying confession.

"Confession of sin, it should be first observed, is first to God and then extended to others only as they've been directly injured by the sin" (Bibliotheca Sacra Volume 93, page 151).

The internal change of thinking occurs first. You admit the Lord is correct and that you are wrong, but not only that you are wrong but that you have changed your thinking by the Lord's convicting. That is how confession and repentance work together.

Consider how this works in healthy human relationships. Dr. Fred Lybrand says, "Good marriages and relationships leave a trail of resolved issues." Confession is one of the critical resolution tools. When you use forgiveness and confession, freedom is also present. Neither confession nor forgiveness results from badgering or bullying someone to admit any wrong they did. That does not include freedom and probably is unlikely to be confession.

Freedom does not expect them to forgive you either! That is between them and God.

Additionally, to keep things simple, it is best to use confession when you have done something wrong rather than "asking for forgiveness." Confession is about you doing something wrong, and forgiveness is about others doing something wrong to you.

That distinction was critical for me when initially studying forgiveness.

Hindrances to Confession

Confession and Investment

> *"He who has the most invested loses the power." —Dr. Marlin Howe*

You often are unwilling to confess sin because you invested so much in it. Allow me to explain. The more you invest in something, the more power it has over you.

Imagine you own an expensive car. Who has the power in this situation? You or the expensive car? Most often, it is the car because you have invested a lot of money and it now has power over you. When you drive it, you take great care in parking where other people will not damage it. The car has power over you. It, not you, dictates your behavior.

That is what sin does to you because you "invest" in it. Now, sin has power over you. It can keep your heart and mind closed to the reality that you have done wrong. However, if you confess, you divest yourself of the sin and have power over it through Jesus Christ.

Getting Right, Not "My Rights"

Another hindrance to confession can be an expectation or demand from a person in a relationship. One person might say, "If someone ever did that, well, the relationship would be over right then!"

You face a dilemma if you are the other person and do what they said would terminate the relationship. The right thing to do is confess to them, but you fear confession because you do not want the relationship to end.

If you think clearly, you will ask, "Do I want my relationship with God more than I want my relationship with them?" Of course, you can easily answer that question when you are not in that situation. But if you were, the order of confession would guide and protect you. Because, first and foremost, your relationship with God must be unhindered. If you do not have that in good order, then none of your other relationships will be in order. That allows you to live the way God wants.

It is essential to add that demands and expectations create problems for relationships. The purpose of most demands and expectations is to control people and relationships. God does not do that.

Yes, God created the Ten Commandments and set clear boundaries for us. But if crossed, He does not separate you from His forgiveness. No matter your sin, you are always free to confess, repent, and be restored with Him. The Bible says that ". . . while we were still sinners, Christ died for us . . ." (Romans 5:8). All relationships experience hurt and sin; do not make them worse with demands and ultimatums.

Demands are another way to get my way or establish my rights. Confession is not about your rights. It is not about doing it your way. Confession is about a change of thinking and removing your investment in sin, leading to freedom.

God wants that for you. He does not want you controlled by the sin in your life, just like He does not want you controlled by the sin that somebody else has done to you. He wants you controlled by His thinking because He knows that is the best path for your life. That is the primary reason you need confession and forgiveness in your life. That is part of the abundant life God gave you when you trusted in Jesus' death, burial, and resurrection.

Satan's Deception

The ultimate hindrance to confession is Satan's deception. He deceives through his primary strategy—"Did God really say . . . ?" Avoiding confession is precisely what Satan wants. If he deceives you into believing that you do not need to confess or that confession does not work, your sin stays powerful in your life. That is why he uses two simple deceptions.

First, Satan deceives you to compare your sin to others and rationalize it. Comparing your sin takes the focus off you and puts it on them. For example, take the marriage problems that my wife Louie and I had. You can watch our testimony online at *https://gr8relate.com/hermann-louie/*.

It's easy for me and others to say, "Louie is the bad one in the marriage. She did some bad stuff. She needs to confess." While that is true, I did bad stuff too. I wounded her in many significant ways, primarily with my controlling spirit, which destroys relationships. I, too, had sins to confess. The difference is my stuff is less visible and, by the world's standards, not as bad.

When you label the other person as worse than you, you minimize the reality of your sin. You distract yourself from your sin and focus on comparing your sin to theirs. Instead of seeing all sins hindering your relationship with God, you rationalize your sin.

That behavior is evidence of walking in the flesh. Satan wants you to explain, defend, and justify your life instead of submitting to God. God wants you to walk with Him and trust your life to His way. His message is the opposite of Satan's. "You don't need to try to defend yourself. Just do it My way. Trust Me; this is the right way to go. I know it may not feel good, but trust Me."

Second, Satan wants you to believe that God will not forgive you. That lie will keep you enslaved to guilt. That lie is often more powerful because it appears more accurate than your rationalization.

Third, and closely connected to the second, Satan wants you to continue to feel guilty despite God's forgiveness and cleansing. This deception is a simple whisper in your ear.

"But you still did it!"

That distracts you from everything God states, and you fall for Satan's primary strategy, which gets you to doubt God—"Did God really say . . . ?" When you focus on what you did, you believe God is still paying attention to your sin. But that is a lie.

The following steps help cement the truth of God forgiving your sins. Satan wants you to trust yourself. He does not want you to accept and trust God's way, which is the best way for you to go.

Confession is trusting God and going God's way.

Defining Real and False Guilt

There is a big difference between *real guilt* and *false guilt*. However, that is not evident because of poor definitions and understanding of guilt. Dr. Paul Tournier stated these two definitions in his book *A Doctor's Casebook in the Light of the Bible*.

**"False guilt" is that which comes as a result of
the judgments and suggestions of men.**

"True guilt" is that which results from divine judgment.

If God has spoken against it and you do it, you are guilty—*true guilt*. Or if God has stated it and you do not do it—*real guilt*. On the other hand, if man creates laws you do not follow, it may be *false guilt*.

That creates important questions like, "What about the government's laws? Aren't those the judgments or suggestions of men? Doesn't Romans 13 state that we should obey our authorities?"

Great questions and answers depend on whether man's judgments or suggestions align with God's. As you learned in the first two chapters, God is THE authority, and everyone else is a channel of His authority. God's authority is the final word, and if man's law goes against what He says, not doing what man says is *false guilt*. God will not judge you for violating that. Here is a clear example of that.

*Acts 4:19-20 (NKJV)—But Peter and John answered and
said to them, "Whether it is right in the sight of God to
listen to you more than to God, you judge. For we cannot
but speak the things which we have seen and heard."*

Satan loves for people to create rules and regulations, especially in churches, that seem correct but are not what God's Word says. Those become tools for Satan to create *false guilt* and use guilty feelings to make you ineffective and say silly things like, "I need to forgive myself."

You need to be aware of the "But you still did it!" deception. Even when you confess your *real guilt* as God desires, Satan's whisper focuses your attention on the slander from his mouth, which is not from God.

There is no defense against *real guilt* without the death, burial, and resurrection of Jesus Christ. You are a slave to sin, unable to be free from guilt. You only have freedom from guilt and condemnation when you accept that Jesus Christ's death paid for your sins. There is no other way to remove guilt and sin. God's Gift of Salvation is the first step to freedom. That is why the Gospel is such GOOD NEWS!

You can be free from both *false guilt* and *real guilt*.

DEALING WITH FALSE GUILT

False guilt originates primarily from lousy thinking, which demands bad feelings and often leads to wrong actions. You may be experiencing thoughts like, "I have a huge feeling of guilt but cannot understand why." Unfortunately, lousy thinking often comes from not being in God's Word enough to see how God thinks about life.

Please accept that *false guilt* does not come from God. He sent His beloved Son to set you free (Galatians 5:1), so He has no desire to manipulate you with *false guilt*. The *false guilt* is from Satan. Most often, *false guilt* is as simple as not accepting God's incredible forgiveness or not accepting forgiveness from others.

"I can't forgive myself" is terrible thinking absent in an *Overcomer's* mind, and it is solved simply by accepting God's forgiveness. You will see more about this later when you learn about forgiveness.

Satan's never-ending messages whisper, "You have failed; you haven't lived up to expectations, and you have disappointed the people around you!" When you experience *false guilt*, you experience Satan's deception and believe a lie. Change your thinking to become healthy and distinguish between *real guilt* and *false guilt*.

Step One: New Family

You are in a new family. Listen to Paul's words to the Ephesians:

Ephesians 1:5-8 (NKJV)—[God] having predestined us to adoption as sons by Jesus Christ to Himself, according to the good pleasure of His will, to the praise of the glory of His grace, by which He made us accepted in the Beloved. In Him we have redemption through His blood, the forgiveness of sins, according to the riches of His grace which He made to abound toward us in all wisdom and prudence . . .

"He made us accepted." You are adopted and accepted by God even though you did nothing to earn it. Nothing. Instead, God did it all! You are in God's family, which freed you from the family and slavery of sin. You may find that hard to believe because it sounds too good.

The great thing about truth is that it remains valid despite your beliefs. You are freed from sin and loved as God's very own child. Hallelujah! However, if you do not feel this is true, Satan is deceiving you. That is another reason it is best not to trust your feelings driven by lousy thinking. Remember the proper order:

1. THINK (know God's truth)
2. ACT (follow God's way)
3. FEEL (allow God's truth to drive your emotions)

Step Two: You Have Been Forgiven

You have been adopted into God's family and forgiven of your sins by God. If you trusted His Son, the Lord Jesus Christ, as your Savior at any point in your life, you stand before God **FORGIVEN**. Completely forgiven. Please accept this truth because it is the foundational truth of the Christian life.

- Jesus Christ bore your sins on the cross (1 Peter 2:24).
- Jesus Christ saved you from God's wrath (Romans 5:9).
- Jesus Christ paid your sin debt in full—**you are no longer guilty**.
- Jesus Christ chose to forgive you and make you His own, **now and forever.**
- Jesus Christ extended His arm of forgiveness and placed a seal upon your heart. You are His for all eternity. Nothing, nothing can erase His seal.
- Jesus Christ will NOT change His mind about us (Romans 11:29).

The Good News of Jesus Christ is you have been forgiven and granted eternal life, as John tells you in John 6:40 (NKJV):

> *And this is the will of Him who sent Me, that everyone who sees the Son and believes in Him may have everlasting life; and I will raise him up at the last day.*

Try this exercise.
1. On a piece of paper, create a list of everything you feel guilty about. It does not matter if it is *real guilt* or *false guilt*.
2. On another sheet, WRITE each of the following verses.

> *1 John 1:9 (NKJV)—If we confess our sins, He is faithful and just to forgive us our sins and to cleanse us from all unrighteousness.*

> *1 Peter 2:24 (NKJV)—Who Himself bore our sins in His own body on the tree, that we, having died to sins, might live for righteousness—by whose stripes you were healed.*

> *Romans 8:1 (NKJV) —There is therefore now no condemnation to those who are in Christ Jesus, who do not walk according to the flesh, but according to the Spirit.*

> *1 John 2:12 (NKJV)—I write to you, little children, because your sins are forgiven you for His name's sake.*

3. Pray to the Lord Jesus Christ.
- Bring each item of guilt, real or false, to Him.
- Imagine you are laying each item at His feet.
- Confess any real sins and even ones that may be false.
- Tell Him you claim His sacrificial death as full payment for your sins.
- Tell Him that you accept His forgiveness (for both real and false guilt).
4. Claim each Scripture you just wrote as His personal promise to you.
- Write one or more Scripture references beside each item.
- Draw a line through every item on your list.
- Write "Forgiven" over the top of each.

When you do the exercise, you reinforce Godly thinking and truth.

Step Three: Remember You Have Been Set Free

Freedom in the Lord is not subjective. You are objectively, utterly free because God says you stand justified before Him in Christ. Justification is a legal term that means "to be declared not guilty." How can this be true? After all, God clearly says that you have sinned and must confess your sins to Him and perhaps even those you have injured.

> In New Testament times when a person was sent to prison, guards posted a ledger outside the cell door declaring his guilt. When he completed his sentence, a certificate was then written and signed "Paid in Full." From that point on there was proof of the debt's payment.
>
> *Dr. Charles Stanley*

God also says you are justified before Him because Christ's death, His blood, paid for all your sins. The spilling of Christ's blood allows you to be found **not guilty** before God's throne of judgment. If you have God's seal upon your heart, you have His forgiveness, which applies not only in this moment but forever. The seal is made possible by the precious gift of the Holy Spirit, who embeds the words "not guilty" upon the seal written in the blood of our Lord and Savior, Jesus Christ.

That does not mean you will not sin once the Holy Spirit has sealed you. You will! And God knows this. That is why He had St. Paul write to us in Romans about his sin.

> *Romans 7:19-20 (NKJV)—For the good that I will to do, I do not do; but the evil I will not to do, that I practice. Now if I do what I will not to do, it is no longer I who do it, but sin that dwells in me.*

If the greatest of the Apostles continued to sin after being saved by Jesus, you, too, could expect to battle sin for your entire life. That is why confession is so important.

Confession of sin restores your fellowship with God because you have aligned your heart with His desires for your life. This restored fellowship allows you to live as the King's adopted, forgiven, and justified child. It is not what you deserve. You deserve to feel depressed, rejected, and worthless. The beauty of God's grace is that you do not get what you deserve. You are not worthy of God's love and forgiveness. No one is! Grace is an unmerited gift from God that allows you to enjoy His favor.

> *Ephesians 2:8-9 (NKJV)—For by grace you have been saved through faith; and that not of yourselves, it is the gift of God; not a result of works, that no one should boast.*

Paul reminds you that salvation only comes from God as a gift you do not deserve. When you humbly trust God, He treats you as a loving father treats His children—with undeserved and unending love.

Having read this chapter section and hopefully understanding *false guilt*, please accept the freedom God has provided you. If the Holy Spirit convicts you and you want God's grace and freedom, consider praying the following prayer:

> *Father, thank You for loving and accepting me. I lay aside all feelings of guilt and self-condemnation and choose by faith to receive the forgiveness of my Savior, Jesus Christ. I realize that through Him, I have unlimited access to Your throne. I know that since You can forgive real guilt, You can also forgive false guilt. I no longer want to be a slave of lousy thinking or Satan's deception. As Your beloved child, I ask You to reveal Your love to me today in a fresh, new way. In Jesus's Holy Name, Amen.*

Now, get the list that you created earlier.
1. Write your name somewhere at the top of the list.
2. Read the following verses.

> *Romans 5:1 (NKJV)—Therefore, having been justified by faith, we have peace with God through our Lord Jesus Christ*
>
> *Romans 5:9 (NKJV)—Much more then, having now been justified by His blood, we shall be saved from wrath through Him*

3. Over your name, write the words "Eternally FREE—Justified."

Remember you are adopted, you are forgiven, and you are justified. And if God can deal with *real guilt*, confess your *false guilt*; He can handle that also.

Dealing with Real Guilt

Real guilt is a gift from God that will turn you from further sin and consequences. God uses *real guilt* to bring you to repentance and experience His forgiveness. It is a marvelous gift from a loving, PERFECT Father God to check your course and change your path.

When speaking about *false guilt*, there were references to your feelings. While feelings will be part of *real guilt*, they are much less important. Why? Real guilt speaks about your relationship with God and His standards. *Real guilt* is objective and a reminder that you . . .

- Have stepped beyond God's boundaries.
- Are no longer walking with God.
- Need to check our course and adjust your sail.
- Require repentance and confession.
- Need to agree with a merciful and Holy God about your sin.

Below are some detailed steps that spell CONFESS. They help you understand how to deal with *real guilt*. The seven steps occur in three phases—Preparation, Application, and Thanksgiving.

Preparation

Step One: Choose Humility

Humility is essential for confession. Without it, you remain defensive, judgmental, and unable to see the real issues in your life. More importantly, when you are humble, you receive God's grace.

> *1 Peter 5:5-7 (NKJV)—Likewise you younger people, submit yourselves to your elders. Yes, all of you be submissive to one another, and be clothed with humility, for "God resists the proud, but gives grace to the humble." Therefore humble yourselves under the mighty hand of God, that He may exalt you in due time, casting all your care upon Him, for He cares for you.*

Who does God give grace to? The humble. The humble person says, "I can't do this alone." The prideful person says, "I can do this by myself." Scripture tells us which person God helps.

Step Two: Own Your Guilt. Do Not Excuse It.

Excuses are a natural part of the sin nature. It is not easy to accept what you have done and the consequences. It is always tempting to blame someone else for your shortcomings and sin. Consider a few of the common excuses. Does the excuse hold up after considering the reply?

Excuse	Answer	Excuse	Answer
It happened a long time ago	It's time to deal with it	They will not understand	Just do the right thing
They have moved away	They can be found	I'll do it later	Later never comes
It was such a small offense	It can create big damage	I'll only do it again	You can confess again.
Things are better	Good, let's resolve it now	They were more wrong	It's about you, not them
I'm just being too sensitive	They may be sensitive, too	I will not do it again is enough	Confess to remove its power
No one's perfect	That's not the issue; sin is	It will get friends in trouble	Confess about you, not them

However, excuses are worthless; as Steven Grayhm says, "Excuses are the tools with which a person with no purpose in view builds for themselves great monuments of nothing."

Step Three: Name the Real Offense

Confession requires honesty, objectivity, and reality. It is about what happened. That is not something you can do in your power. To get to the real issue, ask God to reveal the real hurt, the actual offense.

Bill Gothard says, "It is relatively easy to remember the faults of others, but when it comes to listing our faults, we may discover a lapse of memory." Therefore, you desperately need the wisdom of the Psalmist.

Psalm 139:23-24 (NKJV)—Search, me, O God, and know my heart; Try me, and know my anxieties; And see if there is any wicked way in me, and lead me in the way everlasting.

To get to the real offense, you must know it. Doing so requires asking God to show it to you and then willingly and clearly name it. I suggest a written list. Otherwise, it is too easy to forget and avoid real offenses.

Step Four: Feel the Offense as They Felt It

Empathy involves seeing life from their perspective, understanding their pain, and doing something about it. When it comes to confession, you may feel you are only 10 percent wrong, while they think you are 100 percent wrong.

Often, when you think something is no big deal, they see it as huge. You do not have to understand their pain, but you do need to attempt to see it through their eyes. Be willing to grasp their pain so that you are moved to do something about relieving the pain—like confessing if you were the one who created the pain.

Application

Step Five: Earnestly Repent of Your Sin

Repentance ultimately aligns your heart with God. He wants a close, intimate relationship with you—hearts aligned. The outcome of repentance is fantastic, but the process is not fun because it requires remorse for your sin. In case you did not know, your sin nature hates remorse. However, your internal change of thinking is precisely what you do to experience genuine joy in the forgiveness of God. Simply put, repentance involves a 180 turn—turning from sin and turning toward righteousness.

Faking repentance means you want others to tolerate your sin without changing. It is like saying, "I am just that way; put up with it."

Step Six: Soberly Confess Your Sin

Remember, confession is first to God and then to the person you wronged and injured. Do not forget that **confession is the external act of an internal change of heart**. Internal change is critical but does not remove the requirement for external action.

> *1 John 1:9 (NKJV)—If we confess our sins, He is faithful and just to forgive us our sins and cleanse us from all unrighteousness.*

Thanksgiving

Step 7: Sincerely Thank God for the Conflict

Most people avoid conflict like the plague. It should not be so among believers. Conflict is an excellent time for learning and development. More importantly, God can bless us immensely, even if the conflict is evil. Remember how Joseph's brothers severely mistreated him, but in Genesis 50:20 (NKJV) he said,

> *. . . you meant evil against me, but God meant it for good . . .*

And Paul tells us God is at work in all, even the worst, situations.

> *Romans 8:28 (NKJV)—And we know that all things work together for good to those who love God, to those who are the called according to His purpose.*

Even though it sounds wrong, thank God for what has happened because He alone knows how He will use your sin for His good purposes. He alone is in control of all things.

If you are ready to deal honestly with the *real guilt* in your life, please consider praying this prayer:

> *Lord Jesus, I want to thank You for loving me and accepting me. I want to confess any sin in my life right now, and by faith, I claim Your forgiveness as mine for eternity. Please make me sensitive to the movement of your convicting hand. I thank You that this will make me like You, reflecting Your unconditional love and grace. Amen.*

Use these scriptures to reinforce how God will grow you, desiring the best for you.

> *Psalm 27:5-6, Psalm 27:11-14, Isaiah 41:10-11, 42:6, Lamentations 3:22-5, Habakkuk 3:17-19, Matthew 11:28, John 16:33, Romans 8:37-39, Ephesians 5:20, 1 Peter 1:3-9*

See "Appendix: Forms for Chapter 6" for help preparing for confession.

Discussion Questions

1. Memorize the definition of confession. Explain it.
2. What is the order of confession, and why is that important?
3. Memorize and explain, "He who has the most invested loses the power."
4. What is Satan's primary, maybe only, strategy?
5. What does Satan whisper to you after you confess? What makes that so powerful? How does it fit Satan's primary strategy?
6. What is the difference between Real and False guilt?
7. Is it real or *false guilt* if you do not obey your country's laws?
8. What is an easy way to explain what repentance means?
9. Why is repentance needed as part of confession?
10. Since Christ forgave all our sins at His death, what is the reason for 1 John 1:9?
11. What is the benefit of thanking God for the conflict, even the sin that you confessed?

CHAPTER 7

BUT I DIDN'T DESERVE THIS

George and Sandy have been married for 20 years and serve as worship leaders at a church in a large metropolitan area. They have two kids—Benny, who is 15, and Jade, who is 12. George and Sandy have been with the church for two years and have revolutionized the worship. Rather than two songs, a scripture, and a sermon, the church has evolved to seeking God through worship. Having introduced this more immersive style of worship, they have written four original songs. They have also launched a YouTube channel that features their songs and songs from other worship team members.

Their kids are in public school and have run into some bullying because their parents are worship leaders and have a YouTube channel. On top of that, some of the long-time church members don't like the music and want to go back to the old way of doing things.

These long-time church members call a meeting of leaders and like-minded people who want to get the leadership to go back to the old format. They deliberately do not invite George and Sandy to the meeting. The leader of the dissenters, Harry, starts the discussion this way.

"I've been a member of this church for forty years and have always loved our dependable service format. The old hymns that my parents used to sing were always uplifting to me. Now we have guitars, drums, saxophones, and a violin. I don't mind the violin so much because it reminds me of the symphony."

As Harry is making these comments, many in the meeting are nodding in agreement.

The Lead Pastor, Brock Chambers, responds, "Harry, we appreciate your input because you have been a longstanding and loyal member of this congregation. I know it's hard to adjust to drums in church, but many of the songs that we sing really work better with various instruments."

Pastor Brock then shared some scriptures that validated the format of using different instruments. He also shared some stories of the numerous salvations and moves of God in some large churches in the area that had changed to this same style of worship. Then he explained that the church leadership had recruited him three years ago because attendance was dropping off and membership reflected few younger families in the congregation. Now the membership was growing with new, younger families.

Harry did not take well to what Pastor Brock said but just made a face and went silent. Harry thought to himself, *I'll just have to handle this another way.*

Others who Harry had invited to the meeting looked at each other with a look of resolve, knowing that Harry would not drop the subject that easily. The meeting ended cordially.

Six months later, Harry had managed to stir quite a following. They all smiled and acted like everything was fine, but behind the scenes, they were meeting and gaining steam. Harry scheduled a meeting with all of the leadership and his group of followers. Many of these people donated large amounts to the church.

Harry explained they were prepared to leave and go to a different church if something didn't change. Pastor Brock said he hated to see them go because they valued all these members of the church.

He asked, "What would help you feel more comfortable here?'

Harry, not holding back, bluntly said, "Get rid of those worship leaders. They are more interested in promoting themselves on YouTube. I don't think they really care about this church."

Shocked, Pastor Brock responded, "I can't just fire them because you don't like them. They are making a huge difference in this congregation and in the community."

"Fine," Harry said, "You will not be seeing any of us around here anymore."

Pastor Brock said, "Are you open to discussing options?"

"Like what?' Harry asked.

"What if we added a traditional service with the old format?" Pastor Brock suggested.

Harry rubbed his chin and said, "I'll think about it," before leaving the meeting.

Since the meeting wasn't going anywhere, Pastor Brock adjourned it and assured Harry that leadership would look into it.

The following week, the church bookkeeper noticed a sharp decline in offerings. Some of the automatic drafts for contributions were canceled. She brought the subject up with Pastor Brock and explained that if this continued, the church would have difficulty paying salaries, bills, and maintenance costs.

Pastor Brock panicked and called a meeting with George and Sandy, who were unaware of what was going on. The conversation went something like this.

"George and Sandy," Brock began, "you have made a monumental impact on this church, and I believe your worship has drawn many families here who are seeking a rich relationship with God. I know you have influenced people outside of the church with your YouTube channel as well. Unfortunately, some people are offended by the format of worship, so we need to figure out something to do fast. I thought it would be good to give you and your family a month-long sabbatical until things calm down a bit."

George and Sandy looked at each other in astonishment. George was at a loss for words but was thinking, *It's bad enough that my kids have been bullied in school because we did what God was calling us to do. This man convinced us to give up everything to move here. And now this?!*

Sandy started to cry and said, "I don't understand why you are taking sides against us."

Pastor Brock said, "I know it's hard to understand, and believe me, I'm not trying to shove you out. You will still be paid and I can arrange for some time off with your kids at a friend's ranch not too far from here."

George felt rage well up inside of him and his face got red, but he didn't say anything to Pastor Brock. "C'mon, Sandy, let's go," he said as he stormed from the room.

George and Sandy went away for the weekend and left their kids with friends.

During the time away, though George and Sandy planned to relax, George couldn't help but stew and vent about the situation.

Lots of thoughts raced through his head like, *We don't deserve this. We have given up everything for this church. Our kids have suffered; we left a home we loved. Haven't we made a difference in the Kingdom!? Pastor Brock should have stood up for this. He is forcing me to look for another position! This could not end well for our side. Besides, this is a betrayal that we do not deserve.*

In the weeks that followed, George and Sandy quietly went "undercover" searching for a new position. George found himself often thinking, *I'll show them. I will not let anyone betray us without restitution. I have to protect and take care of my family! We are doing God's work."*

Questions

1. George decides to take care of his family by trying to find another job. Do you think he is acting like an *Overcomer*? Why or why not?
2. How might George's reaction impact his life and the lives of his family going forward?
3. How might you have handled the situation differently?

OVERCOMERS FORGIVE

Key Lesson: *Forgiveness frees you from bitterness, resentment, and grudges.*

SIGNIFICANCE OF FORGIVENESS

The Best Advice

Based on personal experience and working with others, the best advice or counsel to give for most relational problems starts with opening and walking through the gate of forgiveness. Forgiveness heals most relationship problems, but it is unnatural to consider it, especially after someone has hurt you. The pain of what they did typically removes any thinking about forgiveness—the actual cure for you.

Forgiveness is so powerful but underused. You can take advantage of the power if you know the answers to two questions:

1. What is a good working definition of forgiveness?
2. How do you know if you have forgiven someone?

The answers allow forgiveness to become part of your life. The more you know about forgiveness, the more you can use it.

Consider what this Chinese proverb tells you:

> *The men of old . . . first set up good government in their own states; wanting good government in their states, they first established order in their own families; wanting order in the home, they first disciplined themselves; desiring self-discipline, they rectified their own hearts; and wanting to rectify their hearts, they sought precise verbal definitions of their inarticulate thoughts—Chinese Proverb*

For life, clear definitions and clear thinking are imperative. That is true when relationships have problems or someone has hurt you. Your lousy thinking will crowd out what God says is correct and can lead you to wrong actions, worsening the situation.

Two words that people inadequately define are *love* and *forgiveness*. You already have the definition of love.

**Pursuing their best patiently, kindly,
sacrificially, and unconditionally**

And if you love, you will forgive—that definition is coming soon.

Bad Strategies

If forgiveness is the cure, *guilt* is the problem. And guess what—
we are all guilty! That is why Jesus died for us! You have been treated
poorly; I have been mistreated—we all have been wronged. But worse,
we are guilty because we have hurt and sinned against others.

When guilt is present, several unhealthy strategies become active.
For instance, when you are guilty, instead of confessing your guilt to the
Lord and others, you:

- Rationalize— "It really wasn't wrong! They deserved it!"
- Deny— "What's wrong with that? I didn't do anything wrong!"
- Scapegoat (blame) — "I wouldn't have done it if they . . ."
- Self-Punish (shame) — "I'll never be able to get over this. Why
  did I do something like that? How could I have been so dumb?"
- Medicate (alcohol, drugs) — "I don't want to think about it; I
  just want to feel better now."
- Do Penance (good deeds) — "I'll make it up to them by . . ."
- Self-forgive— "I know that others, even God, have forgiven me,
  but I can't forgive myself!"

Every strategy is flawed and will not provide healing.

Self-forgiveness has become the go-to statement for guilt. Suppose
you say, "I know that others and God have forgiven me, but I can't
forgive myself." What does that say about your view of others and God's
forgiveness? Where does that put you, above or below others and God?

See the problem? Others and God have forgiven you, but your
opinion is their forgiveness was somehow ineffective. They and God do
not see the offense as an issue, but you still do. **You decide to hang on
to it because you somehow have become the ultimate decision-maker
when forgiveness is ineffective.**

You have placed yourself above other people and God! You are calling
God a liar when He tells you that you are forgiven in 1 John 1:9 (NKJV):

> *If we confess our sins, He is faithful and just to forgive
> our sins and cleanse us from all unrighteousness.*

When you say you cannot forgive yourself, it implies you are thinking,
"I know that God created the Universe, but He really can't deal with what I
have done." Some people say that is not what they think, "I just feel so bad

that I did it that I just can't get it out of my mind." No matter how you word it, it still comes back to putting yourself in a higher position than God.

The answer for the flawed self-forgiveness strategy will not come from forgiveness—it comes from CONFESSION. The self-forgiveness strategy does not understand *real guilt* and *false guilt.* Go back and review confession.

On the other hand, when others are guilty, you . . .

- Seek revenge—plot, try to, or get even.
- Carry baggage—drag the problem into other relationships.
- Draft others—enlist others to join you against the person.
- Become a victim—"Poor me," everyone needs to rescue me.
- Hold grudges—become bitter and resent the person.

Those strategies lead to a highly unpleasant life. You can understand the essence of resentment, bitterness, and grudges in this statement—"Bitterness is like drinking a bottle of poison and hoping the other person dies!" So true! All those strategies link you to the person and the wrong done to you.

This heartbreaking story shows the far-reaching and destructive nature of bitterness.

> *Ruth has been trying to forgive her mother for years. God knows it is hard to do. She knew early on that her mother never wanted her. She cannot remember ever being held in her mother's arms; as far as she knows, she was never cuddled, never tucked in bed, never kissed. What she does remember is being handed a lot of expensive toys at a stiff arm's length.*

> *When she was eight, her parents' marriage fell apart; her mother wanted a divorce. But there was Ruth, what would become of little Ruth? So for the sake of a child she did not want, she hung on with a man she did not love. But she only resented Ruth more for burdening her twice—first with herself and then with her father.*

> *Ruth, in turn, hates her mother, who locked her out of family love as if she were an enemy alien. She has hated her mother so terribly long. All these years—the hound of her hate always growling in the bottom of her heart! She wishes her mother would die and let her forget, but she knows that her hate will outlive her mother.*

> *Ruth's hate for her mother doesn't stop there—it has a hook in it that catches Ruth herself. In her heart of hearts,*

*she feels as if her mother was right about her from the
start, that she probably was never worth loving . . .*

*How can Ruth break through the matted tangle of
hate that both binds her to and alienates her from
her mother?—Lewis Smedes, Forgive & Forget*

What is your story? Everyone has a "Pity City" or "So Sad" story. You have an account of being wronged. It may be exaggerated or minimized, but it is part of your life.

None of the above strategies work long-term, but one will work—**forgiveness**. It is the *only* cure for wrongs done to you.

*If we could only choose to forget the cruelest moments, we could,
as time goes on, free ourselves from their pain. But the wrong
sticks like a nettle in our memory. The only way to remove
the nettle is with a surgical procedure called forgiveness. It
is not as though forgiving were the remedy of choice among
other options less effective but still useful. It is the only remedy.
The remedy has existed since the first wrong done one human
being by another. Yet, people still punish themselves with the
pains of a past long gone. Or punish others in a futile passion
to get revenge . . . Couples break their marriages and divide
their families into weeping pieces. All because they will not
make use of the means given to us for recovering from . . .
insults and injuries.—Lewis Smedes, The Art of Forgiving*

You face severe consequences if you do not use the forgiveness strategy. Do you want consequences or freedom?

BENEFITS OF FORGIVENESS

Forgiveness Pleases God

*Ephesians 4:32 (NKJV)—And be kind to one
another, tenderhearted, forgiving one another,
just as God in Christ also forgave you.*

Does the verse give any options not to forgive? Do you forgive if the other person has met some specific criteria? No! There are no criteria, only an example to follow—God. Forgiving others is like thanking God for forgiving you! You did not deserve it, yet He asked Christ to pay the penalty for your sin, and Christ agreed.

You feel so "right" not to offer forgiveness to others because of your flashing ME. When you operate in opinion, not truth, you cannot see the boundless mercy God has shown you. Forgiving is obeying God, which pleases Him.

Forgiveness Imitates God

Forgiveness is indeed a Divine action. It is one of those situations where you can be like God. Without the example and grace of God, how many would ever choose to forgive others? Looking at my life, I am unsure how much forgiveness would be there without trusting God's justice, mercy, and omniscience.

Forgiveness not only thanks God but also confirms that you want to act like God, unlike your sin nature. It says you trust what He says, what He has done, and you want to imitate His incredible example.

Forgiveness Escapes Serious Consequences

The above reasons are enough, but you may not consider them important. Why? Because it is natural to ask, "Okay, but what's in it for ME?" (The flashing ME is everywhere.) Ironically, whether self-control or self-absorption is our goal, forgiveness is the **best** option either way! You may be doing it for self-control—God asked me to follow His example so I can be a Godly example. Or you may be doing it for self-absorption—I want out of the pain, to move on; I am tired of this weighing me down. Either way, the benefit is huge because you escape the trap of an unforgiving, bitter heart.

Like all sin, unforgiveness has consequences. If you think clearly, you will want to avoid them. There are probably more, but here are six consequences you can escape.

Loss of a Walk with God

> *1 John 4:20-21 (NKJV)—If someone says, 'I love God,' and hates his brother, he is a liar; for he who does not love his brother whom he has seen, how can he love God whom he has not seen? And this commandment we have from Him: that he who loves God must love his brother also.*

Despite not forgiving, you still have the gift of eternal life. You are still God's loved child. Praise God for that, but your unforgiving spirit separates you from fellowshipping with God, separates you from enjoying the benefits of dependence, and separates you from growing more of the Fruit of the Spirit in your life.

Loss of Health and Vitality

Scholars believe David wrote Psalm 32 after he sinned with Bathsheba and had Uriah killed. While this scripture is about confession, it still provides the precise impact of losing health without forgiveness. Listen to David contrast the joy of forgiveness with the physical suffering of unforgiven sin.

> Psalm 32:1-5 (NKJV)—Blessed is he whose transgression is forgiven, whose sin is covered. Blessed is the man to whom the Lord does not impute iniquity, and in whose spirit there is no deceit. When I kept silent, my bones grew old through my groaning all the day long.
>
> For day and night Your hand was heavy upon me; my vitality was turned into the drought of summer. Selah.
>
> I acknowledged my sin to You, and my iniquity I have not hidden. I said, "I will confess my transgressions to the Lord," And You forgave the iniquity of my sin. Selah

God provides healing and blessing through forgiveness, both for those confessing (seeking forgiveness) and those forgiving. However, when David lacked forgiveness in his life, he suffered physically. How about you? Are your physical struggles spiritual, not medical? That does not mean specific sins in your life cause sicknesses or physical ailments, which forgiveness will cure! But if you continually refuse to forgive, do not expect to be as healthy and happy as before.

Loss of Joy

> It is a simple but sometimes forgotten truth that the greatest enemy to present joy and high hopes is the cultivation of retrospective bitterness.—Robert G. Menzies

The only alternative to forgiveness is vengeance and bitterness. There is no middle ground, no matter how you try to avoid the issue, so ask yourself—do I want to forgive or be bitter and vengeful?

> Proverbs 15:17 (NKJV)—Better is a dinner of herbs where love is, than a stalled ox and hatred therewith.
>
> Hebrews 12:15 (NKJV)— . . . looking carefully lest anyone fall short of the grace of God; lest any root of bitterness springing up cause trouble, and by this many become defiled.

Bitterness and vengeance fuel the wars between Jews, Arabs, Sunni, and Shia in the Middle East. It is the same for you and your enemies. It is probably at the heart of your marriage or family struggle. Bitterness and vengeance always hurt and destroy you as well as others. Forgiveness, though, heals.

Loss of Freedom

Consumed *with the offender*—Isn't it a pleasant experience to be around bitter people? What fun talking about the situation and their emotions, right?

How can you be free when you spend so much time thinking about how they hurt you? Your mind is stuck on resolving something that only God can handle effectively. Spending that much time thinking about them is like building a lovely house for them in your mind and moving them in. You keep it painted and maintained and constantly visit them.

Bitterness and vengeance are a trap. Bitterness blinds you and moves you to a place you never wanted to be. You think it will make you *better*, but it just makes you *bitter*. It is an open wound, draining life from you.

Controlled *by the offender*—Not only are you consumed by them, but worse, they control you. The longer you carry the grudge, the more they control your thoughts, actions, and feelings. The more you desire vengeance, the more energy you lose by plotting, seeking, or getting revenge. And even if you do get revenge, you will often have regrets, second-guesses, or feel it was insufficient.

Conformed *to be like the offender*—Your loss of freedom is complete when your actions reveal you are becoming like them. Consider this. If you want to learn golf or tennis, you spend time playing and thinking about it. If you are going to learn something new, you read and think about it. When you immerse yourself in something, it can become part of you.

The more energy used and time spent thinking about the person who wronged you, the greater the chance they will influence your thoughts and actions. You increase the chances of becoming like them. You are already a slave, and now you are becoming like them. The Lord has a better path for you. He wants you to renew your mind, controlled by His thinking, by truth.

That is why Romans 12:1-2 (NKJV) says,

> *And do not be conformed to this world but be*
> *transformed by the renewing of your mind.*

Remember, your thinking drives your actions and emotions. Bitterness blossoms from lousy thinking, and the harvest is slavery, but forgiveness and freedom flow from a renewed mind.

Loss of Hope

Depression is often born from an unhealthy focus on past events. It was so unfair, and there is no hope for justice. Hope, like joy, does not grow from vengeance, bitterness, or holding grudges. Hope takes root in the soil of forgiveness.

It is exhausting. It takes the life out of you because you focus on trying to control something you cannot, and that even feels hopeless just reading it!

Can you right a wrong that has occurred in the past? Of course not! It happened; it is a fact, part of history, and you cannot change it. But you can accept that it happened, learn from it, forgive, and move on. Why? Because your PERFECT Father God knew about it and will turn it into "best" for you as you trust Him.

That puts hope and a new future into your life, resulting from forgiveness.

Loss of Future Generations' Health

Research shows parents pass unresolved issues to their children. The feuds and hatreds of people and families who cling to bitterness are evidence of the tenacity of sin and its transmission from father to son. Attitudes, words, and actions pass to your children. Even if they learn from your mistakes and do not repeat them, they will still suffer from your mistakes unless they accept the perfection of God.

God clearly states this in Exodus 20:5 (NKJV):

> For I, the Lord your God, am a jealous God, visiting
> the iniquity of the fathers upon the children to the third
> and fourth generations of those who hate Me . . .

However, as God does, He provides a solution. Pay attention to what He says; there is hope, joy, and blessing.

> Exodus 20:6 (NKJV)— . . . but showing mercy to thousands,
> to those who love Me and keep My commandments.

The past is over. Move on! Trust God to redeem your past! He knows what is best. He will use your situation for your best and their best. Doing it any other way will create more problems.

Your Choice

Be controlled by the past or by God. Be controlled by the sins done to you, or forgive and trust that the Lord will take care of it. It is a clear choice. God wants you to live in freedom, not bondage! Forgiveness releases you from the bondage of bitterness and vengeance.

God seems to say, "Forgiveness is the best way to deal with your memory of wrongful pain. It will free you and help others. It is your choice to trust My way or yours. By the way, the alternative to forgiving—bitterness and vengeance—only makes the pain last longer. It will affect you emotionally, mentally, physically, and will even affect future generations. Please, don't choose that."

Forgiveness puts a new future before you and gives you a new way to see those who hurt you. It may be the one act that allows you to imitate God, the original Master Forgiver.

A Process for Forgiving

Forgiveness is like treating a wound.

It is best to forgive, but we have a wrong view of forgiveness and do not experience the benefits. What would you tell someone who asked the following?

> *"Am I supposed to swallow hard; let the murderers of my mother, father, husband, and kids off the hook? Am I to pretend the whole thing never happened? If forgiving is about that, I would rather buy a gun, track them down, and torture them individually."*

> *"Do I just go on with life and ignore that my best friend had an affair with my husband and destroyed my marriage?"*

> *"Do I just wave a magic wand, forget that my partner embezzled money from me, accept him as he is, and BE HAPPY with my dire financial situation?"*

NO—that is not forgiveness! It is not about letting someone "off the hook" or pretending something did not happen! So what is it?

Any wrong done to you is like a physical wound to your body. It may be a bruise or, worse yet, a deep cut. If untreated, you will lose blood, risk infection, and even die if the wound is deep. The basic medical steps you can follow for a wound are:

1. *Stop the bleeding*: Apply gentle pressure with a clean cloth or bandage. If bleeding persists, seek emergency assistance.

2. *Clean the wound*: Rinse the wound well with clear water. Thorough wound cleaning reduces the risk of tetanus. Use soap and a washcloth to clean the area around the wound.

3. *Apply an antibiotic*: After you clean the wound, apply a thin layer of an antibiotic cream or ointment to discourage infection and help your body close the wound.

4. *Cover the wound*: Bandages can help keep the wound clean and remove harmful bacteria.

5. *Change the dressing regularly*: Do so at least daily or whenever it becomes wet or dirty.

6. *Watch for signs of infection*: See your doctor if the wound does not heal or if you see any redness, drainage, or swelling.

7. Enjoy healing!

Just like a physical wound, the wrong done to you needs treatment to heal. When you follow a clear process, forgiveness can be more easily understood. It can help you understand the HOW of forgiveness by looking at the medical and spiritual steps side-by-side.

Preparation

Step 1—Face Their Humanity (Stop the Bleeding)

Estimates say that 80 percent of what you see lies behind your eyes. If that is true, when you look at the offender, you mostly see the wrong and the pain they created for you, not the person. You see "that animal," "that jerk," "that piece of trash," but NOT the person.

If you want to be free of the pain, you can stop the bleeding by taking this first step. Choose to see the person, not just what they did. Rediscover their humanity. Choose to see them differently!

Suppose you saw someone wearing tennis clothes at a formal black-tie event. Tennis clothes would stand out to everyone because they are out of context with the event. What might you think about that person? "How stupid! What a dunce! Do they have any brains!" It would be easy to look at the clothes, not the person wearing them. Your words come from thoughts about the clothes.

Before this first step of forgiveness, we focus on the offense, behavior, or "clothes" instead of the person. In this step, you can get new eyes from God to see the person, not the offense or the wrong done to you.

This step does not release them from accountability for their sin. Right now, you do not have to believe that they will once again be a close friend or a trustworthy spouse or will not do the same harm to you again. But you can choose to believe they are a person and take them back into your imperfect world. That "scoundrel," your enemy, is a faulty, bruised, and flawed human, just like you are. They are still blamable and accountable for the wrong done. There but for the grace of God go you and me!

A great example:

> Yehiel Dinur was a witness during Adolf Eichmann's trial. Dinur entered the courtroom and stared at the man behind the bulletproof glass—the man who had presided over the slaughter of millions. The court was hushed as a victim confronted a butcher.

> Then suddenly, Dinur began to sob and collapsed to the floor. As he explained later in an interview, what struck him instantly was a terrifying realization: "I saw that I am capable to do this . . . Exactly like he."

> The reporter interviewing Dinur (asked), "How was it possible for a man to act as Eichmann acted? Was he a monster? A madman? Or was he perhaps something even more terrifying? Was he normal?" Yehiel Dinur, in a moment of chilling clarity (concluded), "Eichmann is in all of us."

That describes this first step—see them as a person, faulty just like you are. When you see the humanity of the person who wronged you, the bleeding is under control.

Another example:

> A woman had sinned against her husband. The counselor was working through their past sins done to one another. The woman

admitted what she had done, but the man did not believe she was telling the truth. He continued to see her based on what she had done until an extraordinary event occurred. The woman, in great pain and tears, held her hands palms up to the Lord and said, "I know that I am clean! I have confessed it all, Lord." Only then did the man stop seeing only the sins she committed and once again saw her as a PERSON just like himself.

Step 2: Overlook Revenge (Clean the Wound)

Overlook your assumed right to revenge or to "get even." Notice I said, "assumed." You may think you have the right to revenge, but you do not. Vengeance is God's right alone.

> *Romans 12:17-19 (NKJV)—Repay no one evil for evil. Have regard for good things in the sight of all men. If it is possible, as much as depends on you, live peaceably with all men. Beloved, do not avenge yourselves, but rather give place to wrath; for it is written, "Vengeance is Mine, I will repay," says the Lord.*

Yet revenge is cherished, savoring it like a delicious poison, though it kills us.

> *After we have been wronged—wounded in the bargain—been swindled, cheated, abused, or demeaned, no human right seems more sacred that the right to get even with the scab who wronged us. We want to get him back, make him feel— at the very least—as much pain as he made us feel. Nothing could be fairer. Or taste so sweet.—Lewis B. Smedes*

> *Revenge tastes so sweet, we swirl it around on our tongues and let it drip like honey down our chins.—Homer*

> *If you prick us will we not bleed, if you tickle us, will we not laugh, if you poison us, will we not die, if you wrong us, shall we not revenge?—Shakespeare, from The Merchant of Venice*

Forgiveness accepts God's justice and not your idea of justice. You try to "be God" when you assume the role of avenger! You say you want justice, but such a thing is impossible from your hand. And if you are honest with yourself, you know you want to do just a bit more to them than they did to you. When you try to "get even," you multiply your sin toward the other person and God by demanding He gets off His throne and let you sit in His place.

Vengeance grows in the soil of pride. It is a "right" you never had, a lie that Satan wants you to believe.

But forgiveness gives up the sinful desire for vengeance. Forgiveness provides healing, a brighter future, and hope.

Hand vengeance over to God. Hold the assumed right to revenge in your two hands, take one last longing look at it, and let it spill to the ground like a handful of water. Vengeance is of the sin nature; forgiveness is of God.

> *Colossians 3:13 (NKJV)— . . . bearing with one another, and forgiving one another, if anyone has a complaint against another; even as Christ forgave you, so you also must do.*

This step is crucial because you are drawing a line in the sand, handing vengeance to God, and moving forward. You are letting God clean the wound.

Step 3: Renew Your Mind (Apply Antibiotic)

Before you entered the first step of forgiveness, your feelings toward the offender may have been hate, bitterness, and anger. You wanted terrible things to happen to the evil person who did bad things to you. That is what hate is about. Since your feelings are primarily responders, your thinking and actions need to change to revise your feelings. Remember the order: first think, then act or feel.

Choose to believe the truth.

> *Romans 8:28 (NKJV)—And we know that all things work together for good to those who love God, to those who are the called according to His purpose.*

We have trivialized and misused this verse; however, it is still accurate and applicable. God fully understands your situation and was not caught off guard. God controls vengeance and the whole situation.

Choose to see the offender as an instrument of God. Remember that God is using that person to develop and shape you to be more like Jesus Christ. That may be hard to accept, but you are not trusting God if you do not. Further, you miss out on blessings that can only come from trusting God through forgiveness.

Joseph is a good example we can follow. Remember the mistreatment Joseph suffered because of his brothers? Yet his response was completely unexpected when he was in an ideal position to take full vengeance on them.

Genesis 50:19-21 (NKJV)—Joseph said to them, "Do not be afraid, for am I in the place of God? But as for you, you meant evil against me; but God meant it for good, in order to bring it about as it is this day, to save many people alive. Now therefore, do not be afraid; I will provide for you and your little ones." And he comforted them and spoke kindly to them.

When you meditate on truth, you may feel a natural (perhaps reluctant) wish that some good things might come the "weasel's" way. Feeling good about them may initially be hesitant, but it comes as you meditate on truth and God changes your thinking. You may backslide along the way, but persevering with the truth creates the framework for your feelings to respond. Apply the Antibiotic of Truth, and healing begins.

When you forgive someone, you decide never to use that offense against them or pay attention to it again. Unhand the "weapon" that you could use on them. Please give it up; stop holding onto the offense.

It is critical to renew your mind about what forgiveness is. Here is our definition of forgiveness:

A choice to lay the offense down, not mark or pay attention to where you laid it, and never use it against them, not in your thoughts, speech, or action.

Or the short version:

> **Never abusing them with the wrong they did to you – not in thought, word or action**

Application

Step 4: Give it Up (Cover the Wound)

This step is where you make the decision.
- You decide, conclude, commit to—stop holding onto the offense.
- You decide, conclude, commit to—never use the offense against them, to never pay attention to it.
- You decide, conclude, commit to—unhand the "weapon" you could use against them.
- You decide, conclude, commit to—move forward rather than remain stuck in the past.
- You decide, conclude, commit to—bless them and free yourself.
- You decide, conclude, commit to—**FORGIVE**.

Bitterness keeps you stuck in the past, but forgiveness moves you forward into the future. Some people believe that you need to forgive and forget. Forgetting is not part of, or required, for forgiveness, though it can help.

Some people think God forgives and forgets, referencing Jeremiah 31:34 (NKJV).

> For I will forgive their iniquity, and their
> sin I will remember no more.

The word "remember" is critical in this verse. According to Strong's dictionary, "remember" means "to mark (so as to be recognized), or it implies to mention."

> When God is challenged to "remember," the meaning
> is better taken as "pay attention to" since nothing
> ever escapes God's omniscience (Psalms 89:47).—The
> Theological Wordbook of the Old Testament

God does not forget as we do. He does not pay attention to—does not mark our sins against us because He sees us through the blood of Jesus. He accepts us because of Jesus' death, burial, and resurrection—our sins are no longer a barrier between God and us. Thank God for that! We know that when God forgives, He will never use our sins against us again.

For example, suppose you are reading a book and want to "remember" a statement. You could memorize it, but more likely, you use a highlighter pen, underline it, place a sticky note, fold the page, etc., to mark the place to draw your attention to it later.

God the Father will not do that. He has chosen not to "pay attention to" what the Son has covered. God has moved into a different relationship with us.

Just let it go. God knows what is best for you and this situation. Stop "marking it against them." Why keep holding on to the hurt?

> A rattlesnake, if cornered, will become so angry it will
> bite itself. That is exactly what the harboring of hate and
> resentment against others is—a biting of oneself. We think
> we are harming others in holding these spites and hates,
> but the deeper harm is to ourselves.—E. Stanley Jones

It is time to—Give It Up—so you can cover the wound and give it a chance to heal.

Step 5: Apply Your Decision (Change the Dressing Regularly)

Consider the scars on your body. They are memorials to healing! My body has significant scars from a bad accident and two back operations. Those situations were extremely painful at the time but are not painful now because they healed!

I could look at those scars, remember the pain, and put myself back into the pain and difficulty of each situation. But why do that? Those situations are over, and the scars are proof of the healing.

That is why we believe in FORGIVE and REMEMBER. Once you experience the power of forgiveness, you will have multiple healed scars rather than open wounds.

Forgive and Remember helps old wounds as well as new ones. When you remember or reflect on any old "wound," you can remember it is now a scar—healed—and there is no need to reopen it. You can remember the scars and healing from the old wounds when you have a new wound. That will help you consider forgiving again, maybe even now.

Unfortunately, without forgiveness, you leave the wounds open, and they turn into bloody messes. Not what God wants for you!

Once you forgive, create a way to remember it because it is easy to forget in a tense situation. You decide to forgive in Step 4. You concluded and committed to new thinking—no longer revenge—instead, you are letting it go. Now, memorialize your forgiveness with an action and a date. This step is similar to the reason for baptism. Baptism does not save you; it is a testimony, a memorial to the most critical decision you will ever make—trusting God for your eternity.

Here is an application tool when you choose to forgive.

> On a small card or piece of paper, write down the name of the person you want to forgive and what you are forgiving. Take the card and go to a quiet place. Kneel and place the card in your hands, palms up. Hold the card up to heaven. Pray to the Lord what you have written on the card in your own words and tell Him you are forgiving them and want Him to take this event from you. Pray whatever else you desire about the event, and when you finish, write the date and time on the card. Put the card in a safe place to remind you that you have forgiven the person, or throw the card away if there is a chance the person might see it. But remember the date somehow.

Now you have a date, a memorial to remember you forgave them.

Verification

Step 6: Verify Your Decision (Look for signs of infection)

Satan and your sin nature are not happy with forgiveness. There will be many opportunities to move backward toward vengeance and bitterness—the next time you get into an argument, the next time you feel slighted, or the next time you see, hear, smell, taste, or touch something that reminds you of what happened. Anytime you start "Flashing your ME" with them, you may return to bitterness. Most likely, immediately after forgiving, the event will cross your mind. Satan, through your sin nature, wants you to "pay attention to" it, to go back to how life was before Step 1.

How can you deal with the thoughts about what they did to you? You say you forgave, but the thoughts keep coming up. The answer depends on one critical question. Before asking the question, consider these options:

1. You did not forgive when you said you did.
2. You did forgive and need to forgive again.
3. You did forgive, and you need to validate your forgiveness.

All three options need this critical question:

Did I forgive them when I said I did?

The only answers are YES or NO. MAYBE does not help. Did you forgive them when you said you did?

If your answer is NO, that's option one above. Ask the Lord to help you understand forgiveness and prepare you to forgive. Go back to Step 1. You either want to be free or stay in bondage—which is it? You either want to seek revenge or give it to God—which is it? You either want this wound healed or not—which is it? It is your choice.

Your answer could be YES; you know you forgave, remember the date, and used the application tool. But you let your lousy thinking control you, resulting in using the offense against them. You may have wanted revenge in your thoughts or had a moment of anger and spewed hurtful words at them about how bad they are for doing "that" to you. That would be option two above. You are "paying attention to" or have "marked" the location of the "weapon" and have started using it again. The solution is to go back to step 1 and forgive again. It would also help to confess to the Lord and the other person that you have sinned against them for letting bitterness and revenge control you.

Or your answer is YES, but you continue thinking about what happened. Your thoughts are not toward revenge or bitterness; it is just that you remember it and the pain of going through that event. You do NOT need to go back to Step 1. Do these two simple things:

1. Give your thoughts to Jesus. Claim 2 Corinthians 10:4-5. The end of verse 5 says, "bringing every thought into captivity to the obedience of Christ." Ask Jesus to take the thoughts: "Lord, I know that I forgave and did not lie, and You know that. Please take those thoughts from me."

2. MOVE QUICKLY TO STEP 7.

As you give those thoughts to Jesus, you will struggle with them less, and the wound will heal.

Step 7 Enjoy Freedom & Healing

If you have forgiven, this step speeds the healing.

Louie had a severe break in her left arm at the elbow that required a metal plate and screws to give her use of the arm again. Not long after the surgery, the doctor prescribed working with a physical therapist to rebuild the muscles and maximize the flexibility of her elbow. That therapy was painful, but maximizing her arm's healing and use was necessary.

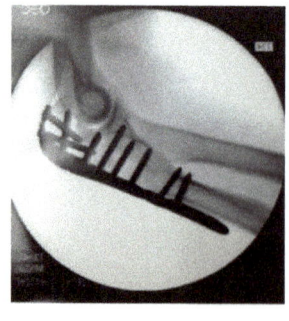

Step 7 may not be easy for you at first, but it is imperative if you want freedom and healing. Here is what this step requires:

- Praying for God's blessing upon them.
- Encouraging them as you can.
- Pursuing their best by finding ways to serve them.

When you come through step 6 and verify that you have forgiven, this step will help you continue to move forward. Without this last step, it will be easy to let the memory of the pain of what they did to you pull you back toward revenge and bitterness. This step has immense power.

You may be thinking, "Really! You just asked me to let the offense go, and now you are asking me to pray that God blesses them!"

Yes, I am because it is what Christ did. This step follows the marvelous example of Jesus Christ.

We participated in the crucifixion of Jesus. He was beaten, tortured, and hung on the cross. As Jesus was on the cross, He asked His Father to forgive us and the people of Jerusalem. He then died, rose again, and appeared to many people. Then He did something we want to imitate.

> *Acts 1:4, 8 (NKJV)—And being assembled together with them,*
> *He commanded them not to depart from Jerusalem, but to wait*
> *for the Promise of the Father, "which," He said, "you have heard*
> *from Me . . . But you shall receive power when the Holy Spirit has*
> *come upon you; and you shall be witnesses to Me in Jerusalem,*
> *and in all Judea and Samaria, and to the end of the earth.*

Jesus sent the Holy Spirit to the disciples to bless Jerusalem, the people who did Him wrong! Blessing people who have harmed you is impossible without forgiveness. Until you forgive those who have wronged you, you will not pray God's blessing upon them, encourage them, or pursue their best. And until you do that, you will not experience the freedom and healing God wants for you.

Ensure healing—pray for them, bless them, and find ways to pursue their best. Enjoy the FREEDOM.

Forgiveness Is Not

Forgiveness Is Not Pardoning.

Forgiveness does not remove natural or legal consequences. It certainly can lessen consequences in many situations, but it does not deal with the justice required by law. Usually, justice is outside our control, so God tells us, "Do not seek revenge (justice); I'll take care of it."

Forgiveness never removes the offense; it means you no longer pay attention to it or mark it against them. Knowing this frees you and potentially the offender from slavery to the pain of the offense.

In another sense, forgiving is pardoning in the broad sense of the word. You no longer require justice and leave it up to God. You "pardon" them so YOU can be free.

Forgiveness Is Not Forgetting

If you can forget a wrong, then forgiveness is not necessary. Forgiveness is only needed because you remember. Forgiveness heals, healing leaves scars, and scars are GOOD!

I have some large scars on my body. When I see the scars, I could think about the pain I went through, the accident, the surgery, and the recovery. I could start picking at the scar and making it a bloody mess. But that makes no sense. It is healed!

Forgiveness does not forget; instead, it remembers that the incident is healing or healed. You only have scars from healed wounds. If there is no scar, there is no, or limited, healing, implying no forgiveness. The scar or incident is to help you forgive again in the future. Praise the Lord; He walks with us through our healing to prepare us for the next time we need to forgive.

Forgiveness Is Not Restoration or Reunion

The focus of forgiveness is the inside of the person. God is for restoration and reconciliation, which may occur but is not part of or required by forgiveness.

Forgiveness	Reunion
· It takes one person to forgive	· It takes two to be reunited
· Forgiving happens inside the wounded person	· Reunion happens in a relationship between people
· We can forgive a person who never says he is sorry	· We cannot be reunited unless he honestly repents and confesses
· We can forgive even if we do not trust the person who wronged us	· Reunion occurs and deepens as we trust the person who wronged us
· Forgiving has no strings attached	· Reunion has strings attached

Restoration is needed in marriages and families to produce healthier future generations, so always pray for the restoration of broken families and marriages. But sometimes a reunion is impossible or not the best. The other person may have moved away, married again, or even died. Sometimes reunion is even harmful; for example, a husband may still be addicted to abusing women. A business partner may still be a crook—a forgiven crook, but still a crook.

Reunion may be such a threat that it keeps us from forgiving. For example, forgiveness is unlikely if an abused woman believes it requires her to return to her abusive husband. Forgiveness is doubtful if a teenage girl thinks it is part of being reunited with a mean-spirited girlfriend. That is why it is essential to recognize the difference. Unforgiveness is terrible, especially if a lousy definition of forgiveness keeps you from forgiving and enjoying freedom.

Forgiveness Is Not Dependent on
the Offender's Repentance

Some say you do not forgive unless the person who wronged you has repented. They may use this passage for support:

> *Luke 17:3-4 (NKJV)—Take heed to yourselves. If your brother*
> *sins against you, rebuke him; and if he repents, forgive him. And*
> *if he sins against you seven times in a day, and seven times in a*
> *day returns to you, saying, "I repent," you shall forgive him.*

But what is Jesus' point? If you cannot forgive unless the other person repents, that presents a big problem because some people who wrong you will never repent. Think of the unforgiveness you would drag around every day if you had to wait for someone to repent before you could forgive. God does not remove your freedom by binding you to the actions of another person. The context of this passage is about the attitude of the forgiver, not the conditions of forgiveness. "If he repents" is not a condition but describes a situation in which someone comes to confess their wrong to you. The same is true when he sins and repents "seven times a day." If I told my child I loved them when they were disobedient, I did not mean only then, but even then! Jesus always wants you to have an attitude of forgiveness.

The "rebuke the offender" is also interesting. Does that mean that rebuking is part of forgiving? The word in Greek means "to rebuke, to reprove, to speak seriously to prevent an action or to bring one to an end." That has nothing to do with forgiveness. It is not a condition to forgiveness but is done in love, pursuing their best, after examining yourself to ensure you are not in sin. If you are sinning, God warns you to be careful about rebuking anyone (Galatians 6:1-2). If someone sins against you, speak seriously to them so that they may change their ways. You can forgive them without rebuking them or requiring their repentance.

> *If you are permitted to rebuke him, you are advised to do so.*
> *Smother not the resentment, but give it vent. Tell him his faults;*
> *show him wherein he has not done well nor fairly by you, and,*
> *it may be, you will perceive (and you must be very willing to*
> *perceive it) that you mistook him, that it was not a trespass*
> *against you, or not designed, but an oversight, and then you will*
> *beg his pardon for misunderstanding him—Matthew Henry*

Forgiveness Is Not Interested in My Rights

Dr. Carl Zimmerman's book, Family and Civilization, details the connection between focusing on self (selfishness) and the decline of a civilization or a society. As people became more focused on their rights, civilizations declined. The more your "flashing ME" is accepted behavior, the more pain you create for all relationships. Of course, I am for freedom and individual rights, but that is not the issue. My rights are not more important than pursuing the best for relationships, the family, and society.

And forgiving others is reduced as individual rights become the focus. For example, as a person moves toward separation and divorce, they say, "My freedom, happiness, and rights are more important than

- the pain I will create for my spouse
- the emotional health of and pain for my children
- the pain created for my extended family
- the scars and pain I create for future generations
- God's Word, which says my actions are not right

"My rights" or the "flashing ME" closes your eyes to forgiveness and THE solution for all relationships—pursue their best, no matter what—just like Christ does for you.

We have seen individuals and couples awaken to this blindness. We also have had couples leave, stating they are going for a divorce. Their eyes are closed, so all they see is how they have been wronged and their rights being violated. They wrongly think dissolving the marriage will make it better. But that is a lie from Satan, just like the lie he told Eve in the Garden of Eden.

Can You? Will You? When?

All this talk about forgiveness comes down to three simple questions—Can you? Will you? When?

Can you forgive? Some of you might say "no" to that question, but that answer is wrong. Why? Think about the definition of "can." That question only asks if you "have the ability" to forgive. Some of you may have answered the question thinking a decision was needed. No, this question is not asking for a decision, only establishing whether you will acknowledge that you "have the ability" to forgive.

Answering "no" is not reality. At some level, anyone who has any mental capacity has the ability to forgive. There is only one answer—Yes. We all have the ability to forgive!

Will you forgive? Why was the "Can you?" question so important? Because it sets up the "WILL you forgive?" question. Think about it. If I ask you, "Do you have the ability to forgive?" and you answer "Yes," you establish that you have the ability to do it, but will you? "Will you?" is a more difficult question because it asks for a decision or commitment to resolve or conclude for or against forgiveness. It is time to choose between "bleeding or healing."

When will you forgive? Finally, if you said yes, you will forgive, then WHEN will you do it? Sometime later next week? Tomorrow? When you feel like it? Please do it as soon as possible, for your good. Remember, the person whose unforgiveness hurts the most is you! Please do not let the sun set today without forgiving!

DISCUSSION QUESTIONS

1. Explain why "I can't forgive myself" is invalid.
2. How does not forgiving hurt your freedom?
3. What example or analogy is used to help you understand how forgiveness works?
4. Explain this statement—"80 percent of what you see lies behind your eyes, not in front of them."
5. What is probably the biggest problem with seeking revenge?
6. Memorize and explain the definition used for forgiveness.
7. How would you explain this statement ". . . and their sin I will remember no more" in Jeremiah 31:34?
8. What is the benefit of "creating a memorial" when you forgive someone?
9. What is the process you use to know that you have forgiven someone?
10. Why is step 7 a great way to know you have forgiven someone?
11. Explain why forgiveness is not pardoning.
12. Explain why forgive and remember is better than forgive and forget.
13. Explain why forgiveness is not reconciliation or restoration of a relationship.
14. Explain why forgiveness is not dependent on the other person's repentance.
15. How does the "Can you? Will you? When?" technique work? Make sure you can explain the difference between can and will.

CHAPTER 8

TRUTH AND JUSTICE

Hilary is 35 and a lawyer at a law firm in a large city. She joined the firm right out of law school, so she has worked in the firm for 10 years. She was raised in a Christian home and went out of her way in high school to defend biblical truth. Sometimes she wasn't very popular because she didn't just go along with the crowd. She stood up against abortion at some community rallies and promoted the importance of marriage between a man and a woman. In high school, she was on the debate team and learned to love "arguing a point" based on the facts.

She attended a state university to get her undergrad degree, then attended law school at a small school in her state. During law school, Hilary relaxed some of her conservative views because of things she was learning in her classes. She loves the rigor of a trial and is so focused on her career as a civil defense lawyer.

Hilary still goes to church, but only when her schedule allows. She has a boyfriend, Ted, who travels quite a bit, so they like to spend their weekends together, which sometimes gets in the way of church. Growing up, Ted's family went to church most of the time, but they didn't really talk about a relationship with God in his family.

After church one afternoon, Hilary and Ted get into a discussion about the sermon.

"Hilary, I know you have an opinion about what the pastor said today," Ted said with a smile.

She smiled back. "Of course I do. I'm a lawyer."

"What do you think about the fact that we should accept everyone in church, and that it's God's Will to accept people with different lifestyles?"

"I suppose you are talking about that he said it was wrong to judge someone with a different lifestyle or sexual orientation. I believe in Truth and Justice for everyone, no matter what. And of course, I think we have to accept everyone. I mean, look at who Jesus hung out with in the Bible. Tax collectors, who weren't very popular. Mary Magdalene didn't have such a pure background, and think of the Woman at the Well. After she found out who Jesus was and He told her everything she had done, she went and evangelized the whole town, and everybody got saved."

She continued, "From what I have read, people can't help their sexual orientation. They are born with it. You know, we are beautifully and wonderfully made in God's eyes. Who am I to judge? So based on all that, I think the Pastor is right. There's nothing wrong with someone with a gay lifestyle. That's just how God created them."

Ted nodded in agreement, "Yeah, that makes sense. You know justice means treating everyone fairly, so it would be unjust to tell someone how they ought to live and say it *in the name of Jesus*. I was wondering because two ladies at work feel like I do not treat them fairly because they are openly gay. I just avoid them so I won't get accused of anything. I mean, I don't understand being attracted to a same-sex person. I totally prefer women over men, but I don't want to get into a discussion with them because I'm afraid HR would pounce on me.

Like a good legal counsel, Hilary said, "Wise move, Ted. No one has time to deal with an over-zealous HR department.

Questions
1. Does Ted sound like an *Overcomer* to you? Why or why not?
2. Does Hilary's view of the sermon from the Pastor seem truthful and just to you? What makes you say that?
3. In pursuing the truth, what else do Ted and Hilary need to do?

Overcomers Pursue Truth

Key Lesson: *Truth and reality are your friends and will free you.*

Opinion Is Common

Fossil Footprints

Imagine you are back in elementary school. You and your classmates are on the playground while workmen remove dirt from a field next to the playground. As you watch, they uncover a patch of rock. The first glimpse of the stone appears to have something on it. The workers look more carefully at the rock. You intently watch as they remove the dirt. Finally, everyone sees the image to the right. As you look at the footprints, your teacher asks, "What do you think happened here?" What would your answer be?

If you are like me, even as a child, you want to understand or explain what happened. You might create a common sense or more imaginative answer, but you conclude what happened.

But here is the problem. You do not have enough information in the picture to know what happened. That means any answer comes from speculation, opinion, or guessing. Determining an answer would require studying the evidence and, most likely, needs assumptions to establish a "most likely scenario."

Think about this statement.

> **When you do not know or cannot find the facts, you tend to "fill in the blanks."**

That is an unfortunate yet consistent pattern—filling in the blanks about what happened rather than looking for the facts. It is also a consistent pattern you have with God, speculating about what He is doing and, worse, who He is.

The word "think" is used 72 times in the New King James Bible. It is often a synonym for opinion or speculation. For example:

*Job 35:2 (NKJV)—Do you think this is right? Do you
say, "My righteousness is more than God's?"*

*Matthew 10:34 (NKJV)—Do not think that I came to bring
peace on earth. I did not come to bring peace but a sword.*

God wants you to know your thoughts to protect you from error. Too often, errors result from depending on opinions, speculations, or guesses instead of facts.

Knowing the times you operate on opinion, not facts, is imperative. Consider a recent difficult conversation, especially one involving elevated negative emotions. How much speculation or opinion was present? What did you claim about them that you did not know as a clear fact? What did they claim about you that was not fact? Did the claims and speculation help or hurt?

My speculations did not help create a solution when I think of conversations like that. Speculations, opinions, and claims often lead to further accusations and actions based on assumptions. A chain of events may be initiated because of opinions, claims, and guesses rather than facts. The worst part is that further problems were created, or the problem was inflamed primarily because of speculating.

If you can learn to "hold the tension," you won't "fill in the blanks." You leave the blank empty until you gather more information. If you search for facts and speculate less, many relationships would benefit. What a benefit when you ask more questions, looking for truth and facts rather than operating on opinion and emotions. What a blessing if the truth was the goal instead of believing the assumptions.

And what a benefit it would be if you pursue the truth rather than speculate about their actions that you do not like. That is where freedom will help dramatically. You will get to see more about that later.

What Is Opinion?

Suppose you could take everything in your mind and download it to a computer. Every thought is on the screen in front of you. As you look at it, you decide to take each thought and put it into one of two categories—Truth or Lie. You start down the list and quickly realize that this is not easy. Assigning some items into one or the other category is difficult because you do not have enough information to determine where it fits.

The finite limits of human knowledge, especially what you know, require a third category—opinion, claim, or guess.

What if one thought you see on the screen is, "When they change, I'll be happy." Which category would you select? Truth or lie? You might place it in the Truth category based on some of your experiences. You might place it in the Lie category if you define "happy" and consider something other than a short time frame.

Unfortunately, most people put that statement in the Truth category. But it is not true. It is opinion masquerading as truth. If you were objective, you would analyze what happens when they change. You are seldom satisfied with that one change. You want more. At best, your happiness is fleeting.

Thoughts are either true or false. But our finite ability makes it difficult to know the difference. Thus, opinion is necessary.

The definition of opinion from Webster's Collegiate Dictionary is

Judgment or belief not founded on certainty or proof; the prevailing or popular feeling or view: public opinion; belief stronger than impression and less strong than positive knowledge. Synonyms—evaluation, estimation, conjecture, supposition, theory

The definition reveals vital information—"belief not founded on certainty or proof," "conjecture, supposition, and theory."

Consider this option to help relationships and clarify conversations. You are about to state something that you do not or cannot know as a fact. You stop yourself and say, "My speculation is . . . ." Better yet, what if you said, "I am only guessing here, so be careful with what I am offering. My guess is . . ."

Overcomers let others know when they are "filling in the blanks." It is okay to have an opinion; everyone has one. Some have lots; be honest about it.

Consider the following:

- Just because I believe something, that does not make it true; your belief does not impact truth.
- Am I guessing about life and relationships, not seeking the truth or facts?
- Is my life based on opinions, maybe even lies I have not verified?
- Do I know the "who said so," the facts, the truth that supports my beliefs?
- My opinion may be false. Do I know the consequences?
- Simple probability says my opinion has a 50 percent chance of being a lie.

Anything in your mind has three options—true, false, or opinion. If it is true, it is not an opinion because it is correct, a fact. If it is false, it also is not an opinion because it is wrong, a fact. Please do not believe false opinions; stop using them. Unfortunately, many people are unwilling to see them as a lie and move it into the opinion or even truth category because it just seems "right."

If something is an opinion, you do not know enough about it to determine if it is true or false. Be diligent and search for the facts; be careful if you use it because it may be wrong. And always remember, **God's Word speaks to you—you do not speak to God's Word**. When you have an opinion about God's Word, be incredibly careful. His Word is eternal and correct even if you do not understand it.

Opinion Is Powerful

What about you? Do you believe something that you have not checked against God's Word? Does it have little or no evidence to support it? Are you operating with common statements like "How can we know the truth?" Do you believe that truth is how you see it? Do you think there are no absolutes? Do you rely primarily on experiences rather than searching for objective data?

You might think that believing the Bible is in the realm of opinion. However, you will see the Bible's trustworthiness and accuracy when you research the evidence. Faith is required, but the facts put the Bible overwhelmingly on the side of reality and truth. Take the time to review some of the evidence by reading some great books like Josh McDowell's *Evidence That Demands a Verdict* and his latest, *The New Evidence That Demands A Verdict Fully Updated To Answer the Questions Challenging Christians Today.*

When your thinking is an opinion, it leads to confusion and, ultimately, sin because **it trusts something other than God**. Opinion often shows up in the traditions of your family, church denomination, and country of origin. Jesus tells you to be careful not to replace what God says with what you think, in other words, your opinion.

> *Mark 7:8 (NKJV)—For laying aside the commandment of God, you hold the tradition of men—the washing of pitchers and cups, and many other such things you do."*

And the Apostle Paul tells you the same thing.

> *Colossians 2:8 (NKJV)—Beware lest anyone cheat you through philosophy and empty deceit, according to the tradition of men, according to the basic principles of the world, and not according to Christ.*

Overcomers believe God is telling the truth—what is best for them. Faith always plays a part in life because that is how God created life to work. At the same time, God does NOT hide anything you need to know because He said in 2 Peter 1:3 (NKJV):

> *His divine power has given to us all things*
> *that pertain to life and godliness . . .*

What is needed **has been given** to all believers!

Overcomers pursue the truth and enjoy the abundant life because they search God's Word for the answers and do not follow the traditions of men.

Additionally, faith is only as good as the object of the faith. Faith in faith will not work. The object of an *Overcomer*'s faith works because it depends on the PERFECT God—Father, Son, and Holy Spirit, and nothing less!

Because all believers have "all things that pertain to life and godliness," God is very interested in "opinion." **He wants you to experience what is BEST for you**, and that is not your opinion, your family's opinion, your church's opinion, or your country's cultural opinion.

The Greek word *dokeo* often translates as "think," but its definition is "to be of opinion, think, suppose, to seem, to be accounted, reputed to be, it seems to me." Jesus uses the word various times when talking to His disciples, demonstrating how much God is interested in "opinion."

For example, in Matthew 6:7 (NKJV), Jesus said,

> *And when you pray, do not keep on babbling like pagans, for*
> *they think they will be heard because of their many words.*

Jesus states that the pagans "think" that babbling with many words is the right way to pray. Jesus is saying, "The pagans have an incorrect opinion about prayer." And it is almost as if He asks the disciples, "Do you think that? Is that your opinion also?"

The Lord knows what you are thinking but uses everyday situations to help you become aware that your thoughts do not match the truth. For instance, He might ask you, "What do you think about your current situation?" He could also ask for your opinion about your job, children's behavior, or finances. If you do not trust God and what He has told you about living and dealing with each situation, then you trust your opinion! Every situation that occurs is an opportunity to trust God and remove opinion.

Remember when Jesus was in the garden with His disciples, and Judas betrayed Him? Judas brings a multitude with swords and clubs, so one of Jesus' disciples pulls his sword to defend Jesus and cuts off the ear of the high priest's servant. Then Jesus speaks directly to that disciple in Matthew 26:53 (NKJV) with these words:

> *Do you think I cannot call on my Father, and He will at once put at my disposal more than twelve legions of angels?*

Wow, the disciple was trying to help! That is true, but that is the problem; it shows he had an "opinion" that Jesus was not in control of the situation and could not defend Himself. Worse yet, it implies that he did not see Jesus as God.

But Jesus corrected the disciple's opinion, which paraphrased might say, "Your opinion about my needing to be defended is wrong. Your opinion about my Father's ability to protect me is wrong. Your opinion about your ability to protect me is wrong. The truth is, I can call my Father and He will provide twelve legions of angels to protect me."

In that situation, a typical human sees a friend in trouble who needs help. If the situation, however, were seen through the eyes of one who understands who Jesus is, the thoughts and actions would be different. The thoughts might be, *"Jesus always does exactly the right thing, so He must have a good reason for not defending Himself. I do not need to step out and start doing anything. I will follow His lead and do what He does. In fact, I can trust that He will do what is right for me also."*

What a contrast! That is how *Overcomers* think and what Jesus wants believers to think about all situations! Are you thinking that way about your concerns today? The best answer you can give is either yes or no.

Here is a final example.

> *Matthew 17:24-27. (NKJV)— . . . those that received the temple tax came to Peter and said, "Does your Teacher not pay the temple tax?" He said, "Yes." When he had come into the house, Jesus anticipated him saying, "What do you think, Simon? From whom do the kings of the earth collect customs or taxes, from their own sons or from strangers?" Peter said to Him, "From strangers." Jesus said to him, "Then the sons are free. Nevertheless, lest we offend them, go to the sea, cast in a hook, and take the fish that comes up first. And when you have opened its mouth you will find a piece of money; take that and give it to them for Me and you."*

Simon stated that Jesus would pay the temple tax, so Jesus took the opportunity to help Simon see the truth. "What do you think, Simon?" is like saying," What is your opinion? Do kings on earth collect taxes from their sons?" The answer is obviously no. Simon's thinking was wrong. Jesus is the son of THE KING OF KINGS, so He did not have to pay taxes, now or ever. Not only son of The King, but He was the King and the Temple was built to worship Him! Why would He pay taxes?!

Common everyday situations are like the conversations Jesus had with His disciples. You are one of His disciples, and Jesus asks you, "What do you think?" You may be struggling with a relationship. Jesus is asking, "Do you think I know about this? Do you think I care about you? Do you think I want what's best for you?" It may be finances, your job, or sickness, but He asks the same questions. "What is your opinion about Me and how I deal with you?"

Opposites Reduce Opinion

Use 2's or Opposites

Everything, except God, is changing, even if you cannot see it. If everything changes, it is getting better or worse. Notice that the statement gives you only two options. That is a "2" or an opposite.

Other examples are yes or no, plus or minus, true or false, up or down, good or bad. It is much easier to be confused when you do not accept that there is a "2" for your situation. When you stay between the true and false, instead of accepting that it is one or the other, expect confusion to dominate.

Without clarity of good and bad, anything goes. Satan wants you confused, thinking that things are not good or bad. He wants you to believe the opinion that things are complex, even when something is plain and obvious. Look at the way he used that strategy with Eve.

> *Genesis 3:1 (NKJV)—Has God indeed said, "You shall not eat of every tree of the garden?"*

What God had stated was plain, straightforward, and simple.

> *Genesis 2:16-17 (NKJV)—"Of every tree of the garden you may freely eat; but of the tree of the knowledge of good and evil you shall not eat, for in the day that you eat of it you shall surely die."*

That statement from Satan introduced the possibility that things are not as simple as they appear. With that seed of confusion came the full blossoming of Eve and Adam trusting their thinking, doubting God, and ultimately introducing sin into the world.

You are faced with that same strategy today. Knowing what God wants is imperative; otherwise, deception is much easier. But even though you know (consider Adam; God gave the command directly to him) and have even applied God's wisdom to your life, Satan, through your sin nature, will introduce options and confusion to get you to think, "It cannot be that clear. There must be room for me to do as I want without violating what God says."

Overcomers do not entertain that thought because that is the slippery slope to sin. The antidote is to know God's Word and think with opposites. ***Every situation pleases God, or it does not.*** Notice that statement is an opposite or a 2. If unsure, get into God's Word or seek counsel, but do not act.

God has provided a clear principle even for things you might consider unclear. More on this principle is coming shortly. But for now, consider these questions.

1. Are you causing someone to stumble? Yes or No!
2. Are you willing to give up your freedom for the good of another? Yes or No!
3. Are you willing to do it privately, not publicly? Yes or No!
4. Are you doing this with a clear conscience, in faith, honoring God? Yes or No!

Asking a closed-ended question using opposites creates a structure that requires a definite answer, like "yes or no." That provides clarity, and often, the truth becomes clear. Is this choice good or bad? Am I willing to live with the consequences? Will this glorify God? Each of those questions requires a clear yes or no.

Be careful not to rationalize your answer. It fits God's principles or it does not.

Sometimes 3 Helps

While not as helpful as a "2," you can use a "3," which allows no change. It is an acceptable option since we cannot or may not see change. A standard "3" is "gets better, stays the same, or gets worse."

	Yes	No	Getting Better	Staying Same	Getting Worse
Meeting expectations?	X				
Project on schedule?		X	X		
Improving my listening?		X			X

For example, look at the chart for the second item, "Project on schedule?" It starts with a digital answer of "No" and then uses a "3" to identify that it is getting better. The problem with a "3" is that you may rationalize your "No" by stating that it is getting better. So it may be best to stick with "2s." The project is not on schedule, so get it back on schedule.

Using 2's and 3's

You can help people discover solutions without advising them when you use opposites.

Early in my career as a leadership coach, the CEO of one of my clients called me to help with a problematic employee. The employee was not performing and constantly used excuses for their poor performance. After talking briefly with the person, I asked, "How do you see your performance at work? Is it adequate or inadequate?"

The response was a list of excuses. I told the person, "I can appreciate that those things happen; we could talk about them, but it is important to know your answer to that question right now. If you would indulge me, how do you see your performance at work? Is it adequate or inadequate?"

After five minutes of more complaints and excuses, I walked over to a whiteboard in the room and drew a horizontal line. Then I drew a vertical line in the middle of the horizontal one. On the left, I wrote "Inadequate," and on the right, "Adequate."

I asked the person to put an "X" on the horizontal line to represent their performance.

Several minutes passed with them recounting excuses, telling their work history and how others constantly created problems for them. I did not state that the excuses were invalid; we talked briefly about a few. Finally, I politely asked, "So considering all that is happening, do you think your performance is adequate or inadequate?" The person stood up, walked over the board, and put an "X" on the "Inadequate" side of the line. They eventually got into reality about their performance without me badgering them or providing advice. Within a few weeks, they quit.

It would be a much better story if the person decided to become a high performer, but that did not happen. When you apply Opposites to your life, I hope you choose to change and live God's way!

Fighting reality is futile, but we still try because we will not give up our flawed thinking. Unfortunately, the battle is often against God's Word, the ultimate reality.

Look at this passage.

> *1 Thessalonians 5:12-22 (NKJV)—And we urge you, brethren, to recognize those who labor among you, and are over you in the Lord and admonish you, and to esteem them very highly in love for their work's sake. Be at peace among yourselves. Now we exhort you, brethren, warn those who are unruly, comfort the fainthearted, uphold the weak, be patient with all. See that no one renders evil for evil to anyone, but always pursue what is good both for yourselves and for all. Rejoice*

> *always, pray without ceasing, in everything give thanks;*
> *for this is the will of God in Christ Jesus for you. Do not*
> *quench the Spirit. Do not despise prophecies. Test all things;*
> *hold fast what is good. Abstain from every form of evil.*

Answer the following questions with a yes or no.
- Are you rejoicing always?
- Are you praying without ceasing?
- Are you giving thanks in everything?

Overcomers have a better probability of answering yes to those questions. Answering no says that you live in a fantasy world, not reality. Why? Because God's Word is the ultimate reality. **Anything God says is real; therefore, He tells you how life works best.** When you do not live by His Word, you live in a fantasy world, thinking you know best—thinking that complaining is okay! WOW, that is convicting to me!

The same is true about how God wants us to see marriage. God says that marriage—
- Demonstrates His Divine Nature (Genesis 1:27, Titus 2:1-5)
- Produces Children (Genesis 1:28)
- Eliminates Solitude (Genesis 2:18)
- Prevents Immorality (I Corinthians7:2, Hebrews 13:5)
- Provides Enjoyment (Proverbs 5:18)

Overcomers believe all five statements. If you do not believe and apply all of them, your marriage is not in reality. Do you want to live in reality or fantasy? Either you are in reality, or you are not.

Earlier, you read the Ultimate 2, but it was called the Fundamental Choice you have in life. It is the decision needed every minute of every day of your life. The Ultimate 2 is:
- Will I depend on God? Or . . .
- Will I depend on something other than God?

Overcomers depend on God. Do you trust Him or yourself?

OBJECTIVITY AND TRUTH, NOT OPINION

Jesus helps you think clearly. But the lack of knowledge about who He is, the lack of reading His Word, leaves you with nothing more than an opinion about Him. He wants you to depend on Him and His Word and stop depending on yourself and other things that do not accurately state who He is. God's Word says this clearly in Proverbs 3:5-6 NKJV):

*Trust in the Lord with all your heart and lean
not on your own understanding; in all your ways
acknowledge Him and He will direct your paths.*

Truth is superior to opinion. Truth needs no defense because it will stand when all else fails. Consider the quote by Robert Fritz in the box to the right—"You know what you know, and you don't know what you don't know." Opinion will not entertain that thinking. Opinion believes and operates like it

> We all dance in a ring and suppose while truth sits in the middle and knows—*Robert Frost*
>
> You know what you know and do not know what you don't know—*Robert Fritz*
>
> Just (correct) definitions either prevent or put an end to disputes—*Nathaniel Emmons*
>
> Truth is rude to opinion—*Unknown*

knows more than it does. Stop dancing around the truth and look at it. Check out the definitions of words and define your problems, issues, and struggles. Without truth, you are not wise; you are weak and vulnerable.

Use these simple definitions to see the difference between objectivity and subjectivity.

- Objectivity—How it IS
- Subjectivity—How it FEELS

Feelings are real but can hide objectivity and truth. They are great but not as great as the truth. Objectively seeing how it is, not relying on how it feels, makes a big difference. ***Decisions based on truth provide reliable, superior results. Decisions based on opinion or feelings provide variable, uncertain results.***

You Can Know

Truth is so powerful that you can remove opinions and assumptions about living wisely and what to do and not do. You might say, "God doesn't outline every thought or action of my life in His Word, so how can I know the truth or lie of each situation?" Or a similar question is often asked: "How can I know if something is right or wrong when God has not spoken about it in His Word?"

Most people think that God has left us with complex situations, and it is difficult to determine what is right or wrong. Is that true? ***No, that is not true***.

Many believers wrestle with things like dancing, playing cards, drinking alcohol, etc. They do not have a way to determine whether those things are good or bad, acceptable or unacceptable, or as some people categorize life—in or out of the will of God.

Overcomers know that every action, thought, or feeling you have is actually "good or bad." That is true for everyone. In these discussions, I like to say, "I know that wearing these socks and shoes is clearly in God's will. How can I know that?"

How Can You Know?

First, God says that there are two options for everything in life.

> *Romans 6:13 (NKJV)—And do not present your members as instruments of unrighteousness to sin, but present yourselves to God as being alive from the dead, and your members as instruments of righteousness to God.*

God's Word clearly states that everything you think or do is righteous or unrighteous, good or evil. In the Old Testament, God referred to the options as "blessing or curse" (Deuteronomy 11:26-28). Since that is TRUE, what you think or do is one or the other.

Second, God clearly defined specific things as unrighteous or righteous. He has clearly stated what is right or wrong in passages like the Ten Commandments, Sermon on the Mount, and even more specific items, such as husbands loving their wives and wives respecting their husbands. When you do not spend time in God's Word, you will be confused because you trust your opinion instead of God's truth. Remember James 3:16? If not, look it up!

Third, God provided a simple principle for everything not listed in His Word. The Apostle Paul provided this truth in Romans 14.

> *Romans 14:19-23 (NKJV)—Therefore let us pursue the things which make for peace and the things by which one may edify another. Do not destroy the work of God for the sake of food. All things indeed are pure, but it is evil for the man who eats with offense. It is good neither to eat meat nor drink wine nor do anything by which your brother stumbles or is offended or is made weak. Do you have faith? Have it to yourself before God. Happy is he who does not condemn himself in what he approves. But he who doubts is condemned if he eats, because he does not eat from faith; for whatever is not from faith is sin.*

God's Critical Principle

So how can you know if something is good or bad when God has not given specific directions about it in His Word? Here are two questions or criteria to determine if you are sinning.

1.   Are you doing something that causes a fellow believer to stumble? Stop doing it or no longer do it in public. Romans 14:22 says, "Have it to yourself before God."

2. Do you have a clear conscience that doing it is okay? If not, Romans 14:23 states, ". . . for whatever is not from faith is sin."

When you take the clear things in God's Word and the Principle of Responsible Freedom, you can know when you are self-absorbed and self-controlled. You can know if your thinking or actions are sinful or not.

Think about the issues in your life—job, career, relationships, and decisions. Think about the above, apply it to each, and see if it answers any of your questions. Applying that principle tells you whether your thinking, acting, or feeling is correct for even the most minor areas of your life.

Seeing life through the lens of RIGHTEOUSNESS or UNRIGHTEOUSNESS *elevates everything you do to a level of significance*. Your belief in Jesus' gift—His death, burial, and resurrection—is the most critical decision in your life. But if you think that is everything, you are trusting opinion, not truth.

Overcomers know there is far more to this life: it determines your inheritance and reigning with Christ in eternity—the prize! The incredible gift of life that Jesus has given you and the energy of the Holy Spirit that energizes the life of Jesus in you gives you the ability to live Jesus' life through you—instead of living your sin nature life. Please do NOT trust me on any of this! Go to God's Word and study to determine whether this is correct. Plant His Word in your life, and it will change you.

If you do not want to hurt your relationships because you are assuming things about others and living primarily in your emotions, consider asking yourself these questions:

- Am I guessing and assuming things about them?
- What standard am I using for Truth? Who is my "Who said so?"
- What do my actions show I value?
- Am I focused on how it is or how it feels?

When you do not depend on God, the only option is to depend on something other than God. Most often, this will be yourself. The Bible contains many examples where people trusted themselves, and the results were not good. The Bible, and specifically the book of Judges, consistently tells the story of people who trusted themselves, not God, over and over, and it ends with this sad indictment.

> *Judges 21:25 (NKJV)—In those days there was no king in Israel; everyone did what was right in his own eyes.*

Do not let that be you. Please do not do that.

DISCUSSION QUESTIONS

1. What is the critical point of the fossil footprints exercise?
2. Explain why we tend to "fill in the blanks."
3. What words may be better than opinion when talking to others?
4. Explain how God is asking about your opinion regularly.
5. Explain what an Opposite or "2" is.
6. What is the benefit of using a "2" with others and yourself?
7. What is the Ultimate 2?
8. How would you use a "3" with an Opposite? What are the benefits and dangers of using a "3"?
9. What are the simple definitions of Objectivity and Subjectivity?
10. Explain a simple way to know if ANYTHING you are doing is right or wrong in God's view.

CHAPTER 9

EXCELLENCE OR EXCUSES?

Darren, 42, works at a large international pharmaceutical company. He joined the company only six months ago as a salesperson. His boss, June, hired him thinking he needed a second chance at sales. In the interviewing process, he admitted to June that he had trouble meeting his sales goals. He explained that bad press came out about the company he worked for soon after he started working there. None of the physicians on his "route" of calls would use the samples he brought them. Finally, some of them asked him not to visit their offices anymore.

Every week, when he turns in his accountability report with the new company, June notices that Darren tends to explain why he wasn't able to achieve something. For example, in a recent report, he said, "I called on 18 offices this week. None of the physicians would meet with me, so I had to talk to a Physician's Assistant (PA). Typically, these individuals do not understand the value of our innovations with the drugs we sell. So I left samples but don't really expect any orders."

June has tried to be understanding, but at this point, she is at her wit's end. She doesn't like conflict, so she has put off the conversation, hoping that Darren's sales calls will pay off at some point. Now, she is faced with a situation where Darren is not producing enough sales to support his base salary. She schedules a meeting with Darren to figure out the next steps.

June welcomes Darren in her office and asks him to sit in the chair in front of her desk. He looks at her like he expects the worst from this meeting.

She asks, "How's it going, Darren?"

He answers in a despondent tone of voice, "It's okay. At least it's Friday."

June thinks to herself, *He doesn't even try to act like he cares. I guess I just need to get this over with.*

"Darren, I know you have tried very hard and you want to make your goals, but I just can't justify your base salary based on what you have sold in the first six months with us."

Darren says, "Yeah, I figured that is what this meeting would be about. I can't help it that I can't get in front of doctors."

June raises her eyebrows and says, "Well, that may be so, but all my other sales reps are figuring out how to get in front of the doctors. Last week, Mary Anne made a huge sale in one of the clinics she calls on."

Darren replied, "Well, she has been calling on them for four years. That's to be expected. That group also has 10 doctors in the practice. I don't have any offices like that. I don't even know what you expect me to sell. You asked me what I wanted to make but didn't give me a target."

Frustrated, June raised her voice a bit, "Darren, I have given you the benefit of the doubt in many ways. You didn't perform well in your last company, and I took a chance on you. I convinced my boss that it would be okay to hire you, but now she's on my case because you have done nothing. We like to project a spirit of excellence at this company, and you just don't fit the bill."

Darren is a little shocked at her tone of voice, which he hasn't seen before, and looks down at the floor.

June, feeling a little guilty, says, "Look, Darren, I'm sorry. I shouldn't have gotten short with you, but I have a job to keep too. Let's give it one more shot. I'll try to expand your territory a little bit, so you can call on some other offices. How does that sound."

Darren looked up and smiled and said, "Yeah, that would help. This is an answer to prayer. I have been praying you would have mercy and show grace toward me."

June stands up to end the meeting and says, "Okay, I'll get back to you in a week regarding changes in your territory if I can get that approved.

Questions

1. Has June promoted a spirit of excellence in the company in her actions with Darren?
2. How do you think this meeting will impact his performance and commitment to doing a good job in the future?
3. Does Darren have a clear direction going forward?
4. What do you feel is missing from the above conversation?

OVERCOMERS PROMOTE A CULTURE OF TRUTH

Key Lesson: *Moments of truth require a clean heart, clear expectations, and clear communication to create a culture of truth.*

MOMENTS OF TRUTH CREATE THE CULTURE

A culture of truth is critical to any organization, especially those who desire to honor God because He is Truth. Overcomers share the truth about an individual's behavior and performance because they love the people, pursue their best, and value them enough to help them grow and develop.

If you value truth, you will build a culture of truth.

> *Ephesians 4:15-16 (NKJV)—But speaking the truth in love, may grow up in all things into Him who is the head— Christ—from whom the whole body, joined and knit together by what every joint supplies, according to the effective working by which every part does its share, causes growth of the body for the edifying of itself in love.*

You share the truth to help people, not punish them! And you not only share truth; you encourage everyone to share truth with you!

A culture of truth encourages excellence in everything. That means you notice when people are not doing what they said they would—tasks they chose and were assigned. If they are not progressing, you share the truth with them and help them make changes. If they are making progress, you encourage them.

Remember, actions show what you value—not your words. Your values show up in your daily activities. If you value a culture of truth, it shows up in moments of truth.

Recognize a Moment of Truth

A moment of truth depends on ***constant awareness and consistent sharing of truth***. When you become aware of a person's behavior or performance that does not match what the organization needs or wants, you talk about it, share the truth, and help them change.

1. *Awareness* that there is a difference between expected and actual delivery
2. *Decision* you make about what to do with that information

That is how you know a Moment of Truth (MOT). The first part, **Awareness**, implies that you make sure everyone is clear about the expected goals, work, values, and behavior. Then you pay attention to see if those expectations show up.

Clear expectations take time and effort. And if you are not doing that with the people you lead, then you are not performing your job as a leader.

The second part, the **Decision**, is more critical. You can provide clear expectations, track progress, know expectations were unmet, and DO NOTHING! Or you can resort to punishing, creating a structure of fear rather than learning and growth.

Neither of those approaches is acceptable. *Overcomers* pursue the best for people and the organization, which means sharing a moment of truth. Either you share the truth and pursue the best for those you lead, or you will not. Either you value truth and developing people, or you do not!

You can build a culture of truth with each moment of truth.

Remember 3 Daily Priorities

Our GR8 Leaders material includes the GR8 Recipe—*6 Critical Values, 5 Essential Capacities, 3 Daily Priorities, 2 Remarkable Skills, and 1 Timeless Process.* The 6 Critical Values are the most important to be a GR8 Leader, and the most critical value is TRUTH. However, there is another part of the GR8 Leaders Recipe that helps encourage excellence and build a culture of truth—the **3 Daily Priorities**: Clear Expectations, Clear Consequences, and Self-governance. The three priorities show up in everything God tells you in His Word. For example, it is in the first command that God gave Adam.

> Genesis 2:16-17 (NKJV)—And the LORD God commanded the man, saying, "Of every tree of the garden you may freely eat; but of the tree of the knowledge of good and evil you shall not eat, for in the day that you eat of it you shall surely die."

God asked Adam to be self-governing (self-control) by not eating from the tree of the knowledge of good and evil (clear expectations). And if Adam ate from the tree, he would surely die (clear consequences). After the sin, God let Adam, Eve, and Satan experience the consequences.

Moments of truth are available daily but depend on whether you pay attention. Remember, awareness and decision. When you put the 3 Daily Priorities into your routine, you create a structure that encourages excellence in you, your team, and your organization.

These priorities apply to you AND to those that you lead every day.

- **Self**—Are you self-governing? Are you clear about the expectations of you and the organization? Are you clear about the consequences of not meeting those expectations?

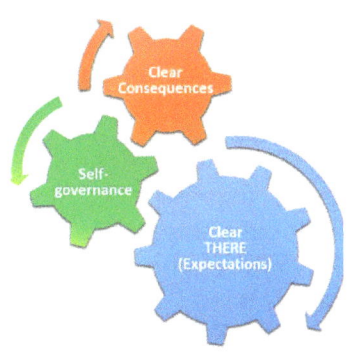

- **Others**—Today, are you encouraging and coaching self-governance? Have you ensured those under and with you are clear about their expectations? Have you made sure they know the consequences of not meeting those expectations?

The three priorities help you work with people and situations before they become big problems. Each time you talk about a lack of self-governance, unclear or incomplete expectations, or vague or ignored consequences that may become a **Moment of Truth**.

Refuse to Work Around the Truth

A moment of truth is misused when you let lousy thinking drive your emotions. Even when you decide to help someone learn and grow, your discomfort can stop you from sharing the truth. Unless you learn to trust good thinking, you will often not share the truth when needed.

Think about when you became aware someone had not done what you had asked them to do. It may have been someone who works for you, with you, or a family member. What did you do when you knew they did not do what was needed? Most people did nothing or handled the situation poorly.

If someone does not meet expectations and you say nothing or handle the situation poorly, it is like telling them that it is OKAY to perform poorly, fall short of expectations, or NOT do what is needed. **You create a structure that says poor performance is OKAY!**

While that may be hard to accept, it is reality. On the other hand, if you handle the situation well, you demonstrate that you want to help people grow and learn, develop and improve, and perform excellently.

What will you do the next time you become aware of something done wrong or incomplete? Remember, your ACTIONS imply what you VALUE!

You may say nothing for at least three reasons:
1. You do not like emotional conflict—hurt feelings, etc.
2. It did not work well when you shared the truth in the past.
3. You have opinions on how things are working.

Those three reasons encourage two common strategies or excuses instead of sharing the truth.

- "I've got too much to do. I don't have the time to deal with them."
- "I'll have to watch the stuff I give them. It can't be important things."

Both strategies hurt you, them, and the organization. You do not grow, and neither do they. That leaves you with the "Work Around Cycle," and nothing changes!

When you use an MOT, it helps you remove those strategies and excuses. Using an MOT will help you deal with corrective situations in a structured, constructive, and less emotional way.

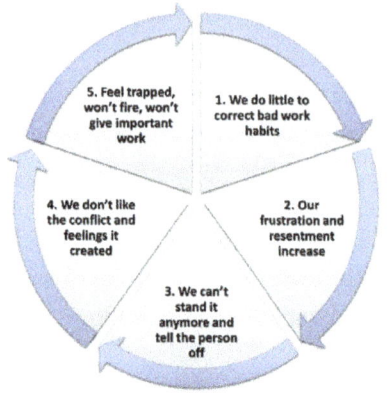

It helps you follow through on your awareness of unmet expectations. Will it help you solve a person's underperformance? Maybe, because this is a tool to help that happen. Other factors are involved, like the person's desire, ability, and the clarity of your expectations. But nothing happens unless you refuse to work around the truth!

Overcomers who provide clear expectations help themselves and the other person. They identify the performance standard and help the team or individual know the target.

That is precisely what God does for us. His Word is clear about what is good and what is not. And He even tells us what is most important.

> *Mark 12:29-31 (NKJV)—Jesus answered him, "The first of all the commandments is: 'Hear, O Israel, the LORD our God, the LORD is one. And you shall love the LORD your God with all your heart, with all your soul, with all your mind, and with all your strength.' This is the first commandment. And the second, like it, is this: 'You shall love your neighbor as yourself.' There is no other commandment greater than these."*

However, leaders who provide vague, unclear expectations make it difficult to know if EXPECTED differs from ACTUAL, and they encourage less objectivity during a performance conversation. Most importantly, leaders who provide unclear expectations demonstrate that the leaders are not doing their job.

One of the basic and best leadership tools you can learn is THP or THERE, HERE, PATH (see "Creates Clear Goals). THERE is the desired end result you want from the person, your expectation.

Resolve to Be a "Catalyst"

Finally, a moment of truth encourages you to be a catalyst. That is a good word that describes every *Overcomer* when they follow the lead of the Holy Spirit. A catalyst is:

**A substance, usually used in small amounts relative to
the reactants, that modifies and increases the rate of
a reaction without being consumed in the process.**

Note three vital elements in the definition.
- small amounts
- increases the rate of reaction (or change)
- not consumed in the process

Jesus is the ultimate catalyst. He does not overpower you, even though He could. He speaks to you with a "still small voice" to get your attention. And He speeds up change and **never** is changed.

How can you be more like Jesus when you decide to have an MOT or a difficult conversation with someone?

Here is God's "catalytic" approach.

*Galatians 6:1–5 (NKJV)—Brethren, if a man is overtaken
in any trespass, you who are spiritual restore such a one in
a spirit of gentleness, considering yourself lest you also be
tempted. Bear one another's burdens, and so fulfill the law of
Christ. For if anyone thinks himself to be something, when he
is nothing, he deceives himself. But let each one examine his
own work, and then he will have rejoicing in himself alone,
and not in another. For each one shall bear his own load.*

That will help you have an MOT that honors God and the people you lead. Most importantly, it enables you to understand where your heart is before you start, how God wants you to talk with the person during the conversation, and how God wants you to think after it.

Check Your Heart Before You Start

An MOT is an opportunity to help someone grow and learn. But it will not work out well if you do not use God's values.

MOT Is NOT...	MOT Is a...
Punishment or a reprimand	Process to create an honest and open environment
Problem-solving technique	Process to enhance learning and performance
Airing "feelings" or opinions	Process to develop people and build capacity

Living, sharing, and encouraging a life built on truth is an opportunity to please God.

> *Proverbs 3:3-4 (NKJV)—Let not mercy and truth forsake you; bind them around your neck, write them on the tablet of your heart, and so find favor and high esteem in the sight of God and man.*

Mercy and truth are a fantastic combination. Mercy provides the relational component, while truth provides the powerful element. Each situation where a person does not meet expectations is an opportunity to "find favor and high esteem in the sight of God and man."

Remember, MOT is best done without emotions and is best when you are using great values. When focusing on mercy and truth, you keep your lousy thinking out of the conversation. Together, they support each other and provide the best results.

If you do not focus on valuing and developing people, you can do an MOT, but it will probably be more about punishment than help. ***Valuing people is critical for moments of truth***. It is unnatural to value people enough to develop them because everyone is more prone to think about themselves, which starts "ME flashing" moments.

You will not do what is good when you have worldly values. ***Focusing on loving, serving, and developing people takes a deliberate choice.*** It reduces your emotions and enhances your ability to work through difficult parts of the conversation. Remember that the other person will tend to be defensive, so if you do not focus on developing them, you will also become defensive and emotional.

Do not let the great opportunity to help someone grow and learn turn into an emotional, subjective, and ultimately destructive interaction. It is your choice, and it all depends on what you value!

Trespass, Not Opinion

> *Galatians 6:1 (NKJV)— ". . . a man is overtaken in any trespass . . ."*

A significant danger in talking to someone about a "trespass" is the difference between your preferences and God's Word.

A trespass is crossing the boundary of what God has stated is right or wrong, not your opinion of right or wrong. Before you go to someone, especially with a difficult matter, verify God's Word about the matter. Have *"chapter and verse"* available for them. Let that passage in God's Word speak to them more than you do.

Again, look at the truth and the facts to remove your opinion or assumptions. Your brain wants to "know," so when you cannot find or do not know the facts, you will FILL IN THE BLANK with opinions, guesses, and assumptions.

Be Spirit-led

*Galatians 6:1 (NKJV)—You who are spiritual
. . . considering yourself . . .*

Paul just finished talking about the fruit of the Spirit, so it seems evident that "spiritual" is about walking in the Spirit instead of the flesh. And during these conversations, it is easy for the flesh to take you in the wrong direction, "lest you be tempted."

What the person says or your flawed thinking can sidetrack you. Difficult conversations only work right when you follow the Holy Spirit's guidance.

Restore

Galatians 6:1 (NKJV)— . . . restore . . .

Restore is the verb, the critical action of ". . . you who are spiritual." That implies that without the Holy Spirit leading, the restoration will not happen. Restore is about mending, so God wants you to walk in the Spirit with a heart that desires to recover and restore people, not leave them broken. Mending is not your responsibility, but God asks us to be His tool. God wants you to say "yes" to the other person, even when they say "no."

Not having a difficult conversation when needed is easy. The thought of the emotional conflict that may happen becomes a big flashing stop sign—stop, do not do it! But trust the power of God and refuse to work around the truth.

God is in the business of restoration and redemption. He wants you to be a channel of His grace, mercy, and truth. You are not doing this alone; His Spirit guides you. Watch how God uses you in this conversation.

Be Gentle

Galatians 6:1 (NKJV)— . . . spirit of gentleness . . .

Gentleness is only possible with humility, which is the context of this passage. Look at Galatians 5:26; the verse immediately preceding verse 1 of chapter 6 says, "Let us not become conceited, provoking one another, envying one another." Gentleness reduces barriers, while force raises them.

Difficult conversations are not about using truth as a sledgehammer. It is about using truth in love, following the Holy Spirit to see how God might use you to restore this person.

Fulfill the Law of Christ

Galatians 6:2 (NKJV)—Bear one another's burdens, and so fulfill the law of Christ.

Not only gentle, but the most critical ingredient to renew your mind is to do this in love.

Love—pursuing the BEST for others patiently, kindly, sacrificially, and unconditionally—is the law of Christ. And you will not bear their burdens unless you want what is best for them. Love requires a decision *before* you enter the conversation, *while* conversing, and *after* you finish. Love makes the difference, not your persuasiveness.

FOLLOW 4 STEPS DURING THE CONVERSATION

Below are four steps for a Moment of Truth conversation. These steps are easy to remember and personalize to fit you. More importantly, they create an excellent structure for your conversation. Of course, like any tool, it requires practice to do it well.

1. Reality	2. Story	3. Plan	4. Feedback
Acknowledge reality	*Analyze how it got that way*	*Create an action plan*	*Create a feedback system*
"Stay on topic"—the topic is expectations were not met	"Not Problem-Solving"—that is next, get the story	"The plan is the agreement for the change."—it is their responsibility	"Feedback is a process, not a single event."

When you share these four steps with everyone, you help build a culture and truth. You share the steps and **tell them how the MOT will help people grow and develop**. MOT is not a secret leadership tool only you know how to use. Everyone needs to know, even if they do not use it. By the way, it is handy at home as well as at work.

Finally, do not start the conversation without remembering what God has told us in Galatians 6:1-2—this conversation is about following the Holy Spirit, restoration, gentleness, and love.

Step 1—REALITY: Acknowledge the Truth

A Call for Help

Suppose you are a consultant and one of your business owners asks you to help with one of their employees who has not been doing what they need to do. You do an MOT with the person while the owner is present, making sure that the expectations are clear and that the person has a clear plan to go forward to meet the expectations. They agree to make the necessary changes.

Then in three weeks, you get this email from the business owner.

> *Doug did not open several emails I had sent him for at least two days . . . which we just now discovered . . . and had not completed some tasks I had asked him to do immediately at least two times. (Burt, COO of ---) emailed me to ask why he had not received his information.*
>
> *Doug still chooses to do things his way but says he has done it.*
>
> *Also, I again asked Doug to learn to call in to check for messages . . . (I am HORRIFIED that he has not been doing so! And he still has not asked anyone to teach him how to do it).*
>
> *EMAILS AND VOICEMAIL MUST BE CHECKED AT LEAST EVERY TWO HOURS!! HELP!!!*

Remember, "Doug" knew precisely what to do and was not doing it. The manager is frustrated and, guess what, not saying anything—not doing an MOT when needed.

Here is a great exercise to do using the above information. Please do it now without reading any further.

> *If you were the manager, what are some STEP 1 questions that you would ask?*

You can see the answers below. **Hints**: remember . . .
- MOT's first step is about REALITY.
- Step 1 is about you and the other person being on the same page.
- Step 1 is NOT about the story.
- Expectations are clear and known by Doug and the manager.

Critical Thoughts

Before going further, please note that some situations of clear sin may only require reading the person a verse or passage in God's Word. Then you remove yourself and rely solely on the power of God to work on their heart to make the changes God reveals to them. That is Step 1, where God reveals the reality and now it depends on whether they agree.

Those situations are like doing Step 1 without asking a Step 1 question. You rely on God's Word to do Steps 1, 2, 3, and maybe Step 4. Of course, you remain available to talk further if they want, willing to be a resource, as you will see in Step 4.

For all other situations, the first question for an MOT is critical. *I believe that if people took this first step, performance would improve!* That is a bold statement, but it is also the power of holding people accountable.

Critical Point: Stay on Topic—It is about Reality

Some other vital thoughts about MOT Step 1 are . . .
- Keep it SIMPLE.
- Do not mix facts with the story of how it got that way.
- Do not go beyond the reality of the situation.
- Do not go beyond what was expected and delivered.
- Do not go into other topics until you agree that expectations were unmet.
- Big Reminder—Stay with facts and ONLY facts!

This step is about reality. You may see reality, but they may not. Until both of you agree that "reality is what it is," the chance that things will change decreases. Either the expectations were met or not. When you start Step 1, it is not about your opinion.

Step 1 is only about the facts: "You were asked to finish the project by November 23, and now it is November 25—so the project is late, right?" The MOT is not about your feelings, so do not say anything like, "You really let me down." The MOT is not about you but about helping people develop and improve. When introducing emotions into the conversation, you encourage defensiveness and fear rather than growth and development.

And it is not about getting the story—that is in Step 2. Step 1 is ONLY about them acknowledging REALITY—how it is. *The only message you deliver is reality, not your feelings, and nothing else.*

Your First Question

Okay, get the question(s) you wrote from the assignment above and compare them to the following. Here is the type of question you would ask a person when you compare expectations to actual results.

- You did not get his lists to him when he needed them; is that correct?
- You have not checked your emails and voicemails every two hours, correct?
- You have not asked anyone to show you how to use voicemail; is that correct?

Notice that the question is not about what a person knows, not about creating fear in them, and not about why they did not meet expectations—it is **ONLY** about the reality that expectations were not met. And the question only needs a YES or NO answer.

You can be direct or relational, whatever fits the situation, their personality, your personality, and your style. Just make sure that both of you agree that expectations were not met. You do NOT talk about the story or how it got to be this way. It is only about REALITY—expectations were not met.

If you wanted to create a more relational question, you could ask something like:

- Since Burt did not get his lists when he needed them, can we agree that is not good?
- I want to talk about the lists you were to send to Burt. Can we agree it is not good for our business that the lists were not sent when Burt needed them?

Now, think about a time when someone did not meet your expectations.

- Create a direct question that requires a YES or NO answer
- Create a more relational question that still requires a YES or NO answer

Try it, and you will do yourself and those around you a big favor because it helps you start sharing the truth constructively. Telling the truth is a critical element in helping a person change.

> *James 5:19-20 (NKJV)—Brethren, if anyone among you wanders from the truth, and someone turns him back, let him know that he who turns a sinner from the error of his way will save a soul from death and cover a multitude of sins.*

How to Handle Excuses

Most often, when you tell people that this conversation is about developing people and sharing the truth about expectations and reality, there are few excuses. But sometimes excuses show up, and there is a simple way to handle them. Suppose, in the example above, the person replied

> *"Yes, but Joe has required a lot of additional training, taking up*
> *a lot of my time, and you know how important his training is."*

How would you handle that? Consider this simple approach:

> *"I want to talk about that, but first, let's ensure we agree that*
> *the expectation was not achieved. Can we first agree on that?"*

Even if they offer a second excuse, you follow the same format. There is no need to get frustrated with them; you will not if you maintain the mindset that this is about growing and developing people. It is not your job to make them change. Your job is to allow them to grow and change if they want it. At some point, that opportunity to grow and change may be closed.

But They Are Just Difficult!

Yes, you will have those people in your life. But this IS NOT ABOUT YOU! It is about following a process that gives them the best chance to grow and develop. When that happens, you increase their capacity, which increases the organization's capacity. Without that thinking, your flawed thinking will result in emotions that hurt the MOT. Your emotions tend to be your most significant obstacle to correcting poor performance. Of course, your emotions are just a byproduct of thinking.

That again brings up what is going on in your mind when correcting someone's performance. You experience a values conflict. Think about it. On the one hand, you value peace and emotional comfort. On the other, you value truth. Which will you choose?

Look at your actions because that shows what you value! In life, truth and reality are more important than avoiding uncomfortable feelings. You would agree with that statement until you needed to do an MOT. Then you will know what you value—look at what you do.

Overcomers share the truth to build a culture of truth that is critical for relationships and organizations. Remember what that implies if you do not share the truth about poor performance? Yes, you are saying, "Poor performance is okay here!"

Here is a good statement that will help build a culture of truth.

It is SAFE to tell the truth around here, but
it is not okay to NOT tell the truth.

Overcomers focus on truth and reality. They are self-governing and value doing the right thing. Remember, telling the truth is an action that shows what you value.

Make "Truth Telling" The Norm

As you have already heard, Step 1, all by itself, can improve performance. That is a big claim, but think about it. Step 1 asks a person to acknowledge that they did not meet expectations.

Holding someone accountable may not be enough to see the change in their behavior, but it is an excellent step in the right direction. This step alone can energize self-governance in people who have reasonable values. Talking about the truth *will not get it done*. Listing value statements *will not get it done*. Teaching and training each person and employee in the organization that telling the truth, even when it is terrible—**WILL WORK! It builds a culture of truth!**

You want to create a structure that becomes more comfortable with the truth. You can call it constructive criticism, but I like the simple word truth.

Before you start sharing the moments of truth, understand that people are probably uncomfortable when the truth is shared. That means you have the wrong structure. If you persevere in sharing moments of truth, you continue to build a culture of truth. In time, people see telling the truth as part of their job. Of course, you always want to reinforce telling the truth with mercy. It is not about trying to punish someone with the truth.

> *Galatians 6:9-10 (NKJV)—And let us not grow weary while doing good, for in due season we shall reap if we do not lose heart. Therefore, as we have opportunity, let us do good to all, especially to those who are of the household of faith.*

Finally, here are the skills you need to make Step 1 work for you.
- Separate how it is from how it got that way.
- Revisit an objective description of reality as needed.
- Get a definitive yes or no. Is the description of reality accurate or not?
- Watch out for qualified answers.
- Watch out for a difference of opinion.
- Recognize the quick deflective "yes."

Those skills will help you master Step 1—REALITY. Try it now.

Step 2—STORY: Analyze How It Got to Be That Way

Your Role

When you see they understand that they missed the expectation, you move from Step 1 to Step 2. In Step 1, you want to determine if both of you are looking at REALITY the same way. Now, you want to get the STORY of how they missed the expectation.

This step requires **your listening skills and the ability to ask questions**. Your ability with those skills helps them think clearly about the events that led to this reality, the missed expectation. Your critical question is, "How can we understand what happened?"

Do not get fooled into hearing about one single event. "Joe had a problem, so I helped him." That would be just one event in the time frame from when they received the assignment to the missed deadline or the poor quality. If that was their first statement, ask, "What were you doing just before he asked for help?" Then you could work back from that event.

You can also start at the beginning. "Let's back up to the beginning. What was your plan of action to make sure you met the expectation?" The better you understand the sequence of events, the more you will help them find a way to do it better next time. You explore and analyze the events to see their thinking and where things went wrong. You want to ask about their decisions, actions, assumptions, and plans followed.

The more you ask questions to see the chain of events, the more you help them grow and develop into a self-governing individual. **THAT IS YOUR ROLE in this step of the MOT!**

And this step is NOT about problem-solving! When you hear the story, you will see problems. Please do not try to solve the issues because this step is ONLY about getting the story. It takes discipline and excellent listening and questioning skills to understand the story. You can mark the situation in your memory or jot a note. BUT DO NOT STOP TO DISCUSS THAT PROBLEM!

Here is how problem-solving happens too often in life. Problem-solving done right is helpful, but most of the time, it is nothing more than an exercise in futility because you don't take the time to get to the root causes or you do not create a better structure.

Often, problem-solving ends up as the graph shows.
- A PROBLEM arises, which
- leads to PAIN, which
- leads to ACTION, which
- leads to less pain, which
- leads to less action, which
- leads to the return of the PROBLEM!

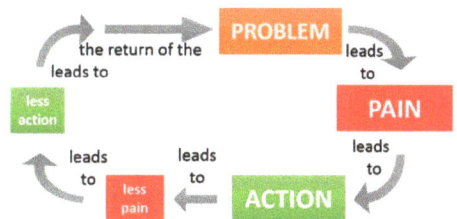

That is an oscillating structure like a rocking chair. That structure shows poor focus on the final solution (THERE) or a lack of persistence toward the final solution, which leads to the return of the problem (HERE).

Picture the THP structure: THERE at the top, HERE at the bottom, and the actions or PATH between. Any time you remove THERE, you only have HERE, where you are, which leads to reacting and responding to whatever is happening. Then with entropy (natural decline of everything without energy applied), you start sliding back to the original HERE.

That repeats the big idea. Step 2 is NOT about problem-solving. It is about the STORY.

Track Their Thinking

Step 2 of a Moment of Truth depends on your ability to OBSERVE what they say. Think about the combination of words Observational Listening. Those two words refer to two different senses—seeing and hearing. You not only listen, but you ask questions about the story that you are developing from what they say. As you track their thinking, you see the sequence of events. You see . . .
- The beginning decisions and actions
- The following events and the outcomes of those
- You see their role and the interaction occurring with others
- You see both their execution and the process they used

That is a process of co-learning as you see the story unfold. And it is better to stay with What, How, and When questions. Before you jump to the "Listen and Ask Questions" chapter, finish this chapter to know the entire MOT process.

Design & Execution

In every MOT story (Step 2), one or both elements—design and execution—appear. When you combine design with execution, you get performance. Your job is to listen for those elements.
- DESIGN—the process used
- EXECUTION—the effort expended

Poor performance means one or both are missing. Good design is undermined by poor execution, and good execution is hampered by poor design. The worst situation is both poor design and poor execution.

Some Design and Execution Elements

Design	Execution
• Sequence	• Competence
• Scheduling	• Assumptions
• Accountability	• Work habits
• Workload-capacity relationships	• Ability to delegate
• Built-in conflicts of interest	• Follow-through with orders
• Contradictory or reinforcing reward systems	• Clarity of roles, outcomes, current reality
• Delivery delays	• Decision making
• Inventory availability	• Creativity
• Workflows	• Flexibility
• Available technology	• Steadfastness

Managerial Moment of Truth, p20

The story will likely not be a situation with good design and execution; otherwise, you would not be doing an MOT. As you listen, make mental markers or take notes on the execution and the processes used. Seeing those two elements will help you dramatically as you work through Step 3—the PLAN.

A Step 2 Conversation

Manager: "What happened that the due date was missed?"

Employee: "Well, I guess I just got too busy with everything I've got to do."

Manager: Is the date we put on this the right date? In other words, did we need to have your part done in the time frame?"

Manager: "Yeah, because Marketing needed the info for their ad campaign. So yeah, that date was part of the larger project.

Manager: "Given that you needed to make the date, how did you think about it when you took on the assignment?"

Employee: "I didn't realize it would take as long as it did."

Manager: "Why not?"

Employee: "Well, I just didn't."

Manager: "Could you have known if you had done better planning?"

Employee: "In this case, yeah."

Manager: "Although you make an assumption about how long it would take, that assumption turned out not to be right. Is it safe to say you didn't think it through?"

Employee: "Yeah, I didn't. I assumed it wouldn't take too long. But as it turned out—when I began to work on it, I suddenly was swamped with everything coming all at once—this and a number of other things."

Manager: "I see. When you thought about how you were going to do this project, did you add the other stuff you were also going to do to the equation?"

Employee: "No."

Manager: "What does that suggest?"

Employee: "To get the whole picture. To consider all the things I've got to do."

Manager: "Is that something you do from time to time: underestimate how long it will take to accomplish your goals without considering all the other things you've got to do?"

Employee: "Yeah."

Manager: "Okay, so one approach we can take is to have a better system to think through the demands of any project. If you had known this project would have been as involved as it turned out to be, what would you have done?"

Employee: "Started about two weeks sooner."

Manager: "Good, that's one idea. Now, sometimes it happens that you can't start sooner for some projects—you need information from someone else, or you need a decision to be made, and so on. If that were true in this case, what could you have done?"

Employee: "I could have moved some of my other work up, so it would have been done well before the other project hit."

Manager: "If you did that, would it have worked in this case?"

Employee: "Yes."

Manager: "What are you noticing about your work patterns?"

Employee: "I need to get a better fix on how much time it'll take to get a project done, and I have to factor in what's on my plate. I've got to create a more realistic schedule for myself."

Manager: "Good."

Managerial Moment of Truth, p, 17

Critical Points

In Step 2, you get the STORY of missing the expectation. You use your excellent listening and questioning skills without becoming emotional. You learned about the design used and how they executed their design or plan. And you do not get sidetracked by trying to solve problems as you listen.

An excellent summary of the skills needed in Step 2 is as follows:

> *James 1:19-20 (NKJV)—So then, my beloved brethren, let every man be swift to hear, slow to speak, slow to wrath; for the wrath of man does not produce the righteousness of God.*

Three additional critical points to remember:
1. Without this step, you will not see how they think and how they can make changes. When you do a good job of listening and asking questions, you see an accurate picture of what happened.
2. Do not discuss who is to blame. The MOT is about developing people rather than blaming them.
3. Ensure you understand the sequence of events that make up the entire story.

Skills needed are:
- Track the story chronologically— that is the easiest way
- Create pictures from the words
- Avoid speculating
- Identify their assumptions
- Look for design flaws
- Notice how they dealt with unexpected events

Develop those skills and master MOT Step 2—the STORY.

Step 3—PLAN: Create an Action Plan

Critical Point: The plan is the agreement for the change.

Recognize the Actions Needed

Toward the end of the STORY, you will know ways the situation could have been different. Those differences could have prevented the missed expectation. You have tracked the sequence of events, held onto your insights for change, and now are ready to move on to Step 3—The PLAN.

This step provides both of you the path for developing additional capacity and ways to help the person grow. The plan is often simple, with one or two items, and only requires a verbal agreement. Other more complex situations need a written plan. Reading the plan will help you know they understood what needed to change. It will also give you another opportunity to discuss any changes required.

Step 3 is the PLAN, and it is the AGREEMENT for change.

Robert Fritz's book, *Managerial Moment of Truth*, has an excellent example of a Step 3 conversation.

Manager: "When's the next time you're accountable for a similar project?"

Employee: "I've just taken one on."

Manager: When's the due date?"

Employee: "In five weeks."

Manager: "Given what we know, what changes to your process would you make?"

Employee: "The first thing is to get a more realistic fix on what it will take."

Manager: "How will you know you have a realistic assessment of what it will take?"

Employee: "Looking at the scope of the work, the resources I have—those kinds of things."

Manager: "That's good. What else?"

Employee: "Well, I don't want to be surprised, so I'd better look at my workload to see my demands. I'd better be a little smarter about scheduling what I do."

Manager: "If you took those steps, does it look likely you'll make your deadlines?"

Employee: "Yeah, it does."

Before reading further, answer this question. What two things do you see as most important in the approach the manager took?

The two items you want to model in Step 3 are 1) the manager only asked questions and 2) the person created the plan. Those are two essential items to remember.

In your next MOT, try it. It will take pressure off you and help the person you are coaching.

Their Responsibility

If you want them to benefit from the MOT, make the PLAN **their responsibility.** You may have the experience to create a better plan but do not do it. That does not help them grow. You can help them with insights as you discuss the plan, but do not make it yours.

You want to think through the plan as they talk about it. Assess whether it is workable, practical, has reasonable assumptions, and helps them change their behavior. If you answer NO to any of those questions, provide your concerns and get them to address each issue. While the PLAN needs to be theirs, it does not mean you do not help them create a good plan. You are a resource; they can discover more insights than being told what the problem is.

> Proverbs 15:22 (NKJV)—Without counsel, plans go awry,
> but in the multitude of counselors they are established.

If you create the PLAN, they may not understand it, commit to it, or use it. Worst of all, if the PLAN does not work, it creates a path of least resistance to blame you. You can help with the PLAN, but do not do it for them.

Win the "Yes, but" Game

It is easy for people to become defensive and resist responsibility for change. You will do the same when you have lousy thinking. The defensiveness can take the form of being a victim, which means they believe they are performing well, but people and circumstances prevent them from doing better.

Defensiveness can be the "Yes, but . . ." game. They do not want to create a plan and constantly find reasons to resist any change needed.

Here is an example of a "Yes, but . . ." conversation from the Managerial Moment of Truth.

> "You could try to schedule your work better to make sure you're spreading things out well." "Yes, but I can't do that because I don't know when other assignments might come in." "Well, you could call the people you are working with and see if they can give you a heads-up." Yes, but I can't do that because they get their assignments at the last minute." "Well, figuring that there'll be some work coming in at the wrong time for you, you could write that into the system and try to plan accordingly." "That's a great suggestion. The thing is, I'm too busy right now with what I am doing to add anything to my already cramped load. No matter how much planning I try to do, it's going to get changed anyway."

And it goes on.

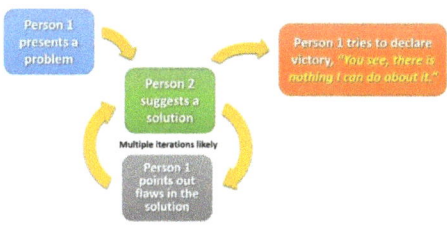

It can be a form of backing away from the Step 1 REALITY that they missed the expectation. You may need to revisit their agreement with REALITY. It can also mean they did not take a good look at the STORY they told. Whatever the reason, they may start playing the game when you try to help them develop a PLAN. The graph above shows the way the game plays out. They believe that providing enough flaws in the proposed PLAN will show they are doing everything possible, but the systems, people, and circumstances are the real issue, NOT THEM.

When you run into this, and you will, it is time to play your "**Manager Card.**"

> *"You know, whenever I suggest something, you find some way it will not work. Since you need to find a better way and increase your self-governance, it's your responsibility to produce and execute a workable plan. I'll expect your plan by tomorrow morning at the latest."*

Use this card sparingly because it is easy to rely on, meaning you are dominating, not leading. But it does need to be used.

Capture the Plan in Writing

An MOT usually does not take long, and the change plan is simple enough for them to tell you what they will do. If the PLAN is more complex or you have had some difficulty with past moments of truth with this person, capture the plan in writing.

Have them write the plan and send it to you.

Manager: "So you are going to spend a little time seeing what this project will take, and you're going to take a step back, look at your entire work schedule, and be more realistic about your process, is that right?"

Employee: "Right."

Manager: "Good. Can you send me an email by Friday that summarizes what we've said, the current pattern, and how we're going to address it so we both have a copy of this talk?"

Employee: "Okay."

Consider this: the written plan gives insight into how they understood the MOT. The emotional conflict may still exist, so they do not think as clearly. They may want to do what is right but wish for the MOT to end. When they write the plan, it can help them clarify it. Additionally, their written version gives you a chance to respond with clarifications.

Finally, this written plan is not for their personnel folder, although sometimes you may need it. Using it to clarify the plan is extremely useful, but most importantly, this shows your resolve to create a change. It shows that you want to see them meet expectations next time, and if the MOT is done well, it demonstrates your desire for them to develop and grow.

Some skills you need in Step 3 are as follows
- Rethink the process
- Identify a similar project
- Picture the plan
- Mentor them with overall insights

Those skills will help you master Step 3—The PLAN.

Step 4—FEEDBACK: Create a Feedback System

Critical Point: Feedback is a process, not a single event. It is a habit, part of being an Overcomer.

The Talk and Plan are NOT Enough

While each step of the moment of truth is helpful, this last step can be critical. Step 1 is about the REALITY of unmet expectations, Step 2 gets the STORY, and Step 3 gets them to create a PLAN.

Now, Step 4 is FEEDBACK. This step is about what you can do to be a resource for them to make the change. Becoming a leader is about being a coach. Leading requires improving your interpersonal skills and your decision to value people enough to develop them.

The first three steps are necessary, and, as I stated earlier, I believe Step 1 alone can create a structure for change. But using all four steps is best.

Getting the STORY about the situation is incredibly good. You both can now see the sequence of events, decisions made, assumptions made, and the level of effort. Having them create a PLAN is extremely helpful because it helps them see that you are committed to the change. It is also their agreement to change.

Now, you can support the need for correction. You need a system to provide a chance for adjustment in REAL time. Multiple meetings may be required, especially if the issue is complex.

Power in this last step

Remember the critical shift every leader must make? You move from doing good work as an individual to doing good work through people. *Overcomers* embrace a consistent approach to feedback. It is best if it becomes a habit rather than just another step in the MOT process.

> *Aristotle says, "Habit differs from disposition in being more lasting and firmly established."*

Feedback is a process, not a single event. That is why it is part of coaching. And it will not happen unless you value people enough to be available when needed.

Skills you need to master in Step 4 are:
- Implement the plan
- Follow-up need not be time-consuming or a big deal
- Follow-up email
- Check for Progress
- Mentor and provide consistent feedback

You now have everything you need to have an MOT with someone. Try it now!

Final INSIGHTS

The following are some great points from Managerial Moment of Truth, pages 157–170.
- Know the Right Time
  - When is the right time for an MOT? When you have time to cover the issues adequately
  - Set the agenda in advance if possible ("The next meeting will address recently missed deadlines.")
  - Choose a time close to the event to cover it while it is fresh
- Be Direct
  - Be clear and straightforward
  - Stay away from strategies that compliment then criticize
  - Those strategies tend to paint you as disingenuous, if, on the receiving end of this conversation, you tend to feel confused or manipulated
- Address Matters Even if Imprecise
  - Make sure you understand precisely what you are addressing
  - Things left vague rather than straightforward make the MOT more difficult
  - When the topic is not precise—discuss it anyway!

- Think Timeliness, Not a Burning Platform
  - The "burning platform" can be used to manipulate people
  - Using a sense of urgency when it does not exist is improper use of the MOT
  - Work toward an understanding of timeliness, getting things done within the proper bounds
- Use MOT to Establish Deadlines
  - Use MOT to help establish deadlines rather than pressuring people into action
  - Deadlines establish real priorities and schedules
  - Use MOT to help people see the bigger picture of the project rather than the "to-do list"
- Work Toward Alignment, Not Just Compliance
  - Establish alignment of individuals and team toward goals
  - Compliance is typically about getting obedience
  - MOT is about personal responsibility, aligning work to the needs of the organization
  - MOT is to help people become self-governing and less about obedience or compliance
- Make It Your Own
  - Do the four steps, but use the form to fit your personality and style
  - Use your experience, personality, and managerial intelligence

That last point is crucial. The more you practice MOT and its structure, the more you can have a simple conversation with someone, but it is an MOT. Make it fit your personality, but do not skip an MOT because you have some emotional conflict.

Rejoice After the Conversation

Rejoice

If the conversation helps them, and they change, it is not because of you. Verses 4 and 5 in Galatians 6 provide some profound insight into how God wants us to think about each moment of truth.

God clearly shows us that a moment of truth is simply about doing what He wants us to do. It is not about being better than others, and it is not about taking credit for helping someone change. It is also not about feeling guilty that someone did not change.

*Galatians 6:3 (NKJV)—For if anyone thinks himself to be
something, when he is nothing, he deceives himself.*

That is a direct reference to you taking the credit instead of giving credit to God for any change that occurred. It also clearly references the PROBLEM in all relationships—thinking about "ME" more than others.

And even if they did not change, God wants you to rejoice. Really? Notice the following verse.

*Galatians 6:4 (NKJV)— . . . rejoicing in
himself alone, and not in another.*

That is not a "ME" flashing, self-absorbed moment. Instead, you did what was right, so you praise God that He is at work in you and thank Him in all things.

*1 Thessalonians 5:18 (NKJV)—in everything giving thanks;
for this the will of God in Christ Jesus for you.*

You have the freedom not to do this, but when you do it, you can rejoice. Your joy is from doing what God wanted, not because they changed. You operate in freedom when your emotions are about pleasing the Lord rather than yourself or others.

Lastly, God reminds you about personal accountability.

Galatians 6:5 (NKJV)—For each one shall bear his own load.

That clearly states that everyone is responsible for their actions, like in Ezekiel, as we see throughout the Bible.

*Ezekiel 18:20 (NKJV)—The soul who sins shall die. The son shall
not bear the guilt of the father, nor the father bear the guilt of
the son. The righteousness of the righteous shall be upon himself,
and the wickedness of the wicked shall be upon himself.*

In this situation, you rejoice for your behavior, and they can rejoice or suffer consequences depending on what they did with the truth shared with them.

Persevere

Finally, keep doing what is right because that is self-governance (self-control) when walking in the Spirit of God (Galatians 5:23). Your self-governance is the life of Christ in you and the Holy Spirit's energy working through you.

Galatians 6:9a (NKJV)—And let us not
grow weary while doing good . . .

Difficult conversations often start the process toward a solution or changed behavior. That means you fulfill the calling of an *Overcomer* and persevere, provide help, and stay available to them as the MOT step 4 asks.

Most situations follow a longer time frame, so hang in there. Do not tire of doing what is right.

Galatians 6:9b (NKJV)— . . . for in due season
we shall reap if we do not lose heart.

You have an unlimited resource to help someone when you are a conduit of God's truth flowing through you.

Rejoice and persevere as you create a culture of truth!

DISCUSSION QUESTIONS

1. How would you explain "Moments of truth are the foundation for a culture of truth?"
2. Explain the benefits of a clean heart, clear expectations, and clear communication.
3. Memorize and explain the definition of a Moment of Truth (MOT).
4. What are the 3 Daily Priorities?
5. Try to link all 6 Critical Values to the 3 Daily Priorities.
6. Try to connect all 5 Essential Capacities to the 3 Daily Priorities.
7. Can you link the 2 Remarkable Skills and 1 Timeless Process to the 3 Daily Priorities?
8. Explain what structure you create when you do not use MOT consistently.
9. What are the two critical parts of the definition of a Catalyst?
10. Why do you need to set clear expectations for an MOT?
11. Which of the 6 Critical Values do you want to verify before you have an MOT?
12. Why do you want to be sure someone has sinned according to God's Word?
13. What is the Law of Christ? How do you fulfill it when you have a Moment of Truth with someone?
14. Memorize and briefly explain each of the four steps of an MOT.
15. What type of question does Step 1 need? Explain.
16. How do you handle excuses from a person?
17. Do you see a relationship between actions and values? Explain.
18. Why might Step 1 help if that is the only MOT step you used?
19. What two skills do you need for Steps 2 and 3? Why?
20. How does problem-solving fit into Step 2?
21. Step 3 is about creating a plan. Why does it need to be their responsibility? Can you help them?
22. What is Step 4 about?
23. Explain the statement ". . . rejoicing in himself alone . . ." in Galatians 6:4.

Chapter 10

The Boiling Point

Dean and Julie have been married for five years. Dean is a CPA, and Julie makes jewelry and sells it online. Both in their mid-thirties, Dean and Julie attend their neighborhood church, which happens to be steeped in solid Bible teaching. Their son Cameron is three years old and a barrel of energy.

Dean's upbringing was emotionally tough. His father was emotionally abusive, favored Dean's older brother, and was unkind to their mother. Dean's father owned a local business in an upscale shopping center in their midwestern town, and his mother did not work outside the home. They did not attend church except at Christmas and Easter.

In contrast, Julie grew up in a loving, peaceful home. No one ever really argued and they laughed a lot. Both her parents worked. Her dad served as a pastor of a small congregation in their small town, and her mom taught math in the middle school. Julie and her younger sister continue to be great friends even though her sister moved away when she got married.

Lately, things at home have been tense. More and more, Dean comes home after work in a bad mood, irritable and exhausted. He works long hours preparing clients' business financial statements, and he has lots of deadlines.

One evening, hungry and tired, he demands, "Julie, why isn't dinner ready?! I'm hungry."

"Oh, hi Dean, Cameron and I played out in the backyard until late, so I had to get him cleaned up, and I just haven't started dinner yet."

"What?" he almost yelled. "This isn't acceptable."

"Well," Julie said in a matter-of-fact tone, "There's nothing I can do about it now. What are you hungry for?"

Impatient, Dean says, "Let's just go out. I don't want to wait for you to cook. I'll be out in the car."

Julie doesn't say anything and gathers up Cameron to go out to eat. Her chest tightens up because this type of scene seems to be happening more and more often. Every day she wonders if Dean's behavior will ever change. He is just so impulsive and emotional.

• • • • •

Six months later, the strain of their marriage has only worsened. Julie and Dean decide to see a marriage counselor. In their first session, Dean says he feels like Julie doesn't "pull her weight" in the household because she just has the little jewelry business that doesn't make much money. He is mad because he had to put himself through college because his dad didn't save money for it, and Julie had her college paid for. He says this is why he's always angry and impatient with Cameron because he didn't have it so easy growing up.

The counselor turns to Julie and asks her how she feels about this. Unable to hold back any longer, she explodes, "Stop blaming me for how you grew up! I had nothing to do with that! I'm sick of you! You are one of the most selfish people I have ever met."

Julie gets so angry she jumps up from her chair and leaves the counselor's office. She calls an Uber and leaves her husband behind at the counselor's office.

Dean looks at the counselor in shock. He has never seen Julie this angry before.

Questions

1. What problems do you see in this marriage?
2. What could Dean change about the way he acts?
3. What could Julie change about the way she acts?
4. Do you think emotions are the problem for Dean and Julie? Why or why not?

OVERCOMERS RENEW THEIR MIND TO TRUTH

Key Lesson: *Your thinking drives your actions and feelings.*
So renew your mind to the truth.

WHICH COMES FIRST?

Feelings

Feelings Will Lie to You

If you would rather live in truth instead of speculation or opinion, then be clear about the interaction of three elements: feelings, thoughts, and actions. The SOLUTION—love—is not emotionless, nor is it emotion-led.

Do you have a favorite scary movie? Maybe the classic film *Psycho*? Mine is the original *Alien,* and even though it is my favorite, I do not like to watch it because it scares me with its special effects and creatures!

Why are you afraid when watching a scary movie? When something frightening happens on the screen, why do you jump? Is it because you are in danger? Of course not—it is just a movie!

Suppose you are watching a scary movie, but you tell yourself, "I am watching a story filmed for entertainment, especially to create fear and excitement. Scenes are created to scare me, but I know that is not happening to me."

That would take all the fun out of the movie, right?

The movie's structure draws you into the story and connects you with the characters. When you remind yourself of reality, you minimize the film's efforts to encourage a fearful response.

There are two important implications. *First*, feelings and emotions are **primarily RESPONDERS**. You respond to the film when you watch a movie and are scared, sad, happy, or crying. Feelings show up as a response to something. *Second*, and most importantly, feelings are **often UNTRUSTWORTHY**. If you can be scared but not in danger (like watching a movie), your emotions are untrustworthy in those situations. Your emotions are real, but they are responding to something unreal. That is why when you tell yourself, "It's just a movie," the emotions are reduced or removed, responding to accurate thinking.

With that in mind, consider the options for three words: Think—Feel—Act. Which sequence do you suppose most people follow? How about you? Like it or not, people typically react and respond like an amoeba—a single-cell organism with little or no thinking ability. Poke it and it will move away. Offer sugar and it will come to you.

Consider the following important scripture passage:

> *Matthew 22:37-40 (NJKV)—Jesus said to him, "'You shall love the Lord your God with all your heart, with all your soul, and with all your mind.' This is the first and great commandment. And the second is like it: 'You shall love your neighbor as yourself.' On these two commandments hang all the Law and the Prophets."*

Which is first in those verses—Thinking, Feeling, or Acting? Everything depends on what "love" is. The construction of the sentence says "love" is a verb; therefore, a decision or action is first. Some say that "love" is a feeling, so their conclusion is God is asking us to act on a feeling.

God is asking you to decide. Review the working definition of love, "Pursuing their best patiently, kindly, sacrificially, and unconditionally." That is a decision! That requires thinking to make a conscious choice. And possibly more importantly, you must read the scripture or have it told you first! The information processing would be first, even if you decided love was a feeling. A reasonable conclusion is that *thinking* is first in those verses.

Before going any further, I think emotions and feelings are great! Correctly understanding emotions allows us to enjoy the highs and lows of life. *Overcomers* understand how their emotions work and use them to help them become more like Jesus.

Feelings Can Create Problems

Feelings will often create problems. Again, it is not that emotions are bad; you will soon hear what is flawed or wrong. Consider these two simple statements:

- Bad can feel good
- Good can feel bad

"Bad can feel good" is easy to prove. You have no doubt experienced feeling good, even excited, as you encounter temptation and sin. But it is followed by an inner conviction that you have done something wrong. That good feeling about doing something bad will always be temporary unless you have a hard heart.

Vengeance is a "bad" that may feel good longer than other sins because your mind is focused on justice and "getting even." Most other sins register quickly with regret or guilt, replacing whatever positive emotion existed. The story of any sin fits the "bad can feel good" statement and is evident in the original sin in the Garden of Eden.

Genesis 3:6–8 (NKJV)—So when the woman saw that the tree was good for food, that it was pleasant to the eyes, and a tree desirable to make one wise, she took of its fruit and ate. She also gave to her husband with her, and he ate. Then the eyes of both of them were opened, and they knew that they were naked; and they sewed fig leaves together and made themselves coverings.

And they heard the sound of the LORD God walking in the garden in the cool of the day, and Adam and his wife hid themselves from the presence of the LORD God among the trees of the garden.

Put yourself in Eve's place and let your emotions follow the story. Eve was swept away by the fruit's appeal—good for food, pleasant to the eyes, could make her wise—so she ate. Apparently, she felt good about eating the fruit, BUT it was terrible.

And to prove it was not good, notice where their feelings go next. "Their eyes were opened . . . knew they were naked . . . hid themselves." Emotions were responding to the reality of what God said would happen.

Most often, the good feelings happen before and during the sin because our desire overrides the conviction of our conscience or the Holy Spirit saying—"Think about this! Do not do it!"

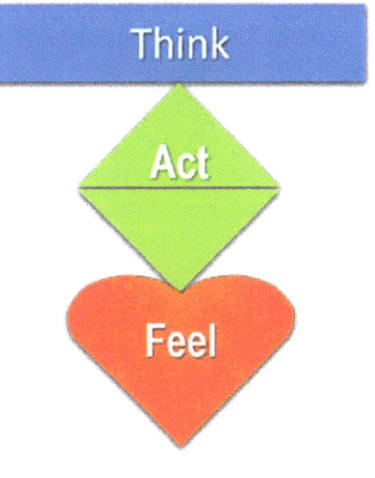

"Good can feel bad" is also real. Consider the emotional conflict you experience when you know a close friend or relative is sinning. You know it is time to speak with them, so you gather your courage but "feel uncomfortable" about doing it and do not follow through. And in those cases where the conversation goes poorly, you experience feelings of regret instead of peace or joy for doing what was right.

A good parent disciplining their child understands that "good can feel bad." Similarly, when a good leader shares the truth with a person because they are not doing a good job, it often does not feel good.

Following your feelings creates an unstable foundation for your life because you are reacting and responding. Your negative emotions indicate that you are in the left circle. (See the Two Circles.)

Consider the following:

**Just because I do right does not mean
I will feel right (at that time).**

**Corollary: Just because I feel right does
not mean I am doing right.**

Acting

Feelings and Behavior

Overcomers know feelings are not the issue because they respond or point to something else. Since feelings are responders, acting or thinking should come first. That makes sense. Ready–fire–aim is not a good option. Acting before thinking can be as bad as "following your heart."

No doubt, thinking belongs at the beginning, so should acting come second or third? There are significant benefits when you act, even when your emotions oppose the action, and you can strengthen your action when emotions are engaged.

What is the connection between feelings and behavior? Do your feelings affect your behavior? Does your behavior impact your feelings?

The answer is yes; both happen. It is easy to see that feelings drive behaviors, but the opposite is also true. For example, researchers have consistently found that people behaving in ways that conflict with their feelings or attitudes will change their feelings to be consistent with their behavior.

Act the Way You Want to Feel

Order or consistency is essential for life and your body. Research shows that if you feel depressed, you can act differently than your feelings to impact the depressed feelings.

> *Isaiah 58:10 (NKJV)—If you extend your soul to the hungry
> and satisfy the afflicted soul, then your light shall dawn in
> the darkness, and your darkness shall be as the noonday.*

When you serve others, your darkness turns to light because you stop focusing on yourself. God wants you to help others, which models His behavior instead of "flashing our ME."

You can experiment with yourself to prove whether actions can alter feelings with a simple technique. Try it the next time you are feeling sad. Three steps—Face, Body, Breathe/Speak. Start with your face. Ask yourself, "How would I like to feel right now?" If you answer "sad," then this three-step technique may not help, but if you answer "happy," "joyful," "peaceful," or other similar words, then put a smile or at least a pleasant expression on your face. Even if you answered "sad," you can still try this.

Next, look at your body. Most likely, your body reflects sadness—slumped shoulders, head down, moving slowly. Change your body to be in a position that demonstrates your chosen emotion. At least sit or stand up straight, with your shoulders back and chin up, and have a good posture. Start moving with more energy.

Finally, think about your breathing and speech. Take some deep breaths and speak with energy and articulation if you need to talk. You will soon see the critical element that makes this technique work.

If you do those three steps, you put your body out of sync with your emotions. So your feelings are sad, but your body is "happy," which leaves you in what researchers call dissonance—emotions and actions are not equal. You have two options—change your feelings to be like your body or your body to be like your emotions. If you let your body remain "happy," you will experience the reality of emotions being responders. They are responding to your actions and, more importantly, to your thinking, which drives your actions.

"But that is just being fake!" That could be the case, but if you decide joy is more critical than sadness or depression, it is not fake—it is being true to your values or priorities. Being depressed is not what you value, the actual "fake" item. This technique can help you to be authentic.

Help Attitudes Change

Behavior can be easier for people to change than an attitude or feeling because it is tangible. If the action is taken consistently, despite the feelings, then feelings will eventually respond.

Changing your feelings through action is somewhat like repairing something broken. The broken pieces need to be realigned and reconnected.

Recently, I needed to repair a wooden chair. Since people would use the chair, I needed to fix it correctly. I aligned the broken pieces, applied glue, clamped the pieces together, and then waited for 24 hours based on the directions on the glue.

After the glue dried, I removed the clamp and saw the two broken pieces were connected and properly realigned. The chair was restored to its intended usefulness.

Actions are like glue, while feelings are like broken pieces. Thinking is the clamp, which keeps the parts aligned while the glue hardens. The thinking component will be discussed later, but for now, consider using actions to help you or others change feelings.

Suppose you have a friend who has a bad attitude toward another person. You could do something like this.

"You've stated that you don't like Joe. Since you are often around him, it would be best to find a way to make the relationship work better than it is now.

Since I know you value kindness, would you be willing to do a small experiment for the next few weeks?

You don't need to become his friend, but would you be willing to smile and offer a pleasant greeting each time you see him during the next month?"

If they say no, you could ask them what they would be willing to do that would honor their value of kindness, then ask if they would be willing to take that action.

Choice and free will are critical! Do not try to convince them to be a better person, shame them into change, or make them do anything. ***You are only calling them to act on their good values***. People will have more energy to perform when they freely act on their values. You can also offer to be an accountability partner, which is often a great help.

People willing to take that action for at least 30 days will see themselves change, even if the other person does not.

Try it on yourself to see if it works.

Thinking

Thinking/Feeling Principle

Which is easiest to change—Thinking or Acting? People often choose acting, but it is thinking. Consider this—thinking about changing your actions precedes the actual actions, right? That does not mean you believe the thinking but act on it anyway.

The more you act consistently with your thinking, the more it will be reinforced, impacting your beliefs and feelings. Life can be simplified when you consider the power of thinking. If you think correctly, it drives good actions and, at some point, good feelings. Unfortunately, if your thinking is flawed, it drives incorrect actions and emotions. What you think is crucial!

Your thinking is the most critical thing in your life—it drives everything you do or feel. What you think about reflects in your actions and feelings. If your thinking about God does not match God's Word, then your thinking is distorted, impacting all areas of your life. Worse yet, you are violating the first commandment.

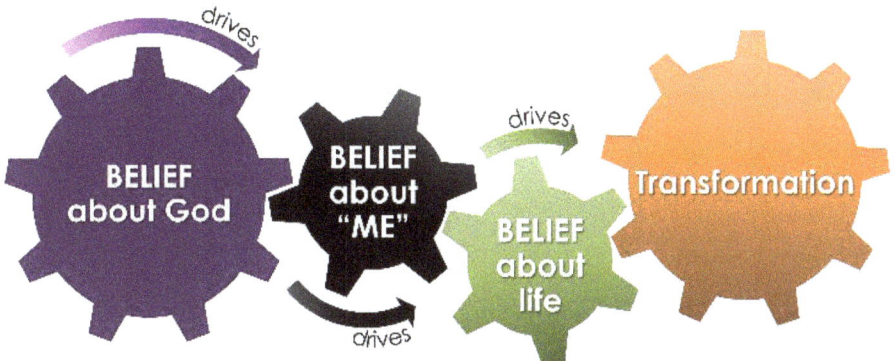

This graphic is critical for an *Overcomer*. It shows the importance of having a proper view of God. Your belief about God is either based on truth or lies. If truth, you understand who He is, who you are, and how life works. Those thoughts transform you into the image of Christ. If lies, you are confused about God, yourself, and life. Therefore, you try to control everything to make you happy.

*Romans 8:6 (NIV)—The mind governed by the flesh is death,
but the mind governed by the Spirit is life and peace.*

Notice that the gears impact each other. If a power source is attached to any gear, that gear will drive the others. If my thinking is about "ME," I alter my thoughts about God, life, and transformation.

Overcomers know the gears work for their best when attaching the power to the "God" gear. That encourages them to learn more about God's ways and desires instead of trying to make God fill their needs.

And please consider this. **Your thinking is the only thing you can control!** You might say, "I can control my actions." Yes, you can because your thinking leads to your actions. You can say, "I can control my attitude and how I see life." You can because thinking about those things creates your attitude and perception. How you think about things becomes your attitude and perspective of life.

The scripture above clearly states that thinking drives you toward life or death. Using life or death shows how critical your thinking is. As seen in many scriptures, what is in your mind is essential. Either renew your mind to God's ways or trust yourself and the world's.

The entirety of God's Word is about changing your thinking to the reality and truth of what God says. If you think things work differently than what God says, one of you is wrong. I am betting that God is right. That is why the Bible

> ...THE MOST CRITICAL THING IN YOUR LIFE IS YOUR THINKING. IT DRIVES EVERYTHING ELSE THAT YOU DO OR FEEL.

constantly refers to the mind. Even passages referring to the heart refer to the "essence of who you are," which is about your thinking.

Two significant passages about thinking are:

> *Romans 12:1-2 (NKJV)—I beseech you therefore, brethren, by the mercies of God, that you present your bodies a living sacrifice, holy, acceptable to God, which is your reasonable service. And do not be conformed to this world, but be transformed by the renewing of your mind, that you may prove what is that good and acceptable and perfect will of God.*

> *Philippians 4:8 (NKJV)—Finally, brethren, whatever things are true, whatever things are noble, whatever things are just, whatever things are pure, whatever things are lovely, whatever things are of good report, if there is any virtue and if there is anything praiseworthy—meditate on these things.*

Your thinking drives your values and beliefs. Your thinking drives who you trust, what you trust, who you respect, and every choice you make. Even if you disagree with the above statement, it is best to recognize that the number of things you can control is minimal.

When it comes to the interaction of thinking, feelings, and actions, it is generally best to

- Think first, then Feel or Act.
- In difficult situations, Think—Act—Feel.

Build a solid foundation of good thinking and good values. Then act based on that foundation. Your feelings will respond—eventually.

Thinking that arises from the sin nature will always focus on satisfying yourself rather than glorifying God. Even if you have studied and practiced good thinking from God's Word, any difficult situation or flawed thinking not subjected to Jesus Christ (2 Corinthians 10:4-5) will follow the sin nature. That is why the Apostle Paul wrote Romans 6, 7, and 8.

Without the power of the Holy Spirit guiding your thinking, your sin nature, which promotes self-seeking thoughts, will introduce **fear, uncertainty, and doubt.** How will this impact me? What is going to happen to my family and me? Satan used that same strategy on Eve—"Has God indeed said . . . ?"

If you do not have a solid foundation in God's Word, specifically that God is PERFECT and will take care of you, then you will be filled with assumptions, speculation, guesses, and opinions, leading to fear.

What Is This?

A Common Pattern for Life Change

Good thinking helps us eliminate the lousy part of a common pattern everyone experiences. This pattern occurs repeatedly, with the outcome of each occurrence leading either to a life that glorifies God or further self-absorption.

We need to determine what THIS is!

The common pattern has three simple statements:

> *"I was living this way. Then one day, THIS happened. Now I live my life differently."*

On closer inspection of many life changes, you will see more detail, which sounds like this:

> *"I was living this way. Then THIS happened . . . it happened again and again and again . . . Then it struck me! I got it! Now, I live my life differently."*

That is the standard form of every testimony you hear at church or any program that helps people change. Multiple examples of this pattern exist in the Bible. One of the more well-known examples is King David in 2 Samuel 11 and 12. There, you can read the story of David and Bathsheba.

A shortened version of the story is David commits adultery with Bathsheba. She later told him she was pregnant. Since her husband, Uriah, was away at war, David arranged for Uriah to come home. That would give time for husband and wife to be together, covering up David's sin. But the plan did not work, so David ordered Uriah to the front of the battle, where he was killed. David then took Bathsheba as his wife to hide the sin.

David did not confess his sin, so God sent Nathan to confront him by telling him a story of a rich man stealing a poor man's sheep. That aroused David's anger to say, "As the Lord lives, the man who has done this shall surely die!" Then Nathan stated, "You are the man!" which awakened David to say, "I have sinned against the Lord."

David could tell us the story with the common pattern.

> *"I was living a life that displeased God—adultery, murder, and unconfessed sin. I made bad choices, allowing my sinful thoughts to lead me rather than doing what was right. I knew it was wrong but did not want to admit it, and I made it worse by trying to cover up my adultery with murder. Then one day, Nathan confronted me with a story that showed how real my sin was. I confessed it to the Lord and experienced the consequences of my sin with my son's death. Now I focus on walking with the Lord, and when I sin, confess it as soon as I know it."*

God called David ". . . a man after His own heart . . ." How could that be when God knew that David would commit such horrible sins? I believe it was because David believed and trusted God first, and when he sinned, he confessed it. That is a person desiring to please God—a man after God's heart.

Options for Change

Since the pattern is valid, the middle part, "THIS happened," is the critical element. The THIS in David's story is when Nathan confronts him, but that is just one way THIS shows up.

Consider three examples from my life.

Category	Former Belief	Current Belief
• Spiritual	• Going to heaven is all that is important	• I will be judged. Eternal rewards are real
• Career	• Climb the corporate ladder	• Work to your strengths
• Social	• I am mostly self-sufficient	• Relationships are critical

I believed in God's desire to conform me to His image, but despite that, I did not understand the connection of this life to life in the kingdom. I thought only going to heaven was important. Now, because I understand Scripture better, my thinking has changed. While going to heaven is especially important, it is not the end of the story. I will also be judged, and eternal rewards (or loss of rewards) are real. This life is an apprenticeship for being a servant king in God's Kingdom.

Another former belief about work and career was climbing the corporate ladder in an organization. That changed to working to my strengths to be most effective for the organization.

Yet another change I have had is social: I used to believe in self-sufficiency, but now I believe that relationships are critical.

Take a minute to think about your life. Consider the categories in the table above, think about what you believe now, and reflect on what you used to believe.

What happened that moved you to change? What THIS happened?

One thing most likely occurred: you adopted different thinking. So consider this great principle.

If people are changed, they are mainly changed because their thinking has changed.

Notice how that statement fits the scripture below.

> *Acts 19:18-20 (NKJV)—And many who had believed came confessing and telling their deeds. Also, many of those who had practiced magic brought their books together and burned them in the sight of all. And they counted up the value of them, and it totaled fifty thousand pieces of silver. So the word of the Lord grew mightily and prevailed.*

Before they knew Christ, they thought magic was the answer. Now that they believe in Christ, they burned an absolute fortune in books about magic.

Why? Their thinking had changed! Their common pattern could have been, "My life depended on whether I had the right magic or potion to make life better. Now that I believe in Christ, I burned my magic books and believe He is the answer." Their life was radically changed, so much that they burned what they used to consider a treasure.

Change can follow three options: get better, stay the same, or get worse. A "Change Table" would be:

Options	Better	Same	Worse
Believe a truth	Believe another truth	Believe the same truth	Believe a lie
Believe a lie	Believe a truth	Believe the same lie	Believe another lie

What is evident about the BETTER column?

Right, it involves believing TRUTH!

Truth is imperative for a "better" life. When lives change for the better, truth is involved somewhere. "Better" in this context does not mean winning the lottery. It can be better for some if they have the correct thinking about stewardship, but it creates a nightmare for most. So "better" is defined as a life that becomes more closely aligned with God's prescription.

Truth is always required to become aligned with God. Consider the definition of truth: "the quality of being true, genuine, actual, or factual; a proven or verified principle or statement; fact."

Let me introduce another word to consider—REALITY. The definition of reality is "an actual fact, the quality or state of being real."

While those definitions are not identical, they show remarkable similarities. Believing truth means seeing what is actual, genuine, and factual. Believing reality is seeing objectively and factually. Lies are real, but the content of the lie leads to what is not true and factual. Truth can be difficult to accept, and reality is often an acquired taste, but both are worth seeking despite any unpleasantness they may create.

By the way, the phrase "perception is reality" is invalid. Reality does not change because we perceive it differently. The phrase is correct if used from the view that people think their perception is reality, but reality does not care about our perception; it is what it is.

Reality and Change

We can build on the earlier statement with truth and reality in mind.

**We seldom change for the better unless we
accept and act on truth or reality.**

What reality/truth are you not applying to your life? Are you willing to ask others for their input? Consider the following as a starter kit to reflect on changes in your life.

- Health/exercise/food/weight
- Financial stewardship/saving/spending/investing
- Prayer life/Bible study

If you took one item and saw its truth or reality, you would have a great chance to make a change. Assume it is your spending. You are not treating God's money as His. You are acting like it is yours (*I was living this way*). Truth or reality is accepted, or you ignore it and act like the money is yours. Your life is better, the same, or worse (*Now I live this way*). See the pattern?

The Critical Element

So what is THIS? It is one of two things:
- Truth and Reality or
- Lies, Deception, and Bad Assumptions

You will know which as you look at where your life goes from that point or get someone to review your decision compared to God's Word.

Lies and deception lead to unexpected consequences, regrets, grief, and even slavery, like addictions. You end up just like Adam and Eve in the Garden of Eden, wondering how things got this way. Deception always looks like something good but ends up bad. For King David, it seemed so right to be with Bathsheba. He rationalized it to be right so much that he had Uriah killed.

It seems so right, just like Eve's statement about the tree.

> Genesis 3:6 (NKJV)—So when the woman saw that the tree was good for food, that it was pleasant to the eyes, and a tree desirable to make one wise, she took of its fruit and ate. She also gave to her husband with her, and he ate.

But there were unexpected consequences.

> Genesis 3:7 (NKJV)—Then the eyes of both of them were opened, and they knew they were naked; and they sewed fig leaves together and made themselves coverings.

Truth or Reality is just the opposite. It often does not look easy. Flawed thinking driving your emotions will tell you it is the wrong way. But if chosen, there are rewards, wisdom, and freedom, which are also largely unexpected.

A good example from my life is when our authorities asked Louie and me to tell the church about our marital problems. I was an Elder in the church, and Louie was the teaching director of a prominent women's Bible study in the community. We were asked to stand before both assemblies and reveal our sins because we were leaders.

We did not want to do that, and our emotions did not support it either. We could only see the humiliation of others knowing the truth about us.

We eventually experienced the massive benefit of not wasting energy trying to hide what had happened. It was in the open, and all that wanted to know could know. It was also a great blessing to restore our marriage because it put Louie and me together, equally blamable, and together as broken human beings.

Even though brutal, that one action was a critical part of providing a faster path to restoration and healing for Louie and me. It was also a crucial element in creating the material in this book.

Reality or truth provides largely unexpected rewards, wisdom, and freedom!!

> *If you look for truth, you may find comfort in the end; if you look for comfort you will not get either comfort or truth—only soft soap and wishful thinking to begin, and in the end, despair. —C.S. Lewis*

It is your choice.

> *Hebrews 3:13 (NKJV)— . . . but exhort one another daily, while it is called "Today," lest any of you be hardened through the deceitfulness of sin.*

The Lord is dedicated to your growth. What are you leaving unchanged, even though it is repeatedly brought to your attention? You have two options: you will make the change or not.

That is why you need to use "Opposites," which you will learn about shortly.

Simple Tools for Better Thinking

Slow Your Emotions (Thinking) Down

Many situations will stimulate your emotions in some way. It can be anything from a near-miss collision with another car, lies being told about you, or a temptation to sin. Whatever it is, something happens and it stimulates your feelings. Your flesh is ready to act.

You have a choice at that moment, but you seldom realize it. Follow the Holy Spirit or your emotions, which may be following your sin nature and flawed thinking. Too often, you do not see a choice; you only react.

That reaction is often from significant events stored in a portion of your brain called the amygdala—two small lobes in the base of the brain, one on the right and the other on the left. The amygdala does not store memories with a time stamp. Therefore, what is stored can be seen as relevant now, even though it is not. When a current stimulus is similar to a previously stored memory, the amygdala prepares your body to react or respond according to that stored memory.

For example, when I was about eight years old, I can remember being bitten by what appeared to be a friendly dog. I was petting the dog, and suddenly, it bit me. I have had numerous experiences with dogs since then, but that memory still creates some caution, especially if I do not know the dog.

Tests of people's brains using MRI (Magnetic Resonance Imaging) show that when a person's amygdala is activated, the connections with the frontal lobe, the "reasoning" part of the brain, are bypassed, and the person responds according to the memories stored.

But when the person was asked to take three deep breaths, that tiny bit of time allowed the connections to be restored to the frontal lobe, allowing rational thought instead of reaction.

Slowing your emotions is calling yourself back to good thinking. It allows you to reflect on what is right. Hopefully, you have been in God's Word and under good biblical teaching so that you can consider Godly principles, Christ-like values, and truth. If you do not have a foundation of good values, then slowing your thinking may only delay the reaction. But having a good foundation allows you to think about and act on Godly principles, truth, and virtues. Eventually, emotions or feelings will follow your thinking, whether good or bad.

Simple, right? That is what you were taught as a child, right? Count to ten, or take a deep breath—those things help you renew your mind to good thinking. What you were taught is correct, and it works.

Magic Question

Another great tool is the "***Magic Question***." This technique has been used successfully for years.

1. Identify a person's issue or problem.
2. Have them rate where they are now with that problem using a 1-10 scale, where 10 is feeling great, and 1 is feeling awful.
3. State, "We only want to move up the scale 1/2 or 1 point."
4. Discuss why that is so important (prevents becoming overwhelmed, progressing in small steps).
5. Ask the MAGIC QUESTION.
   - "Suppose a miracle occurred tonight while you were asleep, and your problem disappeared—no more pain. Since you were sleeping, you did not know that. When you woke up, you noticed some things were different. **What small signs would tell you that the problem is solved?**"
   - The small signs are often the steps they could take now to help.
6. Help them find the small steps to move up the scale ½ or 1 point.

A dramatic example of using this process was a couple who was moving toward divorce. The wife had filed the papers, but due to Louie's friendship with her, she agreed to come to talk.

She and her husband came to our house, and after two hours of going through the basics of GR8 Relationships (forgiveness, confession, freedom . . .), there were signs of hope, so we asked the wife the Magic Question.

After some discussion, she decided these three things would indicate a change.

- She would hug him in the morning when she first saw him.
- She would make him coffee and breakfast if he wanted it.
- She would kiss him goodbye when he left for work.

Once she identified those three small items, I asked. "Would you be willing to do that consistently every day for the next 30 days and see what happens?" After some hesitation, she replied, "Yes."

God's grace eventually stopped the divorce, and the marriage was restored. They also supported their marriage by learning about what God desires for marriage.

Again, these techniques are not what creates the change. They help catalyze the change but are not the reason a couple stops a divorce or why couples start enjoying their relationship and practicing love, freedom, and kindness.

People change because their thinking changes.

Pre-decide

What happens when you do not think and weigh your options? You tend to react and respond. But it is worse than you think. Depending on the situation, you may push your values aside, especially if the temptation is strong. For example, research shows that men with good values toward women and then see pornographic images of women often select lower, immoral, and even illegal actions toward women as they view them.

Those situations let you know if your values or good thinking have become part of you rather than just part of your speech. **Difficult situations show your character. Actions show character, not words.**

An excellent way to prepare for many life situations is to pre-decide. List various temptations or situations where you know you are weakest. Study and reflect on God's Word related to those situations, and then *pre-decide* **to trust God's way by the power of the Holy Spirit** within you.

Immerse yourself in God's Word; meditating on what He says is the best way to live. Mediate on the fruit of the Spirit—love, joy, peace, patience, kindness, goodness, gentleness, faithfulness, and self-control.

Then listen to God about decisions you can make now to display more of that fruit in your life.

And the simplest of all—will this bring glory to God? That is an excellent foundation for good decisions.

Finally, remember the power of deciding *for,* not just *against,* something. Identifying something to remove from your life creates rebellion because you see that as losing some of your freedom. While *stopping* bad habits and wrong thinking is essential, it is **critical** to ***start*** living differently, focusing on adding the fruit of the Spirit or those things that are ". . . pure, just, lovely and true . . ." (Philippians 4:8) into your life.

Discussion Questions

1. What two phrases do you need to remember about feelings?
2. Provide an example showing you can control your feelings or emotions.
3. Can your example be used to support the two phrases? If not, find one that will.
4. Find examples in the Bible for each of these two statements: Bad can feel good; Good can feel bad.
5. What is a crucial action to take when feeling depressed? What verse can you use to support that?
6. What is the point of talking about "Act the Way You Want to Feel?"
7. Explain why the book states, "The most important thing in your life is your thinking."
8. Memorize the statement about God, self, and life.
9. Memorize the Thinking/Feeling Principle and explain it.
10. What is the Common Pattern for Life Change? Simple form and detailed form.
11. What word has a similar meaning as truth? Why is that important to know?
12. What is "THIS" in the Common Pattern?
13. How can you actually "Slow your emotions down"?
14. What does "pre-decide" mean? How does it work?

Chapter 11

Freedom?

Susan and Ed are in their mid-40s and have four teenagers. The oldest is Ed Jr. He is 19 and in his first year of college. The others are in high school and middle school. —

Ed provides well for his family as a director at a Fortune 500 company. This made it easy for Susan to quit her corporate job 10 years ago and homeschool the kids.

Ed Jr. excelled in his studies. As a homeschooler, he was always academically ahead of his friends who attended public school. His parents encouraged this by giving him a financial reward for good grades. Ed always wanted to please his parents, so he was very involved in the high school youth group at church. Ed also excelled in track and won some awards for his running at track meets. He led a Bible study at their home his senior year and always did more than his fair share of chores around the house.

Ed Jr.'s dad always said with a chuckle, "There's no free rent around here."

When Ed Jr. went off to college, he decided not to play sports. He convinced his parents that he was tired of the rigor of getting up at 5:00 am every morning to go run around the track or run through the neighborhood. When he enrolled in classes, he only signed up for 12 hours to make it easy on himself. None of his friends in the dorm went to church. One Friday night, they were sitting around the dorm. Some of the guys had a beer in hand, and some drank soda.

One of the guys in the group teased Ed Jr about getting up to go to church. "Hey, Eddie, why don't you just sleep in on Sunday? Your mom and dad will never know about it. I won't tell 'em," he said with a laugh. The rest of the people in the room laughed. Ed felt a wry smile cross his face.

On Sunday, he decided to hang out at the dorm and miss church. He thought to himself, *I really like this freedom. Nobody is watching to see what I do, and my little brother and sisters are not around to tell on me.*

Ed relished his freedom and sometimes skipped class. He bragged to one of his friends, "I don't need to go listen to boring lectures. I made great grades being homeschooled and was always ahead of my friends who went to public school."

One Friday night, he decided to join the guys for a beer. Pretty soon, he was drinking beer every night. He lost track of how far behind he was in his studies. Finally, when finals came around, he didn't study that much because he figured he could at least get a 3.0 grade point average. He ended up with a 2.8 grade average for the semester. He thought to himself, *My parents won't like this, But hey, at least I'm free.*

Questions

1. Is Ed Jr. really free, as he keeps saying to himself?
2. How do you think his life growing up might have impacted his first semester at college?
3. How could his first semester at college impact his relationship with his parents?
4. How might his actions in his first semester impact his relationship with God?

OVERCOMERS UNDERSTAND FREEDOM AND LOVE

Key Lesson: *When control (manipulation or domination) is in a relationship, at some point, the relationship will become intolerable.*

FREEDOM IS POWERFUL

Imagine a large dog trotting eagerly toward the house, tongue hanging out of his mouth, anticipating dinner. He has been out chasing rabbits and has worked up quite an appetite.

But as he approaches the porch where his food bowl sits, he slows to a halt.

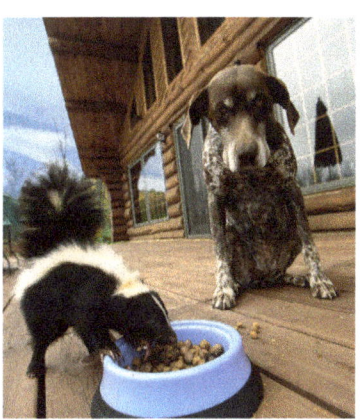

He sees a black-and-white-striped creature with a fluffy tail eating his food! There it is, munching away, thieving nose buried deep in the bowl. The dog slowly comes nearer, careful not to disturb the little thief. The food is tantalizingly near. He can smell it and even see crumbs flying out of the bowl.

He is at least ten times bigger than the skunk and could make it leave. However, he is wise and patient because he knows it is best to leave the skunk alone. After all, it is not worth putting up with the smell.

Overcomers understand that freedom and choice, even irresponsible freedom and bad choices, are part of life. When someone is not doing what you want, manipulating or dominating to get them to change may seem right, but it is wrong.

Freedom Defined

Freedom, used correctly, works flawlessly with love and other critical values. Misused, you ignore or elevate it above love. It can transform your emotions for any action from dread to doing, maybe even delightful doing. That is the massive benefit of freedom and choice.

Definitions are essential for clarity and learning, so here are two from Webster's Dictionary:

- **Freedom**—Absence of necessity, coercion, or constraint in choice or action; independence; quality of being frank, open, or outspoken
- **Free**—Not subject to the control or domination of another; not determined by anything beyond its own nature or being; choosing or capable of choosing for itself

Here is something easier to remember:

> FREEDOM — acting without force or manipulation (or acting without controlling or being controlled)

Freedom Is Real

Freedom is about the reality of your choices instead of controlling or being controlled.

Overcomers accept the critical truth that everyone can make their own choices and are responsible for them. When you choose freedom, it applies to you and those around you. You are free, and so are they. When you understand freedom, you know there is an interplay between freedom and control because both are part of life. Unfortunately, the opponents of freedom choose control because they argue freedom will be misused if broadly applied. That encourages manipulation, domination, and devaluation of people. Freedom offers a better path.

Freedom is the best lifestyle because that is God's example. However, freedom is difficult to grasp and apply, especially for relationships. For example, a husband is frustrated with his wife spending money and says, "I can't take it anymore. I'm leaving." If you asked him if he chose to leave, he would probably say yes. But think about it. Is he saying he could stay or go, and he decided to go? Probably not! He is essentially saying that he must leave because of what she is doing—how she is living her life. He sees no other options. He feels forced into leaving or even divorcing because of her actions. But the reality is, he could choose to stay.

Freedom Is Radically Different

As simple as it may sound, freedom used correctly is a ***radically different way to relate and live***. Unless you accept the reality of freedom and choice, you will react to and be controlled by

> *"Nothing is more wonderful than the art of being free, but nothing is harder to learn how to use than freedom."*
> — Alexis de Tocqueville, Democracy in America

situations like a mouse to cheese. And just as important, you forget that other people have choices, too. When you forget or ignore their freedom, you will try to force or manipulate others to choose what you want.

For example, a wife does not want her husband to make bad decisions! She thinks complaining about each lousy decision multiple times will cause him to do better. She becomes more forceful when he ignores or refuses to accept her input. Why? She wants to prevent his mistakes because those mistakes hurt her, too. That is what makes sense to her—and most people!

But freedom helps her see choices instead of trying to control him. She could offer her insight without complaining when he does not accept it. More problematic, she could keep "I told you so" out of her conversation when his decision creates difficulties for them. That would be like God's option in 1 Peter 3:1: choosing to remain silent is **a no-words strategy!** Unfortunately, even though it is God's Word, it is often ignored or considered a bad strategy.

Why are those options not considered? FEAR! She makes life about herself—her ME starts flashing, driven by the possibility or probability of bad things happening. Control seems to be the only reasonable option; otherwise, bad things will happen unless she steps in.

That is a common issue in relationships! But God asks us to relate to one another differently.

Freedom Is Responsible or Irresponsible

As a Christian, you are entirely free, but that was not always true. You were born with a nature enslaved to sin (Ephesians 2:1) that does nothing good (Romans 3:12).

> John 8:34 (NKJV)—Jesus answered them, "Truly, truly, I say to you, everyone who commits sin is a slave to sin.

But our glorious Savior, Jesus Christ, gave us, His children, a new nature free to choose what is good by His power and grace or what is wrong! Christ died for us to FREE us.

> Galatians 5:1 (NKJV)—Stand fast therefore in the liberty by which Christ has made us free, and do not be entangled again with a yoke of bondage.

What a great verse. Your salvation unchained you from sin and set you free! When used responsibly, freedom helps you see others differently—it changes your focus on others and yourself.

When responsible with your freedom, you see others as having their own choices. It does not mean you like or even put up with those choices, but you know they can choose whatever they want. And whatever their choice, good or bad, it does not control you to try to make them change. You can offer thoughts and ideas for them to consider, tell them the pros and cons of their choice, let them experience the consequences of bad decisions, and help them recover if they want your help.

That may sound like you disconnect from other people. In a sense, that is true. You detach from their behavior by controlling your thoughts about them, but not from your desire to hope, pray, and encourage them to better behavior and choices. You may even exhort and rebuke them, but be careful to walk with the Spirit of God in those conversations; otherwise, there is a marked tendency to sin.

Instead of treating people as machines with buttons to manipulate, you respect their freedom to choose and be responsible for their decisions. It is God's job to change them, not yours. You are more than willing to participate with God in helping them, but you do not become the "Junior Holy Spirit" in their life.

Responsible freedom impacts your thoughts and behavior also. You see more clearly how many options and choices you have rather than thinking you are powerless.

Without that insight, you miss how much freedom you have, turning yourself into a victim, controlled by life, circumstances, and people. Anyone and anything becomes a candidate to control you. But living in freedom, you **refuse** those candidates and choose the *Overcomer* path, a life based on values rooted in God's Word. There, you find your pleasure in doing right, not trying to force yourself or others to do right.

Unfortunately, because of your sin nature, you will use freedom irresponsibly. One massive misuse of freedom is when you fear *others will be irresponsible with their freedom*. That encourages you to try to limit their freedom. Indeed, it has a proper place and time, as you saw earlier with the Freedom V, but please do not set that as your standard.

In the same chapter where God tells you that He sent His Son to die for you to set you free, He tells you not to use your freedom irresponsibly.

> *Galatians 5:13 (NKJV)—For you, brethren, have been*
> *called to liberty; only do not use liberty as an opportunity*
> *for the flesh, but through love serve one another.*

God urges responsible, not irresponsible, freedom.

> *I Peter 2:15-16 (NKJV)—For this is the will of God, that*
> *by doing good you may put to silence the ignorance*
> *of foolish men—as free, yet not using liberty as a*
> *cloak for vice, but as bondservants of God.*

Freedom is often hard to accept, not as much for yourself, but for others. You may push to maximize your freedom while minimizing others' freedom. It is like saying, "We cannot allow freedom for people! If we do, they will be irresponsible and sin even more!"

That is what the Apostle Paul's critics were arguing. He responded to them in Romans 6:1-2 (NKJV), saying:

> *What shall we say then? Shall we continue in sin*
> *that grace may abound? Certainly not! How shall*
> *we who died to sin live any longer in it?*

Have you ever thought about this reality—you can sin all you want! *Overcomers* know the ugliness of that thought, but it is true based on experience. While those sins do not take away your adoption into God's family, they inhibit your growth as an *Overcomer* and, ultimately, your eternal inheritance. Worse yet, your sins imply the death, burial, and resurrection of Christ were not a big deal even though it is the greatest gift of all time and eternity. But you are still free to do just that! It is an irresponsible use of the freedom that God gave you.

Responsible and irresponsible freedom is the difference between what you **can** do and what God invites and encourages you to do. It is the difference between can and will, between the possible and the beneficial. While freedom allows you to sin, it does not condone sin or bad choices. Paul is clear about that.

You can do whatever you want. You are free to do it. But why would you? Once dead and now alive in Christ, why would you want to walk as though you were still dead? This verse points you back to the fundamental choice in life—depend on God or something else.

> *Romans 6:13-14 (NKJV)—And do not present your members as*
> *instruments of unrighteousness to sin, but present yourselves*
> *to God as being alive from the dead, and your members as*
> *instruments of righteousness to God. For sin shall not have*
> *dominion over you, for you are not under law but under grace.*

What is your choice—righteousness or unrighteousness?

Freedom Is Divine

God is THE model for how to use freedom responsibly. Consider a few statements about God. He is the only one with complete control, sovereignty, and power. Everything that happens is part of His perfect plan.

> *Proverbs 16:33 (NKJV)—The lot is cast into the*
> *lap, but its every decision is from the LORD.*

*Proverbs 16:9 (NKJV)—A man's heart plans his
way, but the LORD directs his steps.*

*Proverbs 30:4 (NKJV)—Who has ascended into heaven,
or descended? Who has gathered the wind in His
fists? Who has bound the waters in a garment? Who
has established all the ends of the earth? What is His
name, and what is His Son's name, if you know?*

He could make us do what He wants, but He models responsible freedom in His relationships. On the other hand, we are weak, foolish sheep!

Isaiah 53:6 (NKJV)—All we like sheep have gone astray . . .

We have limited power, yet we try to manipulate or dominate others to get what we want. Notice the irony. God allows freedom, but we try to control (manipulate or dominate). **God can control but does not— we cannot control but tirelessly try.** Freedom is divine! When you are responsible with your freedom, you act like God.

God does not force you to do what is right. He does not make you glorify Him, even though He deserves all glory. Nor does He act as a dictator. He offers a better way and gives energy through His Holy Spirit to live that better way.

He also allows you to ignore what is right and choose to sin! But He never leaves or ignores you. He draws you gently through His love and truth, urging you to make wise choices, desiring eager obedience because that glorifies Him and gives you life! What a great model for you to imitate in your relationships. Your relationships would blossom if you related to others how God relates to you!

Consider this:

*When control (manipulation or domination) is in a relationship,
at some point, that relationship will become intolerable.*

Everyone has freedom built in. When you recognize someone is controlling you, you want to get away. But if you try to control them, you believe it is for their best—and it may be. But that most often turns into rebellion instead of better behavior. Control works against most relationships. God's freedom model works best.

Since God, who is perfect, allows freedom, why deny it in your relationships? You can accept their freedom instead of trying to manipulate and dominate. Please trust that God can do a much better job in their life than you ever could.

Yes, control is required, but consider the power of freedom and stop making control your primary approach. The Freedom V helps you combine freedom and control because both are necessary.

Try this question to help you overcome. *Where is my life not reflecting the fruit of the Spirit?*

That is a powerful freedom question because it focuses on your behavior, doing what is right, and leaving others to God. Being an expert on other people's walk with the Lord is easy! However, freedom focuses attention on your behavior more than theirs. God has given you freedom— use it responsibly (Galatians 5:13). Stop controlling others and start hoping, praying, encouraging, and sometimes exhorting and rebuking. Pursue their best patiently, kindly, sacrificially, and unconditionally.

Control Is Common

Do You Feel Obligated—You Have to Do It?

Whenever you feel obligated, you limit your choices. If you pay attention to what you say, you will notice your use of three words— should, ought, and must. Those words are an excellent sign that you are turning even good commitments into obligations. For example, your marriage vows are a commitment. Are they a choice or an obligation? Do you have to stay married or want to stay married? How about obedience to God? Do you have to obey God, or do you want to? Do you have to love others, or do you want to?

- Obligation de-energizes you—when you no longer see a choice. It makes you complain that you should, ought to, must do it, or have to do it. You "roll your eyes" when you think about it. You do not want to start, so it keeps you busy with other things or in bed in the morning. You end up reacting and responding instead of choosing.
- Obligation removes freedom—when you no longer can see a choice. It is sad that past promises made, even important ones, can become an obligation. Great goals that you set can become an obligation. Any free choice can become a "have to do" obligation.
- Obligation derails commitments—when you no longer can see a choice. Like great goals, the commitments you swore to or solemnly chose can become an obligation. Your former "want to" has now become a "have to," which blocks any sense of choice you have. Then to make matters worse, commitment and obligation are now used to manipulate ourselves into compliance.

For example, your marriage vows are a commitment. Are they a choice or an obligation? Do you have to stay married or want to stay married? How about obedience to God? Do you have to obey God, or do you want to? Do you have to love others, or do you want to?

Commitments are good, but to benefit from them, remember them as a choice. When you focus on a commitment, you seldom remember you are still free, which causes your sense of choice to vanish. "Yes, I chose to commit to this. I can back because I am free to do that, but I choose to follow through."

Second, obligation or "should, ought, must" encourage rebellion. Freedom is in the DNA of every person who has lived or will live. Remember what God said to Adam in the Garden of Eden?

> Genesis 2:16-17 (NKJV)—And the LORD God commanded the man, saying, "Of every tree of the garden you may freely eat; but of the tree of the knowledge of good and evil you shall not eat, for in the day that you eat of it you shall surely die."

God's first command shows He created Adam and Eve with the ability to choose, implying freedom. That is why control creates a structure of rebellion. You can get results through force and fear, but it will not work long-term. People often comply when you introduce control into a system. The problem is that they will tend to do the minimum and no more.

When you tell yourself you "should, ought, or must," you encourage a rebellious heart. That is why Jesus died to set us free. He gave you the freedom to follow Him or not. How about relating to others the same way?

Finally, obligation creates fiction. Obligation is the opposite of freedom, choice, and want.

- Choice means you can "do something" or "not do it"; there is no compulsion for one option.
- Obligation means you must do it; you cannot get out of it, de-energizing, draining.

See if you notice a difference in how you think and feel when you read the following sentences out loud.

- I have to do what is right.
- I want to do what is right.

The two sentences are vastly different. You do not have to do what is right. You have a choice. If you think you do not have a choice, you believe a lie!

*The reality—you are free to choose; you create
fiction thinking there is no choice.*

Do you love people because you "have to" or "want to?" Big difference, right?

Do You Accept That Others Are Free?

Now that you are learning more about freedom, you have another difficult question to answer. *Do you accept that people are free to act however they want?*

(We will discuss clear examples and great reasons to limit others' freedom later. For now, please entertain the thought that you may actually or mentally deny others' freedom.)

When learning about freedom, you may hear yourself say, "I am giving them freedom." However, do you give people freedom?

You may not understand a fundamental element of freedom. You can only give someone freedom when it is in your control. For example, you can give someone a goal to achieve, unlock their jail door, or give them your automobile keys to use your car.

But that does not give them freedom in the way we discuss it. **People are already free to act in any way they want**. That is not something you give—but something you **ACCEPT** is true.

Second, you may not realize how much you try to control others. These questions may help. Are you mad at them without telling them? Are you discouraged, angry, depressed, or resentful when "They just don't get it"? Are their poor values, bad decisions, or flawed thinking causing you to worry and fret? Perhaps you think, "They don't realize how bad 'that' is and what 'that' does to them, the kids, and others (and ME)! Or "If they don't get this corrected, [insert something terrible] will happen to them (and reflect on me)!"

That thinking denies the reality of their freedom to misbehave, even sin, and experience the consequences. Of course, that is why you are trying to limit their freedom, so they will not experience the consequences. And too often, you want to control others' lives for the wrong reason. *If they change, you can relax and be happy—at least for a while.*

Finally, you may claim, "I'm only concerned. Isn't that okay?"

"Yes" would be supported if you see sin in another person's life and do not want them to experience the consequences. If that is the case, you hope, pray, encourage, and perhaps exhort and rebuke. You do those things because God asks you to "speak the truth in love" (Ephesians 4:15). You are not trying to be the Jr. Holy Spirit—you do it because it is pursuing their best.

"No" would be where you feel compelled to *make* them change. That means their behavior controls you. You are in the Left Circle. You may have the right motive, hoping they change not to experience the consequences of the sin, but you see their change as your responsibility—not God's and theirs. Be careful and be objective. Your ME flashing will remove objectivity every time.

Satan and your sin nature can distort the beauty of grace and freedom. Please do not let that happen.

Are You a Good Person Up to No Good?

Control people are typically "good people up to no good." It has created severe damage in all my relationships and is a tricky issue for most people. Practicing freedom is seldom easy but becomes easier once you see the benefits.

If you have good intentions for controlling, you may wonder—since people are free, will they care for themselves? Will they make wise choices? Will they be responsible? If they are irresponsible, how might that hurt me? Can I trust they will make good decisions when they are not as discerning as me? How often will I need to step in and prevent them from making bad choices?

On the other hand, if your intentions are wrong, your questions are different. Will their freedom interfere with what I want? Will they work against me or with me? How can I neutralize or eliminate those who will not do what I want? How much pressure or pain will I need to induce to make them do what I want?

While many people have bad intentions, I speculate that control people tend to have good intentions—GOOD PEOPLE UP TO NO GOOD. They fear bad things will happen if freedom is allowed; therefore, control kicks in—manipulate or dominate—to prevent those bad things. Control people see potential danger in most situations. If others do not agree, they think, "Why don't others see how dangerous things are? They think that it is fun, but it is dangerous. They must not be very smart. They need protection and my help for their good."

> *Of all tyrannies a tyranny sincerely exercised for the good*
> *of its victims may be the most oppressive.*—C.S. Lewis

You may be a control person with good intentions, but it does not matter—it damages relationships. Protection requires rules and regulations. Your fear discounts input from others because they are not knowledgeable enough to see the danger. That puts you on defense, defending yourself and everyone from "potential dangers." Disagreements are often seen as personal attacks because "I know what is right, you don't. Why are you attacking me when I only want what is best for you?" It takes substantial energy to be a control person because people can mess things up or get into trouble in many ways!

They may tolerate your control (manipulating or dominating) for a while, but it will become miserable and intolerable for them. Consider their side, being controlled. They will seldom cheerfully go along with you—instead, they create counter strategies to establish their freedom. Sometimes their strategy would be to counter-control, like altogether avoiding the relationship to maintain their autonomy or independence.

> *If you want total security, go to prison. There you're fed, clothed, given medical care and so on. The only thing lacking . . . is freedom.—Dwight D. Eisenhower*

There is also a downside for you as a control person; you are often the biggest target of your control strategy. You will worry, obsess, warn, criticize, and work hard to keep yourself in line.

You may love and cheer for freedom as a value, but your actions show that you see it as a threat when others have it. "They will not be responsible with their freedom and, therefore, bad things will happen." That drives you to react to imagined danger, devaluing their freedom. If you decide to control, it *will* hurt your relationships.

Are other people really free? Yes, they are, but your actions show if you believe it.

> *You cannot build character and courage by taking away a man's initiative and independence. —Abraham Lincoln*

How to Increase Freedom, Reduce Control

Control people can change! You can stop trying to get everyone to live the way you want. You can lighten your burden and remove the load you have placed on those around you and yourself. However, it only happens when you practice freedom. *Overcomers* primarily trust in the power of the Holy Spirit to practice freedom. They also know these tools can be helpful.

Ask, "Is my fear real or imaginary?"

Please memorize the statement to the right. When you have the urge to control, you think WILL instead of MAY; in other words, it WILL

IMAGINARY fears refuse to use "MAY" for unknown outcomes

happen! That drives more energy to prove the "fact" that bad things WILL happen. The problem with control people is seeing the difference between real and imaginary dangers.

How can you know if fear is imaginary? The answer comes from considering time. Control people see current behaviors and forecast future results of the behavior, and that result is always terrible! That does not mean boundaries and controls are not good because we believe in them. You will see how control, freedom, consequences, and self-governance fit God's ways. We call it the Freedom V!

For example, in my son's early life, his unkempt room irritated me. That unclean room became a huge issue when I mixed truth with speculation. I projected lousy future results that would happen to him if he did not clean his room. "If he is not responsible in small things, he will not be responsible in big things. His disorderly behavior will translate into a poor work ethic, making it difficult to keep a job. He will be unable to support a family, and he will _____ (fill in the rest of the story with heartbreak and tragedy)." But reality says I CANNOT know the future (apart from what God has revealed), so freedom requires me to understand the difference between real and imaginary fears.

You fear having people experience the consequence, or you fear having to initiate the consequence. Neither is an excellent option for you, which drives you to control. "I do not want to see them go through that, so I must prevent it from happening!" Or "I do not want to be the 'bad guy' to put the consequence on them, so I must prevent it from happening!"

F · Future

E · Events

A · Appearing

R · Real

Fearing what *might* happen creates a structure that demands that you control! You may know the FEAR acronym. Our adaptation is in the graphic.

When your fear is in the FUTURE, it is imaginary. The future has not happened! "But the probability of it happening is real!" Yes, there are probabilities and possibilities, but even if it has a 99 percent chance of happening, you still do not know; therefore, it is imaginary. The critical element is—what is the real threat? What are you afraid of right now? Most often, it is not the situation or the other person's behavior but your fear of what **might** happen! Please learn to ask, "Is this fear real or imaginary?"

Along with that question, learn to focus more on NOW! Fear is often irrational—mainly from using your opinion and assumptions. When you focus on now, you learn to see the real threats rather than seeing a horrible future. When you can see a fear is imaginary, not real, you can focus on now.

I moved from speculation to reality when I focused on now and applied it to my son and his room. I could more easily see my options: want his room clean because 1) that is part of the house rules, or 2) *it would eventually lead to heartbreak and tragedy for him and me—a long, lonely, and sad future!*

When I think of those options, the choice is clear, right? Wanting a clean room helps remove the dramatic emotions of "getting that room cleaned or else!" The change becomes his issue, and he chooses the consequences or not.

Remember, change is their responsibility

God allows freedom and says people are responsible for their decisions (Ezekiel 18:20). You can encourage change, but people change because they accept and apply truth or reality. It is their responsibility.

The minute I say that, you may think that I do not care if they change. Wrong! I am incredibly interested in people changing, which is the slippery slope to control. Even if changing is their responsibility, I am responsible for sharing the truth. God may use my sharing with them to help them change their thinking. Consider these thoughts about freedom and change.

- Freedom is into reality; it is NOT YOUR JOB to change them—it is theirs.
- Freedom tells the truth, pursues their best, and invites them to change.
- Freedom hopes, prays, encourages, and sometimes exhorts and rebukes them to change.
- Freedom does not give up on people changing but does not demand it.

This entire book is about helping you grow as an *Overcomer*. And it respects your freedom to reject everything and anything you read. That is how God acts with you and me.

Slow down, remember the "Control Boomerang"

Recognize you can control everything	BUT	accept their freedom to choose
Invite them to change; you are willing to help	BUT	accept their freedom not to want your help
Paint clear boundaries and clear expectations	BUT	accept their freedom to cross the boundary
Explain the painful consequences	BUT	accept their freedom to experience them

What difference would it make if you changed "accept their" to "give them" in the above statements?

This difference is enormous. When you "accept their freedom," you understand they already have it, no matter what. When you change it to "give them their freedom," you are not in reality. They have freedom; you cannot remove it. You can put chains on them and remove their physical freedom, but you cannot control their mind, so they are still free! Think about it!

Change Your Words

Notice how often you think or say "Should, Ought, and Must." Be deliberate and change your words to:

"I choose to . . . ," "I am willing to . . . ," "I would prefer . . . ," or "It would be nice . . ."

Use Primary and Secondary Choices

You can change an obligation to a choice. Any event in life can become an obligation if you do not think clearly. Consider an athlete in training or a mother cleaning up after the kids. What about a family giving up an exciting vacation to care for a dying grandmother? How about just going to work or school?

Since obligations are real, you "have to" do certain things. How can you live in freedom? The answer comes from understanding your hierarchy of values or wants.

It is pretty simple: some events or wants in your life are more crucial than others. It is because of your values. Some are more important than others.

A primary choice is a value, outcome, or vision you want to achieve—your THERE. A secondary choice is what you do to reach the primary choice. Please note that you may not want a secondary choice.

Your current reality, where you are today, most likely is that you have not achieved the outcome you want. Focusing on THERE, the Primary Choice, creates energy to go from HERE to THERE, but only if you want THERE more than HERE. (See the Personal Plan Form for more information on THERE, HERE, and PATH.)

If you are an athlete in training, are you training just to train, or is there a Primary Choice (THERE) to achieve? Olympic athletes train to get the Gold Medal. The training is a Secondary Choice to help them get to the Primary Choice. Training is the PATH to THERE from HERE.

You have more energy when focusing on the Primary Choice instead of the training. That is the power of Primary and Secondary Choices. When you only see your Secondary Choices, you may lose sight of why you are doing them. That is the time to remind yourself of the Primary Choice. "I may not enjoy this training, but I want to enjoy the Gold Medal!"

Moms probably do not want to clean up their kid's sick messes at 3 a.m., but they choose to do it because they love (want the best for) their kids. Of course, a family would not enjoy giving up an exciting vacation to watch someone die. But they choose to because they value family more than entertainment.

Realigning your focus to the Primary Choice adds energy to your life. The highest, most joyful, most energizing primary choice for doing anything is to please and glorify God. With His strength, you can continue completing your secondary choices, not for you but for the ultimate joy of pleasing our PERFECT Father God.

Value and Love People More Than Freedom—choose "WE," not "ME"

Freedom is one of the highest and dearest principles for relationships. It is synonymous with, if not the same as, grace. Yet, it is not the most critical element for superior leadership and relationships. Relationships will suffer from irresponsible freedom if freedom is not underneath at least one other principle.

Consider gravity. Like freedom, gravity is subject to at least one higher principle because heavy planes can fly. How can those giant planes fly even though gravity is real? The one in the picture shown weighs 1.41 million pounds when fully loaded!

There is a higher principle, Bernoulli's principle—which creates a lift force on an airfoil when you apply energy to the airfoil.

> *Bernoulli's Principle can be used to calculate the lift force on an airfoil. For example, if the air flowing past the top surface of an aircraft wing is moving faster than the air flowing past the bottom surface then Bernoulli's principle implies that the pressure on the surfaces of the wing will be lower above than below. This pressure difference results in an upward lift force. Whenever the distribution of speed past the top and bottom surfaces of a wing is known, the lift forces can be calculated.—Wikipedia; Bernoulli's Principle, Real-world application*

Why is that important to know? Because **Love** is to freedom as the Bernoulli Principle is to gravity.

Your freedom is subject to the highest principle—**LOVE**, especially when other people are involved. Love—"pursues their best patiently, kindly, sacrificially, and unconditionally." A good friend, Victoria Printz, once said, "Love trumps freedom." What a great, simple statement to remember. Love does trump freedom—love is more important than freedom and promises, promotes, and provides the ***responsible*** use of freedom.

Love asks for freedom to adopt a higher standard that will limit your freedom. Love sets and respects boundaries, while freedom without love (irresponsible freedom) ignores boundaries. Love does not focus on ME or judge or complain about people, especially those near you. Love does not try to change people. Love never manipulates or dominates others to feel better. Instead, love always promises, promotes, and provides freedom for others to relate to you or not. Love focuses on others—patiently, kindly, sacrificially, and unconditionally pursuing their best.

> *Galatians 5:13 (NKJV)—For you, brethren, have been called to liberty; only do not use liberty as an opportunity for the flesh, but through love serve one another.*

Love sets boundaries and respects others' boundaries. Love also creates consequences for crossing boundaries AND, at the same time, accepts that others are free to cross them. They are free to cross and free to experience the consequences.

- Is your child free to not clean their room? Yes, they are free to obey or disobey. AND if a clean room is a house rule, that is a boundary with probable consequences.
- Is your friend free to curse at you? Yes. You may not like it, AND it is their issue. You are free to associate with them or not.

- Is a person free to rob you? Yes, it is their choice to be evil or not. AND you may protect yourself, your property, and seek justice.
- Is a husband free to not love his wife? Yes. His wife may not like it, AND it is his issue.
- Is a wife free to not respect her husband? Yes. Her husband may not like it, AND it is her issue.

That may appear to be condoning bad behavior. Not true! Freedom is reality. When you ignore reality, you fuel your actions with opinion, subjectivity, and selfishness.

Remember, God allows freedom.

Finally, and this is most important, God is all-powerful, and He created freedom and allows it.

- He controls everything   AND   allows freedom of choice
- He shares what is best   AND   allows choosing the worst
- He paints clear boundaries   AND   lets us cross them
- He shares the consequences   AND   lets us experience them

God knows what will happen and still allows the freedom to choose what is wrong. He can make everyone do what is right, make all evil disappear, and remove all pain, but He does not for His perfect reasons. God knows all the consequences of bad choices yet does not control or prevent people from sin and misery. He has graciously provided clear instructions in His Word for our best, AND He does not prevent us from doing exactly the opposite!

Proverbs 29:25 (NKJV)—Fear of man will prove to be a snare, but whoever trusts in the LORD is kept safe.

RESULT: PROFOUND CHANGE

The above tools do NOT mean you should ignore helping people consider different behavior. It is simply about living in REALITY—moving from a concept of danger to actual risk assessment. That profound change will benefit all your relationships. No longer will you need to try controlling everything. You will see the difference between real and imaginary fear. ***Now, you can practice freedom as a value for yourself and others, too!*** You will have more energy to care for and pursue the best for others rather than control them.

AND you can remove the burden of thinking it is your job to protect the universe. It has never been—you are just into reality to see it.

FREEDOM INSIGHTS

Parents—You Aren't Your Child

Understanding freedom is critical because while you are responsible for being a Godly parent, children ultimately make their own choices. Is the following an accurate statement? Great parents can have bad kids. Is this true? Bad parents can have great kids.

Both statements are factual, right?

The table below is called a "Truth Table." It allows you to take two things you see as linked and provides insight into how they are not connected. That table provides the answers to the questions asked in the first two paragraphs above. Here is how you would read the table.

- Godly parents "+" have Godly children "+"
- UnGodly parents "—" have unGodly children "—"
- Godly parents "+" have unGodly children "—"
- UnGodly parents "—" have Godly children "+"

If you believe that Godly parents will have Godly children, you will have difficulty seeing that the options represented by the four boxes on the right side are

Godly Parents	+	–	+	–
Godly Children	+	–	–	+

valid. The table does not assign probabilities; it only identifies what is TRUE. If you only accept the first four boxes on the left side, you see only 50 percent of reality.

Read Ezekiel 18 to see what God thinks about children and parents. Who does God say is ultimately responsible? It starts in verse 1 with a proverb about fathers eating sour grapes and the children setting their teeth on edge. In verse 3, God says He never wants to hear that proverb again. If you get the picture of the proverb, the father is eating sour grapes, but the children are reacting to the sourness, you will see what is happening. The children blame the father for the way they turned out.

God says He never wants to hear that again (verse 3). Why are the children saying it? Because that is what they think God said in Exodus 20:5: "... visiting the iniquity of the fathers upon the children to the third and fourth generations of those who hate me ..." So it is understandable why the proverb was created.

But God sets the record straight. Even if you experience consequences from your parent's behavior or parents experience consequences from the children's behavior, the real issue is YOUR BEHAVIOR! That is made abundantly clear in verse 20.

*Ezekiel 18:20 (NKJV)—The soul who sins shall die. The son shall
not bear the guilt of the father, nor the father bear the guilt of
the son. The righteousness of the righteous shall be upon himself,
and the wickedness of the wicked shall be upon himself.*

Please listen to what God tells you here. Even if you are a terrible
parent, how your children turn out is still their decision for or against God.
He will hold them accountable for choosing Him or not. And God will hold
you responsible for being a lousy parent, not for your children's decisions.

If you have great children who honor God, that is excellent. If you
have children who dishonor God, that is sad. Either way, focus on your
behavior more than theirs. Are you the parent God wants you to be right
now? If not, God will give you the wisdom to share with your children.

At any point in time, either one of you can change. You might try
to blame your parents for the way you are, or you can blame your
children for how they turned out. God says neither is acceptable. You
are responsible for your decisions, and they are responsible for theirs.
Trust in God no matter the lifestyle of your children. Do you trust that
His plan is PERFECT despite what you see?

Seeking Acceptance

An improper view or belief about acceptance will hinder your
freedom. Worse, it turns you into a follower, not a leader. Where are you
seeking acceptance and praise? Who do you hope will accept you? Who
are you trying to please?

*If you seek your praise, acceptance, and pleasure from
man, you will likely be controlled by and follow man.*

*If you seek your praise, acceptance, and pleasure from
God, you will likely be controlled by and follow God.*

Remember, *"Where you look, you tend to go."* When you focus on
being accepted by or trying to please someone, that person controls
you—probably more than you realize. That is another subtle way your
ME flashes. You want their attention because you think it will satisfy you.

When you want to be accepted by others, you may erroneously think
you can make it happen—but you cannot. It is the other person's choice;
they accept or reject you according to their standards, probably multiple
subjective standards. Unfortunately, even if they tell you the standards
and you meet them, they may not accept you. Ultimately, the standards
do not matter because they either want to accept you or not. If you play

the game, they will continue to control you as their puppet. You cannot make them accept you; it is not within your control!

If you elevate your desire to be accepted, you may compromise your values and beliefs, a clear sign of being controlled or losing freedom. That is one reason gangs work, and good people do bad things.

God is different. Meet His standard, and you become part of His family—totally accepted. The standard is the same for all—**faith alone in Christ alone**. Faith in Christ's death, burial, and resurrection from the dead to pay for your sins allows your adoption into God's family. That is the only criterion for acceptance, and it will not change.

The incredible difference between seeking acceptance from God versus man is how freedom works. With man, you rarely have freedom because the acceptance continues to be conditional, subject to whims and variable standards. With God, your initial acceptance can be classified as conditional if you say receiving a gift or trusting Christ as a condition, but then it becomes unconditional. Once God accepts you, nothing can reverse it!

Romans 11:29 (NKJV)—For the gifts and the calling of God are irrevocable.

It makes so much more sense to seek the acceptance of God because it provides freedom. Seeking man's acceptance hinders freedom. When you understand that being part of God's family is eternal acceptance, you can focus on obtaining the inheritance God has set aside for you. Overcomers know there IS a difference between the GIFT and the PRIZE!

Is Accepting the Same as Approving?

Accepting others can also hinder your freedom. Accepting others may control you because it is erroneously connected to the other person's behavior.

Please think about this carefully. Relationships suffer when you confuse acceptance of the person with approval of their behavior. Those are two separate elements. God's example shows that acceptance and approval are not connected—praise God!

He accepts us when we believe in Jesus Christ, His Son! He makes us new creatures, adopts us into His family, and guarantees us a place with Him in eternity! Nothing can separate us from His love.

Romans 8:38-39 (NKJV)—For I am persuaded that neither death nor life, nor angels nor principalities nor powers, nor things present nor things to come, nor height nor depth, nor any other created thing, shall be able to separate us from the love of God which is in Christ Jesus our Lord.

AND He is either pleased or displeased with our behavior.

Hebrews 11:6 (NKJV)—But without faith it is impossible to please Him, for he who comes to God must believe that He is, and that He is a rewarder of those who diligently seek Him.

His displeasure with our bad behavior does not change the fact that we are part of His family. Isn't that true of you and your parents? God accepts us, and our behavior does not control that; it is governed solely by His chosen standard.

You, too, are free to accept others even when their behavior is inappropriate. It is entirely your choice—separate from their qualifications, actions, or thinking. You do not need to reject and remove someone from your life because of their behavior. Unfortunately, that happens too often.

You can have standards for accepting someone and for their behavior—that is fine, but you can also accept someone just because you want to! Acceptance is totally your choice—with or without standards.

Their behavior, on the other hand, is their decision. They choose what they do. You can be pleased or displeased based on whether they have good or bad values. You can be sad, angry, excited, thrilled, or brought to tears with their behavior because God's Word shows He has similar emotions to our excellent and destructive behaviors. But He does not reject us because of lousy behavior.

Watch out for the emotions trap! As you experience emotions because of someone else's choices, you may let your flawed thinking and lousy emotions control you. That thinking will link accepting them to their behavior. Without the Holy Spirit's energy, you will not accept and love someone whose behavior is terrible, even evil. And the opposite is true—your thinking can drive your acceptance when they behave well. Neither is correct—acceptance is separate from their behavior.

That is the ESSENCE of LOVE! And that is precisely how God deals with us.

Accepting and Correcting

Bad behavior will occur with those that you choose to accept. Demanding change is an option, but it is often more likely to create rebellion than change. And most often, the demand for change is about you wanting relief from their bad behavior. That encourages flawed thinking, damaging the relationship.

There is a better way. Please follow this pattern.

Galatians 6:1-5 (NKJV)—Brethren, if a man is overtaken
in any trespass, you who are spiritual restore such a one in
a spirit of gentleness, considering yourself lest you also be
tempted. Bear one another's burdens, and so fulfill the law of
Christ. For if anyone thinks himself to be something, when he
is nothing, he deceives himself. But let each one examine his
own work, and then he will have rejoicing in himself alone,
and not in another. For each one shall bear his own load.

This pattern is part of the Moment of Truth information. Consider three elements in this context—*a spirit of gentleness, consider yourself,* and *bear one another's burdens.* Further, notice that this behavior will *fulfill the law of Christ,* which is **LOVE**—pursuing their best patiently, kindly, sacrificially, and unconditionally!

Luke 10:27 (NKJV)— . . . love the Lord your
God . . . and your neighbor as yourself.

Pursuing their best encourages freedom instead of fear about sharing the truth. You are gentle. You are honest about yourself and their behavior but avoid condemnation. You do not tolerate sin; neither does God. You speak the truth in love (Ephesians 4:15) but avoid judgment and condemnation. That is God's job, not yours.

Using the standard of love prevents you from trying to control and condemn their behavior. Without love, their behavior occupies your mind, removing energy for more productive thinking, actions, and feelings.

God is the only judge, so be careful when spending energy judging others.

Romans 14:10-13 (NKJV)—But why do you judge your brother?
Or why do you show contempt for your brother? For we shall
all stand before the judgment seat of Christ. For it is written:
"As I live, says the LORD, every knee shall bow to Me, and
every tongue shall confess to God." So then each of us shall
give account of himself to God. Therefore let us not judge
one another anymore, but rather resolve this, not to put a
stumbling block or a cause to fall in our brother's way.

Judging is from your heart's intent, not the words you say. When you speak to someone about their sin, they may accuse you of judging. When you "are spiritual" (Galatians 6:1), you have prayed about the conversation and decided to "fulfill the law of Christ" instead of judge. Your response to their accusation is not defensive and shares God's Word about their behavior, not your opinion or assumption.

That does not mean they will accept what you say, even if it is a direct, precise quote from God's Word. Their response is between them and God, and "each one shall bear his own load." Their load is their sin, while you have no load from this conversation and "have rejoicing in himself alone" since you did what God desires.

God's Word is powerful and freeing. Without it, you will be controlled by reasonable-sounding arguments often distorting God's clear truth.

Remember the five freedom actions to aid gentleness.

When correction is needed—hope, pray, and encourage
change; sometimes, exhort and rebuke.

Because judging is part of the sin nature, rebuke with the wrong intent of your heart is extremely easy. That is why God provided Galatians 6:1-5. You want their behavior to change, which turns into judging instead of restoring them and fulfilling Christ's law.

Consider a friend telling you, "Your behavior does not align with God's Word. You may not like hearing that from me. I hope, pray, and encourage you to change. And whether you change or not, I will continue to love, accept, and value you."

That friend is telling you the truth in love. Judging you is the more likely path for a friend, but God wants you to follow His example. People are free to choose right or wrong. The real issue is whether you will love them even when they choose wrong. Will you hope, pray, encourage, and sometimes exhort and rebuke?

Growth is encouraged with the assurance of love
and the prospect of hope!—Unknown

You can accept someone and still correct them. It starts with following the Spirit and listening to Him as He focuses your attention on your behavior—not their behavior. Consider asking, "Am I pleasing God now?" "Has my behavior been pleasing to God recently?" Those questions are for you, not your neighbor.

Oh, the comfort—the inexpressible comfort of feeling safe
with a person—having neither to weigh thoughts nor measure
words, but pouring them all right out, just as they are, chaff

257

and grain together; certain that a faithful hand will take and sift them, keep what is worth keeping, and then with the breath of kindness blow the rest away.—Dinah Craik

As a further reminder, consider a few of God's invitations.

Micah 6:8 (NKJV)—He has shown you, O man, what is good; and what does the LORD require of you but to do justly, to love mercy, and to walk humbly with your God?

Colossians 1:10 (NKJV)— . . . that you may walk worthy of the Lord, fully pleasing Him, being fruitful in every good work and increasing in the knowledge of God.

1 Corinthians 4:5 (NKJV)—Therefore judge nothing before the time, until the Lord comes, who will both bring to light the hidden things of darkness and reveal the counsels of the hearts. Then each one's praise will come from God.

1 Peter 1:7 (NKJV)— . . . that the genuineness of your faith, being much more precious than gold that perishes, though it is tested by fire, may be found to praise, honor, and glory at the revelation of Jesus Christ.

Hebrews 11:6 (NKJV)—But without faith it is impossible to please Him, for he who comes to God must believe that He is, and that He is a rewarder of those who diligently seek Him.

Each invitation focuses on your growth, which equips you to better deal with helping others grow.

But What If . . .

When you reduce or stop your controlling behavior, you will quickly return because of questions like these. What if they never change? What if they keep their poor values and destructive behavior?

Satan wants you to ask those questions, which encourages worry and fear. The more you worry and fear, the more a return to control appears valid. And what drives you to control? You make it about yourself (ME)! You want the worry gone. You want peace and rest. You want to be happy.

But only God knows the future. Satan wants you to trust your flawed thinking. He wants you driven by fear, but God wants you to trust Him, driven by love (pursuing their best).

You want freedom from worry, so you control to change their behavior. But that enslaves you. Only trusting God can free you from worry!

Worry is not only unnecessary, it is also disrespectful and disobedient to your PERFECT Father God!

When you decide on freedom, it does not mean you give up on them changing! Freedom accepts reality—changing them is *not your job*. Whether they change or not, your job is to tell the truth and love them— pursue their best. Change is their job and dependent upon God's plan.

God wants you to learn patience and trust Him in those situations. Yes, God may use you to help them change, but do not mix up being the instrument versus the cause. In times of trial, you have an excellent opportunity to embrace the pain instead of running from it, and then you will see what God wants to teach you through it! You are responsible for offering the truth and not nagging them about it. Truth can defend itself.

Freedom and Boundaries

If people are free, can they say and do anything they want to me? Are they free to dump garbage in my house? Are they free to steal from me? Are they free to break into my home?

Yes!

Even though you may say or want to say no, people can and will choose to do those things. You know it is correct because the news constantly reports it.

The question is not what you want but about other people's freedom. Each situation above is a product of the other person's freedom of choice and displays irresponsible freedom compared to transcendent values and principles. Irresponsible freedom ignores boundaries.

When someone crosses a boundary and is irresponsible with their freedom, they may receive unpleasant consequences. Why? Because you are also free—free to defend your property and seek justice for them!

While irresponsible freedom ignores boundaries like other people's property lines, responsible freedom respects boundaries. When people cross boundaries, justice, rules, and authority take over.

Freedom without regard for boundaries is irresponsible, self-absorbed anarchy. "I can do anything I want." But responsible freedom considers others, their boundaries, and their freedom. Boundaries help protect freedom, both mine, yours, and others.

However, people still have a choice to ignore boundaries, so we often try to limit freedom for others. When you do that, here is your problem. Trying to limit their freedom may mean you cross a boundary and use your freedom irresponsibly. That is where individual rights are out of control.

What About Individual Rights?

Be careful when promoting individual rights without putting them under love and humility. Without love, you encourage irresponsible freedom. Your "flashing ME" always sees your rights as more important than theirs!

When you push for your rights and freedoms, you create a structure that demands others give up their freedom to get or maintain your freedom. It is like saying you want people to have less independence and be controlled by you to "make you happy."

Isn't that what is happening within a society that promotes limiting things like free speech and fostering lousy behavior and values in the name of tolerance and freedom? That is a misuse of individual rights.

Dr. Marlin Howe gave a pertinent example in his "Hope for the Family" video series. He pointed to the laws established about AIDS in the 1990s. The individual rights of homosexuals were elevated above the good of society, exposing everyone to the devastating effects of AIDS. If a person had AIDS, laws prevented others from knowing about it; therefore, they could interact with society, potentially spreading AIDS to others. Elevating the rights of a select group removed the rights and freedom of the masses, exposing them to a deadly disease. The rights of a few created a detrimental impact on the many.

Individual rights do not stand alone without impacting everyone else. "Everyone be damned who stands in my way" is the argument of those who claim their rights are superior even when it harms society. Anyone who disagrees is intolerant and bigoted. Individual rights issues gone amuck are well documented in *The Marketing of Evil: How Radicals, Elitists, and Pseudo-Experts Sell Corruption Disguised by Freedom* by David Kupelian.

In these situations, you could argue that the structure of the Freedom V is reversed. Control of people, tightening the boundaries, and limiting freedom are promoted as good. Self-governing people are a danger to those structures, so the tight boundaries promote control and rule by the few.

You could also argue that the structure works the same, but the difference is that the authorities redefine irresponsible freedom as responsible. So people following the redefined values are considered self-governing in those corrupt structures and are allowed more "freedom." They will not be "canceled" if they align with the redefined values.

Those things occur when mankind and governments work against Godly values and principles. When anyone promotes a lousy value as good, that is the thinking of fools, like Romans 1:23-31 shows. God allows fools the freedom to dig their own graves. History contains numerous examples of organizations and societies that stray from God's transcendent values.

Whether those situations are the Freedom V in reverse or not, the structure created punishes those who speak up for what is right. That is like the rulers in Acts 5.

> *Acts 5:28 (NKJV)—Did we not strictly command you not to teach in this name? And look, you have filled Jerusalem with your doctrine, and intend to bring this Man's blood on us!*

But Peter and the apostles rejected their redefinition of what was correct.

> *Acts 5:29 (NKJV)—But Peter and the other apostles answered and said: "We ought to obey God rather than men."*

A government built on transcendent values encourages freedom of the individual, but not to the detriment of society. It initiates consequences on those who cross the boundaries when they lack self-governance and adherence to transcendent values. That is why God links self-governance and freedom with love and all other good and Godly values.

Remember, the SOLUTION for all relationship problems is embodied in the definition of love—"Pursuing their best patiently, kindly, sacrificially and unconditionally." Remember, freedom is not as important as love. When you love, you are self-governing and will limit your freedom for the good of others. Isn't that what Jesus did when He came to die for us?

We have the powerful example of Jesus to think about freedom and individual rights. Good thinking about my rights never comes from the sin nature but only from walking with the Lord.

Freedom Changes Relationships

Responsible freedom positively impacts all relationships. When freedom is present, there is a structure for you and those around you to be authentic. Manipulation, mask-wearing, and reacting and responding are no longer valued. Instead, you make choices to relate to others through your Godly values.

Freedom allows everyone to establish their options and express disagreement with you; your ME does not start flashing. Freedom recognizes each person has a responsibility to make their own choices. Most importantly, responsible freedom submits to love, which means you are willing to love someone as they are, to value them as they are, and to accept them as they are.

It is your life—your choice. Freedom puts energy back into your life. All that energy you have been wasting trying to manipulate and dominate is available for a productive activity like pursuing their best. Control removes energy from your life. Will you choose freedom or control? If you do select freedom, when will you start?

Freedom Understands Expectations

Expectations Defined

Does the principle of freedom in relationships mean expectations are bad for relationships? If using "mutual" in a definition of a great relationship drives people to focus on the other person, then that would imply that expectations are wrong. Is that true? No, that is not true. The definition of expectations is—

- The act of expecting, eager anticipation, something expected
- Anticipating with confidence of fulfillment

Some synonyms are "hope, outlook, hopefulness." Most other synonyms are also positive, even when considered for a relationship. From the word's definition, expectations are good for relationships. I can have expectations of you, and you can have expectations of me. That would mean we have hope and eager anticipation of future events.

However, expectations too often hurt rather than help relationships, so it would be helpful to identify when expectations help and hurt.

Expectations Help

Expectations can help relationships when they:

- *Involve All Parties*—The expectations may not be the same for everyone, but each person has expectations that fit their role. They benefit the relationship rather than any one individual.
- *Identify Clear Boundaries*—Expectations identify the limits, norms, guidelines, and rules that will give the relationship the best chance for success. Staying inside the boundaries means sacrificing some of the freedoms you would have if you were not in this relationship.
- *Include Clear Consequences or Outcomes*—If the boundaries are not enforced, they have no "teeth." Those "boundaries" are mostly a wish or a hope and meaningless to those without self-governance. When you have clear consequences (positive or negative), it aids the focus of the people affected. Clarity of the punishment or reward is always great if you are not using them to manipulate people.
- *Inspire Self-governance*—The foundation of inspiring self-governance means the expectation will benefit all parties involved. Self-governance does not require receiving a benefit, but it is still helpful. Expectations met, or boundaries

uncrossed, are a measure of personal responsibility, accountability, trustworthiness, and numerous other excellent values. Expectations provide opportunities for additional growth for those desiring to enhance self-governance.

- *Instigate Service*—Self-governance increases your capacity to serve others. Meeting the expectations of others is serving them and not yourself. Sometimes serving may be motivated by a flashing ME. If that is true, your "serving" is often a form of trying to please others, which tends to be short-lived if you receive inadequate recognition. "Pleasing" benefits you more than the other person, while "serving" benefits the other person more than you. When truly serving, your desire to meet expectations provides practice in sacrifice and humility.

There will be chaos without expectations, guidelines, rules, or norms of behavior. Expectations are helpful when used correctly.

Expectations Hurt

Expectations most often hurt relationships when they:
- *Focus on Others*—The most common way expectations hurt relationships is by focusing on the other person without considering your responsibility. That happens when you create expectations for others but discount or prevent any expectations from being assigned to you. That creates an atmosphere of privilege or an attitude of being served rather than serving.
- *Focus on Judging*—This is a harsher version of the previous statement. The expectations may be well-meaning but written to demand judgment of another person's behavior. The result is finger-pointing, divisiveness, and reduced self-governance. It would be like God asking a husband to determine if his wife respects him. Or God asking the wife to decide whether her husband loves her. That encourages focusing on what OTHERS are doing rather than your actions.
- *Focus on Control*—Boundaries that do not provide appropriate freedom to choose are more about controlling and removing freedom rather than encouraging and developing self-governance.
- *Focus on Freedom*—If you put freedom at the top of the values list, not love, then you may believe it is wrong to have any expectations of other people, and they have no right to put expectations on you. Freedom operating alone does not pursue

their best (love). When you pursue their BEST, you promote and encourage their freedom and limit your freedoms that may harm others or are inappropriate and irresponsible.

In summary, remember the definition of freedom—acting without force or manipulation, not controlling or being controlled. On the one hand, expectations are a tool to control. On the other hand, they are an excellent tool for helping people grow. It is dependent on the intent of your heart, which God knows.

Discussion Questions

1. Memorize the proposed definition of freedom.
2. What makes freedom a "radically different" way to live?
3. How would you describe what Responsible Freedom is? Irresponsible Freedom?
4. Explain what "Internal Freedom is. Give some examples.
5. Explain what "External Freedom" is. Give some examples.
6. Freedom is based on what model? Explain the model clearly.
7. Memorize and explain the quote that starts with "When control...."
8. In the previous quote, which party in the relationship will find the relationship intolerable? Explain.
9. What makes control a problem for anyone?
10. What is the desired result for people who try to control others?
11. What three words are helpful to identify when you are trying to control?
12. What does control encourage in the person being controlled?
13. What is the difference in your energy when you "have to" versus when you "want to?" What example can you use to help someone understand the difference, even feel it?
14. When you "have to," what fiction do you believe? Explain it.
15. What does this mean, "A good person up to no good?"
16. Why does a "good person" feel they are misunderstood?
17. Memorize and explain, "Imaginary fears refuse to use MAY for unknown outcomes."
18. Memorize and quote what the acronym "FEAR" means.
19. What is the benefit of remembering change is their responsibility? What is your responsibility?
20. Explain the control boomerang.
21. Is this phrase correct? "I decided to give them freedom." Explain.
22. How does changing your words from "should, ought, or must" help you?
23. Explain Primary and Secondary Choices.
24. What one crucial value helps you to be responsible with your freedom?
25. What happens to your freedom when you put it underneath love?
26. Explain how to use a "Truth Table."
27. Use a truth table for a husband who says, "She should respect me because I am showing love to her!"
28. If someone asks this question, "What if they never change?" What would you say to them?

.

Chapter 12

The Heart of Covenant

Julia and Steven planned to marry while they were still attending college at a major university. Julia was raised to believe that *"A man is the head of the house, as Christ is head of the church."* (Ephesians 5:23). So when they married, even though she majored in Finance and made good grades in school, she figured she would stay home and manage the household. Steven was working on a degree in Anthropology—his third change of majors since entering University.

They married in the summer (August) after their junior year. Julia only had one semester left because she went to summer school and took extra hours during the regular semesters. Julia and Steven moved into student housing after their wedding. The small "apartment," essentially a run-down mobile home, felt cramped to Julie, but it fit their budget. Julia hoped that Steven would do whatever he could to get them to a better place. She expressed her feelings about their living quarters to him, but he assured her that their love would overcome the cramped space, and she would get used to it.

Julia graduated with honors in December and was offered a job at a bank in their town. She had been waiting tables at night since she and Steven married. Even though Julia still dreamed of being a stay-at-home wife and mother, she decided to take the banking position since she wasn't sure when Steven would graduate. Steven changed majors to Meteorology soon after they married, which meant he needed extra hours to graduate on time in May of the following year.

Julia excelled at her banking job while Steven floundered in school. He loved her dearly and often cooked dinner and ran errands because Julia had such a demanding job at the bank. In Steven's mind, he was an

Overcomer because he supported Julia in her work and performed most of the domestic chores.

At their first anniversary, Steven still was at least two years from graduating. He worked driving an Uber so he could keep up with his studies. Julia kept working and excelling at her job, but she was extremely frustrated with Steven. She was ready to buy a house, quit her job, and have children. Julia continued to work hard to save enough money for a good down payment on a house.

Every time she addressed his education and their living situation with Steven and expressed to him that she wanted to buy a house, he would smile and say, "But Babe, we have each other," and break into the Sonny and Cher song, *I Got You Babe*. Then he would say he wanted to graduate before they bought a house.

Two more years came and went, and Steven still had not completed his degree. By this time, Julia had been able to save enough to afford the down payment for a house. Steven still sidestepped the conversation every time she brought it up. After numerous conversations, Julia just started looking for a house on her own. She had the means to buy a house and was miserable. Steven was so laid back she feared they would end up stuck in a cramped little place. Soon, she found a house and put in a contract under her name.

She arrived home that evening excited and said to Steven, "Guess what?"

He shrugged his shoulders and smiled at her.

"I just bought us a house! I'm so excited. I know you will love it. It has a place where you can grow a vegetable garden and it even has fruit trees in the yard. When we have children, they will have plenty of room to play. And the yard is big enough for a big dog, which I know is something you miss!"

Steven was stunned and looked at her silently. Then he looked at the floor with a dejected look on his face. This was a huge commitment. He was shocked that she went to look at houses, and bought one, without him. He felt like Julia ignored his need to be a part of buying a home.

Annoyed at his reaction, she said in an irritated tone, "Really? I've tried many times to talk to you about this. I've been working hard for this, and you haven't even managed to graduate yet. I try to understand and appreciate you fixing dinner, but I feel like you don't listen to me. I figured if I didn't buy a home, I might never have one . . . whether you live in it with me or not."

Steven looked at her with horror, "Are you leaving me?"

Julia sat down next to him on the couch, looked at him, and said, "I'm sorry, no, I'm not leaving you."

Steven asked, "Do you still love me?"

"I do love you, but I don't like what you are doing. You don't seem to be applying yourself. And I can't keep living in this cramped place. It feels like if anything like buying a house is going to get done, I have to do it."

Steven nodded his head, knowing in his heart that he needed to graduate and get a better job than driving an Uber.

Questions

1. Who do you feel has *overcome* life's circumstances in the story?
2. Who seems to have hardened their heart to their spouse and/or God?
3. Which spouse has violated their covenant before God?
4. As you think about this situation, what emotions arise in you?

Overcomers Oppose Hard Hearts

Key Lesson: *A hard heart separates you from God and prevents you from being an Overcomer because you are not depending on God.*

This chapter is an essential reminder of how easy it is to stray from God and choose sin over the abundant life God provides. That thought is beautifully stated in the hymn "Come, Thou Fount of Blessing."

> *O to grace how great a debtor*
> *Daily I'm constrained to be!*
> *Let Thy goodness, like a fetter,*
> *Bind my wandering heart to Thee.*
> *Prone to wander, Lord, I feel it,*
> *Prone to leave the God I love,*
> *Here's my heart, O take and seal it,*
> *Seal it for Thy courts above.*

Robert Robinson (1735-1790) wrote the hymn when he was 22 in 1757. Later, he wandered away from the Lord.

One day, when he was riding a stagecoach, a young woman entered the coach singing the hymn after having attended a church meeting. Crying, he told her he had penned that hymn years ago as a young believer and would give a thousand worlds to enjoy that feeling again when he first wrote it. The woman replied, "Streams of mercy are still never ceasing," which is another verse in the hymn.

What an excellent reminder for Robert Robinson and all believers! Despite a hard and wandering heart, the ever-watchful PERFECT Father God welcomes a repentant heart back into fellowship with Him. Do not wait; turn back to Him now!

Hard Hearts and the Tree

Our wandering hearts are directly connected to the tree in the Garden of Eden. This book's message would be unnecessary if God's original command to Adam had not been disobeyed.

Have you ever thought about what the "Tree of the Knowledge of Good and Evil" represents? What was the "big deal" about the tree's fruit that got Adam and Eve kicked out of the Garden? Why was knowing about good and evil such a bad thing?

Knowledge of Good and Evil Is Bad?

God did not want Adam and Eve to eat the fruit of that tree because it was terrible for them. But why? The fact that it was horrible is easy to see now, not only because God said so but because we see the consequences daily.

But how could knowing about good and evil be bad since God tells you to choose righteousness, not unrighteousness?

> *Romans 6:13 (NKJV)—And do not present your members as instruments of unrighteousness to sin, but present yourselves to God as being alive from the dead, and your members as instruments of righteousness to God.*

That verse is God's instruction for you NOW because you know good and evil. But that was not true of Adam and Eve when God told Adam about the tree.

> *Genesis 2:16-17 (NKJV)—And the LORD God commanded the man, saying, "Of every tree of the garden you may freely eat; but of the tree of the knowledge of good and evil you shall not eat, for in the day that you eat of it you shall surely die."*

All God's commands are for our protection and invite us to what is BEST (2 Peter 1:3-4)! Since He is perfect, what was God protecting Adam and Eve from if they obeyed that command?

How Is Hard-heartedness Linked to the Tree?

Scholars have written volumes about the Tree, but the purpose here is to understand how the fruit of that Tree is tied directly to Hard Hearts! Two scholars share their insights.

> *All that the text requires is that knowledge followed the eating of that fruit . . . [which] led to an experimental knowledge of the difference. God knew the nature and effects of evil from his omniscience. Adam could know them only from experience . . . the tree of knowledge gave Adam a knowledge which he had not before; he came to an experimental knowledge of the difference between good and evil.—Hodge, C. (1997). Systematic theology (Vol. 2, p. 126-127). Oak Harbor, WA: Logos Research Systems, Inc.*

• • • • •

> *But whatever explanation may be given of . . . the command*
> *given by God not to eat of the fruit of the tree simply served*
> *the purpose of testing the obedience of man. It was a test of*
> *pure obedience since God did not in any way seek to justify or*
> *to explain the prohibition. Adam had to show his willingness to*
> *submit his will to the will of his God with implicit obedience.*

> *The first sin of man was a typical sin, that is, a sin in which the*
> *real essence of sin clearly reveals itself. The essence of that sin*
> *lay in the fact that Adam placed himself in opposition to God,*
> *that he refused to subject his will to the will of God, to have God*
> *determine the course of his life; and that he actively attempted*
> *to take the matter out of God's hand, and to determine the*
> *future for himself.—Berkhof, L. (1938). Systematic theology (p.*
> *222). Grand Rapids, MI: Wm. B. Eerdmans Publishing Co.*

Those thoughts imply that the fruit of the Tree blossomed into self-dependence, self-sufficiency, or independence from God. If Adam and Eve had not eaten the fruit, you and I would depend on God to know what is right and wrong rather than trusting our opinion of right or wrong.

Ponder that last sentence. Does that make it easier to see why God's Word is critical for you? God's Word is His perfect knowledge telling you what is right and wrong.

However, self-dependence and self-sufficiency trust your own opinion or understanding (Proverbs 3:5-6), not God's.

Self-dependence is the seed that blossoms
into hard-heartedness.

When you depend on your opinion, knowledge, and understanding, you encourage a hard heart to become harder, enabling you to ignore God even more!

HARD HEARTS

A hard heart separates you from God, not because God does not want a relationship with you, but because you no longer want one with Him. You choose to depend on yourself instead of God. That deceives you into thinking you do not need God.

God does not force Himself on you! He will not violate your freedom to choose and allows you to depend on yourself. He will not step in the way of the consequences you face for disregarding His truth. Hard hearts are the evidence and result of ignoring God's **complete knowledge** of what is right and wrong. A hard heart proves that you believe you know more than God and would like another serving of the fruit of the Tree of Knowledge of Good and Evil!

Hard, Hardening, or Hardened

* Adapted from Elwell, W. A. (1996). Hardening, Hardness of Heart. In Evangelical Dictionary of Biblical Theology (electronic ed., pp. 324 –325). Grand Rapids: Baker Book House.

God uses different parts of our body to define the whole person, but He most frequently uses the heart. God's Word speaks of the heart as:
- Seat of emotion (Psalms 25:1; Proverbs 14:10; Isaiah 66:14; John 14:1; Romans 9:2)
- Intelligence (Proverbs 16:1; Luke 9:47)
- Morality (Psalms 58:2; Romans 1:24)
- Human choice (Deuteronomy 8:2; Luke 21:34; Acts 11:23)
- Person's religious life (Deuteronomy 6:5; Jeremiah 31:33; Romans 10:9–10; Galatians 4:6)

The heart represents your thinking, feeling, planning, and willingness. Therefore, it impacts everything about you, including your actions and words. When you do not obey God, He calls your heart darkened, rebellious, callous, unfeeling, or idolatrous. Your heart is also a place where God works on you. It is soft or hard as stone.

Ezekiel 11:19 (NKJV)—Then I will give them one heart,
and I will put a new spirit within them, and take the stony
heart out of their flesh, and give them a heart of flesh

Since your heart represents you, a hard heart describes the condition of someone who ignores or rejects the gracious offer of God to partake in the abundant life He has given you.

When you depart from the Lord, you end up in a BAD place.

Jeremiah 17:5-6 (NKJV)—Thus says the Lord: "Cursed is the
man who trusts in man and makes flesh his strength, whose heart
departs from the Lord. For he shall be like a shrub in the desert,
and shall not see when good comes, but shall inhabit the parched
places in the wilderness, in a salt land which is not inhabited."

You can be in that place as a child of God. Overcomers are highly aware of that truth. It does not mean you are not His child, but you chose to "eat with the pigs" instead of dining with the Father, like the Prodigal Son.

As God's child, you are a new creature with a new heart, but you can still choose the ways of the *hard heart*. When you select a hard heart, you are *hardening* your heart, which further creates a *hardened* heart. Jesus says this is a general condition of mankind.

> *Matthew 19:8 (NKJV)—He said to them, "Moses, because of the hardness of your hearts, permitted you to divorce your wives, but from the beginning it was not so."*

Even worse, God says your heart is desperately wicked.

> *Jeremiah 17:9 (NKJV)—The heart is deceitful above all things and desperately wicked; who can know it?*

The desperately wicked hard heart is part of your sin nature, but the hardening of the heart is a choice. You enter the hardening process as you ignore and dismiss God's Word, like in the story of Nebuchadnezzar.

> *Daniel 5:20 (NKJV)—But when his heart was lifted up, and his spirit was hardened in pride, he was deposed from his kingly throne, and they took his glory from him.*

The Apostle Paul warned the Ephesians that their hearts could be like the unsaved.

> *Ephesians 4:18 (NKJV)—having their understanding darkened, being alienated from the life of God, because of the ignorance that is in them, because of the blindness of their heart.*

The writer of Hebrews warned all believers.

> *Hebrews 3:12-15 (NKJV)—Beware, brethren, lest there be in any of you an evil heart of unbelief in departing from the living God; but exhort one another daily, while it is called "Today," lest any of you be hardened through the deceitfulness of sin. For we have become partakers of Christ if we hold the beginning of our confidence steadfast to the end, while it is said: "Today, if you will hear His voice, do not harden your hearts as in the rebellion."*

Each sinful rebellion, bitterness over circumstances, or self-absorption (Exodus 9:34–35; 2 Chronicles. 36:13; Zechariah 7:12) is part of the hardening process.

In some instances—such as Pharaoh and the Egyptians (Exodus 7:3; 9:12), Sihon, king of Heshbon (Deuteronomy 2:30), and the Hivites living in Gibeon (Joshua 11:19–20)—God hardened a person's heart.

That is not something we can understand—it is a mystery. But you can understand that the people rebelled against God in each situation. That implies they chose their way and were part of the hardening process. That is the same thing Paul tells you about choosing your own way. God will give you over to your desires (Romans 1:26-32) and not prevent you from hardening your heart.

God Warns Against Hard Hearts

In His perfection, God accomplishes His purposes despite and even through hard hearts. God's prerogative is to use hard hearts (Romans 9:18–21) for His glorious and perfect plan. At the same time, you are responsible for your inherited, sinful, hard heart condition and all your choices that help harden it.

That is why God warns you not to harden your heart.

> *1 Samuel 6:6 (NKJV)—Why then do you harden your hearts as the Egyptians and Pharaoh hardened their hearts? When He did mighty things among them, did they not let the people go, that they might depart?*

That verse would make no sense if hardening were simply God's act. In Psalms, you read that the wicked have calloused hearts (17:10; 73:7; 119:70), so hard hearts are a willful alignment with wickedness.

Israel's hardening as a nation is a clear example of God's work. Consider the following:

> *Isaiah 6:9-10 (NKJV)—And He said, "Go, and tell this people: 'Keep on hearing, but do not understand; keep on seeing, but do not perceive.' Make the heart of this people dull, and their ears heavy, and shut their eyes; lest they see with their eyes, and hear with their ears, and understand with their heart, and return and be healed."*

God tells Isaiah that Israel's hard heart will reject him as God's messenger when he goes to them. Jesus (Matthew 13:14–15) and Paul (Acts 28:25–27) refer to those verses as prophetic of Israel's rejection of Jesus as God's Messiah.

Consider how God used Israel's hardening in an incredibly beneficial way. It paved the way for Paul to minister to the Gentiles (Acts 28:28). Additionally, because of God's perfect plan, Israel's hardening is not final. When the full number of the Gentiles has come into God's family, all of Israel will be somehow saved (Romans 11:25–27). Now, that mystery asks you to believe in God's perfect plan.

Why is this discussion about Israel's hardening meaningful? For the believers of the Old Testament (Psalms 95:8) and the New Testament (Hebrews 3:8, 15; 4:7), *Israel's hard heart is a warning and challenge not to follow their behavior*.

More specifically, Jesus makes this clear when He warns, maybe rebukes, His disciples for the hardness of their hearts.

> *Mark 8:17-21 (NKJV)—But Jesus, being aware of it, said to them, "Why do you reason because you have no bread? Do you not yet perceive nor understand? Is your heart still hardened? Having eyes, do you not see? And having ears, do you not hear? And do you not remember? When I broke the five loaves for the five thousand, how many baskets full of fragments did you take up?"*

> *They said to Him, "Twelve."*

> *"Also, when I broke the seven for the four thousand, how many large baskets full of fragments did you take up?"*

> *And they said, "Seven."*

> *So He said to them, "How is it you do not understand?"*

What is Jesus telling His disciples? Their hearts somehow did not see the reality that the miraculous feeding of thousands was not about food or hunger; **it was about who Jesus is** and His power over everything. They failed to see His point about the leaven, which Jesus symbolized as the lousy thinking of the Pharisees. *He was saying they were doing the same thing, thinking about Him incorrectly, like wicked hard hearts think! They did not see who Jesus really was!*

But there is good news! God's grace can repair your hard or hardening heart. He can restore you, remove your stone heart, and give you a heart of flesh (Ezekiel 11:18–21).

Hard Hearts Are Everywhere

Of course, hard hearts occur in all areas of life. When you reject the wisdom of God, you put another callous on your heart, which leads you away from God to a self-absorbed lifestyle. You stop seeing who Jesus says He is and stop walking as an *Overcomer*!

Do you have callouses forming on your heart? Like Jesus said, ". . . do you not see . . . do you not hear?" Each callous *prevents you from growing as an Overcomer.* Instead, you become a typical power-hungry, controlling tyrant pursuing what you think is best for ME, not WE!

Finally, accepting your hard heart is one of the wages of sin and hard hearts. You gradually get used to your hard heart until you come to the place where you no longer even realize it is sin. That is the essence of a hard heart. Only the power of being filled with the Holy Spirit can change or prevent the inherent consequences of sin and hard hearts.

Hard Hearts and Consequences

A clear example of the consequences God allows for ignoring His clear truth is Adam and Eve in the Garden of Eden. The table below shows what God did and did not do with Adam and Eve.

DID	DIDN'T
• Allow Eve to talk with Satan	• Stop the temptation
• Allow Eve to be deceived	• Stop the sin
• Allow Eve and Adam to choose to obey	• Tell them they could have a second chance
• Seek them after they sinned	• Ignore the stated consequences
• Maintain a relationship with them	• "Disown" them or say He was going to create some better people
• Show mercy/love by providing a solution to their sin	
• Show justice by initiating consequences	
• Shut the gate to the Garden of Eden and opened the door to Heaven	

If you summarize the information in the table, you could say,

God allowed them to walk away from what was best for them and experience the costly consequences of their decision.

That statement is not easy to accept or understand. It probably sends shivers down the spine of parents and anyone in a position of authority. You might ask, "Why would God let them experience the enormous consequences without stopping them?"

Since God is PERFECT, it was the right thing to do. Instead of questioning it, accept it, at least for now, and see how to use God's approach in your relationships and life.

Right now, someone you know is doing the wrong thing, and there will be consequences. If you were God, what would you do when you learn about what they are doing? Would you try to change their mind to do what is right? Would you put an obstacle in their way to prevent them from doing what is wrong? Or would you accept their freedom to choose to do something wrong, even if it has horrible consequences?

God Rescues Souls AND Allows Sin

Yes, God redeems and rescues souls from hell, **AND** He does not stand in the way of your sinful desires and actions—or mine! ***That is a critical thought that could radically change your relationships.***

Romans 1 is evidence that God allows the worst to happen.

> *Romans 1:24-28 (NKJV)—Therefore God also gave them up to uncleanness, in the lusts of their hearts, to dishonor their bodies among themselves, who exchanged the truth of God for the lie, and worshiped and served the creature rather than the Creator, who is blessed forever. Amen.*
>
> *For this reason God gave them up to vile passions. For even their women exchanged the natural use for what is against nature. Likewise also the men, leaving the natural use of the woman, burned in their lust for one another, men with men committing what is shameful, and receiving in themselves the penalty of their error which was due.*
>
> *And even as they did not like to retain God in their knowledge, God gave them over to a debased mind, to do those things which are not fitting.*

Notice that it DOES NOT say that God tried to stop them from thinking with their vile and hard hearts.

God has a plan, and the sin in the Garden was allowed as part of His plan. How can you know that? Because it happened! God permitted all that has occurred as part of His plan. He is following His plan to its ultimate glorious and perfect end.

The Seed of Consequence

Maybe the consequence becomes the seed planted to grow new behavior!

He is totally in control, and you are free to make choices—no one knows how both are true, but they are. Praise God that He knows how all this works and does it PERFECTLY!

Is He PERFECT when He does not prevent you from sinning and lets you experience its consequences? Absolutely! That may be the most important thing to accept. When you stop someone from experiencing consequences, you may be hindering their growth. Maybe the consequence becomes the seed planted to grow new behavior!

But Freedom Will Cost Too Much!

What if the cost of the consequences is too high? Should you step in and prevent it? That makes sense and appears to be rational thinking.

The difficulty is that in the Garden of Eden and throughout the Bible, God provides clear examples of how He provided explicit instruction, sent prophets to remind and warn of the consequences, and **STILL** let the people experience extremely BAD consequences.

> **The WORST consequence that can happen to any person is separation from God—and God allows that to happen!**

Since God is our model, He created freedom of choice and allows the consequences of bad decisions. He also provides everything for "life and godliness" (2 Peter 1:3) for His children and ***lets us walk away from Him***.

With that as the background, is it correct to say that it is best to—

1. Provide clear instructions and expectations.
2. Draw bright, clear boundaries.
3. Describe clear consequences.
4. Encourage and exhort self-governance and freedom.
5. Allow them to experience the consequences.

When depending on man's knowledge, experience, and thinking, it is easy to argue against those steps. However, that logic is clearly in God's Word. It is easy to say that following that sequence is acting like God. Unfortunately, my behavior, and maybe yours, often violates one or more of those items, which leaves us trying to prevent people from crossing the boundary and trying to control them. Unfortunately, control drives them to rebel and use counter strategies to get across the boundary anyway.

All five steps are essential. Without clarity in steps 1–3, you do not help people know right and wrong behavior. Without step 4, you are apathetic and unloving; without step 5, there is no justice and learning. It is wise to identify which of the steps you tend to ignore.

God Allows the Worst Choices

If you tend to be a "Control Person," trying to control everything and everybody, much of your worry and anxiety is associated with step 5. Based on personal experience, when I did steps 1–4, it provided strength and courage to trust God and use step 5.

What can we learn from this? The only way to model God's behavior is to do all 5 of the steps. The last item is the one that screams at me that it cannot be accurate. It is like fingernails on a chalkboard. But that is what God did, and He is PERFECT!

> **It is evident from God's Word that He lets us experience the consequence of sin, even when it results in a choice for Hell.**

The seed of consequences has often grown and developed my behavior for the better. The worse the consequence, the greater the blossom of changed behavior. Other times, my lousy behavior did not change, and I became angry at the consequences. Those situations, once recognized, blossomed into better behavior, but it took much longer.

Maybe you are trying to rescue someone, preventing the seed of consequences from blossoming into healthy change!

BUT WAIT, THAT IS NOT THE END!

If you stop at step 5, you miss some marvelous actions of your PERFECT God and Father. You miss the salvation message that God provides repeatedly in His Word. It is the cycles you see in Judges and throughout the Bible. The cycles in Judges follow this pattern.

1. **Sin**—You cross the boundary into the realm of pain and consequences.
2. **Enemy**—God allows the pain and consequences that He warned about.
3. **Cry**—You do not like the pain and consequences and cry for deliverance.
4. **Deliverer**—God redeems and delivers you.

The cycle starts over unless you trust God and do not cross the boundary!

However, what are you missing if you stop at step 5?

Forgiveness, Redemption, and Restoration!

Yes, the cycle is real! God allows you to experience the consequences, and since He has already forgiven you, He waits patiently for your return and confession (repentance is part of confession). He waits for your return like the prodigal son's father, rejoices in your changed heart, and throws a party to welcome you back.

The consequences remain because they are part of the process that helps motivate Godly thinking. Even though it may sound strange, as stated earlier, the consequences may be the seed that grows new behavior.

That means the five steps are incomplete. The process is continual, like a cycle or, better yet, an upward spiral. When you apply the teaching

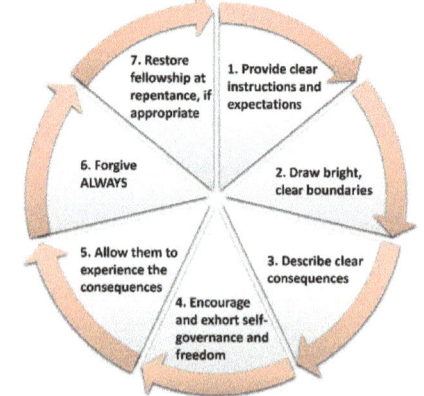

of Jesus about forgiveness in Luke 17:3-10 to the process, a sigh almost comes from your soul—thank you, Lord, that the "game" is not over when experiencing the consequences.

While the first five steps are part of life, the final two are also:

5. Forgive ALWAYS.
6. Restore (and redeem) fellowship at repentance, if appropriate.

The last step is not tied to forgiveness but to their repentance. That is the idea of 1 John 1:9.

Adding these final two steps more appropriately follows the model God demonstrates. In fact, the process displays His Image—

- Powerful—boundaries, consequences, justice
- Belonging—freedom, forgiveness, restoration

The last two steps require a constant attitude of accepting their freedom, a willingness to forgive, and desiring to restore the relationship. Otherwise, you will miss the last two critical elements in the process.

Please pray about this and consider applying it to your relationships today!

Hard Hearts and Discipline

Hopefully, using the Moment of Truth process will reduce the need for discipline in the church. Following a straightforward, Godly process is essential when discipline is needed.

The Belgic Confession (1561) speaks of three ways to know a true church: ". . . the preaching of pure doctrine, the administration of the sacraments, and the exercise of church discipline."

Church discipline is best for the church, but fear of conflict, disunity, and even legal problems leads to not dealing with members living in sin. If it were not the best, God would not give instructions on how to do it! Discipline is God's loving plan for restoring believers to fellowship with Himself and the body of Christ.

Disciplinary action needs Godly thinking and a desire for restoration. That is the purpose of this brief look at the biblical doctrine of church discipline.

The Need

> *The church is called not only to a ministry of reconciliation,*
> *but a ministry of nurture to those within her gates. Part of*
> *that nurture includes church discipline.—R.C. Sproul*

Church discipline is best when you see it as part of discipleship. It ministers to a church member in bondage to sin. When done correctly, you invite them to restore their walk with Christ and experience freedom from the bondage of sin. It is also a clear biblical imperative from Jesus (Matthew 18:15–17) and Paul (1 Corinthians 5:1–13). The Corinthian church is an example of not exercising church discipline and suffering consequences.

The church that neglects discipline is not loving, kind, forgiving, or gracious! That church hinders God's work and advancement of the gospel. It hurts the church's spiritual effectiveness and existence. Be careful; God snuffed out Thyatira's candle because of moral compromise (Revelation 2:20–24).

The Pattern and Purpose

The pattern for discipline is God's fatherly love.

> *Hebrews 12:5–8 (NKJV)—And you have forgotten the exhortation which speaks to you as to sons: "My son, do not despise the chastening of the LORD, nor be discouraged when you are rebuked by Him; for whom the LORD loves He chastens, and scourges every son whom He receives." If you endure chastening, God deals with you as with sons; for what son is there whom a father does not chasten? But if you are without chastening, of which all have become partakers, then you are illegitimate and not sons.*

And love and discipline are connected.

> *Revelation 3:19 (KNJV)—As many as I love, I rebuke and chasten.*

The world often views discipline as punishment, but God's discipline is from His love for a family member. He deals with you "as to sons." All faithful and caring fathers will, when needed, exercise loving discipline! Hebrews 12:10 (NKJV) says that is because God's loving discipline is

> *. . . for our profit, that we may be partakers of His holiness.*

That is hard to accept because going through discipline is sorrowful, not joyful. But there is a reward.

> *Hebrews 12:11 (NKJV)— . . . afterward it yields the peaceable fruit of righteousness to those who have been trained by it.*

If you do not remember that truth, you will become discouraged by discipline or trials coming your way. Also, God provides you with the following two verses in Hebrews 12 to remove discouragement.

> *Hebrews 12:12-13 (NKJV)—Therefore strengthen the hands which hang down, and the feeble knees, and make straight paths for your feet, so that what is lame may not be dislocated, but rather be healed.*

God's purpose in discipline is to heal and restore the repentant to spiritual usefulness. When you accept that, you approach church discipline motivated by love and committed to healing and restoration.

The purpose of church discipline is not judging fallen saints, just like a Moment of Truth is not about punishment. **It is to wake people to their sins and help them return to their former spiritually healthy condition.** That purpose is evident in what you saw earlier in chapter 7, "Create a Culture of Truth."

> *Galatians 6:1 (NKJV)—Brethren, even if a man is caught in any trespass, you who are spiritual, restore such a one in a spirit of gentleness; looking to yourself, lest you too be tempted.*

First, the purpose of discipline is to "mend" and "repair" someone injured or damaged on the battlefield of life. Second, it equips the wounded saint with the spiritual principles needed to avoid further injury and grow in their walk with the Lord. Finally, it helps them return to their former Godly condition. All three elements imply the need for your patience and perseverance.

The Steps

In a survey of 439 pastors about church discipline, 50 percent said they took no action when discipline would have been best. The three top reasons for no action were:

1. fear of the consequences or outcome
2. preference for avoiding disruptive problems
3. ignorance of the proper procedures

The easiest to overcome is the third. Here are the proper steps that Jesus outlined in Matthew 18.

> *Matthew 18:15-18 (NKJV)—"Moreover if your brother sins against you, go and tell him his fault between you and him alone. If he hears you, you have gained your brother. But if he will not hear, take with you one or two more, that 'by the mouth of two or three witnesses every word may be established.' And if he refuses to hear them, tell it to the church. But if he refuses even to hear the church, let him be to you like a heathen and a tax collector."*

The four steps are private reproof, private conference, public announcement, and public exclusion. Before you start the first step with a person, review "Check Your Heart Before You Start" in chapter 7.

1. Private Reproof

In his sermon "Reproof, a Christian Duty," Charles Finney remarked,

> *"If you see your neighbor sin, and you pass by and neglect to reprove him, it is just as cruel as if you should see his house on fire, and pass by and not warn him of it."*

While he sees reproof as a Christian duty, participating with God is better seen as a privilege.

Reproof is first in private, as seen in Jesus' words in Matthew 18:15 (NKJV):

> *. . . between you and him alone.*

You only discuss the sin with the offender. You do not talk or gossip behind their back. Unfortunately, people express concern for a person's sin in the form of "prayer requests" for the person. That is often just gossip! Watch for that and discourage it.

"Reprove" is strong and means "to bring to light, expose, convict, or convince someone." It is the same word Jesus used to describe the ministry of the Holy Spirit in the lives of unbelievers.

> *John 16:8 (NKJV)—And when He has come, He will convict [reprove] the world of sin, and of righteousness, and of judgment:*

When you "reprove" someone, you show them their sin or fault. That will seem risky if you focus more on their response rather than being used by God for their benefit. You do not know how they will respond. But done God's way (Galatians 6:1-5), gently and graciously, they may see their error and not be defensive.

Sometimes there is little or no doubt that the person has sinned. Other times, there is a question. Either way, always follow the guidelines in Galatians 6:1-5 (see chapter 9). If there is some question, explain your concern and ask, "Do I understand this situation correctly? Does a sin need to be dealt with, or a clarification made that I do not know about?"

The last clause of Matthew 18:15 reveals the desired result.

> *Matthew 18:15 (NKJV)—If he hears you,*
> *you have gained your brother.*

The word "hears" is not just hearing with the ear. It means "to agree, follow, heed or obey" (John 5:25; 9:27; Acts 28:28). It can also include repentance because that is what they need.

Believers have debated whether dealing with sin publicly or privately is best. In the first few centuries of the church, persons under discipline privately also made a public confession. However, Matthew's text does not state that it is necessary.

If they repent, turn from sin, and turn back to God, they agree with God that it was sin and settle the issue. But no repentance means that the discipline advances to the next stage.

2. Private Conference

Jesus stated that a brother or sister might sometimes be unwilling to repent in the private rebuke. So He gave the second step.

> *Matthew 18:16 (NKJV)—But if he will not hear, take*
> *with you one or two more, that "by the mouth of two or*
> *three witnesses every word may be established."*

Jesus gave the Old Testament requirement that a person may not be convicted of a crime based on a single witness (Numbers 35:30; Deuteronomy 17:6; 19:15). Several witnesses show that the testimony is truthful.

Some scholars say the additional witnesses must have first-hand knowledge of the sin. But what Jesus says does not require that. More likely, the primary purpose of the additional witnesses is simply to strengthen the rebuke and thus lead the offender to repentance.

The sinner is not forced or coerced to repent. You want to help the offender realize the seriousness of the situation. While adding more people to the process is meant to help repentance, some people become defensive and "hear" less, leading to the third step.

3. Public Announcement

> *Matthew 18:17 (NKJV)—And if he refuses*
> *to hear them, tell it to the church.*

The first two steps were in private. But an unrepentant saint requires stronger, public action.

Notice what Jesus did not say! He did not say, "Tell it to the bishop, synod, or church board." He said, "Tell it to the church." Tell it to the local body of believers gathered in assembly. The local congregation is the final court in church discipline matters.

The body of believers (1 Cor. 12:14–20), including the church leaders (i.e., elders, pastoral staff, or deacons), are the final court to provide loving care for everyone in the body; sometimes, that care is in the form of discipline.

A word of caution. When a church member gives a pastor or leader private information, that information is legally classified as privileged. You cannot repeat that information in a public church meeting without the person's consent. If you violate this confidence, you undermine your integrity as a church leader, which may lead to legal issues for invasion of privacy. You must carefully report to the church without saying anything confidential and private.

Getting the offender's permission to speak about the matter is best. Whether they agree or not, limit the report to what is known publicly rather than what was told privately. **Focus the message on the fact that the offender failed to respond to pastoral instruction concerning known sin.**

However, if you decide to bring the matter of a sinning saint before the church, do it to **encourage the congregation to recognize its part in bringing the brother or sister to repentance.** Encourage people to pray for the sinner, to avoid a critical spirit, and to beware of pride that thinks, "That would never happen to me." The public announcement should be that "God hates sin but loves sinners." Church discipline must reflect this divine perspective.

As you move through these stages, ensure you provide reasonable time for repentance and change at each step. The time between stages depends on the response of the offender. If you allow too much time, it implies tolerance, not love. Too little time means punishment, not love.

4. Public Exclusion

Jesus presents the final step:

> Matthew 18:17 (NKJV)—But if he refuses even to hear the church, let him be to you like a heathen and a tax collector

Disassociate the offender from the church fellowship when you have made every effort to bring the sinner to repentance without results.

The reference to the "Gentile and tax-gatherer" is best understood by considering the first-century Jewish culture. The Jews' popular religious opinion in Jesus' day did not see the Gentiles receiving the divine blessings promised to Israel. A Gentile was not permitted to pass beyond the outer court into the sacred confines of the temple. The penalty for doing so was death! Tax-gatherers like Zacchaeus (Luke 19:2–10) worked for the Roman government. Such Jews were regarded as traitors and outcasts serving Rome at the expense of their countrymen.

Jesus wants you to see unrepentant sinners as outside the circle of God's people. Some churches refer to this as "ex-communication." That means cutting off a person from church membership, fellowship, and communion. No longer is the unrepentant saint allowed to share in the activities and privileges as part of the church fellowship.

Ex-communication is often seen as punishment for the unrepentant saint. A more biblical perspective is to keep loving them (pursuing their best), even as God loves you when you sin. You reach out to them as God encourages you, but not to relate to them as a member of the body of Christ. As strong as this disciplinary step is, it is about a lack of repentance. The attitude of the church members is crucial in carrying out this most severe step in the discipline. As R. C. Sproul says,

> *God Himself, like the prodigal's father, lets people*
> *depart from Him when they are determined*
> *to go, but He lets them go with tears.*

Ex-communication, done correctly, is motivated by love and exercised to encourage genuine repentance and restoration.

The Follow-Up

What if church discipline leads to genuine repentance after public exclusion? How should the church family respond?

Often, the tendency is to keep the repentant offender at a distance and deny full restoration to joyful fellowship with God's people. That was a problem in the Corinthian church. Paul directed the church regarding the discipline of a brother who was sexually involved with his stepmother. He instructed the Corinthians on what to do.

> *1 Corinthians 5:13 (NKJV)—But those who are outside God*
> *judges. Therefore "put away from yourselves the evil person."*

The church did what they were told, and the offender repented. But when Paul wrote 2 Corinthians, about eight months later, nothing had been done to restore the repentant offender to full fellowship with the church family. The Corinthian believers had shared in the disciplinary process. Now, Paul urged them to share in the vital matter of disciplinary follow-up.

2 Corinthians 2:7-8 (NKJV)— . . . so that, on the contrary,
you ought rather to forgive and comfort him, lest perhaps
such a one be swallowed up with too much sorrow.
Therefore I urge you to reaffirm your love to him.

Paul's three instructions to the church body were "forgive," "comfort," and "reaffirm . . . love." The last two steps of church discipline (public announcement and public exclusion) are like a powerful drug that can bring healing or significant harm, depending on how it is administered.

If you want spiritual healing for the offender, then:

- Tell them of the church's forgiveness.
- Encourage them in their Christian life and growth.
- Show evidence that you love them (pursue their best).

When you do not follow those clear instructions, you leave an opening for Satan to "take advantage of us" (2 Corinthians 2:11) and create bitterness, discord, and dissension in the church.

The Precautions

The possibility of litigation is now happening in some churches that exercise biblical church discipline. What can be done to avoid such legal problems?

First, include a clear statement in the church constitution on the church's beliefs and practices regarding church discipline. Second, provide all members and prospective members with the constitution, including the church's procedures for dealing with sinning saints. Third, when discipline is necessary, ensure it is carried out according to the church constitution. Fourth, remember that information communicated in confidence to the pastor, elders, or church leaders acting in their official capacities is privileged information for which there is legal accountability. Fifth, do not advertise any matter of discipline outside the church family. Sixth, if a lawsuit is filed, pursue an out-of-court settlement or an alternative means of resolving the conflict.

Church discipline has certain risks. Yet Christ did not give you, as a leader in the church, an option to ignore sin. Follow the biblical procedures, administer discipline out of love, and maintain a view toward restoration. Doing that means having a clear conscience before God regardless of any earthly court's decision.

Hard Hearts and Marriage

Hopefully, this can clarify confusion about divorce and help anyone who has gone through or is considering a divorce.

I want to be clear that nothing in this section encourages or supports divorce. I passionately believe in God's original intent for marriage—one man, one woman for life. **It is that simple!**

God's Original and Clear Plan for Marriage

When God created man and woman, He gave clear information about marriage.

> *Genesis 2:24-25 (NKJV)—Therefore a man shall leave*
> *his father and mother and be joined to his wife, and*
> *they shall become one flesh. And they were both naked,*
> *the man and his wife, and were not ashamed.*

That verse is God's instructions or criteria for marriage, which involves joining a man and woman together. Of course, people with a same-sex marriage agenda will try to argue differently, but the clarity of the passage and the context is about Adam and Eve—a man and a woman. God's Word offers no support for the same-sex marriage agenda.

In Genesis 2:24-25, God says marriage has four critical elements.

- **Leave**—Commitment and devotion change from parents to the spouse. Now, the spouse is the priority number 2 in your life. God is number 1.
- **Cleave**—It means stick to, keep close, follow closely, overtake, catch, or pursue. The word is more than a picture of holding on to something. It is pursuing your spouse with great energy and clinging to them. That picture shows how much marriage involves work—pursuing the best for your spouse.
- **One flesh**—Nothing is separate between the two people; all things together. Everything is to be one. That has a broader meaning than becoming one from the beautiful sexual union.
- **Naked**—Too often, the only picture considered is the sexual union of a man and woman. But this is much more. It is about having no secrets and being utterly vulnerable to each other. When you are entirely open, it implies purity in your life mentally, emotionally, and spiritually.

How easy would it be to violate those elements? Extremely easy. All of them require a change of mind toward serving your spouse. All of them require a foundation of great values and good thinking. It would be somewhat hard to prove the violation of some elements since it is about values and thinking. You would not be abiding by those criteria when:

- You replace your spouse as your number two priority with another person or thing.
- You do not pursue, cling to, or work at doing what is best for your spouse and the marriage.
- You keep secrets and do not share ownership with your spouse.
- You are not open with your spouse mentally, emotionally, or spiritually.

That is not a complete list but just some examples, and those are easy to violate! But what if there is no confession (repentance) for a violation or no forgiveness by the spouse? Is the marriage terminated? Is it over?

NO! Why? That is the definition of marriage or the criteria for marriage. It is about combining two people, not about separating two people. When you talk about dividing people, that is man's thinking. God's thinking is about "one flesh."

You could argue that this is a contract, and not abiding by the criteria is breaking the contract. But again, that is not the purpose of these statements. The intent of what God tells you here is marriage is "till death do us part." That, of course, is precisely what Jesus says in Matthew 19:6 and 8.

The four elements define God's intent for marriage and **do not include options to terminate it**. As Jesus said, the hardness of man's heart looks for ways out of the marriage. God's original standard provides no path or method to break the one flesh created at marriage.

Man's Hard-Hearted Changes

But hard hearts are unwilling to abide by God's desire. The oldest known civil law, the Code of Hammurabi (1750-1900 B.C.), shows that early in the history of man, there was a desire to get out of marriage. The Code, created by King Hammurabi, became the common law of most of the world and apparently was used during Abraham's, Isaac's, and Jacob's lives. Some scholars believe that God's standard was forgotten during Israel's time in Egypt, and the codes of man became the standard for marriage. It was not until the Mosaic Law was given that God provided better instructions about divorce.

The Code included specific instructions on marriage and divorce.

- Marriage was a simple contract, valid only if written, signed, and witnessed.
- Divorce was allowed and treated variously, but only if the contract had been violated.
- Divorce was verbal, "I put her away," and primarily for men.

> *Hammurabi Code, Paragraph 141: If the wife of a man who is living in his house has set her face to go out, and has acted extravagantly, "has wasted her house" (bit-za u-za-ap-pa-ah), and has neglected her husband, one can bring her to justice, and if her husband formally divorces her, with the words "I repudiate her" (e-si-ib-sa), she goes her own way and receives no uzubu. If the husband does not pronounce this formula, and takes another woman (zinnistu), she remains in his house as a maidservant.—Stanley A. Cook, M.A., The Laws of Moses and the Code of Hammurabi, p120*

- It was risky for a wife to divorce. She had to prove the husband was guilty of violating the marriage contract. She was drowned if the courts disagreed.
- Divorce was prohibited if the wife was incurably sick.

Hard-hearted mankind did not want God's standard and created a way to dissolve a marriage.

Many people talk about marriage as a covenant, not a contract. That is an important distinction because a covenant marriage makes divorce harder than a standard contractual marriage. Unfortunately, it does not prevent hard-heartedness.

God's Plan Has Not Changed

God's original design for marriage in Genesis 2:24-25 is still the standard, and it did not provide separation or divorce as an option. Divorce was a man-made option, and laws were created for it by King Hammurabi. Most importantly, when you read Malachi 2:15-16, you will see that God has not changed His mind about the standard He set in Genesis.

> *Malachi 2:15b-16 (NKJV)—"Therefore take heed to your spirit, and let none deal treacherously with the wife of his youth. For the LORD God of Israel says that He hates divorce, for it covers one's garment with violence," says the LORD of hosts. "Therefore take heed to your spirit, that you do not deal treacherously."*

What Does the Bible Say About Divorce?

God knows our hard-hearted condition, so He made a provision for man's hard heart when married. Jesus talks about hard hearts and marriage in Matthew 19. But before you read the passage, it is crucial to understand the key words used in both the New and Old Testaments.

Key Words

In the Old Testament, study and understand three words—*cepher*, *kerimuth*, and *shalach*. Anyone can use available Hebrew resources to see the definitions of these words. Simply stated:

- *Cepher* and *kerimuth* are about a **Certificate of Divorce.**
- *Shalach* is about **sending away.**

That is especially important because **shalach is not a synonym of the other two words.**

You have Greek instead of Hebrew in the New Testament, so different words cover the same concepts.

- *Apostasion* is about a Deed or Instrument of Divorce
- *Apoluo* is about letting loose, unbinding, separating

Old Testament—Mosaic Law

With the definitions of the words in your mind, look at the key passage in the Old Testament.

> *Deuteronomy 24:1-4 (NKJV)—When a man takes a wife and marries her, and it happens that she finds no favor in his eyes because he has found some uncleanness in her, and he writes her a certificate of divorce, puts it in her hand, and sends her out of his house, when she has departed from his house, and goes and becomes another man's wife, if the latter husband detests her and writes her a certificate of divorce, puts it in her hand, and sends her out of his house, or if the latter husband dies who took her as his wife, then her former husband who divorced her must not take her back to be his wife after she has been defiled; for that is an abomination before the LORD, and you shall not bring sin on the land which the LORD your God is giving you as an inheritance.*

The Code of Hammurabi was created before God gave the Mosaic Law to the Israelites. God seems to be correcting how hard hearts used the Code's statements about divorce.

Divorce was verbal in the Code. A husband could say, "I put her away," and the marriage ended. God made a significant change by stating that a **written document** must accompany the "sending away."

> *. . . writes her a certificate of divorce, puts it in her hand, and sends her out of his house . . .*

Looking up the underlined words, you will see *cepher* and *kerimuth* for "certificate of divorce" and *shalach* for "sends" her out.

God allows divorce and the pain created from divorce, as you can see in Judith Wallerstein's book, *The Unexpected Legacy of Divorce—The 25-Year Landmark Study*.

Well, that is not good news for leaders who fight for marriage and against hard hearts. But it is God's Word. At the same time, God has not changed His statement in Malachi 2:15-16—He still hates divorce. He only permits it because of our hard hearts and freedom to sin.

New Testament—Jesus' Explanation

The best passage about divorce and hard hearts is what Jesus says in Matthew 19.

> *Matthew 19:3-10 (NKJV)—The Pharisees also came to Him, testing Him, and saying to Him, "Is it lawful for a man to divorce his wife for just any reason?" And He answered and said to them, "Have you not read that He who made them at the beginning 'made them male and female,' and said, 'For this reason a man shall leave his father and mother, and be joined to his wife; and the two shall become one flesh'? So then, they are no longer two but one flesh. Therefore what God has joined together, let not man separate." They said to Him, "Why then did Moses command to give her a certificate of divorce, and put her away?" He said to them, "Moses, because of the hardness of your hearts, permitted you to divorce your wives, but from the beginning it was not so. And I say to you, whoever divorces his wife, except for sexual immorality, and marries another, commits adultery; and whoever marries her who is divorced commits adultery." His disciples said to Him, "If such is the case of the man with his wife, it is better not to marry."*

PHARISEES' TWO-PART TRAP

The Pharisees created what they thought was an excellent trap for Jesus when they approached him in Matthew 19. The trap had two parts—a Rabbinic trap and a Mosaic trap. The design of the Rabbinic trap would get one group of Rabbis upset with Jesus, and hopefully, Herod Antipas would get mad at Jesus. The Mosaic trap tried to get Jesus to disagree with Moses.

First, the Rabbinic trap. The Rabbis had two explanations for Deuteronomy 24:1 that you saw earlier.

> *When a man takes a wife and marries her, and it happens that she finds no favor in his eyes because he has found some uncleanness in her . . .*

The difference of opinion is from the phrase "found some uncleanness." Here are the two views.

Hillel—liberal	Shammai—conservative
• Means almost anything the husband did not like—even if the husband found a more attractive woman	• Means some grossly shameful act • Some suggest adultery, but that required death

If Jesus accepts the Hillel view, the Shammai advocates will be mad at him. If He agrees with the Shammai view, the Hillel advocates will be upset with Him. But worse, if Jesus agrees with the Shammai view, Herod Antipas would be mad at Jesus. Herod killed John the Baptist for saying, "It is not lawful for you to have your brother's wife." That means that John the Baptist was taking the Shammai view—and Herod killed him because of it. So ultimately, they were thinking, maybe Herod will kill Jesus if He chooses the Shammai view.

It's a rather good trap. But that is only the first part of the trap. The other was the Mosaic trap. If Jesus disagrees with Moses, then the Pharisees would say that Jesus is not following the Law of God.

By the way, which of the two views of divorce do you think most Jewish men accepted? Yes, the Hillel view. They wanted the easiest path possible to get out of a marriage. Herod, of course, also followed Hillel's view.

JESUS DISMANTLES THE RABBINIC TRAP

With that background, watch how Jesus handled their trap.

> Matthew 19:4 (NKJV)—"Have you not read,
> that He who made them . . ."

That is a powerful statement! Think about who the Pharisees were—scholars of the Old Testament. They had studied and even memorized Genesis through Deuteronomy. Now, Jesus says, "Have you not read . . ." That is like saying to a Biblical scholar, "Have you ever read Genesis chapter 2?"

Jesus called them back to Genesis 2:24-25 to show them that the Law (Deuteronomy 24) does not remove God's original plan and intent for marriage.

> Matthew 19: 4-6 (NKJV)—"Have you not read that He who
> made them at the beginning 'made them male and female,'
> and said, 'For this reason a man shall leave his father and

mother, and be joined to his wife; and the two shall become one flesh?' So then, they are no longer two but one flesh. Therefore what God has joined together, let not man separate."

A concise paraphrase might be

"If you are unclear about marriage and divorce in the law of Moses, make sure you use God's original intent for marriage when you create any interpretations."

Notice that they did not mention any other argument. They knew that their trap had failed, so they quickly moved on to the second part, the Mosaic trap.

JESUS DISMANTLES THE MOSAIC TRAP

Matthew 19:7 (NKJV) —"Why then did Moses command to give a certificate of divorce, and put her away?"

This is the only time in this conversation that *apostasion* and *apoluo* are used. The word for "certificate of divorce" is *apostasion*, while "put away" is *apoluo*. That may be important because it could imply that *apoluo* was used in conversations to indicate or include *apostasion*.

The reply of the Pharisees focused on "command" because that was their trap. If they could get Jesus to violate a command in the law, they would use that against Him. But Jesus was not trapped; they were.

Matthew 19:8 (NKJV)—"Moses, because of the hardness of your hearts, permitted you to divorce . . ."

Jesus did not repeat their word "command," which is extremely important. **The Deuteronomy passage has no command to get divorced**; it is just the process for a legal divorce. That is truly clear based on Jesus' response. **A divorce is an option when a man or woman has a hard heart**. It is an option—an unbelievably lousy option. And Jesus repeats that God wants marriage, NOT divorce.

Matthew 19:8 (NKJV)—". . . but from the beginning it was not so."

Neither of their questions trapped Jesus. Instead, it showed their hard hearts that interpreted God's Word for their benefit.

Conclusion

Through the Mosaic Law, God permits divorce, and it must use a legal document. Please note—**it is ONLY allowed because of hard hearts** that do not want to abide by God's desire for two people to stay together.

> *. . . it requires a CERTIFICATE OF DIVORCE, not just*
> *sending the spouse away. "The word 'divorce' . . . used*
> *today . . . which is issued by a judge without reference*
> *to the guilt or innocence of either party, does not have*
> *its real equivalent in the OT or NT."—Zodhiates*

That is an excellent reason not to get a no-fault divorce. It may be like "sending the spouse away" without a certificate because no valid reasons are provided for the marriage to be terminated.

What About Divorce and Remarriage?

This question would be unnecessary if fewer hard hearts got divorced. However, since divorce is an option, it is essential to ask a second question. **Is remarriage available if you have been divorced?**

4 Options

Below are four possible options.
- Remarriage is permitted in all situations.
- Remarriage is adultery.
- Remarriage is allowed if immorality is the reason for the divorce.
- Remarriage is permitted if it is a Biblical divorce.

The Bible speaks to this question in Jesus' statements in Matthew 19 and the Apostle Paul's statements in 1 Corinthians 7.

Jesus' Explanation

The critical scripture to study is the same one for the first question.

> *Matthew 19:9 (NKJV)—"And I say to you, whoever*
> *divorces his wife, except for sexual immorality, and*
> *marries another, commits adultery; and whoever*
> *marries her who is divorced commits adultery."*

As you saw in Deuteronomy, there is a difference in the words used for separation and divorce. You need to know which Greek word is used for "divorces" in this passage. Is it *apostasion* or *apoluo*?

It is *apoluo*. Each time "divorce" is used in that passage, it is about "sending away," not about a "certificate of divorce." Remember, the critical distinction between the words is *apostasion* is a certificate of divorce, and *apoluo* is just sending her away. While *apostasion* refers to a certificate of divorce, it helps to define it as a "certificate of innocence." When the spouse has this certificate of innocence, it shows the other party has a harder heart. The one providing the certificate is guilty of separating what God has put together. The certificate of innocence frees the other person from the stigma of adultery or fornication as the cause of the divorce.

On the other hand, *apoluo* is only about "sending away."

Keep this key in mind. When Jesus says, ". . . whoever marries her . . ." in the last part of verse 9, He is talking about a dismissed wife who is innocent and deserves a certificate of innocence. Why? **Because He excluded the sexually immoral wife in the exception!**

The passage can be paraphrased like this.

> *"And I say to you, whoever sends his wife away without a certificate of innocence, except when his wife was sexually immoral (the certificate is not needed then), and he marries another woman, he commits adultery. And whoever marries a woman who does not have a certificate of innocence will be committing adultery also."*

With that in mind, look at other scriptures that use the word *apoluo*.

> *Matthew 1:19 (NKJV)—Then Joseph her husband, being a just man, and not wanting to make her a public example, was minded to put her away secretly.*

Joseph wanted to "send her away" (*apoluo*). In this situation, Mary was completely innocent. She was not guilty of improper relations. The Lord intervened and told Joseph about her innocence through an angelic message. Because she was unmarried, it would not make sense for the word "divorce" to be used here.

In this passage, "divorce" is used for the word *apoluo*.

> *Matthew 5:31-32 (NKJV)—Furthermore it has been said, "Whoever divorces his wife, let him give her a certificate of divorce." But I say to you that whoever divorces his wife for any reason except sexual immorality causes her to commit adultery; and whoever marries a woman who is divorced commits adultery.*

Again, here is a paraphrase using the definition of *apoluo*.

> *31 Furthermore it has been said, "Whoever sends away (apoluo) his wife, let him give her a certificate of innocence (apostasion).*

> *32 But I say unto you, that whoever sends away (apoluo) his wife, except for sexual immorality, causes her to be seen as an adulteress when she remarries (because she did not get a certificate of innocence—apostasion); and whoever marries a*

woman that is sent away (apoluo) commits adultery (because she does not have a certificate of innocence and is still married).

What a difference in understanding what Jesus is saying! That makes complete sense when you use the correct words. Also, it is crucial to understand the difference in the tense of the Greek word used for "commit" in the phrase "causes her to commit." It is a passive verb, not an active one like the other "commit" in the passage. That is why my paraphrase says, ". . . causes her to be seen as an adulteress," which is like Jesus is stating the husband who sent her away will be responsible for her sin, not her.

Below is what Strong's Concordance offers.

> *moichásthai, to be considered or counted as an adulteress, and not "to commit adultery," as some translations have it). The subject of this sentence is the licentious person described in Matt. 5:27–30 who constantly looks upon and touches a woman other than his wife. If he consequently dismisses his own wife and does not give her the bill of divorcement spoken of in Matt. 5:31 and Deut. 24:1–4, which amounted to a certificate of innocence for his unjustifiably dismissed wife, he causes her dismissal to be looked upon as adultery on her part. An innocently dismissed wife cannot possibly be conceived of as having committed adultery herself. It is her licentious husband who has dismissed her for a reason other than sexual infidelity who commits adultery against her and, therefore, causes her to be thought of as an adulteress. In addition, the person who would marry such a dismissed woman also assumes her undeserved "adultery."— Zodhiates, S. (2000). The complete word study dictionary: New Testament (electronic ed.). Chattanooga, TN: AMG Publishers.*

The following three scriptures use the same explanation as Matthew 5:31-32. Whoever sends away (*apoluo*) his wife, except for immorality, and marries another commits adultery (because you are still married).

> *Matthew 19:9 (NKJV)—"And I say to you, whoever divorces his wife, except for sexual immorality, and marries another, commits adultery; and whoever marries her who is divorced commits adultery."*

> *Mark 10:11-12 (NKJV)—So He said to them, "Whoever divorces his wife and marries another commits adultery against her. And if a woman divorces her husband and marries another, she commits adultery."*

> *Luke 16:18 (NKJV)—"Whoever divorces his wife and marries*
> *another commits adultery; and whoever marries her who*
> *is divorced from her husband commits adultery."*

Before I go further, please remember God's desire is no divorce. None of the above discussion about *apostasion* and *apoluo* is worth discussing when you eliminate divorce as an option.

Paul's Explanation

What does the Apostle Paul tell us about divorce and remarriage? The following is a key scripture.

> *1 Corinthians 7:10-11 (NKJV)—Now to the married I command, yet*
> *not I but the Lord: A wife is not to depart from her husband. But*
> *even if she does depart, let her remain unmarried or be reconciled*
> *to her husband. And a husband is not to divorce his wife.*

CONTEXT

Good students of the Bible study the context because, without it, you can make almost any verse fit what you want it to say. The immediate context for verses 10 and 11 is in 1 Corinthians 7:1-40, or some people say it is 1 Corinthians 6:12—7:40. The context is about sexual relations and marriage.

More specifically, the context concerns some questions from the Corinthians or some of Paul's previous teachings. Everything revolves around the following statement.

> *1 Corinthians 7:1 (NKJV)—It is good for*
> *a man not to touch a woman.*

The explanation following this verse implies the Corinthians misinterpreted that statement because Paul talks about several issues for men's and women's relationships, both inside and outside marriage.

They seem to have understood ". . . not to touch a woman" to mean sexual relations were bad, even for married couples. That left the Corinthians thinking celibacy was the only proper thing for anyone. So young people were discouraged from marriage, and married couples were separating to live the celibate lifestyle.

With that context, watch how Paul corrects their thinking.

WHICH SITUATION IS BETTER?

Marriage is good. It helps reduce sexual sin, but only when the husband and wife serve one another. Unfortunately, sex becomes a method of control rather than service.

1 Corinthians 7:2-5 (NKJV)—Nevertheless, because of sexual immorality, let each man have his own wife, and let each woman have her own husband. Let the husband render to his wife the affection due her, and likewise also the wife to her husband. The wife does not have authority over her own body, but the husband does. And likewise the husband does not have authority over his own body, but the wife does. Do not deprive one another except with consent for a time, that you may give yourselves to fasting and prayer; and come together again so that Satan does not tempt you because of your lack of self-control.

Paul is extremely clear about the role the husband and wife have when it comes to sex in marriage. It is about benefiting and serving them even to the degree that you do not have authority over your body. That is amazing! And why does Paul say that? Because if that is not true in your marriage, you give Satan an easy way to tempt you to sexual sin, especially when self-control is lacking.

1 Corinthians 7:9 (NKJV)— . . . but if they cannot exercise self-control, let them marry. For it is better to marry than to burn with passion.

Marriage is far better than consuming your life with a desire for sex and having sex outside of marriage. The unsaid implication of "cannot exercise self-control" is a lack of walking with the Lord. Why? Because when you walk in the flesh, not in the Spirit, you do not benefit from His infinite source of self-control (Galatians 5:23).

Celibacy is good. But celibacy is not everyone's gift.

1 Corinthians 7:6-8 (NKJV)—But I say this as a concession, not as a commandment. For I wish that all men were even as I myself. But each one has his own gift from God, one in this manner and another in that. But I say to the unmarried and to the widows: It is good for them if they remain even as I am.

Note that Paul says this is "not a commandment." Paul believes his celibate life would be good for all, but he follows that with "each one has his own gift from God." And you can know if you have the gift based on verse 9.

Single is good. Finally, the Corinthians discouraged marriage and encouraged remaining single. He has already made the case that marriage reduces sexual sin. Now, he makes a broader statement to those who are single.

1 Corinthians 7:25-26 (NKJV)—Now concerning virgins: I have no commandment from the Lord; yet I give judgment

> *as one whom the Lord in His mercy has made trustworthy.*
> *I suppose therefore that this is good because of the present*
> *distress—that it is good for a man to remain as he is:*

He explicitly states that he has "no commandment from the Lord: yet I give my judgment," which is like saying, "Here is my opinion." He adds some weight to his opinion, asking them to seriously consider it, when he says, "as one who the Lord in His mercy has made trustworthy."

Paul is telling them his statement is trustworthy but not required by the Lord. "Because of the present distress" (persecutions), marriage is not the best option. Then he says,

> *1 Corinthians 7:28 (NKJV)—But even if you do*
> *marry, you have not sinned; and if a virgin marries,*
> *she has not sinned. Nevertheless, such will have*
> *trouble in the flesh, but I would spare you.*

Remaining single and marrying is okay—". . . if a virgin marries, she has not sinned." But marrying will create challenges for you, which he calls "trouble in the flesh," especially during this current persecution. If you remain single, you do not experience those troubles.

He states an even better reason to be single—it allows more time for "things of the Lord."

> *1 Corinthians 7:32-35 (NLT)—I want you to be free from the*
> *concerns of this life. An unmarried man can spend his time doing*
> *the Lord's work and thinking how to please him. But a married*
> *man has to think about his earthly responsibilities and how to*
> *please his wife. His interests are divided. In the same way, a*
> *woman who is no longer married or has never been married*
> *can be devoted to the Lord and holy in body and in spirit. But*
> *a married woman has to think about her earthly responsibilities*
> *and how to please her husband. I am saying this for your benefit,*
> *not to place restrictions on you. I want you to do whatever will*
> *help you serve the Lord best, with as few distractions as possible.*

God desires spouses to serve each other with their bodies, which is not needed when unmarried. But a broader service exists when unmarried—serving the body of Christ.

Note also that Paul is not trying to "place restrictions on" them to remain single; it is just an easier way to serve the Lord without the responsibilities of marriage.

So Paul clarifies that the statement in verse 1 for each situation—marriage, celibacy, and being single—is good.

IF MARRIED—DO NOT SEPARATE

In addition to incorrect thinking about getting married, Paul also needed to correct their thinking about remaining married. Apparently, married couples were separating, maybe divorcing, because they misunderstood verse 1. Or they were separating and divorcing because of hard hearts. Both are possible, but the context appears more in line with separating.

> *1 Corinthians 7:10-11 (NKJV)—Now to the married I command, yet not I but the Lord: A wife is not to depart from her husband. But even if she does depart, let her remain unmarried or be reconciled to her husband. And a husband is not to divorce his wife.*

In Jesus' conversation, the Greek words were *apostasion* and *apoluo*. Now Paul introduces two other words—*chorizo* and *aphiemi*- both are synonyms for *apoluo*.
- "A wife is not to depart . . ." (*chorizo*—separate)
- "Husband is not to divorce . . ." (*aphiemi*—send forth or away)
- ". . . even if she does depart . . ." (*chorizo*—separate)

You could paraphrase the passage like this.

> *"Wives do not separate from your husband because you think that pleases the Lord. If you separate, remain unmarried, or reconcile with your husband because you are still married. And husbands, the same is true for you; don't separate from your wife."*

> *Some scholars state that the everyday use of chorizo in Paul's day was another way to refer to a legal divorce. If that is true, it would completely change the paraphrase. It would also support the thought that remarriage after divorce is not acceptable.*

Paul then speaks to the situation where believers are married to unbelievers and uses the same words—*chorizo* and *aphiemi*.
- Unbelieving wife— ". . . let him not divorce her." (*aphiemi*)
- Unbelieving husband— ". . . let her not divorce him." (*aphiemi*)

In both situations, Paul states it is good to stay with the unbelieving spouse if that spouse desires to have them in the marriage. And if the unbelieving spouse leaves, that is okay; let them go.

> *1 Corinthians 7:15 (NKJV)—But if the unbeliever departs, let him depart; a brother or a sister is not under bondage in such cases*

Both times, *chorizo* is used for "depart(s)." However, the more critical issue is the last part, where Paul says they are "not under bondage in such cases." That means they are no longer bound to the marriage. But Paul states a great reason to stay in the marriage. The believing spouse is a channel of grace to the unbelieving spouse. God's mercy and grace somehow benefit their unbelieving spouse. It seems the believer has an opportunity to speak and demonstrate the truth to the unbeliever. But salvation is not guaranteed, just a possibility.

IF MARRIED—DO NOT DIVORCE

Additionally, Paul spoke directly about divorce when he used the terms "bound" and "loosed." Those are not technical terms but are about marriage or the marriage contract. A contract is supposed to be "binding" two parties together in agreement. And "loosed" would be the "unbinding" of the two parties.

> *1 Corinthians 7:27-28 (NKJV)—Are you bound to a wife? Do not seek to be loosed. Are you loosed from a wife? Do not seek a wife. But even if you do marry, you have not sinned and if a virgin marries, she has not sinned. Nevertheless such will have trouble in the flesh, but I would spare you.*

Simply stated, if you are married, do not seek a divorce. And remember, they were separating and divorcing because of misunderstanding Paul's statement in verse 1. Further, he tells those divorced or widowers not to seek a wife. That ties directly to the "present distress" (v26) and "trouble in the flesh" that does not happen by remaining unmarried.

Then he ends with a critical statement. "But if you do marry, you have not sinned." How much clearer can he state it? If you remarry after being "loosed," that is not a sin.

Conclusion

Sending away (*apoluo, chorizo, aphiemi*) **without** a certificate of divorce (*apostasion*) causes the innocent "sent one" and their remarried spouse to commit adultery.

Therefore, remarriage is OKAY!

- Remarriage after divorce (a legal certificate exists) is NOT a sin
- Divorce and remarriage are NOT adultery

If *chorizo* is another way to refer to a legal divorce, as referenced above, then it would be easier to argue that remarriage after a divorce is unacceptable and that reconciliation with the original spouse is the only alternative.

The easy way to avoid these questions and issues is to **follow God's original intent for marriage and stay married.** All the above information about "certificate of divorce" and "sending away" is only necessary to clarify confusion about divorce. **Please do not have a hard heart!**

Unfortunately, the above can support a hard heart. Yes, but a hard heart will do what a wicked heart wants anyway. And God knows my heart—that is not my intent. My desire is NO DIVORCE for any marriage. Divorce creates unnecessary and painful problems.

Finally, **divorce is not a sin; but what leads up to the divorce is sin.** Having **a hard heart is a sin**. Not listening to God and His original intent for marriage is a sin because anything that is ". . . not from faith is sin" (Romans 14:23). Divorce has a prescribed process to use if you follow the sin of a hard heart. But divorce is not a sin. Divorce can introduce many other problems and sins.

It is an unbelievably lousy option, so please do not take it.

DISCUSSION QUESTIONS

1. Explain the theory of what happened when Adam and Eve ate the fruit of the Tree of Knowledge of Good and Evil.
2. What does Jeremiah 17:9 tell you about your sin nature heart?
3. When God talks about your heart, what is He referring to?
4. How does a hard heart get hardened?
5. What is the worst thing God can do to any person?
6. What would you say to someone who says, "This Seed of Consequences idea tells you not to care about people and let them live in sin?"
7. Explain the need for each of the first five steps in the Seed of Consequence.
8. Explain the need for the last two steps.
9. What is the pattern and purpose of church discipline?
10. State the four steps of church discipline and briefly explain what happens in each step.
11. What needs to happen if the person repents many weeks or months after step 4?

Questions for Divorce and Remarriage

1. What is God's original and unchanged standard for marriage, and where is it found in the Bible?
2. Explain each of the four elements of God's standard.
3. What did the Code of Hammurabi imply about what man thought about God's standard?
4. What are the two crucial Hebrew words you need to know in the Old Testament? Greek words in the New Testament?
5. Explain the importance of the differences.
6. What are the critical ingredients for divorce as outlined by God in Deuteronomy 24:1-4?
7. Why did God provide these directions when He says He hates divorce in Malachi 2:15?
8. What are the two views the Jewish leaders had about divorce during Jesus' time? Which was accepted the most and why?
9. What were the two traps that the Pharisees were trying to set for Jesus?
10. What did Jesus say to dismantle each trap?
11. Does Deuteronomy 24:1-4 provide a command for divorce? Explain.

12. Is remarriage prohibited by Jesus' statements in Matthew 19:9? Explain.
13. Study the paraphrase of Matthew 5:31-32. How does that explain why remarriage is not prohibited?
14. Explain the context of 1 Corinthians 7. It is critical to understand what Paul says about marriage.
15. Using 1 Corinthians 7, explain which is best—marriage, celibacy, or being single.
16. Explain Paul's two new Greek words in 1 Corinthians 7:10.
17. What is the conclusion as to why God allowed divorce?
18. What is the conclusion as to whether remarriage after divorce is okay?
19. How do you present this information without encouraging divorce?
20. How would you support or refute this statement: "Divorce is not a sin; but what leads up to divorce is sin!"

CHAPTER 13

BIG DREAMS

From the time Andrew was a young boy, he dreamed of pastoring a large church someday. Growing up in a missionary family in Central America, with parents dedicated to serving the Lord, his life was shaped by faith and a commitment to ministry.

Andrew wanted a church where people could receive healing from emotional wounds. As a missionary, he saw many families torn apart by poverty and war and witnessed many people who suffered from trauma and emotional scars. He wanted to build the church from the ground up rather than go in and try to change what a church was trying to do. He knew he had to create a large church quickly to fulfill his dream and fulfill his calling from God.

Andrew worked through two years of Bible college as an insurance salesman and continued selling for a couple of years to build up his savings. Because he grew up in a family of missionaries, he knew how to stretch a dollar a long way. So he saved enough money to buy a house on a first-time buyer program by the time he was 23.

He started his church in his home, like his father did on the missionary field, and held three meetings a week for family, friends, and his growing network of people in need. After about six months, the church had outgrown the space in his home. He started having six meetings a week, hoping that might solve the problem of space. When the weather was nice, he would have the meetings outside in the yard, but some of his neighbors complained about that. Unsure what to do, he talked to some more mature people who came to the meetings to see if one of them could start hosting some of the meetings.

Two couples gladly agreed and said they would offer a covered dish-type meal since many people came to the evening meetings straight from work. People in the "congregation" gravitated to the meetings with the meals and to the specific couples who hosted because sometimes Andrew had to ask the couples to lead the meeting, including finding a worship leader for the meeting or playing music from their phone or iTunes.

One year after starting his church, Andrew noticed that one of the groups had a lot of teenagers coming to the Sunday night meetings. At first, they were totally focused on getting closer to Jesus in their walk with Him and studying His Word. Some of the older people in the group left and went to another church because they felt left out and because they found out that some of the teenagers were going after the meeting to a group member's house who supplied a keg of beer for them since they were underage. Concerned about the situation, they brought it up to Andrew and he didn't believe them, especially because some of the kids were from families he had known for many years. He couldn't imagine that they would go drinking after church.

Soon after this, Andrew started to feel really overwhelmed. He had not gotten any closer to his dream of having a big church and ministering to emotionally wounded people. He wasn't sure what to do, so he called a meeting with the two mature group leaders to figure out what to do.

One of the couples, Greg and Mary Sullivan, had no kids of their own and were both in their 50s. The other couple, Samuel and June Henderson, had three grown children and six grandchildren and were in their mid-60s. They all gathered at Andrew's house.

Andrew started by explaining his dream based on his experience growing up. He explained why he started the church in his home. Everyone present acknowledged that they knew part of his story based on being friends with him.

At this point, Andrew said, "I dream of having a huge mega-church with a counseling and healing center, but it doesn't seem like I'm going to ever get there."

Greg, a business consultant, said, "Andrew, that is a great and wonderful vision, but things like that don't happen overnight or even within a year or two. You've done a great job building a fellowship, but I see two things missing. One is an overseeing structure and, second, plans for funding something like that."

Andrew said, "Those are good points. I don't really know how to do that."

Samuel said, "If this were about 10 years ago, I would gladly step in and help you build this, but I'm getting ready to retire in a couple of years and want to enjoy my grandchildren. And leading our group is enough for me to handle right now."

June nodded her head in agreement as Samuel talked.

Mary said, "I can help you, Andrew, but I need to discuss this with Greg. How about we meet again in a week or so?"

Andrew said, "Yes, that would be very helpful."

Greg had heard about the teenagers drinking, so he said, "I'm not sure you are aware of it, but some of the kids from the Sunday night group are going to Stephen's house after the meeting and drinking . He always has a big keg and many are getting drunk. "

Andrew, feeling defensive, said, "Someone told me that, but I didn't really believe them. Is it my responsibility what they do once they've left my home?"

Greg said, "If you are concerned for them growing with the Lord, I think you cannot just contain that to when they are at your house."

"Okay," Andrew said, feeling like he just wanted to end this meeting. "So what day next week is good for us to meet again?"

Questions

1. What do you think happened that derailed Andrew's vision of creating a big church with a counseling/healing center?
2. What steps do you think Andrew should have taken when he started the church?
3. Now that Andrew has asked for help, what do you think they can do to help him?
4. What do you suggest Andrew do at this point?

OVERCOMERS CHOOSE AND CREATE

Key Lesson: *Create clear goals and persist until achieved or God says stop. Use and teach THP + ALA + Persist—the creative process.*

PROBLEM AND SOLUTION

Three Common Problems

Three problems consistently show up in people and organizations. There are more problems than this, but these three capture most struggles.

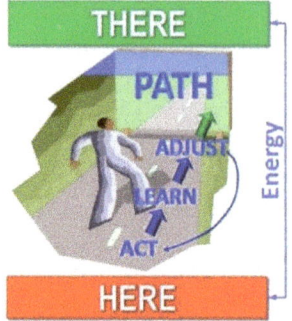

RUDDERLESS—You are unclear about where you are going and what to do. You probably do not have clear goals. You are like a ship without a rudder or a captain without a charted course. You let the day's currents, wind, and tide drive you.

Is that you?

Or you may be BLIND. You do not see reality, "how things are." When you are unclear about your current reality, you believe things are BETTER or WORSE than they are. You are not objective about life. You guess and speculate rather than observe reality.

Finally, UNFOCUSED is the result of the first two. You fill your days, weeks, and months with reacting and responding to what shows up in your life. You are constantly "fighting brush fires." You may be busy but have little to show for your work and effort.

Solution: THP (THERE, HERE, PATH)

Enough about the problem; what is the solution?
- THERE (Future) — "I want to go THERE . . ."
- HERE (Present) — ". . . but I am HERE"
- PATH (Transition) — "That's a PATH I could take."

THP is the beginning of the Creative Process. It has been around for thousands of years and is the foundation for most things created or accomplished. Your brain tends to follow THP, so if that is true, you can learn to master the process.

This quote from Abraham Lincoln shows that he used the THP structure even though he may not have known it.

> *If we could first know there we are, and whither we are tending, we could better judge what to do, and how to do it.*

You create by determining your THERE, then your HERE, and finally, develop actions to move you along the PATH.

There are multiple examples of THP in the Bible; here are two.

> *Luke 5:18-20 (NJKV)—Then behold, men brought on a bed a man who was paralyzed, whom they sought to bring in and lay before Him. And when they could not find how they might bring him in, because of the crowd, they went up on the housetop and let him down with his bed through the tiling into the midst before Jesus. When He saw their faith, He said to him, "Man, your sins are forgiven you."*

What was THERE for the paralyzed man and his friends? Obviously, he wanted to be healed. Can you see the HERE or the current reality they faced? Sure, it is the crowd, the house, and no way to get to Jesus. It is also the rooftop, and maybe some tools and ropes. Finally, what was the PATH? Once they determined the HERE, their current reality, they devised a PATH by going to the roof, tearing away tiles, and lowering the bed into the room in front of Jesus.

The second example is familiar—the feeding of the 5,000.

> *Luke 9:13-17 (NJKV)—But He said to them, "You give them something to eat." And they said, "We have no more than five loaves and two fish, unless we go and buy food for all these people." For there were about five thousand men.*
>
> *Then He said to His disciples, "Make them sit down in groups of fifty." And they did so, and made them all sit down.*
>
> *Then He took the five loaves and the two fish, and looking up to heaven, He blessed and broke them, and gave them to the disciples to set before the multitude. So they all ate and were filled, and twelve baskets of the leftover fragments were taken up by them.*

Can you see THP? Here is what I see.
- **THERE**—Jesus wanted the people to eat.
- **HERE**—5 loaves, 2 fish, 5,000 men plus women and children, a town nearby to buy food, do not know if they had money.

- **PATH**—arrange them in groups of 50, ask them to sit down, ask the Father to bless the loaves and fish, and pass the food to the crowd.

You can see this pattern everywhere in the Bible. For additional examples, look at Noah building the Ark, Moses constructing the Tabernacle, and Nehemiah repairing the wall.

Plan (THP)

THERE—Must Be Clear

Overcomers are clear about what they want to achieve. Without a clear THERE, it is difficult to focus on HERE and build a PATH to get THERE. God gives some clear THEREs for *Overcomers*, and each helps organize your life for overcoming. For example, consider these significant THEREs!

> *Matthew 6:33 (NJKV)—But seek first the kingdom of God and His righteousness, and all these things shall be added to you.*

> *Romans 12:2 (NJKV)—And do not be conformed to this world, but be transformed by the renewing of your mind, that you may prove what is that good and acceptable and perfect will of God.*

> *Philippians 3:13-14 (NKJV)—Brethren, I do not count myself to have apprehended; but one thing I do, forgetting those things which are behind and reaching forward to those things which are ahead, I press toward the goal for the prize of the upward call of God in Christ Jesus.*

> *1 Corinthians 9:24 (NKJV)—Do you not know that those who run in a race all run, but one receives the prize? Run in such a way that you may obtain it.*

Romans 12:2 and the Glorify God structure you saw earlier are some ultimate THEREs to consider. I see the following as *the ultimate THERE for Overcomers.*

Glorify God—Reflect Christ NOW so I can Reign with Christ LATER.

> *1 Corinthians 10:31 (NJKV)—Therefore, whether you eat or drink, or whatever you do, do all to the glory of God.*

Glorify God can be your ultimate or transcendent THERE or the why behind every THERE you set. For example, suppose you want to grow a garden, read a book, learn to drive, or get a new job. Each is a THERE. *Overcomers* would approach any of those items in a way that would glorify God.

You can use the THP tool for anything you want to achieve—big or small. *Overcomers* must be extremely good at creating a clear THERE. That is how you focus your energy and actions.

If you work with an individual, you can help them understand what they want to achieve. When that is determined, you can help them organize their work and effort toward the desired end result. That is a massive help to many people. Those you want to help may have thoughts about what to create but are unclear enough to start. The THP structure enables you to get started and develop actions to take. But for now, only focus on "what do I want to create, achieve, and finish by this time next week?"

One of the first things you can do to help any individual or group is to get them focused on what needs to be done in the next seven days. It is especially helpful if a person is overwhelmed with work or life. It is the best medicine to relieve that tension—focus on one or two things, then move on to the following items.

If you want to create a structure of productivity and achievement with a group, get everyone to list their top three things to do in the next seven days. Then schedule a weekly meeting to discuss results, obstacles, and next actions for the following seven days. The KEY is to have a CLEAR THERE for all items. That requires work because most people do not know how to create a clear THERE. With clarity, you can quickly see if it was or was not accomplished.

If you want to focus on more than the next seven days, use "Learn from the Past and Plan for the Future" at the end of the chapter. It is an excellent exercise to focus on what you want to achieve.

THERE starts with ideas. Then you make it clear. If it is unclear, your actions will be random and unfocused. And you will not know when you finish or if you are making progress. A simple guideline is your THERE (or end result, goal) is a short sentence with a **clear** way to measure it. "Read six chapters by 5:00 PM Monday" is an example. If it is unclear, you create a structure of EXCUSES not to get it done!

As you read and learn about THP, practicing it with something personal is best. Right now, think of a couple of things you want to do, make, or create so that you can use them for practice.

Want List Exercise

Here is an exercise that will help you learn more about "wants." All you need to do is time yourself. See if you can list 10–15 WANTS in three minutes or less. That is all there is to the exercise. TRY IT. You already have a couple listed.

Most people cannot list ten items; few get to 15 in three minutes or less. People assume the instructions ask for more than what is stated. If you understand wants, you can create 10–15 items within 30 to 60 seconds.

Let us start by putting wants or desires into three categories, as shown in the following chart.

Appetites, Impulses, Pleasures	True Values and Aspirations	Vague Hopes and Longings
Close Frame	*Medium Frame*	*Long Shot*
• Too close to see the context—how it fits • Instant gratification • Needs quick resolution or will be abandoned • Time is very short	• Sense of what is and is not important • Most essential organizing principles in life • Values create priorities in our life	• Everything is far away, fuzzy, and out of focus • Difficult to organize into any actions • Someday, it will happen • Time is very long

These categories are like taking a picture with a camera. You can take a picture of something inches away from the lens. You would have an image of that object and not know anything about the surrounding context. That would be the Close Frame.

Or you could take a picture of something far away, so when you look at the picture, you will mostly see everything around the object but will not be able to see the object. That is the Long Shot.

Finally, you could adequately frame an object so that you see both the thing and the surrounding context. That would be the Medium Frame. With that in mind, you can categorize wants or desires.

Appetites, Impulses, and Pleasures (Close Frame) are too often where you spend your life. Some of it is very appropriate—you are hungry or thirsty, so you resolve the tension by eating or drinking. But if that is a constant want, it is unhealthy, driving your life to focus on eating or drinking constantly. That want is about instant gratification, an unhealthy focus on "ME!"

Or you may be in **Vague Hopes and Longings (Long Shot)**. It is equally non-productive because you never get a good picture of what you want so that you can organize your work and effort toward it. It is about "wishing and hoping" instead of wanting. For example, wanting world peace is a monumental desire, but arranging the numerous actions needed to achieve it isn't easy. You need to bring your target closer to home, like peace in our community or at home.

That leaves us with **True Values and Aspirations (Medium Frame)**. These wants focus on what is and is not important to you. It helps you organize your life around values, principles, and priorities.

Now, look at your list. Identify those things that fit in True Values and Aspirations. That is what makes the most sense for a THERE.

Before you go back to your list, here are some additional thoughts.

Are any of these statements true for your list? If they are, it will often keep things off the list or put something on the list you do not actually want.

- I do not know what I want (nothing or few items listed)
- It does not matter what I want (it keeps things off the list)
- I know what I want, but I cannot have it (keeps things off the list)
- It is not right to want this (keeps things off the list)
- I want what someone else wants for me (it may not be what you want)
- I described what I should want (not necessarily what you want)
- I am trying to eliminate a problem (we want to create something)
- I described some vague slogan (you cannot organize actions around it)
- I described a process instead of what I want (talking about the PATH, not THERE)
- I must commit to or work on it if I want it (keeps things off the list that you may want)
- I want something others could keep me from getting (keeps things off the list)

Insights on What You Desire/Want

Sometimes you want what you want; there is no need to justify it. Unfortunately, that can be bad, so pay attention to your values. Additionally, what shows up on your list does not need to be significant but just something you want. Again, consider Godly values here.

Next, and something you may miss, anything that showed up on your list was not by chance. That thought is in your mind for some reason. You did not just pull it out of the air. It represents something you have thought about or made sense to you.

When you take the time to create a list of "wants," it provides insight into what you value or at least implies what you value. If you are honest with yourself, that list may have some things that would be bad to pursue. Your values probably kept most of those things off your list, but when you are honest, you know some things you may want are unsuitable. Be honest about wanting it, and do not commit energy to it.

If you have things on your list like "I want to cover myself in diamonds" or "I want to own a luxury sports car," it may imply you are honest about your wants.

But doesn't that violate some of the values for *Overcomers*? Yes, some of them, but this exercise is about truth and honesty, the essential values. Some of your wants need a pre-decision that you will not pursue them. You do not need to list any sinful wants on the list, but it is best to acknowledge them and not let them derail you.

Of course, the best wants align with God's desires.

> *Psalms 37:4-5 (NKJV)—Delight yourself also in the LORD, and He shall give you the desires of your heart. Commit your way to the LORD, trust also in Him, and He shall bring it to pass.*

Those verses are misused, saying God will give you anything you want. That misses what "delight yourself also in the Lord" means. *Overcomers* know it is about wanting what God wants. When your desires align with God's, He wants to share them with you.

When creating a want list, several things may fit into "True Values and Aspirations." If any of those True Values and Aspirations are made clear, it helps prioritize your life and move away from being RUDDERLESS.

Want List FAQs and Help

If you have difficulty determining something to work on, use the following. Again, be honest and list your thoughts and desires. The following can help create your Values and Aspirations list.

- Personal Qualities—To be who you want to be— what qualities would you have
- Tangibles—What material things would you like to own?
- Home—What is your ideal living environment?
- Health—What is your desire for health, fitness, athletics, and body?
- Relationships—What relationship do you want with friends, family, and others?
- Spiritual—What relationship do you want with God? What change do you want inside?
- Work—What is your ideal work situation? What impact do you want your efforts to have?
- Personal Pursuits—What do you want in learning, travel, reading, or other activities?
- Community—What is your vision for your community or society?
- Other—What else would you like to create in any other arena of your life?
- Life Purpose—Imagine your life has a unique purpose—fulfilled through what you do, your interrelationships, and how you live. Describe that purpose as a reflection of your aspirations.

Two Critical Questions

Now, choose just one item so that you can practice using THP. Once you select something, ask yourself the following question.

Does this matter enough to ORGANIZE my work or life around it and give it my best shot, knowing there is no GUARANTEE?

That does not mean this is your number one life priority. It asks if you will open a slot for it in the 24 hours you have each day. Are you willing to start working on it since you want it?

If you say yes to that question, ask another easier question.

Do I want THERE, the end result, more than I want things to stay the same?

Now that you have said YES to both questions, you can turn this into a clear THERE!

Use SMART

Based on working with people, I speculate that 95 percent of the people think they know how to create clear goals. From my experience, 95 percent of people probably DO NOT know how to develop clear goals. Using the SMART form in the Appendix: Chapter 3 Forms will help. Use it to make THERE clear. It needs to meet all the SMART criteria.

Once you have a clear THERE, use the THP Planning Form in the Appendix. Write your goal in the THERE section at the top and add nothing else to the form.

HERE—Critical for Goals

Starting Point for the PATH

Why is HERE so critical? It establishes the starting point for the PATH! The Biggest FLAW in most planning or goal setting comes from not being CLEAR about HERE—Current Reality.

Suppose a person you just met called you about attending your meeting tonight. They ask, "Can you give me directions on how to get there?"

What is the best question to ask them before you try to give them directions? Many people do not know the best question to ask. Do you know what it is? The best question is, "Where will you be coming from?" or something similar. You cannot create a path of directions unless you know the beginning and endpoints.

Look at the graphic. Notice that it has only 1 THERE, yet 3 different PATHs. Why? Because there are 3 HEREs. If the HERE changes, the PATH will change. So knowing where you are or your starting point is vital.

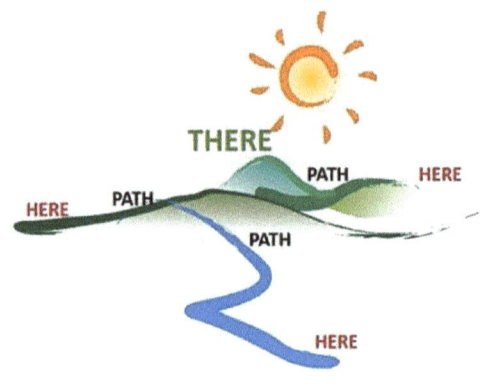

Your HERE is essential when you consider your walk with the Lord. Your sin nature will deceive you into thinking your walk with the Lord is good when it is terrible. Satan does not want you to think about the HERE of your spiritual life. Anytime you examine the intent of your heart, you are doing an excellent thing. You are thinking about your HERE!

Romans 12:3 (NKJV)—For I say, through the grace given to me, to everyone who is among you, not to think of himself more highly than he ought to think, but to think soberly, as God has dealt to each one a measure of faith.

2 Corinthians 13:5a (NKJV)—Examine yourselves as to whether you are in the faith. Test yourselves.

You create energy or motivation for action when you have a clear THERE and HERE.

Determine Your HERE

Like there are three categories of wants or THERE, you have three categories of current reality or HERE.

Immediate Events or Obsessive Details	Objective Shapes and Patterns	Vague Perceptions and True Mysteries
Close Frame	*Medium Frame*	*Long Shot*
• Time is in very short phases • Details and bits of information are the focus • Cannot see what the details imply when put together	• Details AND overall shape are recognizable • See the forest and the trees • See the connection of the present with the past and the future • The future is NOT causal from what we see now, but we see connections	• Time is unlimited • Everything is messy and chaotic • Pondering the distant future is more important than what is happening now

The medium frame—Objective Shapes and Patterns—helps you the most.

When you develop HERE, use the middle section of the THP Planning Form and write facts about your goal's current reality (HERE). Do not write assumptions, estimates, or theories; clearly describe where you are now, your resources, and things relevant to your current goal (THERE). Do not write about history or what you have done; only describe what is happening now.

Use the "HERE (Current Reality) Checklist" at the end of the chapter to help. Do not make current reality better or worse than it is. Just state the facts. Often, some helpful items to list are the things you do not know. That is always true of current reality (HERE).

Finally, write each thought in point form, one statement per box on the form, because that will help when you start working on the PATH.

Return to the THP Planning Form and complete the "HERE" section. Describe the current reality of the goal you selected.

- Provide an objective report, not assumptions
- Describe what you know and do not know
- Describe what is happening now, not what has happened
- Write in point form, one item per line, so that you can use it for developing actions

PATH—Your Actions

Develop Actions

> *The wise man bridges the gap by laying out the*
> *path by means of which he can get from where he*
> *is to where he wants to go. — JP Morgan*

It is time to start working on actions. Again, notice that you assessed both THERE and HERE before working on actions.

As said earlier, most goal-setting processes miss the power of working on a clear HERE before starting on the actions or PATH. Without clarity about HERE, you may be guessing about your actions.

The easiest way to identify actions, or the PATH, is to ask one question about each point in your current reality (HERE).

"Does this imply an action is needed?"

Suppose someone had these statements in their HERE section.
- I do not have an accurate measurement of the table.
- The workers say they do not know what to do.
- The customers are not completing the order form correctly.

If they looked at the first item and asked, "Does this imply an action is needed?" the answer is yes. They would write at least one action like, "Measure all dimensions of the table at least two times."

Now that you know the simplicity of how it works, develop 3 to 5 actions by looking at the HERE section and asking, "Does this imply an action is needed?" Keep the list of actions to a minimum so that you can practice how THP works.

Like THERE, ensure the PATH or actions are clear so you know what to do. Be like Nehemiah when speaking to the King. He did not make some vague statements about what he needed. He listed the items that would help him get to his THERE.

> Nehemiah 2:7-8 (NKJV)—Furthermore I said to the king, "If it pleases the king, let letters be given to me for the governors of the region beyond the River, that they must permit me to pass through till I come to Judah, and a letter to Asaph the keeper of the king's forest, that he must give me timber to make beams for the gates of the citadel which pertains to the temple, for the city wall, and for the house that I will occupy." And the king granted them to me according to the good hand of my God upon me.

A clear THERE and a clear HERE make it easier to create a clear PATH—at least the initial actions or steps you need to take.

Measures, Partners, Due Dates

Finally, you will see on the form that each action has a Progress Measure, Partners, and Due Date. That helps get each action completed. You can have more than one person as a partner working on it with you or being an accountability partner.

Once you have the actions, organize them by the Due Dates. Start working on the one with the earliest due date. Like the due date you wrote for your THERE, these dates are not for creating urgency. You establish the due date based on your best estimate of when you can complete the task.

EXECUTE (ALA)

Action Is Required for Results

"The beginning is half of every action."—Greek proverb

Completing the THP Personal Planning Form is a significant first step, but you need action for results. THP helps you create a plan, but you need to execute the plan to get THERE. We like to say, "Good plans generate action at some point!" That is because the clarity of THERE and HERE creates energy to develop the PATH. Now that you see some initial actions to take—get started!

Some people have the energy to experiment without much of a plan. Others create detailed plans before they act. The creative process requires plans but needs action to get something done.

If you want to create great plans and reduce risk, that is excellent! Remember, planning is great, but action is the only way to know if the plan works. Some people plan and look for the "perfect" plan. That is a waste of time because it does not exist. Please understand that plans bog down when looking for "perfect."

The quote from General Carl von Clausewitz is worth memorizing. He was the father of strategic battle planning, so he believed strongly in plans, but look at what he said.

> No campaign plan survives the first contact with the enemy...It is even better to act quickly and err than to hesitate until the time of action is past.—*General Carl von Clausewitz*

Plan, but move quickly to acting!

Always keep in mind that God is entirely in control. He may not allow it to work, no matter how great your plan is. Do not assume that God should support your goal. Instead, constantly remember that your plans are subject to God's will. He is the authority, not you.

> *James 4:15 (NKJV)—Instead you ought to say, "If the Lord wills, we shall live and do this or that."*

Iterative Actions and Adjustments

"Action without reflection is mindless" - Henry Mintzberg

The creative process is not a manufacturing process. Other people may have done what you are trying to do, but you probably have not. That means you are trying to create something new for yourself.

While the creative process has the engine of THP, it is fueled by ALA once you start on the PATH. Because it is the creative process, you want to LEARN from each action as you execute.
- ACT—Look at the result of the action
- LEARN—Did it help? Did it hurt?
- ADJUST—or act on the next step

Using ALA helps you . . .
- gain knowledge and experience by acting
- see what does and does not work

- revise plans to fit the current situation
- keep moving toward the Result—one Action at a time

Abraham Lincoln beautifully illustrates ALA in the following statement.

> **Focus on the Next Step**
>
> When President Lincoln was asked how he would approach postwar reunification he said, "I'm going to use the same system as the Mississippi riverboat captains. They look out as far as they can see, which typically is just the first bend in the river, and they navigate to that point. When they get to that point, more of the river opens up and they can navigate to the next point...That's the only way I can see managing such a massive change: navigating from point to point." —*Harvard Management Update, July 2001*

That is ALA's essence: navigate from one action to the next, always keeping THERE in mind.

Sometimes as you work toward your clearly defined THERE, you get off-track, even become confused about what you are doing. You may feel overwhelmed, like you are in a maze and cannot escape. That can happen when the actions are complex or just tiring. Your focus turns from THERE to the task or details you are working on. If you are not careful, you will no longer see beyond the current tasks and forget why you are doing them—THERE, your end result.

When that happens, you may need to assess yourself using HALT. That is a good acronym from 12-step programs. When you are working, be careful of the times you are too . . .

Hungry Angry Lonely Tired

And sometimes, S is needed (Sick). In those times, your focus turns from wants based on values and aspirations to your appetites, impulses, and pleasures.

Regroup with some rest and refocus on THERE. You escape the overwhelm and confusion and move back into clarity, enabling you to recommit to THERE.

Tools to Help You Act

These tools will help you continue to act until you reach THERE. Forms for numbers 1 and 2 are in the Appendix: Chapter 3 Forms.

Daily Focus Form: This form can help you every workday. Hopefully, the instructions are clear enough for you. The first time you use the form, it will take more effort because of the time to list your goals. Start by identifying your goals and actions you want to complete in the next seven days. Do not list anything in that column if you do not plan to work on one of your goals during the next seven days. But you can record what you want to accomplish in the Next 30 Days column.

After you start, review the form every morning and identify the top 3 things you WILL DO that day. I created an electronic version, which works great for me.

Accountability Partners: You will get more done with an Accountability Partner. Look at the research in the chart. It shows

Action Taken	Probability of Implementing
Listen to an idea	10%
Consciously decide to adopt an idea	25%
Decide when to act on the idea	40%
Design a plan to act on the idea	50%
Commit to another person to act on the plan	65%
Get a specific accountability appointment with the person to whom you made your commitment	95%

American Society for Training & Development

the power of using an accountability partner. If you want to get something done, this is your tool, so please use it.

Learn from the Past, Plan for the Future: This helps determine a THERE or identify obstacles hindering your progress. It is an every-once-in-a-while document, not like the Daily Focus Form. Follow the instructions to see what you can learn.

Persist

2 Physical Laws You Must Know—Entropy & Inertia

These physical laws impact more than the physical! Consider entropy. First, what is it?

A measure of the disorder or randomness in a closed system.
The inevitable and steady deterioration of a system or society

Entropy is a scientific word for a physical law resulting from the curse on the ground.

Genesis 3:17b-19 (NKJV)—"Cursed is the ground for your sake; in toil you shall eat of it all the days of your life. Both thorns and thistles it shall bring forth for you, and you shall eat the herb of the field. In the sweat of your face you shall eat bread till you return to the ground, for out of it you were taken; for dust you are, and to dust you shall return."

Entropy is at work on the chair you sit on. It is decaying, rotting away as you sit there. No energy is being applied to the chair, so it is deteriorating very slowly. The same is true of your *Overcomer* values! If you do not regularly put energy into your *Overcomer* values—they are DECAYING! Every good thing you do will not last for long without applying more energy!

You experience this every time you learn something new. You will not remember it unless you think about or review that new learning. And think about your work. Just because you were productive today does not mean you will be productive tomorrow.

God's creation groans because of sin and the curse on the ground, which I think is the same as entropy.

Romans 8:22 (NKJV)—For we know that the whole creation groans and labors with birth pangs together until now.

And inertia will either help or hurt you. But what is that?

A body at rest will tend to stay at rest. A body in motion will tend to stay in motion unless an external force is applied.

You experience this when living excellent or awful values. Inertia works for you with your *Overcomer* values when you are not putting energy into them. They do not go away immediately (a body in motion will tend to stay in motion), but they slowly erode due to entropy. And inertia works against you when you have lousy values because it is difficult to stop a bad habit.

Additionally, inertia will tend to work against you if you want to start something new. It is like a massive truck tire you want to roll down a road. It is tough to get that huge wheel moving, but inertia helps keep it moving once it is moving.

Persistence

You started by identifying a clear THERE, something that you want, your desired end result. You commit to it and then determine where you are (HERE). Then you create actions (PATH) and act, learn, and adjust (ALA) to help you get closer to THERE.

Like Overcoming, you need persistence as you travel the PATH, especially when you get closer to THERE. As you get closer to THERE, you change from traveling to arriving. In the traveling mindset, you need persistence to keep pressing forward to reach the destination. But when arriving, you need persistence to finish strong instead of stopping or starting work on another THERE.

Persistence is a close cousin to commitment, which you started with when you chose THERE. The synonyms of "tenacity, dogged determination" provide an excellent picture of what you need on the PATH, especially as you get closer to THERE.

Persistence is the third part of the creative process (THP, ALA, Persist) and a critical part of overcoming. You need it to progress, make tough changes, and demonstrate COMMITMENT instead of talking.

Persistence produces momentum and encourages you to go beyond understanding the need to change to MAKING THE CHANGE.

Galatians 6:9 (NKJV)—And let us not grow weary while doing good, for in due season we shall reap if we do not lose heart.

Project MOOD Curve

Working on any project, especially more difficult ones, it helps to remember how most projects change over time. There is often a big difference between expectations and reality.

Try this exercise with your project group or team. They only need a blank sheet of paper and a pencil or pen. Ask them to write START on the left side of the page and FINISH on the right. Then ask them to draw a line from START to FINISH on how they think the project will go.

You will get lines that go straight across, down then up, up then down, and various other options. Once they have talked about it, tell them that the basic shape will most likely be like a "U."

The MOOD Curve can help you and others persist. It is a simple tool that people will easily understand because they have experienced it. Please share this with any project team you lead.

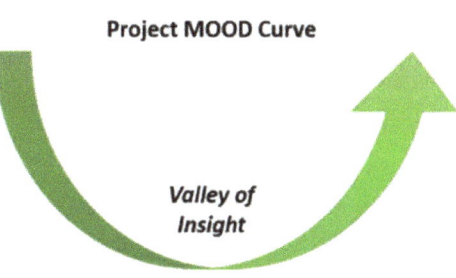

When you start a project, you may have early success, but then you see obstacles you did not anticipate. That can feel like failure; you will think you are in the "Valley of Despair." If you are not self-governing and willing to overcome obstacles, there will be finger-pointing and blaming. But the reality is, those times are not the "Valley of Despair;" they are the "Valley of Insight."

Whenever things are going poorly, help people learn to ask, "What are we learning?" That encourages moving forward, even though it feels like failure. Because of lousy thinking, people start blaming others because they dislike association with failure. However, failure is a part of success, and the MOOD Curve helps your group get through those times more quickly.

To develop good thinking, follow what Paul told the Philippians.

> *Philippians 4:6-8 (NKJV)—Be anxious for nothing, but in everything by prayer and supplication, with thanksgiving, let your requests be made known to God; and the peace of God, which surpasses all understanding, will guard your hearts and minds through Christ Jesus. Finally, brethren, whatever things are true, whatever things are noble, whatever things are just, whatever things are pure, whatever things are lovely, whatever things are of good report, if there is any virtue and if there is anything praiseworthy — meditate on these things.*

And your thinking shows up in your words.

> *Proverbs 16:23 (NKJV)—The heart of the wise teaches his mouth, and adds learning to his lips.*

Teach your mouth not to blame and complain when things are not going well. Instead, look for ways to help others and be part of the solution like Jesus would. And what you say is what you are thinking!

The MOOD Curve is a simple tool that explains a lot. Make sure that people know about it at the start of a project. Reinforce learning and reduce blaming with the great question, "What are we learning?"

Persistence Takes Time

The Creative Process is like exercise—the benefits accrue over time. Exercising, not watching exercise videos, creates benefits. Developing a clear THERE, a clear HERE, and a PATH of actions are the first steps in the process. Then acting, learning, and adjusting take time and persistence to reach THERE.

You will become more adept with the Creative Process by using it and persisting with it. Are you PERSISTING to get to the finish and help others finish?

Discussion Questions

1. What are the three common problems for everyone?
2. What is the name of the process that includes THP? Explain how the whole process works together.
3. What are the three frames of THERE? Explain each frame.
4. What is the purpose of the Want List exercise?
5. What are the two critical THERE questions? Explain why they are needed.
6. Memorize SMART and explain each.
7. Why does HERE need to be second when considering creating something?
8. What are the three frames of HERE? Explain each.
9. What crucial thinking is needed when you complete the HERE section on a THP chart?
10. What is the key question you ask to help develop the PATH while looking at HERE items?
11. Why are there so few rows for the PATH on the THP Planning Form? (See Chapter 3 Forms in Appendix)
12. How would you explain ALA? Why do you need ALA?
13. Memorize the first part of the quote by General Carl von Clausewitz.
14. Explain how to use these three tools: 1) Daily Focus Form, 2) Learn from the Past, and 3) Accountability Partners.
15. Explain Entropy and Inertia—know the definitions of each.
16. Why does anyone need to know about these two physical laws?
17. What is the MOOD Curve? How does it work? When should it be used? What question do you use instead of blaming?

Chapter 14 – *Overcomers* Listen and Ask Questions

Key Lesson: *Humility + Focus + Curiosity = Listening. Asking questions is the most powerful skill and requires excellent listening skills.*

A Formula for Listening

Curiosity Makes the Difference

Few consider listening a critical leadership skill, much less one of the most critical. Why is it so important? Without it, you have much less chance to see inside another person's mind. And when you combine asking questions—**the most powerful leadership skill**—you have an unbeatable combination to understand people and situations better.

> *Luke 2:46-47 (NKJV)—Now so it was that after three days they found Him in the temple, sitting in the midst of the teachers, both listening to them and asking them questions. And all who heard Him were astonished at His understanding and answers.*

Yes, Jesus is God, but His example shows us how to learn and grow.

Below, you will learn the "formula for listening." Curiosity is one of the three parts of that formula. It helps you listen because it is the leverage point to move from being defensive, "making everything about ME," to being open enough to start learning.

Look at the chart below and notice the yellow highlighted portion in the middle. It says, "Choose curiosity about the other person's perspective." That is the tipping point to move away from defensiveness because it helps you move away from thinking only about yourself.

Curiosity helps you change your behavior rather than defend it.

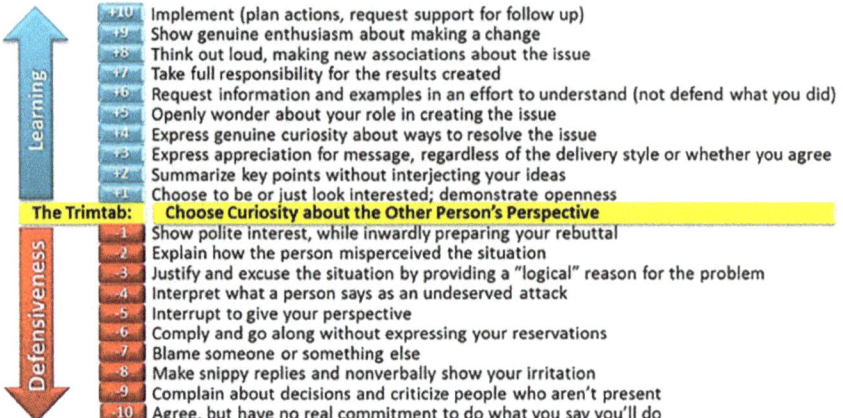

Learning	+10	Implement (plan actions, request support for follow up)
	+9	Show genuine enthusiasm about making a change
	+8	Think out loud, making new associations about the issue
	+7	Take full responsibility for the results created
	+6	Request information and examples in an effort to understand (not defend what you did)
	+5	Openly wonder about your role in creating the issue
	+4	Express genuine curiosity about ways to resolve the issue
	+3	Express appreciation for message, regardless of the delivery style or whether you agree
	+2	Summarize key points without interjecting your ideas
	+1	Choose to be or just look interested; demonstrate openness
The Trimtab:		**Choose Curiosity about the Other Person's Perspective**
Defensiveness	-1	Show polite interest, while inwardly preparing your rebuttal
	-2	Explain how the person misperceived the situation
	-3	Justify and excuse the situation by providing a "logical" reason for the problem
	-4	Interpret what a person says as an undeserved attack
	-5	Interrupt to give your perspective
	-6	Comply and go along without expressing your reservations
	-7	Blame someone or something else
	-8	Make snippy replies and nonverbally show your irritation
	-9	Complain about decisions and criticize people who aren't present
	-10	Agree, but have no real commitment to do what you say you'll do

Try it and see what difference it makes when you feel your defensiveness rising.

Work alone and answer the following questions.

	Often	Some	Rarely
When people ask me something, I have trouble saying, "I don't know."			
I find ways to let people know that I know more about the topic than they do.			
I exaggerate the extent of my knowledge and experience.			
I try to keep my problems covered until I find a way to solve them.			
I deflect attention from anything that makes me look bad.			
I act like I understand something when I am actually confused.			
I try to project an image of decisiveness even when unsure of what to do.			

You can assess your answers below.

Curiosity Is the Spark

It is easy to assume that listening just happens because you can equate listening with hearing. Sounds enter the ear naturally, even without your choice. That makes it easy to think that listening does not require skill and development, just like speaking with clarity and persuasion.

Of course, that is why most people value speaking more than listening. Both are extremely important for leaders, but you will seldom see listening raised to the highest level of importance.

And listening does not need to have sound involved. How does that happen? You "listen" to your conscience; at least, I hope you do. You listen to what you read, even when not speaking a word. You listen to your thoughts and assess your feelings!

By the way, here is how to score the assessment above.

If you checked OFTEN . . .

- 2 times—reasonable
- 3 times—you may be limiting your learning
- 4 times or more—it is time to adjust your style

It may help you, as it did me, to consider listening as a formula.

Listening involves all six Critical Values seen in Chapter 2. You demonstrate self-governance, humility, and sacrifice. You limit your freedom and accept others' freedom to speak. And you value others enough to pursue truth by listening to their side of the story.

Here is another way to see the formula.

- Humility is the KEY—"Will I make this about them, not ME?"
- Focus is the FUEL—"Will I pay attention to them?"
- Curiosity is the SPARK—"Will I be curious about their thinking?"
- Listening is the result—"Do I see what they see?"

Find a signal that alerts you to start using the formula. For me, it is eye contact—deciding to look directly at someone is a signal to me that it is time to listen. When a conversation is more than "small talk," I make eye contact with them, reminding me this conversation is not about me (Humility); it is time to focus on what they say and be curious about what they think. That helps me not only listen but also ask good questions.

Our life depends on this formula when reading God's Word and hearing His wisdom. Sadly, we often listen to our sin nature, not God.

Isaiah 28:23 (NKJV)—Give ear and hear my
voice, listen and hear my speech.

The Most Underrated Skill

Listening Becomes Difficult

Listening is not only underrated; it is not easy to do it correctly. Listening is just like any skill; it takes practice to become good. It is not easy and seldom occurs when

1. **You learn that talking is rewarded, not listening.** Those who make the most noise get the most attention—"The squeaky wheel gets the grease." Numerous people and businesses earn money from speaking engagements. Speaking gets rewarded because it communicates in a "one to many" model. That is not true of listening. Listening is much more of a personal one-to-one skill. Even with many people in a large crowd, the speaker's words are unique to you as the listener. Because of the nature of listening, it is not rewarded unless you are in the counseling or coaching business.

2. **You believe you know more than they know.** "A little learning is a dangerous thing," and most often, a lot of learning is worse when it comes to listening. We fall into the trap of thinking they do not have much, if anything, to contribute because "I know more than them." That tends to drive the belief and action, "Those who know nothing have nothing to say."

3. **You think while others are talking.** Our brain processes five to six times faster than people speak, which makes it easy to stop listening. Then we start thinking about what to say next or wondering what our next question will be. On the positive side, we can concentrate more on what they say. Yes, you can process five to six times faster than they can speak, so put all that additional power into turning their words into pictures. You can start seeing a video of what they say, which expands your ability to understand. Or it gives you much better questions to ask.

4. **You are not teachable/humble.** Making everything about ME is the biggest problem for all relationships. We also easily believe we are more important. Of course, we seldom consciously admit this, but it still leads to limited attention to others.

5. **You and others speak without clarity.** Not all problems are the listener's because poor speakers make it difficult for listeners. That means when you become an Observational Listener, you help the communication process by asking questions to help clarify what the speaker says if you can access them.

If you want to improve your listening, it takes discipline and energy!

Listening Insights

Listening seldom occurs when

- **You are angry**: When was the last time you listened (humble, focused, and curious) to a person when you were mad at them? The only "listening" that happens is searching for ways to use their words against them.
- **You want to punish rather than help**: If you focus on revenge or punishment, you have already decided about them. No more facts are needed or wanted because the jury and judge have already declared the verdict.
- **You are unwilling to remove your opinions**: When we have an opinion, it is an assumption, estimate, conjecture, or theory about them and their actions. If you place your opinion at the same level as facts, you will not listen. You already know, so no listening is needed.
- **You feel a need to give direct advice**: One of the biggest deterrents to listening is our need to talk. It is worse the more that you know. You become the "guru" and will typically feel the need to provide the answers to the world. You think they need to be listening to you and all that you know, not vice-versa.
- **You are in a hurry and do not explore what they are saying**: Listening takes time, and it most often takes energy, too. If you are not willing to accept the need for both, you will not be listening.
- **You are not willing to serve**: Remember the formula for listening? Humility is a critical component. And if you remember, serving is one of the most practical ways to know if you are in the arena of humility. Listening is truly a giving of time and energy to another person. It is often sacrificial.
- **You make everything about "ME"**: Now we get to the most significant reason listening does not happen. It is tied directly to humility. Listening requires making it about them, not you.

How many of the seven items above are preventing you from listening? Watch yourself in your next conversation to see which ones show up. Remember what James tells us.

> *James 1:19-20 (NKJV)—So then, my beloved brethren, let every man be swift to hear, slow to speak, slow to wrath; for the wrath of man does not produce the righteousness of God.*

Listening helps people even if you are not even trying. People who have someone listening to them tend to see it as a positive experience. Research shows that people are helped if a person just listens and offers no advice. When people can express their thoughts to others, they often gain clarity about their thinking. Listening also helps people feel understood, supported, and even challenged. All of that by taking time to listen. It gets even better for the other person when you know how to listen and interject helpful questions.

Finally, listening reveals your attitude toward people because

- **Listeners Value Others**—Listening does not just happen; it takes time and energy. And you derail it when you "Make it about ME."
- **Listeners Know When to Focus**—Not all conversations are created equal. You need to decide which conversations will have your focused energy.
- **Listeners Find Time for Conversations**—Effective listeners invest time in conversations because they know they can better understand others using that skill. Effective conversations will likely take time, so plan for and accept it.

Hopefully, you are becoming convinced of the power of listening.

Listening DON'Ts

Listening is not something that happens! It is not like hearing something. It takes energy to listen, especially if you are picturing what people say. The best way to listen is to turn their conversation into a video. You will learn some basics of that approach soon.

Here are six DON'Ts that violate some part of the listening formula.

Don't control the conversation

Keep the focus on what they are saying. Let them take the conversation where they want. When you do that, you learn about them. One big exception! When you coach someone, that is not a normal conversation. Interrupting helps clarify the story they are telling you.

Don't give advice

Giving advice tends to meet your needs, not theirs. You may be very insightful and wise, but this is not about what you know unless the conversation requires it. Even if you are wise, pride in your knowledge can quickly get in the way of listening. Unfortunately, that brings your listening and observing to a complete stop.

Sometimes people are not interested in you helping them gain clarity; they want you to agree with their perspective. When you see that happening in a conversation, a simple tool to use is to ask, "What advice were you hoping I'd give you?"

Don't judge

The foundation of good listening is keeping your values out of the conversation unless needed. That does not mean you are not living your good values as you listen; it means do not let your values cloud your ability to listen to them. Suspend your judgment about what they say because listening done right observes and looks at what they say.

You can quickly tell when your values are involved because you think or say words like should, should not, good, bad, right, wrong, etc. Again, listening is about understanding what is happening inside their mind. Your values are mostly irrelevant until the conversation changes to how they can change.

Don't replace the speaker's story with yours

It is so easy to hear someone's experience and hijack the conversation with, "Yeah, I had that happen to me. I . . ." Wrong move if you want to value other people rather than making everything about you. Letting them know you had a similar experience is not bad, but immediately turn the conversation back to them.

Don't try to talk the speaker into or out of feelings

Do not discount the speaker's experience by saying, "Don't feel bad," "It's not so serious," "Things will get better," or, "C'mon, give me a smile." Those tend to help you, the listener, rather than them because you may feel pressure to help them feel better.

Just be careful. Many times, people only want someone to listen to them. They do not want advice or even help. Those are the times that you show up and relate to them. No coaching is needed.

Don't sympathize

The following is tricky until you review the definitions of two words - empathize and sympathize.

- Empathize—the action of understanding, be aware of, see it the way they see it
- Sympathize—an affinity, association, or relationship wherein whatever affects one similarly affects the other; an inclination to think and feel alike

While the words are synonyms, I use them to help me listen. I use it this way. When I sympathize, I see it their way and feel it like they do. That will make me less objective. On the other hand, if I empathize, I see it how they see it, but I remain objective and do not let my feelings take over. I can understand how they feel without having the same feelings. That will become a pity party or a "so sad story," which we all have.

Too often, listening and sympathizing can support an inclination toward "poor me." You help them live in a "victim's" world, encouraging inaction and dependence. Yes, sometimes people need mothering; just do not let them indulge in it for long.

Focus Levels

All conversations are not created equal, so you will be at different levels of focus depending on the conversation. But I encourage you to work on your listening by practicing Observational Listening in all discussions. Try it in a conversation today. Tell the person you want to practice listening, and it is okay to discuss anything. You can use some of the skills you learn later during that conversation.

Since I had the privilege of studying under Robert Fritz (robertfritz. com) to learn how to "picture" conversations, it is now more common for me in most discussions. Why? It is a natural way for our brains to work.

Since listening by picturing is rarely taught, most people underutilize a natural brain function and often operate at the Sporadic Attention or Hearing focus levels shown here.

Sporadic Attention	Hearing	Observational Listening
• Tune in and out	• Not understanding	• Empathetic, non-judgmental
• More interested in "ME"	• Hear words, not meanings	• See their point of view
• Follow the discussion to talk	• Little effort to understand the intent	• Acknowledge and respond
• May be quiet, non-responsive	• Surface communication	• Not distracted
• May be faking attention	• Appear to be listening	• Suspend own thoughts, feelings

To be a GR8 Leader, listening is one of the two most critical skills needed. Look at the three different levels and be objective about where you are.

Listening By "Seeing"—LISTEN

"Observational Listening" combines the two senses of hearing and seeing to give you the more remarkable ability to be clear about what you hear. It does not mean you immediately understand what the other person says. But when combined with questions about what you are "seeing," you will more accurately see what the other person is trying to tell you.

Proverbs 1:5 (NKJV)—A wise man will hear and increase learning, and a man of understanding will attain wise counsel

Observational Listening works best when linked with the skill of asking great questions and summarizing what you see. This chapter is inadequate for you to become proficient at picturing what a person says. For me, that continues to be a skill to enhance. If you want to improve, you need instruction from people like Robert Fritz (robertfritz.com).

For these purposes, here are key points to help you start developing this fantastic skill.

Start with a "Clean Canvas"

To help you listen better, you must "start with a clean canvas." What does that mean? Imagine you wanted to draw or paint a picture. Would you get a piece of paper with scribblings, a canvas with markings, or another picture on which to paint your picture? Most likely not. Why? You are painting something new. You do not want the new picture cluttered with the old shapes and objects.

That is precisely how you approach a conversation with someone when you want to practice Observational Listening. What does it mean to have a "clean canvas?"

- Do not put your ideas, assumptions, or thoughts on the canvas.
- Keep ALL your values OFF the canvas.
- Clear your mind of everything else and focus on what they say.

If you review the formula for listening, then this conversation is not about you. It is about them, focusing on what they say and being curious about what they say. You want to see a picture of what they are thinking, and that is exceedingly difficult when you put things on the "canvas" or in the video that are not their thoughts and ideas.

The following is far too little to develop your listening skills, but it is a great beginning. The last point is critical!

To help you do this, follow this acronym—LISTEN.

L—Limit Your Focus to ONLY the Speaker

- Listeners commit to hearing and understanding the speaker.
- Listeners make the conversation about the speaker.
- Listeners use semi-verbals so they know you are listening.
- Listeners maintain appropriate eye contact.
- Listeners need energy, discipline, and focus.
- Listeners make a deliberate choice to focus on the other person.

I—Image Pictures More Than Hear Words

- Listeners "see" the conversation—your mind loves pictures.
- Listeners create movies of their words.

- Listeners "see" best when neutral—not judging: 1) "I will accurately report what I observe" 2) "I will turn my ears on and mouth off" 3) "I will not suggest or correct" 4) "I will not praise or criticize."
- Listeners are not always neutral, but you seldom listen without being unbiased.

S—Seek Facts with Good Questions
- Listeners use 4 Types of Questions (Information, Clarification, Discrepancy, and Implication).
- Listeners use the Rulers of Discovery (What, How, maybe Why).
- Listeners use Open more than Closed questions.
- Listeners test assumptions, opinions, and claims.

T—Trust Simple and Single Questions
- Listeners ask straightforward, understandable questions.
- Listeners believe simple questions are elegant.
- Listeners ask one question at a time.
- Listeners focus on one topic at a time.

E—Ensure Clarity and Connection with Summaries
- Listeners check how well they are tracking with the speaker.
- Listeners summarize what the speaker has said.
- Listeners follow with a question, "Is that a fair summary?"

N—Need Practice
- Listeners practice listening to learn how to listen.
- Listeners desire to ask the best question.
- Listeners ask themselves the Ultimate Question: "What's a better question?"

The above points will not make you an observational listener, but you can see what it requires. Find ways to practice those items to develop this incredible skill your mind is wired to do.

Try "Slow Motion Listening"

Try the following "Slow Motion Listening" exercise to help you develop the skill.

The ultimate result of Observational Listening is understanding what the speaker is saying by asking great questions. That requires you to ask excellent questions based solely on what you see. Doing this exercise will improve your ability to see and ask BETTER questions.

Practice requires another person to get the most benefit. It is not a conversation with the person; it is practice. Ask someone willing to spend time with you to help you. It is often best if the person has a real issue they want to work on or understand. If you cannot get another person, listening to audio without video is another option. Stop the audio at a specific point as you picture what you heard, then take some time to determine what would be a good question to ask from what you heard. While not as good, it will help you focus on listening.

When you are with another person, it is easy to feel pressure to ask another question. PLEASE DO NOT DO THAT! Take your time. When doing exercises like this in Robert Fritz's training, it took 15 minutes and sometimes an hour before asking the next question.

If you want to practice picturing, use paper and pencil and draw a picture of what was said. Most of us are not artists, but do the best you can. The picture does not need to be beautiful; it just represents what you see.

Try it, and you will start developing a different view of listening.

The Most Powerful Skill

What Makes Questions Powerful?

Ask people what they think is the most powerful leadership skill. From my experience, few people list Asking Questions. Most people think about leadership from the opposite side of the communication process. In most of what I have researched and studied, people believe that the most powerful skill is related to motivating people to action with skills like persuasion or casting a vision. Those are valuable and incredibly beneficial skills, but I believe the most potent skill is

ASKING QUESTIONS.

That may sound strange, even unbelievable, but here are three reasons I see Asking Questions as the most powerful leadership and relationship skill.

First, questions engage the mind, answered or not. When someone asks you a question, what happens? I just did it to you. It does not have as much impact in written form as in personal communication, but it still works. You will likely read further to see the answer, right?

Notice in the following passage how Jesus' question engaged the minds of his critics.

*Luke 20:3-7 (NKJV)—But He answered and said to
them, "I also will ask you one thing, and answer Me: The
baptism of John—was it from heaven or from men?"*

*And they reasoned among themselves, saying, "If we say,
'From heaven,' He will say, 'Why then did you not believe
him?' But if we say, 'From men,' all the people will stone us,
for they are persuaded that John was a prophet." So they
answered that they did not know where it was from.*

God wired our minds to want to know or learn. Your mind pursues
the answer when asked a question, even when the topic is unimportant.
Making statements engages a person's mind to a degree, but questions
help grab a person's attention.

Try it and see what happens. Stop depending on persuasion through
statements and work on asking relevant, simple, and essential questions.

Second, questions encourage growth and discovery. Because your
mind wants the answer, you can use questions to energize your growth
and those around you.

That was a big problem with Jesus' critics. They were not interested
in learning; they used questions to trap Jesus.

*Luke 20:39-40 (NKJV)—Then some of the scribes
answered and said, "Teacher, You have spoken well." But
after that they dared not question Him anymore.*

That is an effective use of questions, but it is better to use them to
learn. Learn to observe what is happening and be curious about it. One
of the biggest obstacles to asking questions is how often we assume we
know the answer. It is easy to speculate, assume, or opine about an issue
or a person's actions rather than ask questions to discover facts.

Third, questions help you see how other people think. That is the
most valuable element for leaders. It is critical to understand how people
think if you want to persuade them. Asking questions does that when
you use Observational Listening. Yes, people can lie to you, but if you
ask enough questions and picture what people say, it becomes evident
that something does not "add up."

*Luke 9:20 (NKJV)—He said to them, "But who do you say
that I am?" Peter answered and said, "The Christ of God."*

As you read earlier about opinion, Jesus wants to know if your thinking
matches the truth. That is why he asked the disciples the question. Jesus
knows the thoughts of people—you and I do not. We need questions.

When asking questions, sometimes the question you ask is terrible. It is usually easy to tell because the person has difficulty with it. That means you must always think about the "Ultimate Question," which is

"What's the better question?"

When you develop your listening and questioning skills, you create powerful yet highly underrated skills. Try asking questions to see if you might agree it is a powerful skill.

Four Types of Questions

You may not realize that you can use different types of questions. Most of the time, you just ask questions, but the following can help you ask better questions.

Information Questions

Information you cannot "picture" needs more specifics to "see" it. These questions are like watching a movie; suddenly, the screen has no picture or sound. Then it comes back on a minute or two later. You need information to figure out what happened in that blank space in the video.

Ask questions until you can "see" what you are missing.

EXAMPLES:
- Statement: Our sales were great last year.
- Information Question: How much were they over the previous year?
- Statement: Our expenses are not as low as expected.
- Information Question: How much higher than expectations?

Clarification Questions

These help you get the information to understand what the person is saying. Use them to clarify definitions of words or even acronyms. You may not ask a question about a word a person uses because you assume they define the word as you do. That is a terrible mistake, especially when you want to understand someone.

EXAMPLES:
- Statement: We were looking at the AVR when it happened.
- Clarification Question: What is an AVR?
- Statement: We were deft flexing through the trials
- Clarification Question: What does "deft-flexing through the trials" mean?

Implication Questions

You need these to expand your knowledge of a situation without the person explicitly telling you. When a person shares some information and it suggests something else, that is the time to use an implication question. You want to verify if the implication is true.

EXAMPLES:

- Statement: We did not pay attention to the competition
- Typical question: Why not?
- Implication: If we had paid attention, things would be different
- Implication Question: What would be different if you had?
- Statement: For this project, we spent a lot of time planning
- Typical question: How much time?
- Implication: For other projects, less time was spent planning
- Implication Question: Is that unusual?

Discrepancy Questions

Sometimes a person says something in a conversation and then provides you with conflicting information later. These questions are unused because people do not track complete conversations like you can when you picture them. If you see what appears to be conflicting pieces of information, ask these questions. It helps you determine if some or all the information is false or if you are missing some information.

EXAMPLES:

- Statement: The project went really well, but we lost $500k
- Discrepancy: Went well vs. a loss of $500k
- Discrepancy Question: How is a $500k loss good?
- Statement: He is the right manager for the project, but he communicates and relates poorly
- Discrepancy: Right manager vs. communicate/relate poorly
- Discrepancy Question: Given that he communicates and relates poorly, how is he the right manager?

Rulers of Discovery

Here is a simple way to ask better questions without using the four types of questions.

What, How, and Why are the Rulers of Discovery. Who, When, and Where are still valuable, but What, How, and Why are the essentials. In fact, *What* can easily replace most of the others. It is the Swiss Army knife of questions. You have a powerful combination for discovering information when you follow What with How.

Be careful with *Why*. It is overused and easily misunderstood, which creates defensiveness or speculation. Here are some fundamental reasons to use What, How, and Why.

WHAT—Best

What can help identify issues, either open or specific.

Open	Specific
• What should we talk about?	• What is the problem?
• What things were interesting?	• What is your vision?
• What did you discuss at the meeting?	• What is your goal?
• What did you do today?	• What is the decision?

What can be used to probe thinking or facts.

Thinking	Facts
• What would be the consequences?	• What services do you provide?
• What do you mean precisely?	• What are the facts?
• What examples can you give?	• What resources do you need?

What can replace the other "Rulers," which makes it unique, but it is okay to use the Others. Just be careful with Why (more later).

What Question	Replaces
• What are your reasons?	• Why?
• What about?	• Why not?
• What methods did you use?	• How?
• In what ways?	• How?
• What are your feelings?	• How do you feel?

HOW—Second Best

How initiates a search for specifics, helping the discovery process.
- How can we help them?
- How can we increase morale?
- How can we improve this product?

Typically, use it after *What* to expand your discovery. Using *How* helps you probe a person's thinking; adding it broadens the search.
- Q: What are the consequences of the decline in demand?
- A: First, inventory is growing. Also, it is affecting our cash position with fewer sales and beginning to affect morale.
- Q: How can we reduce or limit the damage?

You can also use *How* to establish numbers or numerical facts.
- How many do we have?
- How old is the boy?
- How much does it cost?

WHY—Useful, But Be Careful

When asking for an explanation, the biggest downside of *Why* is the tendency of most people to assume it is criticism, whether intended or not. That can easily create a defensive attitude in them.

Another problem is *Why* can encourage speculation. *What* and *How* help drive for specifics, but *Why* allows more room for speculation.

Instead of *Why*, use:
- "To understand the situation better, what were your reasons for doing this?
- "That is an interesting suggestion. Tell me how you see that as the way to go forward?"
- "So what were you assuming when you made that decision?"

On the other hand, a good use for *Why* is the "5 Whys Process." It helps get to "root causes." It is not a magic formula, but it helps you and others think through issues. For example, if the problem is declining sales.
- Q1: Why are the sales declining? A1: The quality of the product has deteriorated.
- Q2: Why has the quality deteriorated? A2: Our Quality Control Officer resigned.
- Q3: Why? A3: There are fewer career opportunities here.
- Q4: Why? A4: The company has downsized recently.
- Q5: Why? A5: We are not creating new products or enhancing our best sellers.

When using the *5 Whys*, generate a question from the answer you just received. That helps you get to deeper issues that often are causal.

Question Templates
- 5 Questions for Clarity & Focus
  ○ What result do we want?
  ○ Where are we now?
  ○ What steps are needed to reach the result?
  ○ What is the next best action to take right now?
  ○ What are we learning?

- 7 All-Purpose Questions
  - Why?
  - What is the purpose?
  - What method will be needed to accomplish this?
  - Will the customers care about this at all?
  - What is your premise, theory, or assumption?
  - What data do you have?
  - Where does your data come from?

- 4 Questions to Prepare for Leading
  - Am I focused on RESULTS, not my comfort?
  - Am I living according to my VALUES, not reacting/responding to others?
  - Am I focused on SERVING others, not SELF?
  - Am I seeing reality objectively and LEARNING from what is happening, not rationalizing?

- Learn More About Team Members
  - What challenges you most at work?
  - What things upset you at work?
  - What do you appreciate about your work?
  - What are your concerns about work?
  - What helps you feel appreciated at work?
  - What parts of work are more difficult for you?
  - What talents/strengths do you think you contribute to the team?
  - What concerns do you have for the team?
  - What talents/strengths would you like to have?
  - What else does the team need for success?

- Questions for Customers
  - What do you need that you are not getting?
  - What are you getting that you do not need?
  - What motivates you to do business with us?
  - What motivates you to do business with our competitors?
  - How and when have we made it hard for you to do business with us?
  - If you were me, what is one thing you would change about my organization?

- Ask Employees About the Business
  - How do we make money?
  - How does your work contribute to our success?
  - How could we save money?

- How could you make your job more effective?
- What else could we offer our customers?
- Who do you see as our competition, and what do you know about them?

- Questions Leaders Need to Answer
  - How often do I communicate the organization's vision (& goals)?
  - Am I clearly focused on the three key priorities needed to achieve the vision?
  - Have I communicated, clearly and often, the three key priorities?
  - If asked, could my direct reports articulate the vision & goals? How about their reports?
  - How am I spending my time?
  - Does it match the vision and the three key priorities?
  - How are my subordinates spending their time?
  - Does it match the priorities of the business?
  - How many subordinates would tell me things I may not want to hear but need to hear?
  - Do I give timely and direct feedback that they can act on?
  - Have I, at least in my mind, picked my successor?
  - Am I coaching them and giving them challenging assignments?
  - Am I spending sufficient time developing ways to expand the capacity of my subordinates?
  - Am I delegating sufficiently?
  - Have I become a decision-making bottleneck?
  - Is the design of the organization sufficiently aligned with the vision and goals?
  - How would it look if I had to design the organization with a clean sheet of paper?
  - How would it be different from the current organization?
  - What types of events create pressure for me?
  - How do I behave under pressure?
  - What signals am I sending to my subordinates when I am under pressure?
  - Is that behavior (q21) helping or hindering?
  - Is my leadership style comfortable?
  - Does my leadership reflect both aspects of results and relationships?

- Does my leadership style play to my strengths and allow me to be who I am?
- Am I sufficiently results-oriented, or am I becoming tentative?
- Am I focused on results, not my comfort?
- Am I focused on political correctness and not hurting people's feelings?
- Does worrying about bonuses and promotions cause me to hesitate to express my views?
- Am I focused on how it IS or how it FEELS?
- Am I living according to my values, not reacting/responding to others?
- Am I focused on serving others instead of my self-interests?

Essentials for Resolving Conflict

Most people believe conflict is destructive. The emotions created by a conflict are seldom enjoyable, primarily because we develop bad thinking about it. If you adopt better thinking, conflict becomes an opportunity to grow and develop. Then conflict becomes substantially different for you. That does not mean you enjoy the conflict, but you will more easily look for ways to resolve the conflict constructively for all parties.

The best starting place is to adopt 4 critical principles, 3 cardinal rules, and use the 2 essential skills. Remember 4 + 3 + 2 for the Conflict RESOLVED Essentials.

Below is an outline of the first step in the Conflict RESOLVED process. This information helps you change your mind about conflict and encourages you to move beyond confession and forgiveness to resolution.

4 Critical Principles

Follow these four principles and approach any conflict with better thinking.

RELATIONSHIPS: Preserve Relationships—WE, not just ME
- Relationships are worth saving.
- Relationships, NOT just results.
- Relationship building and conflict resolution are connected.
- Good relationships "leave a trail of resolved issues."

FUTURE: Look to the Future; Learn from the Past—The Past is OVER.
- The Past is OVER, so learn from it.
- You can visit Pity City, but please do not move there!

- The Present is here—show personal responsibility and own your part of the conflict.
- The Future is coming—find ways to make it better.

FREEDOM: Have No Agenda to change them—Change Yourself, NOT Them.
- Freedom does not try to get the other person to fit your agenda or fulfill your expectations.
- Freedom helps prevent flashing your ME.
- Freedom encourages thinking first; think about your values and discount your emotions.
- Freedom aids in gathering facts, not trusting assumptions.

KINDNESS: Kindness Instead of Winning—Kindness Helps Lower Barriers and Defenses.
- Kindness considers the other person—winning considers you.
- Kindness is generous—winning is mostly stingy.

3 Cardinal Rules

Use these three guidelines or rules when meeting with the other person.
SLOW the emotions down
- Think—Act—Feel
- Time out if it gets heated

TALK until a solution is found.
- Persevere; stick with it
- Solutions are possible

Seek **TWO**-sided solutions
- Not about ME winning
- Not about a power play

2 Essential Skills

Always use these two skills in conflict situations to help you remain objective.
- ***Listening***—Observe the conversation
- ***Asking Questions***—Learn how they think about the issue

Conflict RESOLVED Process

The graphic is a summary of the Conflict RESOLVED process.

Use the first two steps **before** the meeting, the following five steps **during** the meeting, and the last step **after** the meeting. Two forms in "Appendix: Forms for Chapter 14" are a simple guide for anyone in a conflict. The first is the Recipe Card, which summarizes critical elements in the RESOLVED process. The second is a worksheet to use before, during, and after you meet.

Conflict Resolution Styles

Few people see conflict as an opportunity to grow and learn because most people fear conflict. However, when you accept that conflict can be beneficial, it helps develop deeper understanding and unity.

Kenneth W. Thomas and Ralph H. Kilmann researched and identified five common styles people use to handle conflict. They developed the Thomas—Kilman Conflict Mode Instrument (TKI) to help people determine how they tend to use the five styles.

Please remember this—***all five styles are helpful and appropriate***. Focusing on using just one style, thinking it is better than the rest, will create problems for you. Everyone tends to overuse and underuse styles. It is best to use a style when the situation needs it. After reading about the styles, you might guess which ones you use the most and which ones you use the least. Taking the assessment is best, though.

Compete: When competing, you exclusively pursue your concerns. Competing might mean standing up for your rights, defending a position you believe is correct, or simply trying to win. Always use competing when standing for your values.

Accommodate: When accommodating, you neglect your concerns to satisfy the other person. This mode has an element of self-sacrifice. Accommodating might take the form of selfless generosity or charity, obeying another person's order when not preferring it, or yielding to another's point of view. It can also give in just because you fear providing your thoughts. It is best used when you see the other person's points are better than yours.

Compromise: When compromising, the objective is finding a quick, mutually acceptable solution that partially satisfies you and the other person. Compromising falls on a middle ground between competing and accommodating, giving up on competing and accommodating by mixing them. It addresses an issue more directly than avoiding it but does not explore it in depth as collaborating. Compromise might mean splitting the difference, exchanging concessions, or seeking a quick middle-ground position.

Avoid: When avoiding, you do not immediately pursue your concerns or those of the other person. You do not address the conflict. It might be diplomatically sidestepping an issue, postponing it until a better time, or simply withdrawing from a threatening situation. The most critical element in using this style properly is this thought—now is not the time, but we will discuss it soon. A simple statement is, ***"Not never, but not now."***

Collaborate: When collaborating, you work with the other person to find a solution that fully satisfies both concerns. It involves digging into an issue and spending time and energy to find a solution that fits both of you. Collaborating between two persons might take the form of exploring a disagreement to learn from each other's insights, resolving some condition that would otherwise have them competing for resources, or confronting and trying to find a creative solution to an interpersonal problem. The downside of collaborating is the extensive amount of time and energy required.

Discussion Questions

1. What helps us think listening is not valuable?
2. Memorize the formula and explain the reason for each element and its order.
3. Explain each DON'T, especially "Don't judge" and "Don't sympathize."
4. Explain the term "Observational Listening."
5. What does "Start with a clean canvas" mean?
6. Explain the three reasons why questions are powerful, especially the first reason.
7. Which of the three reasons dramatically benefits you, the listener?
8. Explain each of the four types of questions, especially the fourth one.
9. What are the Rulers of Discovery?
10. What makes "Why" less desirable than What or How?
11. How would you help someone remember 4+3+2?
12. What are the 5 Conflict Styles?
13. Which style is best or most beneficial?

Chapter 15 – *Overcomers* Communicate Clearly

Key Lesson: *Muddled thinking equals muddled speaking. Use the Rule of 3s & 4s, Classic Form, and Basic Communication Recipes.*

Learn, Apply, Serve

You are learning great truths from God's Word, so here is some help to communicate clearly to others.

When you look at 2 Peter 1:5-7 (NKJV), you see eight steps to personal transformation.

> *But also for this very reason, giving all diligence, add to your faith virtue, to virtue knowledge, to knowledge self-control, to self-control perseverance, to perseverance godliness, to godliness brotherly kindness, and to brotherly kindness love.*

You can organize the eight steps—faith, virtue, knowledge, self-control, perseverance, godliness, brotherly kindness, and love—into three categories.

1. **Learn**—Faith, Virtue, Knowledge
2. **Apply**—Self-control, Perseverance, Godliness
3. **Serve**—Brotherly Kindness, Love

Reading this book helps you learn and apply the information, and you may be serving others with it already. This chapter will help you SERVE others even more through clear communication.

Clear speaking and writing are hard work, at least for me. This material will make clear communication easier.

Requires Clear Thinking

Clear thinking is the essential element for clear speaking and writing. Imagine trying to communicate important information, yet your brain cannot focus. The chance of sharing something that others could understand is unlikely.

You will learn simple and critical information to communicate verbally and in writing clearly. *Overcomers* are excellent listeners and clear, brief, and persuasive communicators.

This chapter will help you present and preach the gospel clearly—the most incredible message ever.

> *Romans 10:14 (NKJV)—How then shall they call on Him in whom they have not believed? And how shall they believe in Him of whom they have not heard? And how shall they hear without a preacher?*

Big Picture

Keep It Simple

Dr. Fred Lybrand has some excellent material to help kids and adults learn how to write. You can see his approach by visiting http://advanced-writing-resources.com/get-the-writing-course.

Here is some of the simplicity he gets you to consider.

- **Write Something**: Keep in mind as you start writing that "you are NOT what you write!" Writing something terrible does not mean you are a bad person or any other negative you put in your mind. And the vice versa is true - it does not mean you are a great person. Consider your writing just practice, meaning you are free to write something "okay," but it does not have to be great.
- **Get Help**: Now that you have written something, get feedback from others and revise as needed.
- **Make It Better**: Focus on workable, then aim for great. Please do not focus on perfection because that hill is a mountain that is impossible to climb. Wanting perfection in your writing is seldom helpful, but it is primarily an obstacle. And remember, "You are NOT what you write!"

Please consider how important the last point is. Most people associate their identity with what they write, present, and do. If someone says what you wrote is not good, you may take that as them saying YOU are not good. And if they say what you wrote is good, you may associate that with YOU being good.

It seems silly to read that, but you know it is true. You will continue to have that lousy thinking unless you learn to see yourself as distinct and separate from what you create.

You are not what you write or create.

Focus on 4 Pillars

Clear communication has four essential elements—Clarity, Brevity, Simplicity, and Humanity.

Clarity—When you communicate clearly, you reduce the audience's effort needed to understand. But clarity does not come from just articulating your words and using good sentences. It comes from using a good structure that creates a path of least resistance to understanding.

Brevity—This is a blessing to any audience. As the communicator, you may think the audience needs all the information. Instead, it is better to help people with the essential information you can provide in the time allowed. Most people learn in small bits and pieces over time. Focusing on a specific topic increases the ability of the audience to retain the critical point. So focus on just those points that will benefit them most now.

Simplicity—While you may have wrestled with the idea you will communicate, others have not. It will often seem somewhat complex unless you provide them with ways to see it through what they already know. Simplicity is not the time to try to sound smart because that makes your communication worse. Simplicity is one of the big aids in helping your audience understand. And the best tool for simplicity is to remove the clutter.

Humanity—Make your communication sound like you rather than a machine. Put personality into what you say to help you connect to the audience. If you prefer providing many facts, humanity may be challenging for you.

Aim for all four, but please get at least three out of four. See if all four are in the Lord's Prayer.

> *Matthew 6:9-13 (NKJV)—In this manner, therefore, pray:*
> *Our Father in Heaven,*
> *Hallowed be Your name.*
> *Your kingdom come.*

Your will be done
On earth as it is in heaven.
Give us this day our daily bread.
And forgive us our debts,
As we forgive our debtors.
And do not lead us into temptation,
But deliver us from the evil one.
For Yours is the kingdom and the power
and the glory forever. Amen.

Eliminate 2 Big Mistakes

Finally, before you start writing, commit to constantly 1) fighting clutter and 2) not thinking about your audience. That second mistake begins before you start writing or preparing for your presentation. Think about what your audience wants to hear instead of just talking about what you want to share.

Clutter	Not thinking about your audience

Yes, you can share what you know, but make it fit their emotions, thinking, and backgrounds as best you can.

Eliminate Clutter

Clarity is Hard Work

It is easier to ramble about a lot of disjointed facts and data. However, presenting and communicating data is clearly hard work. Clarity does not just happen; it requires energy, hard work, and time. Before you tackle clutter, here are six reasons clarity is hard work.

1. Clear Writing Is Not Natural. When writing, you are not naturally clearheaded. Most of us need time and effort to write something reasonably clear. Clear sentences are no accident, so be prepared to write them more than once.
2. Clear Writing Is Not Like Speaking. Writing like you speak can be a reasonable place to start and capture some thoughts, but please do not use that as the end product. Even when you transcribe what seems to be clear spoken communication, you will see many ways to revise it to make it better for reading.
3. Clear Writing Allows the Reader to Follow Easily. It may sound clear as you read what you wrote, but you have been thinking about the information a lot. Please read it with their perspective in mind. Work to remove thoughts that assume further knowledge about the topic or anything that could hinder

their understanding. If something is unclear, most readers will be tenacious at first. They may blame themselves for not understanding, but they often finally give up and stop reading.

4. Clear Writing Comes from Clear Thinking. The same is true about clear speaking. All clear communication comes from clear thinking. One cannot exist without the other. The more you work with the sentences you write, the greater your chance to create better and clearer thinking about your topic. As you process your thoughts into sentences, you aid them, helping them get clearer. If you want to enhance your clarity, learn to ask these two questions:
   ◦ "What am I trying to communicate?"
   ◦ "How would someone new to the subject hear it?"

5. Clear Writing Is Not About Trying to Sound Important or Smart. Why not say, "It may rain," instead of "We anticipate experiencing considerable precipitation?" If your writing seems simple, you may think something is wrong, but it may be the best way to communicate the subject. Often, the more education, the worse the writing.

6. Clear Writing Requires Subtraction to Add Clarity.
   ◦ Remove unnecessary words serving no function.
   ◦ Remove long words that could be short.
   ◦ Remove adverbs with the same meaning as the verb.
   ◦ Remove passive construction that leaves a reader unclear of who is doing what.

Those six reasons may be too much to remember, so **_here is the SECRET for clarity_**.
   • If you read it and it could be misunderstood, it is probably unclear or the wrong construction.
   • For example, "I once knew a man with a wooden leg named Smith." (What was his other leg's name?)

The Bracket Tool

Clarity is hard work, and the Bracket Tool will help. It is pretty simple. Whatever you have written, put brackets around every part that may confuse or is more information than needed. For example, look at the following:
   • Order [up]—unnecessary preposition
   • Smile [happily]—adverb has the same meaning as the verb
   • [tall] skyscraper—adjective states the same meaning as the noun
   • [a bit], [sort of]—qualifiers that weaken the meaning

In some of your writing, whole sentences may need brackets. Have the courage to do it.

Use Punctuation for Clarity

The bracket tool will help you eliminate confusing or unnecessary information. But do not forget about the way you punctuate what you write. Here are three simple ways to use punctuation without returning to English class.

1. Punctuate with Sound, Not Rules. Listen to what you write, preferably read it aloud. Does it read the way you want it to read? If it does not sound right, it probably is not. Take the time to read good writers out loud to hear how good writing sounds.

2. Break Your Thoughts Up—Highlight with Punctuation
   - **. Period**—a long pause at the end of a sentence. Usually, your inflection goes down (your voice drops and stops)
   - **, comma**—a short pause in the sentence that goes with lists or to divide pieces of a sentence into its appropriate parts for how you want it to SOUND when read
   - **; semicolon**—a longer pause (between a period and a comma) is often used to set off a further explanation of something in the first part of the sentence, or when you need a break, but not a period. For example, "Leaders value and develop people; they serve rather than seek service." "Listening makes the difference for most relationships; speaking is also needed."
   - **: colon**—a longer pause than a semicolon often used to separate lists. For example, "Leaders recognize the importance of humility, how underrated listening is, and the use of four types of questions: information, clarification, implication, and discrepancy.
   - **— dash**—a pause that creates an abrupt or hard break but leaves a connection between what goes before and after the dash. For example, "Dealing with underperformance is difficult—it is also critical."
   - **"_" quote marks**—usually read aloud with a "different than normal" voice.
   - **? question mark**—used for a question; inflection typically increases when read aloud.
   - **! exclamation mark**—used for emphasis; the voice usually gets louder when read aloud.

3. Use the Above as Guides, Not Rules

Language is democratic; it is always about how people use it. Rules are not rigid; otherwise, we would still speak Elizabethan English. Consider e.e. cummings — he gave us poetry without capital letters! Punctuation will help you develop the proper pauses, helping your sentences work.

Think About Your Audience

Change Your Thinking about Speaking

One of the speaking issues is the "ME" problem. You tend to focus on yourself and what you plan to say. That comes from our hypersensitivity to being upfront when presenting, "Will people like what I say?" "Will I help or hurt myself by doing this?" "What will people think about this or me?"

But that thinking is 180 degrees wrong. The first and foremost thought for presenting is

**Think about helping people RECEIVE—
Not about you transmitting**

That can be the most critical first step to speaking or presenting in a way that not only is best but will also remove some fear.

The "3 Ps" that Dr. Fred Lybrand teaches will help.

- **Passion**—Be energized about your topic or at least something in your topic. What always helps is to speak about what you are interested in and what you know.
- **Personality**—Be you; you can do that better than anyone else. When you are yourself, you come across as a real person. Remember the fourth pillar for writing—Humanity.
- **Practice**—Be prepared; some people require less practice than others. Again, you need to follow your wired-in tendencies. Practice provides familiarity and helps reduce nervousness. When you practice, you help prepare for this talk and increase your ability for future presentations.

Start thinking about how your audience may RECEIVE what you want to communicate and then use the 3Ps.

4 Questions—Before You Start

Since your mind focuses too often on what you will be "transmitting," you will not think enough about how the people will be "receiving." Ignoring your audience's view is a big mistake. Use these four questions to help you before you start writing or preparing your presentation.

WHO IS MY AUDIENCE? Who will be attending? Are they a diverse or relatively clear segment of the population? Get as much information about who the people are, their age, their education range, their backgrounds, and their interests. The audience is still a big mistake of mine, especially if I think I know enough about them. Take the time to get more about your audience. It will help you adjust your message.

And when speaking, do not just speak from your point of view. Do your homework. Talk to some of your audience to learn what they think about the information you plan to present.

WHAT DO THEY KNOW (ABOUT THIS TOPIC)? Of course, this can be a "best guess," but with this question, you may identify sources that provide more information. Most often, you are asked to present a specific topic. Start with the person who invited you. Second, you may have a reasonable idea of their knowledge, so start by capturing those ideas and thoughts. Finally, while this question is essential, do not assume that the audience knows more about the topic than you do. Be careful to get the reality of what they know as best you can.

WHAT HOPES MIGHT THEY HAVE (ABOUT THIS TOPIC)? This question and the next will help you find the best information. As you think about your audience, try to get their view from what they hope to learn or hear as you speak about the topic. When you know your information can touch the audience's emotions, values, and desires, you have made it easier for them to listen.

WHAT FEARS MIGHT THEY HAVE (ABOUT THIS TOPIC)? Since fear is such a powerful motivator, look at your subject from their eyes through that emotion. Please do not use this in a manipulative way; use it to identify how to focus your topic to help remove that fear. Often, the biggest fear is this will be a waste of time. That is where the Thought-TALK structure below is an excellent help. You tell them clearly about the topic and the 3 or 4 points you will cover.

Suppose you can identify an apparent fear that most people would have about the topic. That will be a significant organizing element for your topic and an excellent help with the title of your subject.

For example, note how Jesus spoke to the Sadducees. He knew they did not believe in resurrection or angels, so He directed His answer at their lousy thinking.

*Luke 20:34-38 (NKJV)—Jesus answered and said to them,
"The sons of this age marry and are given in marriage. But
those who are counted worthy to attain that age, and the
resurrection from the dead, neither marry nor are given in
marriage; nor can they die anymore, for they are equal to the
angels and are sons of God, being sons of the resurrection.
But even Moses showed in the burning bush passage that
the dead are raised, when he called the Lord 'the God of
Abraham, the God of Isaac, and the God of Jacob.' For He is
not the God of the dead but of the living, for all live to Him."*

Identify Patterns and Words from Your Answers

With the answers you have for those four questions, you can look
for common words, patterns, and ideas that will help you determine the
topic you will present or the topic and some key points that may need to
be covered. Pick three that may be most interesting to the audience and
develop your topic and structure from that.

Remove Confusing Traps

MACHETE

The machete is famous for hacking one's way through an untamed
tropical jungle. When a speaker uses a machete, it is a flailing attempt
to hack from one part of a topic to another. The machete violates the
need for milestones and strategy, another example of a disordered mind
showing itself with a disordered presentation.

SNAKE OIL

Snake Oil refers to a presenter who communicates like he is selling a
product that nobody wants or is too good to be true. It is an over-the-top
explosion of every pushy-sales-con-man stereotype. Authenticity is far
better and comes out easily when one uses the Thought-TALK System
Recipes.

SHE'S A WITCH

This failed strategy fits with any mistake based on flawed logic.
When we do not make sense, we do not make sense. However, people
are tricked because they do not analyze what is said. You are far better
off making sure your reasoning works for important events. There is no
recovery from goofy logic (unless you are an elected official).

The following scene from Monty Python and The Holy Grail says it all.

BEDEMIR: What makes you think she is a witch?

VILLAGER #3: Well, she turned me into a newt.

BEDEMIR: A newt?

VILLAGER #3: I got better.

VILLAGER #2: Burn her anyway!

CROWD: Burn! Burn her!

BEDEMIR: Quiet, quiet. Quiet! There are ways of telling whether she is a witch.

CROWD: Are there? What are they?

BEDEMIR: Tell me, what do you do with witches?

VILLAGER #2: Burn!

CROWD: Burn, burn them up!

BEDEMIR: And what do you burn apart from witches?

VILLAGER #1: More witches!

VILLAGER #2: Wood!

BEDEMIR: So why do witches burn?

[pause]

VILLAGER #3: B-- . . . 'cause they're made of wood . . . ?

BEDEMIR: Good!

CROWD: Oh yeah, yeah . . .

BEDEMIR: So how do we tell whether she is made of wood?

VILLAGER #1: Build a bridge out of her.

BEDEMIR: Aah, but can you not also build bridges out of stone?

VILLAGER #2: Oh, yeah.

BEDEMIR: Does wood sink in water?

VILLAGER #1: No, no.

VILLAGER #2: It floats! It floats!

VILLAGER #1: *Throw her into the pond!*

CROWD: *The pond!*

BEDEMIR: *What also floats in water?*

VILLAGER #1: *Bread!*

VILLAGER #2: *Apples!*

VILLAGER #3: *Very small rocks!*

VILLAGER #1: *Cider!*

VILLAGER #2: *Great gravy!*

VILLAGER #1: *Cherries!*

VILLAGER #2: *Mud!*

VILLAGER #3: *Churches—churches!*

VILLAGER #2: *Lead—lead!*

ARTHUR: *A duck.*

CROWD: *Oooh.*

BEDEMIR: *Exactly! So logically . . . ,*

VILLAGER #1: *If . . . she weighs the same as a duck, she's made of wood.*

BEDEMIR: *And therefore--?*

VILLAGER #1: *A witch!*

CROWD: *A witch!*

The easiest way to make sure your logic is sound is to ask others who are objective. Asking people who agree with you is like letting the villagers decide.

Requires Clear Structure

Rule of 3s & 4s

The rule of 3s and 4s is everywhere. It simply states that information is clearer, funnier, more impactful, and more memorable when organized around the number 3 or 4.

When you communicate with 3s and 4s, you use a structure guaranteed to help communication. Consider the ways 3s and 4s show in our world:

Threes	Fours
• Past, present, and future	• Knock Knock...Who's There
• Government of the people, by the people, for the people	• Personality Tests: Assessments often break into four types.
• Mind, will, and emotions	• Four Corners of the World
• Friends, Romans, Countrymen	• Four Seasons
• Blood, sweat, and tears	• Four suits in a card deck
• Father, Son, and Holy Spirit	• Four Gospels
• Faith, Hope, and Love	• The four elements—earth, air, water, fire
• Mind, body, spirit	• KISS—Keep It Simple Stupid
• Stop, Look, and Listen	• Four sides of a square

Jokes often run in a three-step format:
- A Priest, a Politician, and a Cowboy . . .
- "I celebrated Thanksgiving in an old-fashioned way. I invited everyone in my neighborhood to my house, we had an enormous feast, and then I killed them and took their land."—Jon Stewart
- Open . . . Set Up . . . Punchline
- Connection . . . Conceal . . . Reveal: "One morning, I shot an elephant in my pajamas. How he got in my pajamas, I'll never know."—Groucho Marx

The Rule of "Mile-Markers"

The Rule of Mile-Markers is helpful when speaking. It keeps everyone focused because it maintains a sense of time. Each element of a 3 or 4 is a "mile marker," letting your audience know where you are.

When we travel, especially in a car, mile markers give feedback on the distance traveled and remaining. Knowing this distance allows for all kinds of effective decisions about stopping or enduring. In a way, you know where you are, which tells you a rough sense of arrival.

Imagine members of an audience or a meeting knowing exactly where you are in your presentation; that gives them clarity and patience. But without markers, they often do not know where they are or when it will end.

The classical approach in communication has been this "Rule of 3."

- Tell them what you are going to tell them.
- Tell them.
- Tell them what you told them.

This simple structure starts with the Point (what you will tell them) and moves to the Parts (the details). It also uses the power of Repetition to reinforce their understanding and memory.

Why Use 3s

3 is Persuasive	3 is Thoughtful	3 is Memorable
• Not too much to browbeat, enough to convince • 3-legged stool: 1 or 2 is not enough, 4 adds stability	• Suggests objectivity • Implies thought about the topic	• Not too much for most to remember • Not too much to create confusion

Classic Form

Why Use the Classic Form?

Here are four great reasons to use the Classic Form when speaking.

- Aids memory; a gift to the speaker and especially the audience
- Removes common mistake of not repeating or recapping.
- Reduces the impact of your listener's mental vacations—some research shows that people take mental vacations every six seconds.
- Reinforces the strategy of "Tell them what you are going to tell them, tell them, then tell them what you told them."

While you do not need all of it for every communication recipe, it is still best to use it to organize your thoughts. Some recipes, like the "Swing," do not need it, but the other three do.

4 Parts of the Classic Form

CAPTION—A thoughtfully worded statement about the essence of the talk. It is often called the Lead, the Title, or the Headline.

Example: What It Takes to Be an Amazing Employee

CONTRACT—The talk outline is given as one- or two-word summary points and is an implied promise to the audience at the beginning of a presentation. The Contract establishes the Mile Markers you are committing to follow.

Example: You're a fantastic employee if you honor the three cardinal themes—Professionalism, Progress, and Profit.

CONTENT—The actual talk, where you give the information you promised.

Example: Professionalism means that you do your job because you agreed to receive money as compensation for the effort. Your work is about doing what the boss wants and is never about your agreement, happiness, need to be stroked, etc.

Progress means a commitment to improving your skills and the area for which you are responsible. You constantly look for how things can be "a little bit better," etc.

Profit means that you realize the company's money is not Monopoly Money. You know there are no employees if a company does not make a profit. You constantly ask yourself about revenue and expenses and how decisions affect both, etc.

RECAP—The recap of the essential points of what was said. It is a quick review that restates those points.

Example: In summary, being constantly professional, concerned about progress, and careful about profit will make you a fantastic employee.

Get one of your recent presentations, put it into the Classic Form, and see if it would have made a difference. Try it the next time you make a presentation. Structure will help you.

Recipes (4 Basic Recipes)

Talking about structure, each of the four communication recipes below will help you create the CONTENT portion of the Classic Form.

What Is a Recipe?

Webster's tells us that a recipe is:
- A set of instructions for making food
- A way of doing something that will produce a particular result

A recipe is a process or formula that produces
a particular result and allows the result to be
successfully repeated over and over again.

Great chefs use recipes to keep their quality intact. Even though they invented the recipe for the best soup in Manhattan, they constantly refer to it because mistakes are so easy to make.

More than just a means to consistent and quality results, recipes are also empowering. A recipe allows an average Joe to create a dish a Master Chef would like. Following the recipe of a great culinary artist can produce essentially the same result.

A recipe is also a good analogy for your goal of communicating clarity or persuading others. You will use a recipe to guide people effectively from Point A (Hello, my name is Harry, and I want to help you . . .) to Point B (. . . save the day) with a "how to" (. . . by sharing with you the three uses of the wand).

In our THOUGHT-Talk workshop, you will see six essential recipes that should be in every communicator's tool bag. Only four of them are below. Recipes have a variety of names, such as strategies, plans, or templates. They are powerful tools because of the underlying principle of structure.

Since these have been tested and proven, you can comfortably rely on them to organize your intention in communicating with others. Recipes also make use of the universal principle that Limits Yield Focus. In other words, when you limit your approach to a specific recipe, your brain naturally looks for a way to organize your communication to match the recipe. In this way, even an arbitrary use of a recipe will help you organize your thoughts for the benefit of others.

Why Use a Recipe?

It's Faster	It's Easier	It's Reliable	It Creates Structure
It is a template to complete. You just follow the directions	Allows "painting by numbers"	Not a fad, used for 100's or 1,000's of years	Provides clarity Helps you persuade

Borrowing from the STORY Recipe you will learn about later, the four recipes are organized with the questions **What, How,** and **When.**

TIME—Structures information in steps or time

WHAT

A recipe that structures what you want to communicate around time. And it is not just about the past, present, and future. Time is also about what happened (or will happen) in comparison. Sometimes things get better, stay the same, or get worse.

For example, you can describe an organization in its infancy, young adult life, and old age. Using the TIME Recipe is simply a matter of organizing the change that has or will happen concerning your topic.

Einstein once quipped, "The only reason for time is so that everything doesn't happen at once." Showing that your subject did not all happen at once is the heart of the TIME Recipe.

HOW

- What was before?
- What was after?
- What happened in between?
- Where were we?
- Where are we?
- Where are we headed?

WHEN

The TIME Recipe gives perspective to others. Understanding where we stand in a larger story tends to calm and focus people.

The TIME Recipe also tends to give rise to action plans, so it is valuable for rallying people to a new future.

STORY—Structures information into essentials
(Who, What, Where, When, Why, and How)

WHAT

The STORY Recipe is a simple way to distill what matters. These are the same questions everyone in your audience wants to know—the answer to Who? What? When? Where? Why? and How? Often called "5 W's and H" or simply "5 W's."

HOW

Newspapers and news services use it. Take a moment to think about your subject or goal in communication; then, all you need to answer are the 5 Ws and the H. From those answers, you can derive a structure for your talk.

IMPORTANT: You do not have to use all six. Putting together your talk with three questions (and answers) may be all you need.

WHEN

Journalists use this structure because it is an efficient way to tell the whole story. Anytime you need to relay a story to an audience, use this Recipe. It is imperative when bringing others up to speed on a project, crisis, or celebration. Use it as an overview (introduction or just a quick update), to outline details (great for websites and brochures), and for voicemail (who you are, why you are calling, and when you will be available).

BASEBALL—Structures information into any 3 or 4

WHAT

Baseball is a sport of 3s and 4s. 4 Bases (1st, 2nd, 3rd, and Home); 3 strikes and you are out; 3 outs and your team's at-bat is over; 4 Balls and you can walk to first. Baseball becomes an easy picture to recall when trying to remember the Rule of 3s and 4s.

HOW

Remember that you can explain any topic in 3 or 4 major parts. It may be the number of items (4 bases, 3 strikes), the progression (get on base, steal a base, score on a hit), or the people (first, second, and third baseman).

To keep it simple, consider your Mile Markers as bases (items, reasons, elements) or players (people, their views, how different people see the topic).

WHEN

Anytime. It is your fallback recipe. If you cannot apply other recipes, use this one. When you organize your main communication idea with 3 or 4 sub-points, you instantly use the Rule of 3s & 4s and can provide Mile Markers for your audience to focus on and remember.

It also gives the impression that you spent effort and time thinking about the subject. It also helps people agree with you by presenting your view as "obvious," so it "makes sense."

SWING—Structures information by contrasting or blending extremes to a middle

WHAT

The SWING Recipe is a picture of the playground or tree swing. As you swing, you move from one extreme to the opposite extreme, or you can rest in the middle. The SWING Recipe stresses the extremes to show that a third (middle) option is better.

HOW

SWING moves from presenting one extreme then to the other before offering a third option, avoiding the ditches. It has a form of
- One way to go is _____
- The other way to go is _____
- I believe we should consider _____ (a middle, consolatory, or gracious option)

The SWING Recipe intensifies or softens as the need arises by simply elaborating on how and why the extremes are undesirable.

WHEN

Use it in situations where there is polarity and adversarial posturing. One side against the other tends to only call for a winner and a loser. The SWING Recipe allows for alternatives to enter the discussion, which also has the advantage of making you the voice of reason, inventiveness, and leadership to both sides. Furthermore, simply as a means of looking for alternatives, you can use the SWING Recipe to stimulate your thinking and find a new answer when one is not yet in sight.

DELIVERY BASICS

Finally, here are some basics on delivering your message to your audience.

Voice

Project your message clearly and compellingly without filler words (uh, ah, um, you know, etc.). It can hurt your credibility and the audience's memory of your message if they cannot understand you.
- *Note:* If you have filler words, here are ways to expel them: swallow them, close your lips, say "pause" silently to yourself, and change your delivery pattern by pausing, taking a breath, and reaching for water. Stop, be silent, and start speaking again without the filler words.
- *Exercise:* Leave yourself a voicemail message. Without preparation, talk about any subject for one minute. Play the message, identify your filler words, and count the number you use. Do the same thing weekly to track your progress.
- *Remember:* Filler words dilute your message and impact

Vary your delivery and maintain a delivery rate between 140-160 wpm. Deliver your message like a broadcaster with clear articulation, measured speed, and slow delivery for impact.

- *Note:* If you feel you are speaking too quickly, slow your eye contact for a count of 1000, 2000, or 3000, and your voice will often follow.
- *Remember:* Slower delivery + Lower tone = More Credibility

Eye Contact

Eye contact is a critical way to connect to your audience. It shows interest and the willingness to engage with your listener.

- Hold eye contact for a count of 1000, 2000, 3000, or more.
- Rebound your eyes off one person to another around the room. Do not pan or bounce back like you are watching a tennis match. Be aware of those sitting close to you on either side to include them with eye contact.

Try not to read the screen or your notes. Reading does not engage the listener as eye contact does.

- Step away from the screen and do not talk to the slides. Face and speak to the listener.
- While the projector is on, avoid walking in front of the projected image. Turn it off before you move. Step away from the screen or flip chart and try not to block the view of the image.

Touch—Talk—Turn when using a flip chart or whiteboard

- Write on the flip chart or whiteboard, turn to your listener, and then talk so that you can be heard. Position your body on the left of the chart if you are right-handed and on the right if you are left-handed, facing your listener to avoid showing your back or blocking their view as you write.
- Stick to the basics on a flip chart—three columns across, six items deep. The 3×6 rule allows for large print and adequate white space. Avoid writing in the lower third of the page.

Gestures

Use a chart marker or remote, then put it down, if possible. Please do not hold paper, eyeglasses, chart markers, projector remotes, or pens. Free both hands to add energy to your message. Frequently, your audience can only see you from the waist up, so natural, open gestures will reinforce your message.

Position your hands at waist level with palms open and fingers relaxed. Visualize holding a tray of drinks or a frame and use them often to illustrate your points. Clasped hands may suggest to your listener that you are nervous or uncomfortable with your topic. The resting pose is just below waist level.

Think of your palms as positive magnets—hands cannot touch together except to illustrate a point.

Stance

Avoid side-to-side or up-and-back rocking — it distracts your audience. Position your feet at shoulder width and your dominant foot slightly forward to help edit out any rocking or swaying you may have. Stand tall with your feet facing your listener and move with purpose.

Use props to assist you in moving with purpose, i.e., reach for water, step toward the projector to advance a slide, or work on a flip chart with audience involvement.

*How you assist your listeners, connect with them, and engage
their feelings makes it easier for them to remember after your talk.*

Discussion Questions

1. What is the critical element for clear speaking? What makes that accurate?
2. Explain, "You are not what you write!" How will that help you?
3. Explain the four pillars. Which of them do you need to improve?
4. What happens to the four pillars when you have clutter in your writing or speaking?
5. What happens to your thinking when you remove clutter in what you wrote?
6. What is probably the biggest problem when speaking or presenting? Why?
7. Which of the "4 Questions—Before You Start" is probably the best way to connect with your audience?
8. Explain 3s and 4s and what makes them so valuable.
9. What is the classical, time-proven approach to speaking and writing?
10. Explain the four parts of the Classic Form.
11. Explain the Time Recipe and provide some 3s or 4s mile markers.
12. Explain the Story Recipe and some 3s and 4s Mile-markers.
13. Explain the Baseball Recipe and some 3s and 4s Mile-markers.
14. Explain the Swing Recipe and some typical Mile-markers.

FORMS

Forms for Chapter 6

Six Guidelines When Confessing to Others

1. Right Attitude

- Always think of them as more important than you (Philippians 2:3-4).
- Have NO Agenda or expectations about changing them.
- Go with a heart that knows you wronged them and will confess your wrong, no strings attached.
- Be humble and defenseless.
- Believe resolution is possible.
- Slow your thinking (emotions) down!

2. Right Words

- When confessing, be careful of the words you use.
- If you have not confessed to God, you will not like using the words required here.

Agree	...that it was a mistake
Acknowledge	...how it has affected others
Admit	...regret and repentance
Announce	...steps you will take to rectify the situation

- A Pattern for Right Words
  - AGREE: I was wrong when I (describe attitude and actions).
  - ACKNOWLEDGE: I realize this hurt you (and others).
  - ADMIT: I regret my actions and repent before God and you.
  - ANNOUNCE: I plan to (state actions) to help me not do that again.
- Thank you for listening. If I need to clear up any other items, I am willing to discuss those also, now or later.

3. Right Method

- A personal visit is probably the best overall.
- A phone call can be helpful for difficult issues.
- A letter is the least preferred.

4. Right Time

- Is the time to talk convenient for the other person?
- Is it a time when you would not likely be interrupted?
- What is a danger when thinking of the right time?

5. Right Communication Style

- Deal gently, even if they are not gentle with you.
- Slow your thoughts (emotions) down!
- Prepare before and even role-play gentleness.
- Use speech seasoned with grace.
- Take 100 percent responsibility for communicating.
  - Communication is cursed.
  - Communication is delicate.
  - Understand first, then disagree.
  - Do not assume they understand you.
  - Look at them during the conversation.
  - Speak the "Truth in Love"—(Ephesians 4:15).

6. Right Meeting Guidelines

- Create a handout (like the following page) for the parties that will be participating.
- Ask permission from the other party to send the guidelines to them.
- In some situations, select a trusted, wise third party to facilitate.
- Use the guidelines even if there is no third party.
- Look up all the verses in "Meeting Guidelines" before the meeting to refresh your mind to the truth.

Galatians 6:1 Brethren, if a man is overtaken in any trespass, you who are spiritual restore such a one in a spirit of gentleness, considering yourself lest you also be tempted.

James 3:17 But the wisdom that is from above is first pure, then peaceable, gentle, willing to yield, full of mercy and good fruits, without partiality and without hypocrisy.

Colossians 4:6 Let your speech always be with grace, seasoned with salt, that you may know how you ought to answer each one.

Proverbs 15:1 A soft answer turns away wrath, But a harsh word stirs up anger.

Proverbs 6:16-19 These six things the Lord hates, Yes, seven are an abomination to Him: A proud look, a lying tongue, hands that shed innocent blood, a heart that devises wicked plans, feet that are swift in running to evil, a false witness who speaks lies, and one who sows discord among brethren.

The 4 A's of Apology

Agree that it was a mistake.

- Own the mistake; do not excuse it.
- Requires humility; pride will derail you.
- Frame the mistake in the past.

Acknowledge how it has affected others.

- See the situation through their eyes.
- You may be 10 percent wrong, but they see you as 100 percent wrong.
- The Splinter and Beam concept.

Admit regret and repentance.

- Communicate a genuine, heartfelt desire not to repeat the mistake.
- Communicate a change of heart and mind.
- Communicate a 180° turn, turn from that mistake, and turn toward doing what is right.
- Do not fake it; that means you want TOLERANCE without changing.

Announce steps you will take to rectify the situation

- This is not about just "trying to do better."
- Identify specific actions that lead to change.

Thank you for listening. If other items need to be cleared up, I am willing to discuss those also, now or later.

Using Apology to Help You Change

Step 1: Apologize for your current behavior

EXAMPLE

1. "I am sorry that I haven't communicated clearly to you and the team in the past.
2. "I realize this has hurt the effectiveness of the team.
3. "I regret not seeing this mistake earlier and am committed to change.

4. "Considering the change I need, would you mind giving me one or two specific ways to communicate more clearly and effectively with you and the team?"

5. After they answer, you are allowed only one response!! THANK YOU! (No discussion)

Step 2: Use each person's ideas to build a change plan. They help you build the plan, which becomes very personal once you go to step 3.

Step 3: Periodically ask individuals a simple question: HOW AM I DOING with . . . ? (. . . = one of the ideas they offered)

Meeting Guidelines

Be Thankful in Prayer
- Thank God for the conflict—1 Thes. 5:18
- Accept that God has been and is at work in the conflict—Gen. 50:20, Rom. 8:28
- Praise God for allowing the sin. Sin is the root problem, not the other person and not God—James 4:1, Rom. 6:12-13
- Accept confession and forgiveness are God's answer to conflict
- Eph. 4:32, Col. 3:13, I Pet. 3:8-9

Be Humble
- James 4:6; I Pet 5:6-7
- Allow God's grace to permeate your lives—James 4:10
- Recognize both of you are depraved apart from Christ—Rom. 3:10-12, Eph. 2:1-6
- Each person accepts personal responsibility in the conflict. (Offer no defense. Pride is defensive.)

Be Just & Merciful
- Micah 6:8

Be Gentle
- Deal gently with each other—Gal. 5:22, Gal. 6:1, James 3:17
- Consider the other person as more important than yourself; Phil 2:3-4
- Do not try to change the other person. (You are responsible for YOU. Pride causes you to focus on their faults.)

Be Gracious
- Use speech seasoned with grace
- Col. 4:6, Prov. 15:1, 6:16-19

Be Considerate
- Eph. 4:15, Prov. 21:10

Be Renewed
- Christ's Life (your new life) and the Holy Spirit's energy are the keys to any resolution
- Gal. 2:20, 5:16, 24-25; 2 Cor. 5:17

Be Clear
- Speak about the problem, not about the person
- Use the "Speak to the Center of the Room" communication style

Be Honest About both Facts and Feelings
Use the "I + feel + when" technique
1. Begin the conversation with a qualifier
    a. "I want to tell you how I feel."
    b. "I am not asking you to agree with me."
    c. Never use BUT after those statements (it can be manipulative)

2. State your feelings ("I am really upset")
3. Always use observable behavior
    a. "I was hurt when you didn't speak to me last night."
    b. NOT, "You always are hurting me."

4. Reframe or "mirror" what is said
    a. "What I hear you saying . . ."
    b. "I am not sure I understand, but let me tell you what I heard."

FORMS FOR CHAPTER 13

Exercise: Learn from the Past; Plan for the Future

Question 1: What were your most significant accomplishments in the last 12 months? Even if the previous 12 months were the worst of your life, odds are, if you look hard enough, you have something somewhere to be proud of. If it was great, that makes answering the question even easier. After listing all your accomplishments, think about each in detail. Identify several takeaways for each—what you learned or were reminded of by it.

Question 2: What were your biggest disappointments in the last 12 months? Practically every company and individual resists analyzing their mistakes. That is a shame because this is where great learning can happen. No matter how well everything is going, everyone makes mistakes. The trick here is to examine what preceded them, what you could have done differently, and how you can prevent making the same mistakes in the future. Even though the last 12 months were great, you will likely have some personal and professional disappointments. As you did with your accomplishments, list your biggest disappointments—and then identify several takeaways for each one.

Question 3: How did you limit yourself in the past 12 months, and how can you remove those limits in the next 12 months? Did you take or not take specific actions that came back to haunt you? Bring these actions to the surface, shine a light on them, and, most importantly, determine what you want to do differently now and in the future. Once again, make a list and identify the takeaways. For example, when I do not review my goals daily, I react and respond, getting pulled into what is happening and distracted from what may be more critical. That reduces my actions on my goals. The takeaway: Commit to using the Daily Focus Form and schedule key items on my current day calendar to remind me.

Question 4: What did you learn from your answers to the first three questions? That is where you can get the best benefit from this exercise. Remember, the purpose of the exercise is not simply to know you and your business better but to use what you learn to help over the next 12 months. What are your main takeaways from the first three questions? What do you now know about yourself or your business that you did not realize or were not thinking about before? Here are two items from my list.

- Creating products, coaching, and teaching are my most significant accomplishments. Therefore, it is easy to spend time daily creating materials and clarifying how to improve the material.
- A limiting factor is not focusing on attracting and acquiring more people to the material that I love to create. Marketing is inadequate, often ignored, and difficult for me.

Get as many takeaways as possible because that is how you put your learning into reality. These takeaways can help make the next 12 months outstanding. Of course, it is not enough to make your list (although that will get you part way there). You still need to take this information and USE IT! And that is where our final question comes in.

Question 5: How can you use this information to make the next 12 months great? The idea is to take everything that surfaced in your answers to the first four questions and build it into your schedule, interactions, management style, etc. That may alter your goals or help you achieve them. Whatever you do, make sure you create goals first. For example, after creating my goals, I added specific actions to help me accomplish them.

- Start each morning with my Daily Focus Form.
- Block out marketing time on my weekly calendar
- Connect to some good marketing resources

Make Your Goals SMART

S—SPECIFIC: It is imperative to use specific details
- Clear, specific, and picturable
- Exactly what you want in concrete terms
- You will know your objective is specific enough if:
  - Everyone involved knows the specifics of their involvement
  - Everyone involved understands and is clear about the desired end result
  - Your objective is free from jargon
  - You have used only appropriate language

- The following are not clear objectives
  - Increase production and reduce costs
  - Improve report writing skills
  - Increase knowledge by year-end by more comfort in peer reviews
  - Create a more positive work environment

- On the other hand, these are better
  - Drill 4 water wells at less than $1,500 each by March 31
  - Reduce report preparation time by 30% by December 31 and maintain an "excellent" feedback rating from the peer review team.
  - Achieve an "excellent" rating by peers on teaching by November 15.

M—MEASURABLE: Critical Element
- You will know you have achieved your objective because the metric is the evidence. Others can know, too! It becomes your statement of success.
- Objectives have some method of tracking progress, measuring success over time.
- Objectives are not masters; they are servants supporting personal/organizational values and purpose.
- Define the deliverables, documents, products, and desired results.

A—ACCEPTABLE (Most people like to use Achievable): linked to measurable
- If you know you can measure it, you can more easily determine whether you are willing to tackle or put effort into it.

- Limit the scope to your roles and responsibilities. Define the scope within your control and influence because it needs to be something you can make or help happen.
- You may not know if it is achievable or attainable, but do you still want it? Am I willing to be accountable for this, knowing I have no guarantee of getting there? Something you agree that you will put your effort into achieving, even though there is no guarantee you will reach it.

R—RESULT-ORIENTED (Relevant): not about actions
- Even if it is achievable or acceptable, it may not be relevant. That is where alignment with purpose, mission, and strategy happens. A key reason it can be achievable but irrelevant is if it is not a high priority. Often, something else needs to be completed first. If so, set up other objectives in priority order.
- Questions: Is this in line with overall organization activities? Will this contribute to the goals and objectives of the organization? Is there a higher priority to focus on now? Will this add to, even multiply, as opposed to subtract or divide, the organizational efforts?

T—TIME-BOUND: What is the deadline?
- You must include a deadline, or your objective is much less measurable.
- Without the target date, the measurement of the objective is incomplete.
- Set deadlines based on when the project is needed or wanted. Not to manipulate you or give you too much time.

Do your best to meet all the SMART criteria, and you will increase your focus and clarify what you want into an actual value and aspiration!

THP Personal Planning Form

1. THERE—Goals, Desired Outcomes (Picturable, Measurable, Specific)	Due Date	

2. HERE—Current Reality	

3. PATH—Actions	Progress Measures	Partners	Date

Date Prepared:	Approved by:

HERE—Current Reality Checklist

Did you use your Future Result as a reference point in describing current reality?

End Result	Current Reality
100% on-time delivery	89% on-time delivery in last 3 months
$48 million in annual sales	$31 million in sales in the past fiscal year

Have you described the relevant picture?
-It must be relevant to the Future Result. No unrelated details.

End Result	Irrelevant Details
100% on-time delivery	Product is packaged in a blue box
$48 million in annual sales	Sales tax is captured at the point of sale

Have you included the whole picture?
-Not enough to say, "I don't have (my future result)."

Rather Than	Write
We do not have a quality program	We do not have a formal system, although people see a need for more quality in our products. Customer surveys report dissatisfaction with our current quality. We have an in-house training specialist who has had some experience with quality, and the management team is overworked and a bit resistant to any change.

Translate assumptions and editorials into objective news reports
-We just want facts. Objective current reality allows design of effective actions to create the results we want.

Editorial	Facts
We do not have any business trying to go after business outside our niche market	We have tried to do business outside of our market, but we got only a small return on our investment. We did not know how to do it.

Have you told the story without exaggeration?
-Better or worse than reality is not helpful.

Exaggeration	Current Reality
Our products are rated the best	One of three product surveys rated us #1. Two rated us #4.
We have the worst record on safety	We had 9 near misses and 1 minor accident this past year

Did you state what reality is or how it got that way?
-Just describe "right now", not the past.

"The Journey"	Current Reality
We bought a new kettle for the plant, and by the time we installed it, the sales guys had drummed up so many new orders that we could not keep up. So we had to put on a new shift, but they were untrained, and we did not make a lot of headway, but our costs went up. The customers were not getting their orders when we promised, and everyone was mad at us and blaming us, but it was really the fault of the sales guys overpromising again.	Capacity is strained, more orders than we can handle. Sales and manufacturing are not coordinated. New people have taken more time than we thought to come up to speed. Costs up from adding a new shift.

Have you included all the facts you need?
-Leaving an element out of current reality is the same as not giving the whole story.

Current sales	Current management strategies and attitudes
Current market trends	Current job market and hiring practices
Current market share	Current systems
Current competition	Current talent of members of the organization
Current financial conditions	Current core competencies
Current product quality	Current decision-making process
Current distribution system	Current business approach
Current capacity	Available resources
What you need	What you do not know
What could help	What could hurt

Daily Focus Form   Date: _____ / _____ / _____

Directions	Time Principles
1. Do MY PROJECTS and MY CONTACTS before you do MY TODAY.	1. Limited Resource
2. Schedule three 60-minute slots today for the items below.	2. Inflexible Resource
3. Write and review items for 7 and 30 days for your projects.	3. Always More Things to Do Than Time Available
4. Write all intends or ideas on the other side of this sheet.	4. Focus (Not Efficiency) is the Key to Mastering Time
5. 1-week rule—Delete, Do, Schedule, or list on the back.	

MY FOCUS FOR TODAY (No more than 3!)

Top 3	Next 3-5

MY CONTACTS

People I need to contact today to help me accomplish my goals and projects.

Could Help My Goals / Projects	Follow Up or Waiting on Them
•	•
•	•
•	•
•	•

MY PROJECTS

3-5 things I need to do in the next 7 and 30 DAYS to move each project forward.

Next 7 Days	Next 30 Days or Notes
PROJECT 1—	
PROJECT 2—	
PROJECT 3—	
PROJECT 4—	

MY MAYBE LIST—IDEAS or Thoughts for Projects or Goals

Directions—Capture your thoughts and ideas for current projects and add new projects below.

PROJECT 1—

PROJECT 2

PROJECT 3

PROJECT 4

PROJECT 5

OTHER PROJECT IDEAS and OTHER THINGS TO DO

FORMS FOR CHAPTER 14

Conflict RESOLVED Recipe Card

Remember 4+3+2 Essentials

4 Critical Principles	3 Cardinal Rules	2 Skills	5 Styles
RELATIONSHIPS: WE, not just ME **FUTURE**: The Past is OVER **FREEDOM**: Do not try to change them **KINDNESS**: Focus on kindness instead of winning	**SLOW** the emotions down **TALK** until a solution is found Seek **TWO**-sided solutions	Listening Questions	Accommodating Avoiding Collaborating Competing Compromising

Evaluate the Conflict: Questions...

About the Conflict	For You	About Them	About Meeting
What is it about? What are the components? How will it impact the relationship? Will we 1) battle until the other changes? 2) disagree and end the relationship, 3) disagree and keep relationship, 4) resolve and keep the relationship, 5) resolve and end the relationship	What was my role, contribution? What resolution do I want? What are my needs, goals? Do I need them? Are my expectations reasonable? What misperceptions might they have of me?	Am I defining them by their negative behavior? What are their needs? Do I understand their side? What misperceptions might I have of them? What buttons do they have?	What Method? What Time? What Location?

Set the Ground Rules

3 Cardinal Rules	General Rules		Good Values
SLOW the emotions down **TALK** until a solution is found Seek **TWO**-sided solutions	Be Clear "Speak to the center of the room" No attacking or blaming One person speaks at a time	Look at each other when speaking All ideas are valid when presented Build on each other's ideas Explore each idea	Be Fair Be Honest Be Responsible Be Respectful Be Considerate

Open the Conversation

Open and honest about seeking a solution	Partner with them; create a WE atmosphere	Encourage options through shared effort	Narrow the scope—agreement on everything is not required

Listen and Clarify

Focus only on them	Observe what they say	Seek facts with good questions	Summarize; check what you heard	Summarize often	Seek Permission

Value and Seek Options

Criteria for Good Options	Meets one or more shared needs	Meets one or more needs not incompatible with other party	Potential to improve future relationship	Can be supported by all parties
Uncover Options	Seek their options first	Learn from the past	Keep your ears open!	

Establish A Solution

WE (2-sided solutions) Thinking (Slow emotions down) Facts (talk)	Focus on shared needs Increase the size of the pie	Behavior specific	Document it

Decide to Follow-up

Conflict RESOLVED Worksheet

The Conflict	You	Them	Meeting
			Method
			Date/Time
			Location

Openings

Options

Solutions

Do-ables

Solution(s)

Follow-up

www.ingramcontent.com/pod-product-compliance
Lightning Source LLC
Chambersburg PA
CBHW051256120626
46547CB00015B/1972